MW01154642

For the Wild

For the Wild

*Ritual and Commitment
in Radical Eco-Activism*

Sarah M. Pike

UNIVERSITY OF CALIFORNIA PRESS

University of California Press, one of the most
distinguished university presses in the United States,
enriches lives around the world by advancing scholarship
in the humanities, social sciences, and natural sciences. Its
activities are supported by the UC Press Foundation and
by philanthropic contributions from individuals and
institutions. For more information, visit www.ucpress.edu.

University of California Press
Oakland, California

© 2017 by Sarah M. Pike

Library of Congress Cataloging-in-Publication Data

Names: Pike, Sarah M., 1959– author.
Title: For the wild : ritual and commitment in radical
    eco-activism / Sarah M. Pike.
Description: Oakland, California : University of
    California Press, [2017] | Includes bibliographical
    references and index.
Identifiers: LCCN 2017013715 (print) | LCCN 2017015386
    (ebook) | ISBN 9780520967892 (ebook) |
    ISBN 9780520294950 (cloth : alk. paper) |
    ISBN 9780520294967 (pbk : alk. paper)
Subjects: LCSH: Animal rights—Moral and ethical
    aspects—United States. | Animal rights movement—
    United States. | Animal rights activists—United States. |
    Environmentalists—United States—Attitudes. |
    Nature—Effect of human beings on. | Environmental
    ethics—United States.
Classification: LCC HV4708 (ebook) | LCC HV4708 .P565
    2017 (print) | DDC 179/.30973—dc23
LC record available at https://lccn.loc.gov/2017013715

Manufactured in the United States of America

25 24 23 22 21 20 19 18 17
10 9 8 7 6 5 4 3 2 1

For my children, Dasa Grey Schill, Jonah Paul Schill,
and Clara Bergamini, with all my love

Contents

Acknowledgments

This book has been over ten years in the writing and many people have helped it along the way.

I owe much to the many activists who took time to speak with me or shared their stories by mail from prison. I am particularly grateful to Jeffrey Luers, Rod Coronado, Peter Young, and Chelsea Gerlach for the letters they wrote that set me along certain paths I never would have taken without their insights. Thanks to Nettle and Darryl Cherney for hanging out with me for hours and telling me about their lives. The *Earth First! Journal* and its many editors over the years of my research had a profound effect on this project. The artists included in *EF!J* and the authors of letters, articles, pleas, complaints, reportbacks, and poems shaped my understanding of activism and confirmed much of what I saw and heard during fieldwork. Many other activists generously tolerated being interviewed, taught me medic and climbing skills, accompanied me to gatherings, told me about their childhoods, shared meals with me, and welcomed me into their communities. This book would not have been possible without their hard work and passionate dedication to the lives of other species.

Much appreciation goes to Max Lieberman for fieldwork assistance and his thoughtful perspectives on a number of thorny issues.

Eric Schmidt at the University of California Press was positive and encouraging towards this project from the moment I first mentioned it. Thanks to Maeve Cornell-Taylor, Kate Hoffman, and others at the press who worked on the book during various phases of its production.

California State University Chico provided me with several leaves that supported the initial phases of research for this book. The Department of Comparative Religion and Humanities at CSU, Chico, has been a warm and supportive academic home. The University of Oslo hosted me as a visiting scholar and it was during my sabbatical in Oslo that much of this book was written. The Norwegian Research Council generously funded this research as part of the multiyear, international, collaborative project based at the University of Oslo, "Reassembling Democracy: Ritual as Cultural Resource." I owe much to the scholars who participated in REDO, whose questions and suggestions enriched this book: Michael Houseman, Marion Grau, Morny Joy, Donna Seamone, Jens Kreinath, Graham Harvey, Paul-François Tremlett, Gitte Buch-Hansen, Lotte Danielsen, Kjetil Hafstad, Birte Nordahl, Tony Balcomb, Grzegorz Brzozowski, Cora Alexa Døving, Ida Marie Høeg, Samuel Etikpah, Sidsel Roalkvam, and to the other participants in REDO France, REDO London, and REDO Berkeley workshops. Thanks especially to project director Jone Salomonsen, a companion on various adventures over our professional years, who has made much possible for me. The time and ideas shared with all of you in special places far from California transformed this book.

The work of religious studies scholar Bron Taylor has been invaluable to my understanding of radical environmentalism. He saw a richly lived spiritual world in radical environmentalism when others labeled these activists "terrorists" or dismissed them as "tree-huggers." I am deeply indebted to Bron's work. Much of the territory I explore here echoes themes and ideas he has written about in many books and articles over the past twenty-five years.

Mentors and friends who have been important in my personal and professional life read and commented on parts of this manuscript. The care and support of three of them has been essential. David Haberman, my fellow lover of forests, has been urging me for years to finish this book and was the first person to read it all the way through. Bob Orsi has always read my work like no one else and has shaped my scholarly life in more ways than I can possibly put into words. Ron Grimes has inspired and pushed me in the right ways, both compassionate and challenging. Reading for U.C. Press, Adrian Ivakhiv and Evan Berry provided excellent critiques and questions on the entire manuscript. To the other colleagues and friends who read and commented on portions of the book—Jason Bivins, Graham Harvey, Lisa Sideris, Robert Jones, Heather Altfeld, Gretel van Wieren, and Sarah Fredericks—I am grateful for the insight and sensitivity with which you read (and edited in Heather's case) my work, even if I did not always follow your good advice!

I was fortunate indeed to be able to write Chapter 3 at Sally and Rich Thomason's cabin in Montana and edit chapters 3 and 4 at Laird Easton's dining room table. Thanks to the changing personnel of the Chico writing group and my colleagues at Chico State in addition to Laird who joined me in various venues around Chico when I was working on early versions of some of these chapters: Vernon Andrews, Jason Clower, Daniel Veidlinger, Heather Altfeld, and Troy Jollimore.

My parents, Thomas Howell Pike III and Lucy Grey Gould, always met my reports on the progress of this book, and all my other adventures, with curiosity and encouragement. They nurtured my love of the outdoors when I was a child by leaving me alone to roam outside and taking us hiking in many beautiful places around Louisville, Kentucky. I am truly blessed to have had parents such as these!

Thanks to my husband Rob for his easy toleration of long separations due to my forays into the field and for not minding the many hours I spent in my study reading and writing. Our life together gives me much pleasure, and his presence in the days and nights since this book began has been a great gift.

Much of the writing of this book took place while my three children, Dasa, Jonah, and Clara, still lived with me, before they left home to make lives of their own. Their existence has enriched my life and given me more joy and delight than I can ever say. This book is dedicated to them, with all my love.

Introduction

For All the Wild Hearts

In July 2000, federal agents raided an environmental action camp in Mt. Hood National Forest that was established to protect old-growth forests and their inhabitants, including endangered species, from logging. High above the forest floor, activists had constructed a platform made of rope and plywood where several of them swung from hammocks. Seventeen-year-old Emma Murphy-Ellis held off law enforcement teams for almost eight hours by placing a noose around her neck and threatening to hang herself if they came too close.[1] Murphy-Ellis, going by her forest name Usnea, explained her motivation in the following way: "I state without fear—but with the hope of rallying our collective courage—that I support radical actions. I support tools like industrial sabotage, monkey-wrenching machinery and strategic arson. The Earth's situation is dire. If other methods are not enough, we must not allow concerns about property rights to stop us from protecting the land, sea and air."[2] Murphy-Ellis speaks for most radical activists who are ready to put their bodies on the line to defend trees or animals, other lives that they value as much as their own.[3]

For the Wild is a study of radical environmental and animal rights activism in late twentieth- and early twenty-first-century America. I set out to explore how teenagers like Murphy-Ellis become committed to forests and animals as worthy of protection and personal sacrifice. I wanted to find out how nature becomes sacred to them, how animals, trees, and mountains come to be what is important and worth sacrificing for. This work is about the paths young activists find themselves follow-ing, in tree-sits and road blockades to protect old-growth forests and endangered bird species, or breaking into fur farms at night to release hundreds of mink from cages. These young people join loosely organ-ized, leaderless groups like Earth First! and the Animal Liberation Front (ALF), coming to protests from contexts as different as significant child-hood experiences in nature and the hardcore punk rock music scene. Various other experiences also spark their commitments, such as viewing a documentary about baby seal hunts or witnessing a grove of woods they loved being turned into a parking lot. What their paths to activism have in common is the growing recognition of a world shared with other, equally valuable beings, and a determined certainty that they have a duty to these others.

In their accounts of becoming activists, emotions play an important role in shaping their commitments. Love for other-than-human species, compassion for their suffering, anger about the impact of contemporary human lifestyles on the lives of nonhuman species, and grief over the degradation of ecosystems—each of these emotions are expressed through and emerge out of what I describe as *protest rites*. This is a study of how radical activists make and remake themselves into activists through pro-tests and other ritualized activities. It is at the sites of protests that activ-ists' *inner histories* composed of memories, places, beings, and emotions come together with social movements such as environmentalism, femi-nism, anticapitalism, and anarchism, to provide these young people with the raw material out of which they fashion activist identities and com-munities. *For the Wild* is concerned with fundamental questions about human identity construction in relation to others, human and nonhuman. It investigates the role of childhood experience and memory in adult iden-tity and the contours and meanings of our multiple relationships with the more-than-human world. It attempts to understand the connections between individual worldviews, collective ritual, and social change. I explore what the case of radical activists tells us more generally about memory, ritual, commitment, and human behavior, about how the lives of other-than-human beings come to matter, and especially about young adult behavior, since most activists first become involved with activism during their teenage years or early twenties.

Radical activists may be living out their most deeply held commit-ments, becoming heroes to each other in the process, but to outsiders they are often seen as "eco-terrorists."[4] Cable Network News reported in 2005 that in the view of John Lewis, an FBI deputy assistant director and top official in charge of domestic terrorism, "The No. 1 domestic terrorism threat is the eco-terrorism, animal-rights movement."[5] A few years earlier, *Rolling Stone* reported that FBI director Louis Freeh testified before a Senate subcommittee that "the most recognizable single-issue terrorists at the present time are those involved in the violent animal-rights, anti-abortion and environmental-protection movements."[6] According to the FBI, groups like the ALF and the Earth Liberation Front (ELF) have "committed more than 1100 criminal acts causing more than $100 million in damage."[7] Since the beginning of the twenty-first century, environmental and animal rights activists have been aggressively pursued by the FBI, as journalist Will Potter illustrates in his account of the persecution of "eco-terrorists," *Green Is the New Red.*[8] In 2005 the federal government made highly publicized arrests in what FBI agents dubbed "Operation Backfire," the largest round-up of eco-activists in American history. Two years later, ten defendants were convicted on federal arson and vandalism charges, receiving sentences ranging from three to thirteen years. Although no one was hurt or killed in any of the acts, federal prosecutors had argued for life sentences. Even with the threat of prison time, after Operation Backfire radical environmentalists and animal rights activists continued to operate both clandestinely and through aboveground protests. The two movements increasingly converged during the second decade of the twenty-first century. However, the primary focus of this book is on the second half of the 1990s and the early 2000s, when those activists who received significant prison sentences were participating in direct actions in the United States.

For the Wild considers the following questions: How do young people become activists in a network of relationships with trees, other activists, nonhuman animals, and landscapes, acted on by and acting upon different agencies, human and other-than-human? What are the most central emotional and other kinds of experiences from childhood and young adulthood that inspire extreme commitments and shape protest practices? What idealized and desired relations between human and nonhuman bodies are implicated in and emerge from protests? What forms of gender and ethnic identity are contested, deployed, constructed, and negotiated during ritualized actions involved with protests, and what kinds of fractures and conflicts within activist communities are revealed? What bearing do activist protests on behalf of the environment have on social and political change or new forms of democracy in terms of spatial practices and decision-making structures? How do activists express and deal with the grief and loss that accompany environmental devastation and climate change? In order to address these and other questions about radical environmentalism and animal rights, I focus on the role of childhood experience, youth culture, embodied ritual actions, and the emotions of wonder, love, anger, compassion, and grief.

SCHOLARLY CONTEXT AND BACKGROUND

My study is situated at the intersection of a number of disciplinary fields, including religious studies, environmental studies, cultural anthropology, ritual studies, critical animal studies, and youth subculture studies. *For the Wild* is very much an account of youth, a stage of life after childhood that extends through the early twenties.[9] Young people are often disregarded in scholarship on religion and spirituality, even though teenage and young adult years are formative in shaping spiritualities and worldviews.[10] The intersection of youth culture, religion/spirituality, and activism has been particularly neglected by scholars, including by cultural studies research on youth subcultures.[11] Moreover, the small body of work on teenagers and religion is almost completely focused on Abrahamic religions, particularly Christianity, and rarely includes religious experiences of the natural world or beliefs about animals and the environment.[12] My emphasis is on the ways in which spiritual orientations and experiences are intertwined with other shaping factors as young adults come to believe that they must put their lives on the line for nonhuman animals and the natural world.

It is particularly interesting that spiritual aspects of these movements have been ignored, since many representations of activists by the news media and law enforcement focus on their moral lack. Activists do feel a lack, but it is not the absence of morality. Spring, an activist I met at an environmentalist gathering in Pennsylvania, touched her chest and told me, "I always felt an emptiness . . . because the earth is being destroyed and I needed to work to do something." Part of the problem, she explained, is that our society "denies our spiritual connection to the earth."[13] In depictions of activists as terrorists, they are shown to be morally deficient, when in fact it is deep spiritual connections and moral commitments that result in actions that sometimes land them in prison.

This study is ethnographic in nature, but also informed by other types of approaches that focus on how environmental and nonhuman animal issues are entangled with human ways of being in the world. These different disciplinary orientations help me address the ways in which activist youth come to express and practice their spiritual and moral commitments through rites of protest against environmental devastation and animal suffering. My work draws heavily on recent trends in anthropology, environmental humanities, and science studies that suggest new ways of thinking about relationships with other species as well as with the material world.[14] I have been helped by revised understandings of animism, the new materialism, and other approaches that decenter the human and work on the boundary (or lack thereof) between human and other-than-human lives.[15] Like activists, these scholarly approaches challenge strict distinctions between the human and the larger-than human world. They ask how we should think about our relationship to other species and landscapes when we share so much of our lives and even our very cells and selves with them. Our bodies and identities are not easily distinguished from those of others, even matter as inanimate as the rocky assemblages and mountains some of us call home.[16] *How* we come into being and *who* we identify as a person or significant presence in the world are processes that take place in particular cultural and historical contexts.

In addition to twenty-first-century developments, there are ancient examples of ways in which humans come into being in a world of relationships with other-than-human beings and landscapes. Aspects of Asian traditions such as Taoism and Confucianism, as well as many indigenous worldviews, express similar orientations towards human entanglement in and inextricability from the more-than-human world.[17] Many activists are informed by and/or borrow from these traditions.

In the opening decades of the twenty-first century, views of our responsibility for and entangled relationships with species and landscapes have even been expressed in the political realm, such as through movements to bestow legal rights on nature. In 2008 Ecuador became the first country to include the rights of nature in its constitution. These rights include the following: "Rights for Nature. Rather than treating nature as property under the law, Rights for Nature articles acknowledge that nature in all its life forms has the *right to exist, persist, maintain and regenerate its vital cycles*. And we—the people—have the legal authority to enforce these rights on behalf of ecosystems. The ecosystem itself can be named as the defendant."[18] In a similar fashion, in the global North, science studies scholar Bruno Latour and other scholars, students, and artists prepared for the 2015 Paris climate talks by creating an event at a Paris theatre called "Paris Climat 2015 Make It Work/Theatre of Negotiations" in which natural entities like "soil" and "ocean" were given representation and "territorial connections" were emphasized over nation-states. During the event, nonspeaking entities from fish to trees to the polar regions were spoken for and included in negotiations around climate and geopolitics.[19] Like radical environmental and animal rights activism, these efforts might be seen as a ritualized politics of the Anthropocene. They are responding to widespread recognition that human reshaping of the planet and its systems through nuclear tests, plastics, and domesticated animals, among many other examples, has been so profound that we have entered a now geological epoch.[20]

Like the Ecuador constitution and participants in the Theatre of Negotiations, animal rights and environmental activists speak *for* natural entities. Activist bodies and identities emerge within specific kinds of relationships with other beings in a variety of complex ways that lead activists to protests. For this reason, I want to emphasize activists' "becoming with" other-than-human beings, both intimate and distant. I approach young adults' transformation into activists as *a biosocial becoming*, to borrow a term from anthropologists Tim Ingold and Gisli Palsson, a process in which activists should not be understood as clearly bounded "*beings* but as *becomings*" in relationship to many other beings.[21] Science studies scholar Donna Haraway's view of co-becoming also emphasizes the complex and dynamic ways we relate to other species and the life we share with them, even at a cellular level, because human nature is fundamentally "an interspecies relationship."[22] Activist identities emerge from their interactions with many species and landscapes through childhood and young adulthood, as they become human with these others over time, reactivating themselves, so to speak, as they relate to trees, nonhuman animals, and landscapes where they find themselves at protests. It is through these ongoing relationships that they come to know these others' pain and suffering as their own, that they come to fight "for the wild" and "for the animals," as they often sign letters and press releases.

For many activists, caring arises from encounters with an objective reality of suffering and devastation that they experience in the world, an encounter with a mink in a cage or what is left of a mountain after its top has been removed to get at the coal inside. Encounters with humans affected by devastation play a part too in moving them towards action. For anti–mountaintop removal activists such as RAMPS (Radical Action for Mountains' and People's Survival), for example, the faces of people in poor communities affected by polluted water are as important as ruined mountains plowed over for the coal beneath them.[23] For these beings and places, activists must act; they have no other choice. Theirs is a politics of intimacy with these others that emerges from direct encounters with a living, multispecies world. *For the Wild* uncovers and explores the deep experiential roots of activists' political commitments as a reaction to the profound reconfiguration of planet Earth and its beings by industrialized civilizations.

My exploration of the role of ritual and emotion in the commitments of radical activists pushes towards a broader understanding of the stream of American thought and practice historian Catherine Albanese has called "nature religion."[24] Like many of the examples Albanese discusses, activists are more interested in this-worldly than otherworldly concerns, or as activist Josh Harper put it when explaining his disinterest in religion: "this world is primary."[25] They are likely to say they are agnostic or atheist, yet approach activism as a sacred duty, putting into practice a nonanthropocentric morality. Animals and the natural world are what they care about most, although they link environmental and animal issues to struggles for social justice.

As a study of spiritually informed activism, among other things, this book investigates activists' lived experience of nature and nonhuman animals as central to their worlds of meaning. I draw especially on Robert Orsi's definition of religion as "a network of relationships between heaven and earth involving humans of all ages and many different sacred figures together."[26] In what follows, I will suggest some of the ways that radical activists make special, and even sacred, relationships between human and nonhuman *earthly* others, including not only nonhuman animals and trees but also other activists who have become comrades and martyrs in a holy crusade to save the wild. While some activists may see the Earth's body as Gaia or trees as gods and goddesses, they are more likely to emphasize the *sacred relationships* we have with other species and the *sacred duties* and responsibilities we consequently owe them. Trees and nonhuman animals, or even the Earth itself in a more abstract sense, are regarded by activists with awe and reverence. And what these activists set apart from the sacred as profane are the human actions and machines that threaten these beings and places. In the context of activism, "sacred"—a sacred crusade to save the wild or the sacredness of a forest—designates those for whom activists will *sacrifice* their own comfort and safety.[27] These beings and special places are worth the discomfort of many days in tree-sits and the risk of long prison sentences. It is the meanings and origins of these sacred relationships and duties that I focus on in this work.

A number of activists told me they do not like the term *activist* for various reasons, but I have chosen to retain it because I am most interested in *actions* that express their commitments and desires. This study is practice centered and focuses on what activists do and how they came to do it, as well as the beliefs behind their actions. For the purposes of this book, I define radical activists as those who reject anthropocentrism and speciesism and practice direct action.[28] Through direct action they challenge assumptions about human exceptionalism and boundaries between species used to exclude nonhuman species from moral consideration. They also think of themselves as "radicals" in ways I will explore at length, but that include identification with anarchism and the strategies and beliefs of earlier radical movements like the Black Panthers and gay rights. Animal rights activists and radical environmentalists are also closely affiliated with contemporary anticapitalism radicals, such as the Occupy movement. For some radical environmentalists such as Earth First!ers, being radical is about getting to the *roots* of environmental destruction: our very ways of thinking and acting as human beings on a planet where we coexist with many other species.[29] Being radical separates these activists from more mainstream environmental groups—the Sierra Club, for example—and animal rights organization such as the Humane Society (HSUSA). They critically point to the compromises made by mainstream environmental and animal rights organizations and highlight their own refusal to compromise. They engage in direct action and promote an "every tool in the toolbox" approach to environmental and animal issues. Such a toolbox includes illegal acts of property destruction such as arson, occupation of corporate offices, sabotage of machinery, and animal releases, differentiating them from organizations that eschew illegal and confrontational tactics. The refusal to compromise is a hallmark of radical commitment: if eco-activism is a sacred crusade for the wild and for the animals, ideally, then, nothing should prevent activists from acting for them.

THE ROOTS OF RADICAL ACTIVISM

Late twentieth- and early twenty-first-century radical animal rights and environmental activism's origins are complex, the background of participants is diverse, and the two movements have somewhat different genealogies that I trace in more detail in Chapter 2. Radical environmentalism draws on seven main sources that have contributed to expressions of activism seen in Earth First! and the ELF:

1. What historian Catherine L. Albanese has described as "nature religion": ideas and practices as diverse as those of Native Americans and New England Transcendentalists like Emerson and Thoreau, that make nature their "symbolic center."[30] Religious studies scholar Bron Taylor further specifies a strain of American nature religion that he calls "dark green religion," that includes radical environmentalists and is characterized by adherence to the view that "nature is sacred, has intrinsic value, and is therefore due reverent care."[31] Taylor discusses the nature religion of radical environmentalists in a number of articles where he argues among other things that ecotage itself is "ritual worship."[32] This view is shared by sociologist Rik Scarce, who characterizes tree-sitting as a "quasi-religious act of devotion."[33] Historical studies by Evan Berry and Mark R. Stoll broaden this tradition of nature religion by suggesting that nineteenth-century and early twentieth-century American environmentalism was shaped in important ways by Protestant forms of Christianity.[34]

2. The secular environmentalist movement that emerged in the 1960s, built on earlier activities, and was expressed in initiatives such as the Wilderness Act (1964) and Earth Day (1970).[35]

3. Deep ecological views, particularly the work of Arne Naess, Bill Devall, and George Sessions, that have shaped and been shaped by nature religion and the environmental movement. Norwegian philosopher and mountaineer Naess coined the term "deep ecology" in 1973, as a contrast to the "shallow" ecology movement. Deep ecologists promote an ecological self and eco-centric rather than anthropocentric values.[36]

4. The fourth source is a related set of social and political movements that also emerged out of and were significantly shaped by the 1960s counterculture and include the antiwar movement, feminism, and gay rights, as well as environmentalism.[37]

5. Contemporary Paganism/Neopaganism. While many activists do not consider themselves religious or Pagan, nevertheless, contemporary Paganism had a significant influence in the 1980s and 1990s on forest activism in the Western United States, and on important activist organizations like Earth First![38]

6. Indigenous cultures. Activists are also influenced by their understanding of Native Americans' relationships to other species. However, they tend to be sensitive about appropriating these

views for their own use in fear of perpetuating European colonialism and a mentality characteristic of "settlers" who are not indigenous to North America. Activists' appropriation of indigenous beliefs and practices as well as their desire to support indigenous people's struggles has been a significant but contested subject in the history of radical environmentalism, which I discuss at length in Chapter 6.[39]

7. Anarchism, especially global anticapitalist movements like Occupy Wall Street and green anarchism, or anarcho-primitivism, especially the writings of John Zerzan, Derrick Jensen, and Kevin Tucker.[40]

Radical animal rights activism developed in the United States alongside radical environmentalism. Both movements emphasize direct action, criticize speciesism and anthropocentrism, often link their concerns to social justice struggles, and situate themselves within a lineage of radicalism. While many animal rights activists have also been influenced by deep ecology and some by contemporary Paganism, radical animal rights in the 1990s and 2000s was more significantly shaped by anarchism and the hardcore punk rock subculture, especially a movement called straightedge that I explore in detail in Chapter 5. Radical animal rights activism is also one of many expressions of shifting changes in understandings of the relationships between human and nonhuman animals in the United States and in the global North in general, which I discuss in Chapter 2.

SOURCES AND METHODS

For the Wild is informed by multiple methods, but most centrally by ethnographic fieldwork. I have supplemented ethnographic research with a variety of other sources of information about activists' experiences and commitments. I base my exploration of radical animal rights and environmentalism on several kinds of primary sources. The first is written, emailed, or in-person correspondence and interviews with environmental and animal rights activists, including those serving prison sentences during our correspondence. Some of them were organizers for activist groups or gatherings, including the Buffalo Field Campaign, North Coast Earth First!, Earth First! Rendezvous, the Animal Rights conference, and the North American Animal Liberation Press Office. I also conducted informal and recorded interviews with a number of activists, either during gatherings (never recorded), at coffee shops and restaurants (usually recorded), and at the *Earth First! Journal* collective (recorded).

I supplemented correspondence and interviews with participant-observation at five gatherings, some of which featured direct actions, including the annual Earth First! Round River Rendezvous, which I attended in 2009 (Oregon), 2012 (Pennsylvania), and 2013 (North Carolina); Wild Roots, Feral Futures in 2013 (Colorado); the Trans and Womyn's Action Camp 2014 (TWAC, California); and the Animal Rights conference in 2009 (Los Angeles). These gatherings, usually held annually, are primarily for sharing information and experiences, creating community, getting various kinds of training, and airing conflicts. The Earth First! Rendezvous and TWAC gatherings usually include preparing for and engaging in direct actions, such as blocking a road to a hydraulic fracturing ("fracking") site. In each instance I contacted the organizers in advance, explained my project and let them know that I would not be making any recordings, visual or audio, during the gatherings, because anonymity and privacy are important to activists. I have used pseudonyms or "forest names" for my interlocutors, depending on their preference and have disguised other identifying features. In the case of well-known activists, such as those who have served prison sentences, I have usually retained their real names so as to be consistent when discussing references to them in the news media and elsewhere. I did not interview or contact any minors; instead, I focused on young adults' reflections on their teenage years.

I participated in all aspects of activist gatherings: I used gathering ride boards to find riders to travel with me to gatherings, ate meals in the communal dining areas, prepared food, washed dishes, went through a street medic training, volunteered in the medic tent, learned how to climb trees, went to workshops and direct action trainings, learned chants for protests, and held signs and sang chants at protests.

As a participant and observer I often struggled to balance my two roles. In many ways I blended in with activists in terms of my values and interests. I consider myself an environmentalist who travels by bicycle as much as possible, who does not own a dryer, who composts, reuses, and recycles. As a long-time vegetarian, vegan food and arguments for veganism and vegetarianism were familiar to me. My own story intersects with the stories of activists at a number of other junctures as well. At nineteen, while in college, I became involved with nonviolent direct action during the antinuclear movement of the late 1970s, participating in antinuclear collectives and protests in Kentucky and North Carolina. During those years I was introduced to some of the practices used by contemporary environmental and animal rights organizations, such as nonviolent direct action, talking circles, consensus decision making, and affinity groups. In the early 1980s, I spent many hours at punk rock and hardcore shows. A few years later I entered graduate school, earning a doctorate in religious studies at Indiana University, Bloomington, where I also minored in women's studies and taught in I. U.'s Women's Studies program while finishing my dissertation on contemporary Pagan festivals. In these and other ways, I was involved with practices, movements, and ideas that shaped radical environmentalism and animal rights activism a generation later.

On the other hand, I was an outsider at activist gatherings, not currently working on a direct action campaign and over twenty years older than the majority of participants. I did not blend in. There were activists around my age, but not many, and some participants probably suspected I was spying on them, even though it is unlikely someone trying to gather intelligence on activists would look like me. Informants such as "Anna," a twenty-one-year-old FBI agent who infiltrated an ELF collective, do their best to blend into the crowd, which I did not. My visibility as an outsider was both an asset and a liability. I was not privy to some of the more secretive conversations, especially involving actions, and thus missed out on negotiations and concerns at that level of involvement. On the other hand, being treated a bit suspiciously worked in my favor in that I was less likely to be told about anything illegal. I made it a point not to ask about underground actions, only those actions activists had already been sentenced for or that were public, above-ground, and covered by the news media. All of these experiences had a profound influence on how I related to what I heard and saw during my research and have contributed to how I have written this story about radical activism.

My age and life experience turned out to be useful. Because of a stint working in restaurants as a young adult, I could easily follow directions and make myself useful in community kitchens at gatherings. Given years of dealing with a variety of classroom dynamics, I handled situations that required a calm demeanor, such as helping in the medic tent or filling in as a police liaison when the assigned liaison was needed elsewhere during an action. No doubt the police treated me differently as well. As I became more familiar to the communities by participating in all aspects of the gatherings, most activists eventually seemed to accept my presence. They were open with me in as many ways as they were suspicious of me, and many of them shared details of their lives, explaining what mattered to them and why in ways I could understand.

For the Wild is very much the result of intersubjective understandings that emerged from my conversations with activists and from the interfaces of my sensory, embedded experiences with activist communities. You will read my view of what emerged from our conversations, checked against other sources and other views. Any attempt at objectivity would be fragile and incomplete, and mine is no objective portrait of activism, although I try to fairly represent multiple views on most issues. No doubt activists would tell some of these stories differently. But their narratives would be multiple and varied too. Like me, many of them moved in and out of campaigns, returning to work and school in between, while others remained full-time activists. Some of those I spoke with had only been involved for a few months or were attending a protest for the first time, while others drew from many years of experience on campaigns to save wild places and nonhuman animals. There is no central organization in the anarchistic groups I learned from and participated in, no authority to turn to for an official interpretation. Meaning and authority in these movements emerge from what is happening on the ground, between people, in concert with landscapes and other species, and in essays about movement strategies and practices online and in print.

In addition to interviews and participant observation, I draw on three different kinds of primary print sources: published memoirs by environmental and animal rights activists, such as Paul Watson's *Seal Wars*; print publications such as the *Earth First! Journal* and *Satya: Vegetarianism, Animal Advocacy, Social Justice, Environmentalism*; and self-published, photocopied, and usually anonymous "zines" that I picked up at gatherings. These zines ranged from reprints of activist publications to self-authored essays such as those collected in the zine *Reclaim, Rewild: A Vision for Going Feral & Actualizing Our Wildest Dreams*. The final type of primary source was online documentation of actions and gatherings, including photographs, videos, and written accounts of actions and news stories on activist websites, particularly the Earth First! Newswire.[41]

Activists whom I met at gatherings or whose articles I read in print and online are incredibly diverse and difficult to generalize about. While there are well-known figures in these movements, such as Earth First! founder Dave Foreman or PETA founder Ingrid Newkirk, they are as likely to be criticized as emulated. Renowned activists like Jeff Luers and Marius Mason (formerly Marie), who served time in prison, were often referred to with awe and respect by other activists I met. But the communities I spent time with are leaderless; they have policies (such as nonoppressive behavior) that participants mostly agree on, but no

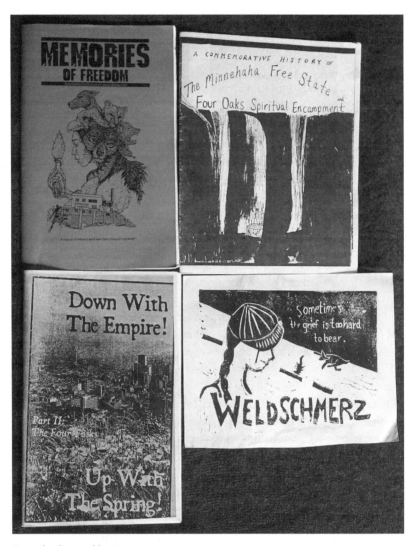

From the distro table: zines.

central organization. In what follows, I describe and analyze important trends and common views and experiences. While my observations will not fit every activist, it is my hope that activists will recognize their communities as I have depicted them and that I have accurately captured many of the values and experiences they share.

In my journey through the worlds of activists, two concepts have particularly troubled me: "nature" and "the wild." I try to use these words in the ways activists use them. But "nature" and "the wild" are, of course, constructions situated within a particular set of late modern conditions, including nostalgia for an imagined past in which humans lived more harmoniously with other species. "Nature" might be seen to include toxic chemicals and clearcuts as well as human beings, even human beings who have no respect for other species, but obviously this is not what activists mean when they refer to "nature." When activists say they want to protect nature or are "for the wild" and "for the animals," they mean they want to protect trees, animals, and relatively wild places from human interference to the greatest extent possible. Sometimes this means making animal testing illegal, getting an area designated as wilderness, or halting logging in old-growth forests and areas inhabited by endangered species. Of course imagining forests or any wild landscape as a place of human absence, a place apart from culture, also depends on erasing the cultures that dwelt and sometimes now dwell there. Some activists have a more sophisticated understanding of history than others; they know that Native Americans managed forests and grasslands, that the "wild" as we understand it in contemporary North America has been made over by humans for millennia. Others see our encroachment as more recent. But in both cases the "most important thing we can do," according to Rabbit, an editor at the *Earth First! Journal*, is "protecting what we have left that is wild . . . and trying to rewild the rest . . . The world without so much human involvement had worked for a long time."[42]

In addition to extending rights and protection to other species and wilderness areas, many activists emphasize human animality and the need for us to "rewild" *our* lives, in order to become more feral than civilized. "Nature" and "the wild" then, tend to mean places and states of being that are not domesticated, not controlled by humans, and usually set in opposition to industrialized "civilization," an opposition that I describe and analyze throughout the following chapters. Rewilding of the human self in a community of other species is a personal transformation that mirrors the transformation of ecosystems by rewilding and reverses domestication. Such transformations come about through particular kinds of embodied practices and experiences, often ritualized.

RITES OF CONVERSION AND PROTEST

I turn to ritual as another perspective on activism.[43] In order to best understand how activists express their commitment to the wild, the tools of ritual studies have been particularly helpful to me. *For the Wild* is about two kinds of ritual: conversion as a rite of passage or initiation into activism and protests as ritualized actions. Conversion tends to take place on an internal and personal level, while protests are usually participatory and collective. In the context of conversion to activism, I explore the ways in which the love, wonder, rage, and grief that motivate radical activists develop through powerful, embodied relationships with nonhuman beings. Conversion to activism can happen in a matter of moments, during what some activists describe as a tipping point, or it can be a longer, more subtle internal process of shifting one's worldview.[44] It may happen within a protest setting such as a tree-sit or road blockade, when listening to vegan hardcore punk rock, as a result of the death of a nonhuman animal friend, or while watching a video about seal slaughter, to name some of the examples described in this book.

Protests like tree-sits and animal liberations are ritualized actions or events. In this study I understand ritual as a distinctive way of enacting and constituting relationships among humans, as well as between humans and other-than-human beings (animals, trees, etc.) or "nature" writ large.[45] Protests call into question destructive relationships between humans and other species. They also suggest new kinds of relationships between humans and the others with whom we are entangled on this earth. Our human situatedness in terms of gender, class, ethnic background, age, and ability also shapes the kinds of relationality we experience with other beings, human and other-than-human. The relationships that are expressed in and emerge from protests challenge human superiority as well as lines dividing us from other species. Protests create and express particular kinds of bonds among activists (such as bonds of love and solidarity or bonds of animosity and difference) as well as between activists and loggers, construction workers, animal researchers, and law enforcement. These latter are often but by no means always oppositional. In these ways, protests express and create a world of interrelated life forms, co-shaping each other. What emerges during protests is a larger-than-human world brimming with diverse forms of life and full of meanings and spirit, a world composed of relationships between many different kinds of humans, various species, bodies of water, rocky assemblages, and landscapes.

Environmental and animal rights protests feature at least some of the following aspects: (1) a particular focus, orientation, and/or way of participating; (2) a reconfiguration of space; (3) the danger or vulnerability of participants; (4) an enactment of particular realities and ideals; and (5) experiences of both collective solidarity and tension/conflict.[46] I wanted to explore a range of environmental protests in order to think through what happens in protest rituals and what theoretical tools might help us understand the ways rituals constitute social relationships and bring about or do not bring about change, such as legal protections for wild places or nonhuman animals. What kinds of boundaries are called into question by particular protest rituals? What boundary crossing takes place in the ritual space? What or who is transformed when boundaries are crossed? How are boundaries we all take for granted dissolved? Will that dissolution continue after the ritual protest, and how will that dissolution manifest?

Protests involve a number of intentional actions and specific modes of participation that carry special meaning within the context of activism. These may include playful practices such as "radical cheerleading" in which chants and dance moves are focused on the issues at hand, such as fracking or coal mining. Other modes of participation might be climbing trainings held before or during tree-sits to teach techniques of the body and skills that require a specific focus on the danger and meaning of climbing in an event. Recreation is not the reason activists learn chants or how to safely climb trees; theirs is a different focus and mode of interaction in relation to these activities. While it may be challenging or enjoyable, activist climbing is about climbers' intentions, about getting into a tree or onto a building to drop a banner in order to disrupt or prevent logging, mining, road building, and so on. Activist medic trainings include learning how to flush out protesters' eyes after they have been pepper sprayed. Confrontations with law enforcement officers are rehearsed in order to defuse potential violence and avoid being triggered into reacting violently. Before and during protests, these practices happen within specially focused spaces. While some of them may be continuous with everyday activities such as climbing trees for fun or working in a hospital, they carry particular meanings at activist gatherings and events. Ritualized actions within specific spatial and temporal contexts negotiate and express activists' orientation to the world and relationships with many other beings.

Protest actions usually involve reconfiguring space. This can include actions such as overturning a van to which activists lock themselves in order to block a logging road or building a tree village with platforms and ropes in a grove of trees to prevent trees from being bulldozed for a natural gas pipeline or a new highway. This reconfiguring may even involve the destruction of certain kinds of spaces, such as an ELF action against a wild horse corral that involved both the release of horses and the burning down of the corral. In these cases, what activists change constitutes another way of being in relation to the logging road (resisting its use by logging machinery) and to the horses (preventing their captivity rather than supporting it).

During such protests, activists' pain and sacrifice may play an important role, just as the suffering and pain of nonhuman others shape activists' commitments. Activists put themselves in danger, committing acts of arson that could carry lengthy prison sentences, splaying their bodies on the ground in front of bulldozers, or hanging precariously from redwood canopies. These ritualized actions are intended to challenge assumptions about what and who is of value. Most forest actions that try to delay logging and draw attention to endangered old-growth forests involve positioning human bodies between loggers and trees, so that logging cannot occur without hurting or killing activists. Some animal rights actions involve risky night-time exploits to free animals from locked and guarded research facilities.

These protests work in part because of the risks protesters take, what communications scholar Kevin DeLuca calls their "utter vulnerability."[47] Risky protest tactics heighten suspense and increase the identification between activists and those on whose behalf they are acting. These protests are ritualized interventions, ruptures that rearrange the taken-for-granted order of society by placing value on the lives of redwood trees and spotted owls and by risking one's own body for these other bodies. In this way, the danger and precarity involved in protests enact activist ideals, including a reality in which the more-than-human living world is valued and protected, even at the cost of human flourishing. Activists' precarious protesting bodies also remind viewers of the vulnerable species they identify with.

Protest rites continually remake activist identities that come about through conversion to a set of commitments. In his classic study of adolescence, Erik Erikson observed that identity formation is the primary task of adolescence. Young people must forge a sense of self that will eventually allow them to leave their families. These new selves are formed in a *liminal* space, a space of transformation according to Victor Turner's, Arnold van Gennep's, and more recently, Ronald Grimes's research on rites of passage. Drawing on van Gennep, Grimes argues that rites of passage are "pivots, at which one's life trajectory veers, changing direction." These pivots, observes Grimes, "are moments of intense energy and danger, and ritual is the primary means of negotiating the rapids."[48] Activists' lives pivot in this way during intense and dangerous protests that inscribe identities on their bodies.

Earth First! Elliott Forest blockade bipod. Photo: Margaret
Killjoy. Licensed under Creative Commons 2.0.

In many cultures there are clearly defined steps that bound adolescent
liminality, but in contemporary American culture, these bounds are anything but clear. As Grimes puts it, "we know so few authentic and compelling rites," that adolescent rites of passage in the West often take a
"postmodern, peer-driven form" that can be vague or uncertain.[49] But
for many activists, there is nothing vague about the life-changing transformations they undergo when they become committed to activism.
Their initiation into activism is an irreversible change that effectively
divides their lives into a "before" and "after," a common feature of initiation rites.[50] While I use "conversion" and "initiation" interchangeably
here, initiation might be seen as more of a public process during which a

community of others, human and nonhuman, work on activists' lives. On the other hand, conversion is more of an internal process during which the shaping forces of human and nonhuman others are taken "deeply into the bone," to borrow Grimes's phrase.

Activists' accounts of how they became committed to activism tend to fall into two categories. For some, becoming an activist was a gradual process of being more true to themselves, confirming what they had always believed. For others, activism marked a critical point in their lives when they rejected many aspects of their upbringing or social status and chose activism. Both types of conversion involve a before and after, and different understandings of self-identity. The activist self is either completely different, or a new version of someone who was "always there." Throughout this book, I discuss both processes in detail, drawing attention to the different forces working on youth as they become activists. During their young adult years, activists-in-the-making do not become successfully socialized into what they describe as capitalist, anthropocentric American society. Instead, they experience conversion to a contrasting set of values and beliefs that shape their activist commitments. They reject many aspects of the culture around them in favor of anarchism, animal rights, and environmentalist commitments and they choose to break human laws in favor of what they consider a higher morality. I argue that their developing commitments to activism are a kind of *internal revolution* that marks a conversion to or initiation into activism.[51]

Rites of passage into activism are not entirely dissimilar to the rites activists have rejected from their pasts and criticized in the broader society. Activist conversion stories may incorporate the language of conversion common to some forms of Christianity, such as being "baptized" or "born again." Accounts of how they became committed to radical activism suggest that they express their conversion through the ritualized actions involved with protests.[52] Although activists typically move away from Western religious traditions, conversion to activism nevertheless sometimes includes the return and reincorporation of the language of Christian rites of passage such as "baptism," even when there are no accompanying ritual actions such as immersion. American Evangelicals are more typically identified with the born-again experience, but activists who reject Christianity redefine being born again in an unexpected context in which nature and animals, rather than God, become the sacred centers of their lives. Being born again as activists is a fundamental reorientation of meaning in which the lives of other-than-human beings come to be as valuable as their own.

The notion of a second chance or new life after conversion in which one's old ways are left behind is such a pervasive metaphor in American cultural history and American religion that it lends clout to conversion stories. At the animal rights conference in Los Angeles I attended in 2007, plenary speaker Alex Pacheco, one of the founders of PETA (People for the Ethical Treatment of Animals), told the audience that he was "baptized" into animal rights through his involvement with Paul Watson and Sea Shepherd (a direct action organization of activists formed to protect marine mammals and featured in the series *Whale Wars* that premiered in 2008 on cable station Animal Planet). He went on to describe his "second baptism" working with the underground ALF as a further stage in his initiation into activism. Another participant in the Los Angeles conference, who said she grew up as a "born-again Christian" and later left Christianity, also described being "born again" into the animal rights movement as beginning a new phase of her life.[53] In various sessions and workshops, other conference-goers identified a "tipping point" that set them moving towards their commitment to nonhuman animals, often the final stage in a series of experiences that had already prepared them for such a commitment.

These activists, while painted as extremists, might also be seen as expressing concerns that cut across a broader swathe of the U.S. populace. Activism is one of many possible ways that young Americans, who experienced the greatest growth in the category of "spiritual but not religious" or "unaffiliated" in the early twentieth century, express spiritual and moral values outside religious institutions in unexpected places.[54] The widespread and surprising support among American youth for Bernie Sanders's campaign for the Democratic presidential nomination in 2015–2016 speaks to young people's dissatisfaction with the social and political status quo, including attitudes toward the more-than-human world. For instance, in September 2014, over 300,000 people converged on Manhattan for the peaceful People's Climate March that included mainstream environmental and animal rights activists, a large contingent of interfaith groups, and politicians such as former U.S. vice-president Al Gore, secretary general of the United Nations Ban Ki-Moon, and New York mayor Bill de Blasio.

By the second decade of the twenty-first century, concerns about climate change were not only the purview of environmentalists, just as the rights of sentient creatures were no longer only the concern of animal rights activists. These activists are the radical wing of a broader cultural shift in understanding humans' place in a multispecies world and a planet in peril. Their actions express trends in contemporary American spiritual expression and moral duties to the nonhuman at the turn of the millennium. Their beliefs and practices reflect a way of being in the world that decenters the human and calls for rethinking our appropriate place in the world vis-à-vis other species. They further our understanding of how younger Americans, in particular, situate the needs of human beings within a world of other species that they see themselves as closely related to and responsible for. I read radical activism as an important expression of social and political trends in the beginning of the twenty-first century that call into question American government and social institutions, as well as fundamental assumptions of what democracy means in the United States in this era and what it might mean in the future.

A READER'S MAP

Chapters 1 and 2 provide introductory material and context for the other chapters. Chapter 1 introduces the reader to activists' lives and work as well as background on the communities I most often interacted with. Chapter 2 lays out some historical context for the other chapters by charting the convergence of youth culture, North American spiritual and political movements, and environmental and animal rights activism. Radical activism among young adults emerged from the conjunction of a number of historical forces. These forces shaped the particular ways activism has come to be expressed within the radical environmental and animal rights movements of late twentieth- and early twenty-first-century America. In this chapter I suggest that activists travel through *networks of affiliation*, including the Occupy movement, hardcore punk rock, gender studies classes, veganism, anarchist infoshops (bookstores, rooms, and/or meeting areas where radical literature and other information is shared), and Food Not Bombs. I place these networks within the historical trajectories of social, religious, environmental, and political movements, including anarchism, feminism, gay rights, deep ecology, contemporary Paganism, and youth cultural movements. More than anything else, the radical activist communities I explore in this book are composed of young adults grappling with the realities of the present and imagining a different kind of future in an era of global environmental change. In this chapter I argue for thinking about youth conversion and commitment in ways that avoid demonizing youth. To do so will involve understanding the deep historical roots of young adults' concerns about the plight of other species as well as their own.

Chapters 3 through 7 cover a lifespan of activism, beginning with childhood experience and ending with mourning the deaths of human and other-than-human beings. Each of these chapters also considers the ways in which particular kinds of emotional experiences shape activist commitments. Chapter 3 focuses on the experience of *wonder* within the landscape of childhood and introduces the notion that activists' inner histories composed of memories and childhood experiences are brought to and emerge during activist gatherings and direct actions. The extent to which the remembered childhood landscape is imbued with wonder may affect the intensity of activists' grief over destroyed landscapes and mistreatment of nonhuman animals. At activist gatherings and direct actions, activists revisit and reconstruct childhood experiences. Rather than severing their lives from childhood, some of them engage in a creative reworking of childhood experiences by creating a deep ecological politics of action.

Chapters 4 and 5 present two possible ways that young people might undergo a rite of passage in the process of becoming activists: one in forest action camps and the other through participation in urban straight-edge/hardcore punk rock scenes. Chapter 4 describes the ways in which some activists' deepening commitments to other species are shaped by *love* and feelings of kinship in the context of forest activism. In this chapter, I suggest that tree-sits and other actions act simultaneously as rites of passage and rites of protest. Activists travel to forests and experience a sense of belonging in these separate spaces away from a society most of them have rejected. They create action camps and protests as spaces apart, as the larger-than-human world becomes more real to them and the human society they were born into becomes more distant. In these spaces apart they often seek to decolonize and rewild what has been domesticated and colonized. Through complex relationships of intimacy and distance expressed in rites of identification and disidentification, they draw closer to the wild and farther away from other humans outside activist communities. Their vision is one of a feral future in which the wild takes over cities and suburbs, as well as their own bodies and souls, reversing what they see as the relentlessly destructive movement of a doomed civilization.

Chapter 5 explores the interweaving of music, Hindu religious beliefs, and activism motivated by *anger* in the context of hardcore punk rock. In this chapter, I describe the unlikely convergence of hardcore punk rock, Krishna Consciousness, and animal rights in youth subcultural spaces in order to understand how the aural and spiritual worlds created by some bands shaped the emergence of radical animal rights in the 1990s. At times these music scenes nurtured the idea of other species as sacred beings and sparked outrage at their use and abuse by humans. Bands made fans into activists who brought moral outrage and the intensity of hardcore to direct actions in forests, at animal testing labs and mink farms, and against hunting and factory farming. In this chapter I also explore the extremism sometimes associated with radicalization that can emerge from oppositional stances as activist and hardcore communities negotiate a variety of tensions concerning gender and ethnicity.

In Chapter 6 I explore conflicts within activist communities more intently by considering how activists both *soften and sharpen the bounds of inclusion* through ritual and spatial strategies, the ways in which they include and exclude self and other as they make and remake sacred and safe spaces within their communities. Chapter 6 analyzes the efforts of activists to create community among people with different agendas and backgrounds and the resultant tensions and conflicts that come about in the process. I look closely at activists' work to build communities that bring together environmental and animal rights activism with concerns about social justice, especially with regard to people of color. Activist gatherings are imagined as free and open spaces of inclusivity and equality, and yet they set up their own patterns of conformity and expectation. This chapter looks closely at how putting the "Earth first" comes in conflict with "anti-oppression" efforts and vice-versa, as activists work hard, drawing on empathy and *compassion*, to "decolonize" their communities and "dismantle patriarchy" and transphobia within their movements.

Finally, Chapter 7 describes activists' *grief* and despair over loss and extinction. Through the study of grief over lost places, tree friends, whole species, and human comrades, I suggest that protests can be understood as rites of mourning. Memories of childhood wonder, feelings of love and kinship for other species, empathizing with oppressed human communities, raging at injustice with hardcore bands, all make the loss of friends and other species even more keenly felt as activists face the realities of mass extinction and climate change. I explore their experience of environmental devastation and species loss as a kind of perpetual mourning from which they cannot escape. And yet, in all this loss, many of them find hope for a *primal future*, beyond the human. This chapter looks at how they make losses visible to each other through their own ritualized vulnerability and martyrdom and to the public through ritualized protest and media exposure.

In the book's Conclusion, I consider the *after-lives* of activists and activism. What does it mean, after all, to act "for the wild" and "for the animals" throughout one's lifespan? What comes after youthful conversion, if that life-changing experience is irreversible? What kind of long-term human existence and moral life does radical activism entail? If activism is a kind of liminal existence, an extended rite of passage, what kind of life do activists pass into, and what kind of world do they work to usher in? What commitments and communities take shape and endure? How might radical animal rights and environmental activism be seen in relation to other radical protests of the early twenty-first century, including Black Lives Matter and the Standing Rock Dakota Pipeline protest, as well as antigovernment protests on the Right. I conclude by suggesting what this study has, in the end, to say about youth culture, ritual, memory, and contemporary spirituality in the contexts of radical environmental and animal rights movements and broader political and social shifts in the early twenty-first century. These movements are significant signs of changing times as human and other-than-human communities face and respond to powerful social, political, and climate challenges.

CHAPTER I

Freedom and Insurrection around a Fire

To act is to be committed, and to be committed
is to be in danger.

—James Baldwin, *The Fire Next Time*

My first involvement with a direct action took place in 2012 in western
Pennsylvania on the last day of Earth First!'s annual week-long Round
River Rendezvous, the largest gathering of radical environmentalists
from across North America.[1] The gathering was sponsored by Marcellus
Shale Earth First!, one of many regional Earth First! groups that alternate in hosting the Rendezvous. Every year, Earth First!ers come together
for workshops and opportunities to share local struggles with a nation-
wide community of activists working on diverse environmental and
social justice issues. The annual Rendezvous offers activists a space to
express their most deeply held beliefs and debate controversial issues, as
well as learn practical skills such as tree climbing and nonviolent resistance. The Rendezvous and other similar gatherings are open to anyone
and include newcomers to direct action as well as veteran protesters, and
participants in illegal underground actions as well as legal protest
marches. The focus of the Pennsylvania gathering was on hydraulic fracturing ("fracking"), which had been responsible for displacing communities and polluting groundwater in western Pennsylvania.[2]

Earth First! is the most prominent radical environmental organization in the United States today that focuses on direct action. For over
three decades, Earth First!ers have regularly engaged in actions "in
defense of Mother Earth" and have supported a variety of other related
causes, such as animal rights and indigenous land rights. Earth First!
has no central structure and is composed of a network of affiliated

groups in the United States and around the world, a journal run by an editorial collective, and two annual gatherings: the Round River Rendezvous and the Organizer's Conference, both planned by different collectives every year. Earth First! was founded by Dave Foreman, Mike Roselle, Howie Wolke, Bart Koehler, and Ron Kezar in 1980. It began as a wilderness protection organization, campaigning to maintain roadless areas under the motto "No Compromise for Mother Earth." Its founders were inspired by Edward Abbey's novel *The Monkey Wrench Gang* (1975), and according to journalist Susan Zakin, they made "ecotage—burning bulldozers, spiking trees, yanking up survey stakes—an attention-grabbing tactic in their no-compromise approach to saving wilderness."[3] Moreover, for Foreman and some of the other founders, direct action was part of "a sacred crusade" to protect the wild from encroachment by humans and their industries.[4]

In addition to Earth First!, the Animal Liberation Front (ALF) and Earth Liberation Front (ELF) were the most widespread and active radical direct action animal rights and environmental groups in the United States at the turn of the twenty-first century. They are also the groups most often mentioned by law enforcement and news media.[5] In the 1990s ALF and ELF became known for their confrontational tactics, acts of animal liberation, and property destruction, especially arson. These networks of activists have no central leadership and few rules. Both ELF and ALF condone property destruction and have guidelines against causing harm to living beings.[6]

From the 1980s into the twenty-first century, Earth First!ers and other radical environmentalists have advocated a "no compromise" commitment to "the wild." They have not only practiced monkeywrenching (sabotaging bulldozers and other heavy equipment, etc.), but have also placed their bodies between trees or nonhuman animals and destructive forces such as logging and fur farming. Environmental actions include a range of activities, such as tree-sits and road blockades to prevent logging and resource extraction. They drop banners in public places, occupy offices of timber or oil companies, and interfere with hunting. *The Earth First! Direct Action Manual*, available by mail, includes detailed instructions for ground blockades across roadways, aerial blockades such as tripods and tree-sit platforms, hunt sabotage, banner drops, destroying roadways and disabling tires, among a host of other ways to protect the environment and nonhuman animals. More extreme actions may include arson, such as the 1997 arson of the Cavel West horse slaughterhouse by the ELF. Radical animal rights activists such as the ALF also use arson to destroy animal research laboratories or other buildings. They release animals from fur farms and research facilities and set free wild horses that have been corralled. They harass animal researchers, sometimes also destroying their work.[7] In order to better understand the ways in which activists arrive at their "No Compromise" stance, and what exactly it means to them, I participated in some of their gatherings and protests.

As the sun was going down on a July evening in 2012, I navigated the back roads of western Pennsylvania, following directions downloaded from the Earth First! Rendezvous website. I missed the last turn and drove several miles before realizing my mistake, as the sky became darker and thick clouds gathered. With relief, I finally drove up to a "Welcome Home" banner and a couple of participants monitoring the gate, who welcomed me and gave me a program with safety warnings about ticks and dehydration, a map of the site, and an "Anti-Oppression and Consent Policy" addressing sexual harassment and other kinds of proscribed behavior. After driving down a gravel road into the forest, I reached a long line of cars parked along the side of the road, apart from the main camp that organizers wanted to keep car-free. Pennsylvania license plates were joined by those from New York, Florida, Massachusetts, North Carolina, Indiana, Oregon, and Ohio, among others, indicating that many activists had traveled from out of state to reach the gathering. Their cars displayed bumper stickers like "I 'heart' Mountains," "Local Food," "Collective Bargaining," "I'm Marching to a Different Accordion," "Eden Was Vegan," and "Comfort the Disturbed, Disturb the Comfortable."

As these bumper stickers suggest, the several hundred participants at the Rendezvous had diverse goals and interests. They came to the woods to learn from each other, share strategies, have fun, and participate in a culminating action at the end of the week designed to draw attention to hydro-fracking concerns in the region. Some had dropped out of high school and had been full-time activists for several years, while others were homeless young travelers who spent their time train hopping and hitchhiking around the country. These travelers sometimes participated in tree-sits or other direct actions; they also worked on farms to make money or busked in towns for change. Other participants were on summer break from elite private colleges, state universities, and community colleges. Some activists lived in permaculture communities or worked on organic farms, while others were from squatted houses in New York City. The majority lived in towns and cities, while fewer lived on farms or in rural areas. These activists came from a range of different class backgrounds, including the very poor and the wealthy, but the majority grew up in white middle-class households. I also met activists from working-class backgrounds, such as Thrush, whose family members were factory workers. He too worked in a factory, until one day he quit to join the Buffalo Field Campaign that monitors buffaloes around Yellowstone Park to keep them from getting shot by ranchers when they venture out of the park. Most activists I met were young (18–30) and most were white, with slightly more male-identified than female-identified and a handful of participants who were transgender, gender nonconforming, or people of color. Older participants do show up at these gatherings, but radical activism is overwhelmingly populated by young adults: few activists in the treetops and locked down to blockades are older than thirty.

Gatherings like the Rendezvous are approached as places apart from the world outside and at the same time as homes away from home, hence the "Welcome Home" banner. At gatherings, activists want to feel they can be at home in ways they may not be able to beyond the gathering boundaries. Even as they work and live in it, they tend to believe that industrialized civilizations, and especially American capitalism, are doomed. "I kind of think we're toast," climbing trainer Lakes told me.[8] For this and other reasons, some activists have separated themselves from the institutions and lifestyles they blame for environmental devastation, choosing to be homeless, living in their cars, or traveling from anarchist squat to action camp. For participants with more conventional lives, the Rendezvous may be a temporary escape from jobs at the heart of a society they feel at odds with. At the Rendezvous and other gatherings I also met nurses, lawyers, teachers, counselors, farmers, and small business owners.

That summer of 2012, deep in the Allegheny forest, I set up my tent on my first night just as the rain began to fall. Because of the weather, I stayed inside until dawn. The free communal breakfast, prepared by a collective called Seeds of Peace, was my first chance to join the larger community. The Seeds of Peace kitchen offered three meals a day, which allowed everyone an opportunity not only to eat but also to network and share what they had learned in the workshops, or where they had found an edible plant or swimming hole. Free meals and a volunteer-run kitchen are important features for those who travel alone to gatherings or are new to the movement, since eating together is an easy way to make friends and feel part of the community. Much of the food for the kitchen is donated or dumpstered (dumpstering is the practice of rescuing edible but overstocked or out-of-date food found in dumpsters behind grocery stores). Like everything else at these gatherings, food preparation, cooking, and dishwashing are done by participants who volunteer each day, even though a handful of people are in charge of the kitchen and responsible for bringing stoves, pans, and other supplies to the gathering site. Communal meals are healthy, varied, and include vegan options, as well as the occasional meat dish if someone donates a dumpster find of hot dogs.

Animal rights activists have national gatherings too, but the ones I attended were more like conventions than the Earth First! Rendezvous, charging a fee for attendance and featuring a room of vegan products for sale. They draw from a spectrum of the animal rights movement, including business owners, mainstream activists involved with letter writing and lobbying, and radical activists taking part in illegal activities. The largest gathering I participated in, the Animal Rights National Conference, took place in hotel convention rooms and was held alternately in Los Angeles or Washington, DC. Property destruction tactics used by the ALF and other radical animal rights activists were more controversial in this context than at the Earth First! Rendezvous.[9]

At radical environmentalist gatherings, animal rights campaigns were discussed and a number of activists participated in both movements, especially in organizations that defend *wild* animals, such as the Buffalo Field Campaign. The *Earth First! Journal* covers animal releases and other ALF actions in its pages, and animal rights campaigns are familiar to many radical environmentalists, especially because some of them have been involved with both movements.[10] In theory, participants at the Rendezvous supported animal rights, but tended not to be as focused on factory farming, and thus on dietary practices, as animal rights activists. Opposition to factory farming is a cornerstone of animal rights, along with other issues such as vivisection (experimenting on animals for medical research or product testing), killing animals for fur, and keeping wild animals in captivity at zoos and animal parks.

While many activists are omnivores, just as many are vegetarian or vegan, for both moral and environmental reasons. As Paul Watson, founder of Sea Shepherd and a long-time campaigner for marine animal rights, put it, "A vegan driving a Hummer contributes less to global greenhouse emissions than a meat-eater riding a bicycle."[11] In addition to Watson's environmental argument, activists are also motivated to become vegans or vegetarians as a result of personal experiences with nonhuman animals or horror over the conditions of factory farming.

After breakfast each day of the Pennsylvania Earth First! Rendezvous, someone blew a horn and participants hanging out in the dining area yelled, "Morning Circle!" As the daily community forum and gathering of the entire camp, Morning Circle served to help organizers find volunteers to handle security, work with medics or as conflict mediators, dig latrines, or help in the kitchen. It also allowed for the airing of more general community concerns, often about safety issues or exclusionary practices and oppressive attitudes among Rendezvous participants. Workshops were held in designated areas throughout the camp that had been given names like Indiana Bat, Bog Turtle, Wood Rat, and Allegheny. Because Earth First! aims to be a leaderless movement, anyone can propose a workshop at these gatherings. There is no selection committee: other participants either show up for a workshop or they do not. Workshops on skills involving safety such as climbing training or medic training are, however, conducted by people who are recognized as having the appropriate skills and experience.

Workshops at Earth First! Rendezvous I attended included the following topics, which I list at length because of what they reveal about the diversity of activist interests in both ecological and social justice issues:

- Action Legal Training
- Practicing Good Security Culture
- Environmental Racism and Solidarity
- Media for Actions
- Unconventional Hydrocarbons
- Know Your Rights
- Men Challenging Sexism
- Propaganda for Revolutionaries
- Cob Building
- Direct Aid on the Border
- Uniting Anti-Extraction Movements
- Cultural Appropriation
- Edible Plants for Wellness
- Mountaintop Removal
- Misogyny in the Catholic Church
- Radical Mycology

- Basic and Advanced Climbing
- Silk-Screening
- Dismantling Patriarchy
- Non-Violent Communication
- History and Future of Animal Liberation
- Red Wolf Re-introduction
- Restoring the American Chestnut
- Women and Trans Self-Defense
- Radical Mental Heath
- Banners and Art
- Plant Walk
- Intersectionality of Oppressions
- Warrior Poets Workshop
- Police Liaison Training

These workshops indicate the many concerns of activists at the Rendezvous and their desire to link environmental campaigns to social and political issues. They also reveal the ways in which activists prepare for protest actions at the same time that they create the kinds of communities they want to live in.

Although many participants at the gatherings I attended had been active in forest campaigns and antiextraction protests, they were also involved in other kinds of activism. Activists' interests bridge social justice and environmentalism and include working in solidarity with Native American communities, providing food and water to illegal immigrants crossing the southern border, and organizing coal mining communities in West Virginia. At the Rendezvous in Pennsylvania, workshops to educate attendees on fracking issues included identification of risks to human health as well as to the environment. The Rendezvous also featured workshops on the following topics: "indigenous solidarity" through Black Mesa Indigenous Support; mountaintop removal campaigns in West Virginia; and No More Deaths, a coalition of religious groups and other concerned activists who make water drops in the desert along the Arizona border.[12] These workshop topics suggest that stereotypes of "tree-huggers" and profiles of the "eco-terrorist next door" miss the extent to which radical activists are involved in a wide range of activities that challenge governmental policies and corporate practices that have an impact on humans as well as the larger-than-human world.

Raising serious social and personal concerns at gatherings often results in fraught discussions and long, frustrating workshops. Trainings for dealing with police during actions stir up difficult emotions; sessions of letter writing to prisoners serving long prison sentences, planning for jail support, and poems written in memory of activists who have died at protests remind everyone of the risks involved in what they are doing. Nevertheless, the atmosphere at gatherings and many actions is also one of serious play.[13] At the 2012 Rendezvous, a puppet show on "security culture" used humor to instruct the audience on what *not* to talk about with their friends in order to protect themselves and others from arrest and prosecution. Talent shows at gatherings showcase a variety of performers, from slam poets knocking capitalism to banjo players singing old coal mining songs. Humor is especially important in the atmosphere of repression that has haunted activist communities since stiff sentences were handed down to some of their comrades during the "Green Scare," a roundup of activists by U.S. government agencies.[14] A sense of humor also infuses the actions themselves. While one or two activists are in precarious positions on blockades, nearby a group of "radical cheerleaders" may be cheerily performing dances and songs to a drummer corps passionately beating on five-gallon plastic buckets. Serious play entertains participants and conveys activists' message with a lighter hand.

One road blockade by Earth First!ers in 1996 to protest logging of ancient forests in Washington State's Olympic Peninsula involved a mock living room in the middle of a logging road. Here, as often, humor and performance art worked together in the context of an action that activists also took seriously as part of their struggle to prevent ancient trees from being logged. They called the blockade "The American Family." It consisted of activists locked to an immovable living room composed of couch, chairs, and a table filled with cement and facing a television. In this action, "Uprooting the familiarity of the domestic sphere into the unpredictable vastness of the old-growth forest directly confronted the conceptual separation of nature from culture," according to one observer. Locked to their seats, activists faced off against logging trucks and forest service personnel in a setting reminiscent of performance art.[15]

Activists approach protests with a mixture of excitement, humor, fear, pride, anxiety, and contestation. Not everyone agrees on tactics, and many elements of actions can be unpredictable, especially with over a hundred people involved. It is uncertain if anyone will be arrested or injured and whether the news media will show up to publicize the action. Not everyone at the Rendezvous stays for the action. Some have records for previous actions and cannot risk arrest; others have young children at home or have come to the gathering to learn and share information but do not want to be involved in direct action, even if they support those who do.

Preparations for the 2012 action in Western Pennsylvania took place throughout the week of the Rendezvous, though details of what we would be doing and where we would be going remained vague. Participants divided into affinity groups and decided what level of risk they wanted to take during the action: green, orange, or red, with red carrying the highest risk of arrest and green the least. Some of us volunteered to serve as legal and jail support, or media and police liaisons. Medics paired up with other medics to work in teams. Other participants made banners, posters, and bucket drums or practiced chants.

On the morning of the action, we set out before dawn. It was a lovely but nerve-wracking drive through the rural hollows and thick forest as we tried not to lose the taillights of the car in front of us on the dark and mist-covered road. Through the mist, in a long caravan of cars, the five activists I was riding with talked quietly. We finally arrived at our destination and parked along a rural road near the entrance to a fracking site in the Moshannon State Forest. As a member of the "green group," I was stationed at the entrance to the forest, in front of the first blockade, but far away from the main action site. We sat in chairs in the middle of the entrance road with a banner reading, "Our Public Land is not for Private Profit." Other banners at the protest were "We All Live Downwind" and "Marcellus Earth First!, No Fracking, No Compromise."[16] We got out our bucket drums and held up signs while one of our members played guitar. A young woman from New York City sprinkled some "holy water" around the protest site that had been "blessed by a medicine man" and given to her by a friend who could not participate in the action. "It can't hurt," she told us. Like many activists, she was practicing a spiritual eclecticism that borrows from and melds together bits and pieces of various religious traditions and worldviews, in this case Catholicism ("holy water") and indigenous traditions ("medicine man").[17]

The center of the action, which we could neither see nor hear, was up the road from where we were stationed. Earlier in the morning, a couple dozen activists had hiked through the woods and constructed barricades of fallen trees and branches across the road. Two activists in the "red group" climbed about sixty feet into some trees and drew their

Fracking site road blockade. Photo: Marcellus Shale Earth First! Used with permission.

support lines across the road. One of them was in a hammock rigged so that if anyone tried to get through the lines, the hammock would fall. Meanwhile, some "scouts" went ahead to see what was happening at the drill rig farther up the road. The seventy-foot-tall rig was operated by EQT Corporation, one of the largest drillers in Pennsylvania, with about 300 active wells in the western part of the state across what is called the Marcellus Shale.[18] Activists approached the workers who were already at the site to let them know that the action was intended to be nonviolent. Before long, Pennsylvania state police arrived and walked around with assault rifles. "You are supposedly adults," one of the officers told activists, "and you're acting like children." As law enforcement personnel became increasingly frustrated and tensions seemed to be escalating, an activist locked his head to one of the anchor lines with a bicycle u-lock to help protect those in the trees.

Back down by the entrance, members of the green group, including myself, were trying to draw attention from locals driving by on the county road. We spent hours chanting and banging on drums every time a car passed us. Most of the cars slowed to look at us since there was probably not much else happening on a Sunday morning in rural Pennsylvania. In the afternoon, some local farmers showed up with a big basket of blueberries. They sat down with us on the side of the road and described how a nearby fracking operation had polluted groundwater on their organic farm. Local politicians had ignored or dismissed the seriousness of their concerns, so they were hoping our presence might help raise awareness about the issue.

Periodically, someone would come down the forest road to update us on what was happening at the barricade as the situation there continued to escalate. Marsh, who had his head in the u-lock, told me later, "there was a lot of drama, everyone yelling, because the police weren't being careful."[19] By early evening the police decided to act. In a video made of the action, a cherry-picker (a bulldozer-like machine with a lift) and a group of police officers started to approach the blockade where the two activists were perched. As the cherry picker followed behind them, officers approached the support lines while frantic activists yelled at them to back off: "Don't touch the line!" We're nonviolent," shouted one activist, "and what you're doing is violent." "Please listen to my friends," called the activist from the hammock, "my life is at extreme risk right now. Please think twice before you cut that line. I'm begging you." The bucket of the cherry picker hit the support line, but eventually they brought the activists safely down to the ground and arrested them. Three arrests were made at the action, but in less than an hour, all three activists were released without serious charges.[20]

After a long day in the forest, I drove away from the 2012 action, joining other participants leaving camp. Some activists went back to clean up the campsite, while others journeyed to other actions near and far or hitched rides to the homes of new friends. Still others drove home to their families or work lives. Many participants returned to campaigns in their local regions, from antifracking in Maine to antilogging in Oregon. Two participants in the 2012 Rendezvous told me they were heading back to their hometown, inspired to start an Earth First! group in their bioregion.

The 2012 Rendezvous action was the first shutdown of an active fracking site in the United States, although the site was up and running again the following day. In the several years following the Rendezvous action, Marcellus Earth First! and other antifracking activists held rallies and educational meetings about fracking and the Marcellus Shale.[21] In March 2014, they organized a road blockade during which protesters in the middle of a forest access road locked themselves to a tube full of sixty pounds of cement. Shalefield Justice Spring Break, modeled on a similar program in West Virginia to fight coal mining, brought college students to the area for activist training and to support the blockade. During the blockade they organized a simultaneous rally at Anadarko Petroleum's corporate offices.[22] In January 2015, Pennsylvania governor Tom Wolf announced he would sign an Executive Order "restoring a moratorium on new drilling leases involving public lands . . . ending a short-lived effort by his predecessor to expand the extraction of natural gas from rock buried deep below Pennsylvania's state parks and forests."[23]

Direct actions are defined as successful or unsuccessful in various ways. In this case, widespread concerns about fracking facilitated by activists' public actions and educational efforts seemed to make a difference. In tree-sits to prevent logging or pipeline construction, sometimes areas are protected (as was the case when a timber sale in Warner Creek/ Cornpatch Roadless Area in Oregon was dropped after an eleven-month blockade that began in 1995). Other times they are long running in nature, such as the 2012 Tar Sands Blockade tree village in Texas, which eventually failed to achieve activists' immediate goals (construction continued by going around the tree village).[24] Yet even the Tar Sands Blockade was effective on some level. Publicity helped bring attention to links between oil spills and pollution, between fossil fuels and climate change, and activists forged coalitions with local landowners and churches, suggesting possibilities for a broad-based movement against extraction industries.[25] The Earth First! 2012 action in Pennsylvania, which was covered by national news sources, also served to draw attention to fracking, making visible what might otherwise be hidden deep in forests or rural areas away from critical eyes.[26]

CHAPTER 2

At the Turn of the Millennium

Youth Culture and the Roots
of Contemporary Activism

Youth, though it may lack knowledge, is certainly
not devoid of intelligence; it sees through shams with sharp
and terrible eyes.

—H. L. Mencken

Youth as menace symbolizes both the collective fear
and the changing face of America. . . . They represent
the emergence of new forms of community, national identity,
and postmodern citizenship.

—Henry Giroux

INTERSECTING PATHS

The paths activists took to arrive at the Earth First! Rendezvous in western Pennsylvania in 2012 were varied and circuitous: from childhood love of the wild to hardcore punk rock scenes. Many of these activists shared the feeling of being at odds with society and the experience of finding a sense of belonging with like-minded young people in activist circles. They rejected the typical goals of the majority of their high school and college peers and developed critiques of capitalism, predictions of societal collapse, and a desire to work for change. In this chapter, I trace some of the ways in which young adults in the 1990s and early 2000s became involved with animal rights and environmental direct action through various *networks of affiliation*. Nettle, who was an editor at the *Earth First! Journal* for six years, arrived at the Rendezvous by way of feminism, anarchism, Paganism, tree-sitting in Scotland, and a tour of the United States with a jug band in a vegetable oil–powered van. I met Nettle at the first Earth First! Rendezvous I attended in Oregon in 2009, talked with her at subsequent gatherings, and visited her in Lake Worth, Florida, in 2014. First at the *Earth First! Journal* office and then at her home, Nettle spent several hours with me, describing in detail the path she took to activism. While no one person's story is typical of radical activists' lives, Nettle's reveals some common themes in activist biographies. Her account offers a starting point for understanding the convergence of historical trends in the late twentieth and early twenty-first century that created a milieu in which radical activism thrived.

Nettle grew up the youngest of three children in a nominally Jewish family in Chicago. Her mother was Canadian and her father Israeli. Her family recycled and composted, and her parents were avid gardeners. As a child she "enjoyed being in nature," camping with her family or exploring forests outside the Chicago area, especially by bicycle. Her older brother and sister were politically active and exposed her to environmental causes, gay rights, feminism, and critiques of capitalism. Not only did her brother support Greenpeace and the World Wildlife Fund, but he also organized buses for a gay rights march in Washington, DC, in 1993. Most of Nettle's high school friends were "jocks," and she remembers being the "weirdo" in the popular crowd. She felt as though she did not fit in and saw her high school years as "years of departure" and depression: "I was an angsty teenager . . . internalizing all sorts of bad things that were going on in the world . . . I would go in and out of depression, I painted my room dark purple, listening to Nirvana." When she went to college, she took courses on feminism and especially feminist art, decided to study abroad, and ended up at an art college in Scotland.[1]

While studying in Scotland, Nettle began a journey into activism that was shaped in part by her family background. Young Americans like Nettle reject common notions of what it means to become a successful adult (making money and owning a house, for example) and convert to radical activism as a kind of subversive rite of passage. Activists often describe their conversion to activism in relation to a protest march or an illegal act of sabotage that expresses their commitment to forests and nonhuman animals rather than to U.S. legal codes and lucrative careers. For them, conversion is a threshold experience, a movement from one existence (the taken-for-granted one) to another (countercultural activism).[2] For many environmental and animal rights activists, conversion takes place during adolescence or young adulthood, which is itself a liminal, threshold-like experience. During this transitional time, young people move from a world that was carved out for them by parents and their social context into a world that they have chosen for themselves, a world in which other species are as important as other humans.

In Scotland at the beginning of her journey to activism, Nettle decided to be a "blank canvas" and start over, so she cut off all her hair and got involved with a collectively run vegetarian art café in Edinburgh. Through the café she was exposed to contemporary Paganism, anarchism, antiwar activism, and environmentalism. Discovering Paganism was for her like finding something she "always believed. Just like finding feminism and anarchism, things I internally already was." Although she liked the communal and ritual aspects of Judaism and some of the Christian churches she had visited as a child, she could not relate to their theology: as a feminist she "was not connecting with this white male god." Paganism resonated with her concerns because she already believed "we are all divine, no hierarchy among individuals, plants and animals." Armed with this affinity for Pagan perspectives, she went into the woods to join an antiroads tree-sit.

Although she had helped organize a protest against the 2005 G-8 summit in Auchterarder, Scotland, Nettle really came home to environmentalism when she "fell in love" with the Bilston Glen tree-sit, one of the world's longest running tree-sits. Bilston Glen changed her life.[3] At the tree-sit she rediscovered her "inner child and this really sacred connection to nature that had been suppressed through the school system, through my own teenage angst and depression." She felt at home in the woods, reconnecting with "the raw and the animalistic part of the human psyche that craves nature and to really be immersed. The thing that I really connected with the most was that I could live here, I could live in the woods and I didn't have to pretend that I had to have a car and a house." She started living at the tree-sit in her own treehouse and taking a bus to her college classes.

From then on, Nettle embraced her "weirdness": "At twenty-one I was waking up from the nightmare of trying to be normal. In high school I was trying to be normal, but I was never normal, I've always been weird. I have to love that and accept that, that's what fuels depression, when I try to fit into society's box." Life at the protest in the forest offered a community in line with her interests in Paganism, anarchism, and feminism. At the same time, her experiences there eased her inner struggles with depression and belonging.

Nettle first encountered the U.S.-based *Earth First! Journal* at Bilston Glen and attended her first Earth First! gathering in the United Kingdom. After graduating from college, she moved back to North America and began to tour with a jug band. During the tour she visited the *Earth First! Journal* collective and not long afterwards was hired there. She thought, "This is what I want to do forever," and was a mainstay at the *Journal* for six years, which was when I got to know her at Earth First! gatherings.[4]

Nettle's story reveals some common themes in activists' accounts of how they became involved with environmentalism or animal rights. Some of the most important influences on radical environmentalism and animal rights during this time included anarchist anticapitalist movements, contemporary Paganism, and understandings of gender shaped by feminism, gay rights, and transgender activism. Nettle's account of her attraction to anarchism and powerful connection to the forest points to the important convergence during the 1990s and 2000s of the anticapitalist movement with strains of deep ecology and biocentrism.

Radical activists charged and sentenced during the first decade of the twenty-first century for actions committed from 1996–2001 (during the FBI's Operation Backfire) came of age at a particular moment in the history of Americans' relation to nature and nonhuman animals, as well as to earlier liberation struggles, so I want to place their actions in a broader historical context. Young activists are influenced by books and films, lovers and friends, anarchist collectives like Food Not Bombs, ecology clubs and volunteer work for the Sierra Club, college courses on deep ecology and gender studies, contemporary Paganism and American Indian worldviews, the Occupy movement and social justice struggles, veganism and hardcore punk rock. Through these disparate activities and interests they find their way to gatherings and direct action campaigns in forests and on fur farms. In this fashion, activist movement through various gatherings, campaigns, and communities traces lines of affiliation and influence across regional, national, and international boundaries.

Like Nettle, Tristan Anderson exemplifies the ways in which many activists are situated within international, as well as American, networks of affiliation. In 2009, Anderson was critically wounded in Palestine during a campaign for Palestinian rights. Previous to his time in Palestine, he had traveled to war-torn Iraq with a circus to entertain traumatized children. He was involved with the Headwaters campaign to save redwood trees, Food Not Bombs, Nevada nuclear weapons test site protests, and a tree-sit in Berkeley to protect oak trees from being bulldozed for a new football stadium.[5]

The loosely organized national and international networks that activists move through also include street medics from mass protest marches in urban areas, Rainbow Gatherings, non-Native people who worked on reservations with Native organizers on a number of issues, other activist groups like Greenpeace, and guerilla gardeners from New York City who grow food in vacant lots.[6] These networks consist of social justice as well as environmental and animal rights communities and organizations. The 2012 Earth First! Rendezvous, for instance, featured a workshop presentation by activists working with No More Deaths in Arizona. No More Deaths is a social justice coalition, composed of both Christians and non-Christians, providing water and food for illegal immigrants along the southern border of the United States. These activists presented a workshop that explored the convergence of environmental and social justice issues in this context.[7]

As these intersections suggest, radical activism of the 1990s and early 2000s emerged within a particular configuration of constructions of youth, feminism, global anticapitalism critiques, social justice concerns (including prison issues), Paganism, deep ecology and other biocentrist approaches within environmentalism, and changing understandings of the appropriate relationships between humans and other animals. Animal rights and environmentalism thus belong to a lineage of radical movements in North America, spearheaded by young people and dating back at least to the civil rights and antiwar movements of the 1960s.

REGARDING THE NONHUMAN: A BRIEF HISTORY OF ENVIRONMENTALISM AND ANIMAL RIGHTS IN THE UNITED STATES

The historical trajectories of radical animal rights and environmentalism in North America are distinctly different, even though twenty-first-century activists often bridge both movements. Radical environmentalists emphasize "the wild," while most animal rights activists are seeking "animal liberation," which includes domesticated nonhuman animals. Radical environmentalists, for example, often sign their letters and communiqués "For the Wild," while animal rights activists are more likely to invoke the slogan, "For the Animals." The animal rights movement in the United States did not emphasize protecting wild animals until late in the twentieth century. Hunt sabotage, for instance, was not common in the United States among animal rights activists until the 1990s, although it was in Britain. A notable exception was Greenpeace, an environmental organization founded in 1971, which focused on direct action against whaling. By the second decade of the twenty-first century, activists in both movements were emphasizing the necessity of working together. During the period of my research (2006–2016), most issues of the *Earth First! Journal*, the most widely read radical environmentalist publication, included articles on animal rights issues and actions.[8] Animal rights activists have been slower to encompass both struggles and combine efforts.

Although it has often shared common cause with the animal rights movement, radical environmentalism has a distinct lineage in the United States. It is particularly indebted to early influences such as eighteenth- and nineteenth-century Romanticism and the writings and lives of Transcendentalist Henry David Thoreau (1817–1862) and naturalist John Muir (1838–1914).[9] Like later environmentalists, Transcendentalists included Buddhist and Native American understandings of nature in their writing.[10] Muir and Thoreau were sensitive to the "interdependence of all life," rejected Christianity and anthropocentric views of nature, admired Native Americans, and underwent pantheistic and animistic experiences in nature.[11] Muir's biocentrism was also influenced by Romanticism and Transcendentalism, as well as personal experiences in wilderness areas. Like other Americans in the late nineteenth century, Muir appreciated nature for being everything that civilization, and urban life in particular, was not. He recognized the intrinsic value of wilderness and the dangers human interests posed to its integrity. Like later radical environmentalists, Muir was devoted to wilderness protection, and his concerns were often in opposition to those of the U.S. Forest Service. Along with Thoreau, Aldo Leopold (1887–1948), and Edward Abbey (1927–1989), Muir is considered by many activists to be one of the "grandfathers" of radical environmentalism.[12] Yet Muir, like other nineteenth- and early twentieth-century wilderness lovers, viewed wild places as pristine and devoid of humans, especially indigenous people who had roamed and shaped the land long before the arrival of Europeans.[13]

Americans' concern for "wilderness" untrammeled by civilization, and especially agriculture, grew during the nineteenth century and led to the creation of Yellowstone Park in 1872, the first time Congress put limits on the spread of agriculture.[14] By the end of the nineteenth century, the fear and hostility many European Americans had felt towards nature in earlier eras was now leveled at cities.[15] Nature appreciation became more common in the late nineteenth and early twentieth centuries, as Americans began to react to disturbing consequences of the industrial revolution and urbanization. With more people living in cities at a distance from the wild, attraction to nature as a place of respite from urban life grew, as did urban dwellers' support for national parks.[16]

Radical environmentalists share this attraction, while at the same time appreciating wild places and beings for their intrinsic value. A tendency of radical environmentalists to view opponents of wilderness protection as "desecrating agents" became a strategy from Muir on, according to religious studies scholar Bron Taylor.[17] Taylor identifies a radical environmental lineage running from Muir and Thoreau through a number of early twentieth-century figures such as Aldo Leopold (1887–1948), David Brower (1912–2000), Ansel Adams (1902–1984), and Rachel Carson (1907–1964), who held somewhat pantheistic views of nature, even though their spiritual beliefs were not as explicit as Muir's and Thoreau's.[18]

By the 1950s, a more militant and anarchist version of this lineage appeared in the West, most significantly in the figures of poet and bioregionalist Gary Snyder (1930–present) and writer Edward Abbey (1927–1989). Snyder's back-to-the-land anarchism and Abbey's pantheism and support for antidevelopment direct action were important precursors to later radical activism. The decade of the 1970s was key for the convergence of these important figures with conservation biology, deep ecology, and other shifts in the new discipline of environmental philosophy. Some of these developments came about in response to the publication of historian Lynn White Jr.'s famous argument identifying developments in medieval Christianity as "The Historical Roots of Our Ecological Crisis" (1967).[19] Not long after the publication of White's essay, the term *deep ecology* was coined by Norwegian philosopher Arne Naess in 1973, further developed by Bill Devall and George Sessions in their book *Deep Ecology* (1985), and adopted by Earth First!ers in the early 1980s.

Due to the spread of these and other views challenging anthropocentrism and promoting wilderness protection, American environmentalist organizations experienced rapid growth in the 1970s. They also became increasingly professionalized, hiring managers rather than activists. Some activists reacted against this trend, which they saw as diluting their cause, and chose more radical tactics. One of Earth First!'s founders, Dave Foreman, quit his job lobbying in Washington, DC, in 1979, and co-founder Howie Wolke was a disenchanted former forestry student.

Foreman and Wolke practiced tree spiking and other direct action, drawing inspiration from Edward Abbey's fictionalized account of ecotage, *The Monkey Wrench Gang*, published in 1975. Deep ecologists like early Earth Firsters! believed nature had intrinsic value regardless of its benefits to human beings. For them, preserving wilderness for its own sake became a moral matter, even a "religious mandate" in the words of Dave Foreman.[20] They adopted the language of holy war, or as journalist Joe Kane put it, "waging guerilla warfare in the name of Mother Nature."[21] Dave Foreman described their monkey wrenching tactics as "a form of worship towards the Earth" and his own role as "a religious warrior for the Earth."[22] In addition to the language of warfare, these years found environmentalists increasingly framing environmental issues as urgent, even on an apocalyptic scale.[23]

Environmentalists from Henry David Thoreau to Earth First!'s Dave Foreman have also freely borrowed from and been inspired by indigenous cultures. The influence of Native American orientations to nature runs throughout radical environmentalist thought and practice, even when troubled by concerns about colonialism and cultural appropriation. Moreover, environmental and animal rights activists have sometimes fought side by side with indigenous people, as when activists supported Navajo and Hopi people at Black Mesa, a sacred mountain that was also the site of controversial strip-mining. As Gary Snyder described the coalition of Native and non-Native activists in *Turtle Island*, "defense of Black Mesa is being sustained by traditional Indians, young Indian militants and longhairs [hippies]."[24] Supporters of the Black Mesa Defense Fund, founded by Jack Loeffler in 1970, engaged in monkey-wrenching during the 1970s when a sabotage campaign was directed at the mine. Dave Foreman, one of Earth First!'s founders, was involved with the campaign at Black Mesa during the 1970s, before the founding of Earth First![25] In other instances, activists and Native Americans have been at odds, as in the case of animal rights protests against members of the Makah (a northwestern U.S. tribe), whose cultural revival included traditional whaling practices.[26]

Since the 1970s, there have been many cases of radical environmentalists joining Native Americans to protest threats to tribal lands, such as the Standing Rock Dakota Access Pipeline protest that began in 2016. RAMPS (Radical Action for Mountains' and People's Survival, organized to fight coal mining in Appalachia) members and friends traveled from Appalachia to North Dakota to work with Red Warrior Camp, a direct action camp at the Standing Rock protest.[27] I discuss issues of solidarity as well as tensions with Native people in more depth in Chapter 6.

In contrast to Earth First!'s campaign for wilderness protection, early animal rights struggles in the United States tended to be urban and focused on domesticated and lab animals. American animal activists inherited these emphases from British animal protection and animal liberation movements. From at least the eighteenth century on, animal rights activism in Britain coincided with other expressions of political and religious radicalism that were already present in towns and cities. The early twentieth century antivivisection movement in Britain appealed to feminists, labor activists, vegetarians, spiritualists, and other radical activists who posed alternatives to the social (and species) order.[28] Like contemporary activists, they saw themselves as the vanguard of social change, advancing a moral crusade. Animal rights was just one of many causes to be addressed in order to usher in a better, more civilized (and for some, more godly) society.[29]

In a similar fashion, mid-nineteenth-century American "animal defenders" often held other radical political and social views and were inspired by Britain's RSPCA (founded in 1824), the antislavery movement, and Darwin's views on evolution set forth in *The Origin of Species* (1859).[30] As was the case in other nineteenth-century reform movements, women played prominent roles in animal rights advocacy during this period.[31] Alongside other nineteenth-century reform causes, such as child welfare and temperance, a variety of organizations were formed in American cities to take up the plight of nonhuman animals. This included addressing slaughterhouse conditions, cruelty to urban workhorses, animal experimentation, and homeless animals. After the end of the Civil War, with the abolition of slavery on their minds, activists began a new campaign of rights advocacy, this time for nonhumans rather than human slaves. Not long after the end of the war, New York's American Society for the Prevention of Cruelty to Animals (ASPCA) was founded in 1866, the American Humane Association (AHA) in 1877, and the American Anti-Vivisection Society (AAVS) in 1883. Debates emerged in and around these nineteenth-century organizations between those who advocated more humane treatment of animals (welfarists) and those who focused on the *rights* of nonhuman animals (liberationists). These debates would continue through the history of animal rights activism into the twenty-first century.[32]

Although wilderness protection and animal rights were political and moral issues in the early part of the twentieth century, the late 1970s were watershed years for American environmental and animal rights campaigns. This development was due in part to increasing standards of living in the United States, more opportunities for contact with nature, a growing tendency to see nature and animals as having intrinsic value, and a sense of ecological precariousness described in widely read books like Rachel Carson's *Silent Spring* (1962).

Environmental and animal rights concerns sometimes converged in the 1970s, as in the founding of Greenpeace in 1971, an organization that campaigned against whalers and sealers as well as nuclear power and deforestation. Greenpeace engaged in direct action, putting activists' bodies at risk for nonhuman animals and creating public spectacles, continuing the legacy of nineteenth-century animal rights movements.[33] After 1975, both animal rights and environmental activists became increasingly confrontational, or "radical," largely out of frustration with above-ground activism that did not seem to be effective: animals continued to needlessly suffer and old-growth forests continued to be logged.

Radical animal rights and environmentalist organizations in the United States, gained significance in the early 1980s: both People for the Ethical Treatment of Animals (PETA) and Earth First! were founded around 1980.[34] Factory farming and fur industries joined vivisection as central concerns of late twentieth-century animal rights activists. During the 1980s, PETA emerged as the radical face of animal rights in the United States, although other more radical groups like the Animal Liberation Front (ALF) would appear on the scene a decade later and see PETA as too willing to compromise and not radical enough.

In its early years, PETA focused attention on primate experimentation and cosmetic testing at the same time that Earth First! engaged in direct action tactics to defend roadless areas in national forests. Both organizations sometimes created spectacles to attract news media attention during protests, dressing as animals or throwing pies at industry officials. For instance, the "Biotech Baking Brigade" threw a dumpstered chocolate cake in the face of a GM scientist at conference dinner.[35] An Earth First! gathering in 2007 ended with an action during which protesters stormed a store owned by a company building a dam in Mexico, with protesters dressed as clowns, otters, and beavers chanting outside the store.[36] For Earth First!ers engaged in these protests on the behalf of other species, forests and waters had inherent rights, while for PETA activists, primates in laboratories did as well. In their parallel histories, both Earth First! and PETA sought to decenter humans and broaden moral and political interests concerning the more-than-human world.

In the early 1980s, some Earth First!ers were dedicated exclusively to protecting wilderness in the United States, while others were fighting against the World Bank and fast-food restaurants that used rainforest beef, linking environmental and nonhuman animal concerns. The *Earth First!*

Journal, published in various formats since the first years of Earth First!, became a central resource for networking and sharing information about environmental and animal rights struggles across the United States and internationally.[37] In the late 1980s, Earth First! was a substantial presence in struggles against logging in northern California, Oregon, and Washington, especially in campaigns to safeguard old-growth forests. Earth First!ers voiced concern for trees as well as the many nonhuman animal species that lived in and around them. Tree-sits and road blockades emerged as the most effective tactics during the forest campaigns of the 1990s. Julia Butterfly Hill's two-year tree-sit in a redwood called Luna brought tree-sits and threatened redwoods to national attention. After considerable coverage by local and national news media, Hill's tree-sit eventually won modest protection for an area of old-growth redwoods.[38]

By the second decade of the twenty-first century, most radical activists I met did not consider PETA to be radical, although Earth First! with its anarchistic organization continued to fit that moniker. PETA has a centralized organization, a significant budget, and celebrity sponsors while, true to its anarchist roots, Earth First! is decentralized, organized through collectives, and uninterested in celebrities. By the 1990s, more radical and clandestine movements (the ALF and the Earth Liberation Front [ELF]) that concentrated on property destruction and used tactics such as arson emerged from within and alongside PETA and Earth First! By the twenty-first century, pie throwing, theatrical urban protests, and other kinds of public disruptions existed on one end of the direct action spectrum, with hidden night-time lab raids and sabotage by hooded and masked activists on the other.

The ELF was founded in the United Kingdom in 1992 by Earth First!ers and the first U.S. action claimed publicly by the ELF took place in 1996.[39] Some Earth First!ers and other activists involved with forest campaigns on the West Coast, borrowing tactics from the ALF in England, began to engage in underground actions, including arson, during the late 1990s.[40] Around the same time that ELF emerged as the most extreme direct action wing of the environmental movement (using arson for property destruction, for instance, not a tactic adopted by most Earth First!ers), animal rights was becoming more militant as well. Many of the radical animal liberation actions of the 1990s were claimed by the ALF or by those who adopted ALF-like tactics of working alone or in small anarchist cells.

The ALF, founded in England in 1976 by Ronnie Lee, garnered media attention for acts of sabotage and animal releases and spread in popularity in the United States during the 1980s and 1990s.[41] From 1979 to 1993, the ALF was reportedly responsible for 313 incidents of break-ins, vandalism, arson, and thefts associated with animal liberation.[42] Although law enforcement agencies and animal researchers see activists as dangerous, the ALF has explicit guidelines about taking precautions during actions to avoid harming humans and other animals.[43] The ALF typically functions as a decentralized, anonymous movement organized around informal and temporary cells, often as small as two people. As a leaderless movement, it has no offices or directors, no fundraising initiatives, and no employees. As one activist puts it in the film *Behind the Mask* (2006), "ALF only exists in people's hearts and minds."[44]

During the 1990s, the hardcore punk rock subculture influenced radical animal rights and environmental activists, as bands like Earth Crisis and Shelter stressed the urgency of environmental and animal issues. Many young activists came out of this scene with its focus on anarchist anticapitalism critiques and Do-It-Yourself (DIY) approaches to music, art, and social change.[45] These concerns were partially driven by a movement within hardcore referred to as "straightedge," which advocated veganism and discouraged drug use, drinking, and promiscuous sex.[46] Many aspects of the straightedge scene helped to create an audience receptive to the message of animal rights. It was inspired by punk rock's anarchistic critique of consumer capitalism and imperialism, the physical intensity of hardcore shows, and bands' and fans' desire to change a flawed world, especially a world characterized by the existence of animal suffering. These influences coalesced in hardcore scenes across the country during the 1990s at the same time that ALF's message began to spread. I explore these developments in detail in Chapter 5.

The influence of hardcore on radical animal rights and environmentalism in the 1990s is just one example of the ways in which radical activism during and since the 1990s has largely been a youth movement, even though activists of all ages participate in protests. Most of the activists serving prison sentences at the turn of the twenty-first century were sentenced for actions committed when they were teenagers or in their early twenties. A large number of activists in the 1990s and early 2000s were introduced to activism through youth subcultures like straightedge, high school clubs, and friends, or during college through campus environmental and animal rights groups. As parental and family influences became less important in these extrafamilial contexts, young people were more likely to be exposed through friends and lovers to activist groups and campaigns. The personal and historical trajectories of young activists in the 1990s exemplify an ongoing dynamic in American culture of the societal marginalization of youth on the one hand and teenagers embracing marginalization and acting as agents for social change on the other.

MISFITS AND REBELS

Like Nettle, whose story I began with, many activists recall being teenage misfits or rebels who were seen and saw themselves as outsiders. Rod Coronado wrote to me from prison that during his teenage years he did not fit in and had "little interest" in what was popular with other teenagers: "Not a lot of teenagers thought it was cool to want to 'save the whales,' so I struggled with wanting to fit in . . . I simply could not focus on wanting things or a career while I knew whales were being slaughtered and baby seals clubbed." Coronado heard about the ALF and became even more convinced that "the only career for me was as this sort of person." During high school he recalls "simply biding my time until I was done with school and could join the struggles." At seventeen, he left home and moved to Seattle to start working with Paul Watson and the Sea Shepherd Society, an activist organization focused on protecting marine mammals.[47] Like Coronado, many activists felt like outcasts until they found activist organizations, the vegan straightedge subculture, a school's ecology club, feminism, contemporary Paganism, or other causes and movements that gave meaning to their ostracism and nurtured their activism.

Even when they felt at odds with other students, high school offered some activists a separate space away from parental influence in which activist identities could emerge. Chelsea Gerlach, who was sentenced in 2007 to eight years in prison on twenty-five charges, including arson at a Vail, Colorado, ski resort, joined her high school's ecology club and was only sixteen when she experienced her first arrest for civil disobedience. In a 1993 South Eugene (Oregon) High School yearbook, her sophomore picture depicts her wearing a black T-shirt with white letters reading "RESIST." In a short article about the school's environmental organization she is quoted as saying, "Our generation was born to save the earth . . . if we wait until we're out of school it might be too late."[48] Between 1996 and 2001, Gerlach's ELF cell was supposedly responsible for setting fire to more than twenty lumber companies, a wild-horse corral, and genetic engineering facilities.[49] For teenagers like Gerlach who find a high school niche and embrace their own identities as outsiders, who become involved with animal rights or environmental issues with teenage peers, high school and its associated extracurricular activities may serve as an important space in which activist identities are forged.

Like other social movements before them, radical environmentalism and animal rights in the United States have been significantly impacted by the historical contingencies of middle-class white high school and college-age youth at the turn of the millennium, even though not all activists come from white middle-class backgrounds. Post–World War II radical youth movements like the antiwar movement of the 1960s and the animal rights movement of the 1990s were in part made possible by a separate youth culture that developed in the United States during the decades after World War II. This separate youth culture developed not only as a market force, but also as a space in which the forces of capitalism could be questioned and challenged. In this historical trajectory, "teenager" and "youth" became charged and ambiguous categories. Youth culture made possible by high schools provided opportunities for young people to identify with their own visions and values.

The emergence of "teenage" as a special stage of life with symbolic and economic importance did not come about until the nineteenth century, even though urban youth groups appeared in America as early as the 1770s. The term *juvenile delinquent* was coined in the 1810s, a foreshadowing of what would become a difficult assumption to shake: that youth gathering in groups and/or outside adult supervision were socially and politically dangerous.[50] Representations of vulnerable and threatening youth from at least the nineteenth century on tended to identify teenagers as quintessential liminal or boundary figures. Cultural critic Henry Giroux argues that young people are "condemned to wander within and between multiple borders and spaces marked by excess, otherness and difference. This is a world in which old certainties are ruptured and meaning becomes more contingent, less indebted to the dictates of reverence and established truth."[51] In this way, the demonization and othering of some youth created a space for dissent and protest in which taken-for-granted truths such as human exceptionalism could be questioned.

Teenagers accumulated economic and cultural power throughout the first decades of the twentieth century. Although "teenager" as a category had emerged in the late nineteenth and early twentieth centuries, it was introduced in the popular lexicon only in 1941.[52] Sociologist Talcott Parsons coined the term "youth culture" in a 1942 article; the magazine *Seventeen* aimed at teen girls was launched in 1944; and in 1945, *Vogue* magazine heralded a "teen-age revolution."[53] After World War II there was a significant shift from what historian Oded Heilbronner calls a "culture *for* youth to a culture *of* youth."[54] The culture of youth, recently empowered, would follow at least two divergent courses: those who embraced their market role and facilitated America's economic and geographic expansion, and those who pushed for revolution against what they saw as an out-of-control industrial nation, both racist and imperialistic.

During the 1950s, teenagers increasingly came to inhabit a world of their own due at least in part to the growth of the high school and an expanding culture of teenage consumption. Their autonomy became a source of tremendous anxiety for the adults who had created high schools and the accompanying separate teen culture in the first place. With the baby boom (1946–1964), youth definitively displaced age as a source of power in the United States.[55] Even though the 1950s are often seen as being family oriented (at least for the white middle class), in fact, a parallel trend during this decade was the increasing importance of "extrafamilial institutions" in socializing the young.[56] For this and other reasons, teenagers were looked on suspiciously as being increasingly outside of adult control and inhabiting their own spaces.[57] From their parents' perspectives, there was reason for concern, since it was often in these autonomous teenage spaces that teenagers encountered activism and other subversive activities.

Many scholars have identified "the unique susceptibility of youth to social change" as a shaping factor in youth activism.[58] According to historian Christopher Lasch, young social reformers in the early twentieth century were also in rebellion against the middle class.[59] This rebellion established a pattern for later youth revolts, such as those of the 1960s, that also rejected middle-class values. Youth activists have been characterized by scholars as educated, middle class, the offspring of loving parents who fostered independent thinking, and members of subcultures who are cynical towards the larger society.[60]

In the 1950s, dissatisfaction with suburbia and capitalist ideals was simmering across diverse populations of American youth. The 1950s Beat movement of artists and writers and the involvement of youth (white as well as African American) in the civil rights movement during the 1950s and early 1960s are two examples.[61] As anthropologist Margaret Mead explained the situation in an interview, the Beat generation consisted of young people "not interested in the kind of society we have."[62] Mead's "uninterested" young people flourished in the 1960s, when protest movements took up many themes that remain salient to twenty-first-century activists, especially the rejection of middle-class aspirations.

By the 1960s, Americans in their teenage years and early twenties increasingly had autonomous lives and separate spaces in which to express and experiment with new political identities. Within these separate youth spaces, as in earlier eras, they also called into question structures of power and authority. Some white middle-class youth dropped out of college in the 1960s and 1970s to pursue a different kind of American dream than that of their parents. Many of them engaged in new forms of protest. The 1960s saw the emergence of environmentalism, feminism, radical politics, and unconventional expressions of religiosity, all of which were influenced and/or made possible by youth culture. These movements, with their roots in the 1960s, would later shape the concerns of radical environmentalism and animal rights activism.

The following sections offer a genealogical account of radical environmentalism and animal rights in the United States within the context of late twentieth-century youth culture. Here I focus on the emergence of radical politics since the 1960s, with a nod to earlier direct action movements, followed by a discussion of the feminist and antinuclear movements of the 1970s and 1980s. I also explore later expressions of radicalism that draw from these movements, particularly anarchists' involvement in the Seattle World Trade Organization protests in 1999. The third section explores anarchism in practice, such as Food Not Bombs and similar organizations, and its impact on environmental and animal rights direct action. Finally, I discuss the role of religion in youth movements since the 1960s, focusing on contemporary Paganism and radical environmentalism in the 1980s and 1990s.

POST–WORLD WAR II ANTECEDENTS OF TWENTY-FIRST-CENTURY RADICAL ACTIVISM

After watching a documentary on the radical 1970s antiwar group the Weather Underground, in which one of the members explained he was so obsessed with Vietnam that he thought about it every waking moment, animal rights activist Peter Young realized that he felt the same way about caged and slaughtered animals. In a letter he wrote me from prison, Young recognized Weather as an important antecedent and inspiration for the animal rights movement of the 1990s.[63] In the 1960s and 1970s, rebellious youth, especially college students, flocked to the antiwar movement and serve as exemplars to late twentieth-century activists like Young. The 1960s helped to shape the course of radical activism in the 1990s and 2000s by providing models for action, often explicitly invoked, as in Young's reference to Weather.[64] A 2005 book on the anticapitalist movement of the 1990s and early 2000s, *Letters from Young Activists: Today's Rebels Speak Out*, makes this connection explicit in a preface by former Weather Underground member Bernadine Dohrn. One of the volume's co-authors is Chesa Boudin, son of two Weather members.

Like 1960s youth movements, contemporary animal rights activism and environmentalism act as "the conscience of society," attending to ethics and justice issues, rather than "bread-and-butter ones."[65] Activists in the 1960s rejected the careers their parents saw as respectable. They believed that the social values of their parents' generation were becoming increasingly irrelevant and irrational.[66] In this way, while youth-led political movements may involve a minority of the national population, they tend to be representative of more widespread sentiments.[67] Like Weather Underground, radical activists are the extreme wing of broader societal trends around environmental commitments and animal rights. And, like Weather, contemporary radicals link their issues of special concern with other struggles: feminism, antiracism, antiauthoritarianism, egalitarianism, moral purity, and anti-institutionalization.[68] Weather organized as collectives and made decisions by consensus, confronted "white privilege," was adamantly opposed to racism, and supported gay rights and equality for women, at least in principle. All of these remained important concerns of activists I met in the 1990s and 2000s.

The Weather Underground was a largely (though not entirely) white middle-class youth movement of self-proclaimed "freedom fighters" challenging the U.S. government's policies, especially those concerning the Vietnam War and African Americans. They modeled themselves after revolutionaries like Che Guevara, the Argentinian Marxist.[69] Weatherman Bill Ayers remembers that they "imagined that the survival of humanity depended on the kids alone . . . We wanted to break from the habitual and the mediocre, to step into history as subjects and not objects. We would combat the culture of compromise, rise up and act decisively on what the known demanded—we could think of no basis on which to defend inaction, and so our watchword was simple: Action! Action! Action!"[70] Weather Underground members were frustrated after petitions, demonstrations, and other above-ground strategies failed to bring about any real change. Some members came from the larger SDS (Students for a Democratic Society, founded in the early 1960s), but they thought SDS nonviolence modeled on the civil rights movement was ineffective. In order to "step into history," they believed that more confrontational tactics were needed to resist American involvement in the Vietnam War and the oppression of African Americans.[71]

Weather was characterized by a tension common among contemporary radical activists: Weather members rejected dominant American values and institutions, but placed themselves within an American tradition of resistance going back to the Boston Tea Party. "In Weatherman," recalls Bill Ayers, "we had been insistent in our anti-Americanism, our opposition to a national story stained with conquest and slavery and attempted genocide."[72] And yet, they identified with an American activist lineage. They had read Malcolm X and their heroes and models were "Osceola and Cochise, Nat Turner and Marcus Garvey, Emma Goldman and the Grimke sisters." According to Ayers, "We located ourselves in history and found a way at last to have a little niche at home."[73] Looking back, claims Ayers, most Americans now "accept the importance of the Boston Tea Party, Shay's Rebellion, Nat Turner's uprising, Denmark Vesey's revolt, John Brown's attack, the Deacons for Self-Defense, the Freedom Riders, the theft of the Pentagon Papers . . . most of us can imagine ourselves throwing tea into Boston Bay or even throwing ourselves in front of that fateful bullet flying toward Martin Luther King Jr."[74] In this understanding of an American tradition of radicalism, Weather and other earlier revolutionaries are all part of a legacy often invoked by contemporary activists who see themselves as heroes of a history not yet told.

After the Vietnam War ended and members of Weather surfaced from their underground lives, the group disbanded. Many of the activists who had protested war and racism in the late 1960s and early 1970s had by the mid-1970s turned to the women's and environmental movements, including the antinuclear movement of the 1970s and 1980s, which I take up in the next section.[75] Two decades after the Weather Underground, radical environmentalists like the ELF would revisit some of Weather's tactics: organizing into cells, emphasizing solidarity with oppressed minorities, issuing communiqués, building explosive devices, carrying out symbolic property destruction, living fugitive lives underground, and identifying with resistance movements in Latin America.[76]

RELIGIOUS RADICALISM

Religious radicalism is also part of the legacy of the 1960s and 1970s that shaped the context out of which late twentieth-century radical environmentalism and animal rights emerged. Religious radicalism from the 1960s on includes Jews and Christians involved in the civil rights movement, radical Catholics like Philip and Daniel Berrigan protesting during the Vietnam War (while they were not young, their tactics of resistance were influential among young antiwar protesters), and Quakers and Neopagans in the antinuclear movement of the late 1970s.

Religious radicalism based on issues of conscience and social justice concerns has a long history in the United States, from nineteenth-century Quaker abolitionists to twentieth-century Pagan antinuclear protesters. The 1960s was a crucial time for the joining of religious commitment and radical action in the antiwar movement, alongside secular movements like the Weather Underground.[77] Catholic antiwar activists were among the most prominent 1960s religious radicals. For instance, radical Catholics in the Catonsville Nine engaged in a famous act of antiwar property destruction. They risked time in prison because they had to act; their moral commitments gave them no other choice. The compulsion to act would continue to echo through direct action movements of the 1970s and into the 1980s as similar moral concerns were taken up by environmental and animal rights activists.

In 1968, the Catonsville Nine (nine Catholic protesters, including Daniel and Philip Berrigan) took six hundred individual draft files from the Catonsville, Maryland, Selective Service office and burned them with napalm. Daniel Berrigan, who was also famous for pouring blood on the Pentagon steps, explicitly placed the protest in an American tradition of civil disobedience, including the Boston Tea Party and "abolitionist and anarchist traditions." During the trial of the Catonsville Nine, Berrigan told the court that "From the beginning of our republic good men and women had said no and acted outside the law" and would be vindicated by time.[78] Another of the protesters, Thomas Lewis, "was not concerned with the law" but with the "innocent"; like the others, he believed that "a person may break the law to save lives."[79] These protesters told the court that they could not rest, knowing that innocent people in Vietnam were suffering because of U.S. military actions. They argued to the jury that they answered to a "higher law" that took precedence over human laws.[80] These antiwar protesters felt that peaceable protests had failed and imperatives had been placed on them by the ongoing suffering of American soldiers and innocent people in Vietnam.

If there is one theme that unites many different forms of religious radicalism, it is the idea of "moral passion" that drives commitment to justice for other humans, nonhuman animals, and the environment. Animal rights and environmental activists belong in the context of this morally passionate American lineage of resistance to injustice. It is a lineage that runs through the antislavery movement, the civil rights movement, the antiwar and Black Power movements of the 1960s, and the antinuclear movement of the 1970s and 1980s. On websites, at protest marches, and at animal rights and environmental gatherings, imprisoned activists' numerous supporters have praised them as "warriors" and "abolitionists," explicitly placing them in the tradition of Martin Luther King Jr., Malcolm X, Gandhi, Sojourner Truth, and other revolutionary leaders.

Social justice movements of the 1960s and 1970s such as the Black Panthers and the American Indian Movement serve as important models for twenty-first-century activists. Henry Spira (1927–1998), an early animal rights activist who organized direct actions against animal testing, explains that "We wanted to adapt to the animal movement the traditions of struggle which had proven effective in the civil rights movement, the union movement and the women's movement."[81] In a 2015 talk on "Purity Politics: How Animal Liberation Is Keeping Us from Animal Liberation" at the International Animal Rights Conference, Stop Huntingdon Animal Cruelty (SHAC) activist Jake Conroy described the Black Panthers as the "most important social justice movement in the history of the United States." When Conroy was released from prison (he was sentenced to four years for his role in SHAC), he sought out activists from the 1960s, including one involved with the Weather Underground. He spoke with them to better understand his own experience and the historical context for his work with the twenty-first-century animal rights movement.[82] By emphasizing their place in an American lineage of social change movements, radical animal rights and environmental activists argue that their activism is on a historical scale with other liberation movements. They believe that decades from now, instead of being remembered as terrorists, they will be seen as freedom fighters, ahead of their time.

"OUR ENEMIES AND THEIRS ARE ONE AND THE SAME"

Politically motivated radical environmental and animal rights activists at the turn of the twenty-first century are committed to a far-reaching program of social change, as well as a future where animals and wilderness have rights and protections. They argue that their concerns intersect in important ways with racial justice and gender equality. Intersectionality was emphasized in activist communities I participated in, which I discuss in more detail in Chapter 6. Activists' critique of American environmental policies and practices concerning nonhuman animals goes hand in hand with a denunciation of consumer capitalism, racism, imperialism, and gender and economic inequality. As the author of a "Report Back" from Earth First!s Rendezvous puts it, "Remember that our enemies and theirs are one and the same."[83] For this reason, the biographies of many radical environmental and animal rights activists are characterized by involvement, often from an early age, with a variety of social change movements and social justice campaigns.

In 2000–2001, Lauren Gazzola became involved in SHAC, the campaign against Huntingdon Life Sciences.[84] Three weeks before she planned to take the LSAT, she was arrested and charged with "domestic terrorism" for her participation in SHAC. In 2006, Gazzola was sentenced to four years and four months in prison for "Conspiracy to Violate the Animal Enterprise Protection Act, Conspiracy to Stalk, three counts of Interstate Stalking, Conspiracy to Harass using a Telecommunications Device."[85] The website she contributed to supported animal liberation, even though she herself was not involved in these actions. As she points out, "The speech on our website was indeed controversial. When anonymous activists liberated 14 beagles from the lab, we cheered. When protesters demonstrated outside lab employees' homes, we applauded."[86] After forty months in federal prison, Gazzola was released in 2010.

While in prison, Gazzola completed most of the work for an interdisciplinary MA in the "Law, History, and Philosophy of Free Speech and the First Amendment," through Antioch University. After her release, she became involved with the New York–based Center for Constitutional Rights, working in the position of communications associate for publications, drafting press releases, writing newsletter articles, and managing the Center for Constitutional Rights blog. She continued to be outspoken about free speech issues around animal activism and the unconstitutionality of the Animal Enterprise Terrorism Act (AETA) that allows for protesters to be prosecuted as "terrorists."[87]

Radical environmental and animal rights activism draws on a range of political currents, usually from the left of the political spectrum. Like Gazzola, Darryl Cherney, one of the leading radical environmentalists in the West Coast "Redwood Wars" of the 1990s, "was political right off the bat." He worked on various political campaigns in New York City where he grew up from age eight on. He came to Earth First! with a music and theatre background, organizational skills, and an appreciation for working-class issues from living in New York. When Cherney met activist Judi Bari, an advocate of workers' rights as well as forest protection, her combined interest in deep ecology and socialism was a natural fit.

Bari infused some Earth First! campaigns with a concern for workers' and women's rights. An article in *Earth First! Journal* describes "the second phase" of Earth First! during the early 1990s (following the original "rednecks for wilderness" phase with its emphasis on biocentrism) as a time of coalition building with loggers and other workers.[88] During the 1990s there was a marked split between some radical environmentalists who wanted to stay focused on wilderness protection and others like Bari and Cherney who felt that environmentalism had to be linked with other causes, such as anarchism, workers' rights, and feminism.[89] Former *Earth First! Journal* editor Panagioti Tsolkas argues that "Judi Bari's anti-capitalist analysis increased EF!'s appeal to crowds of college students and anarcho-punks."[90] In the early decades of the 2000s, a tension between these emphases characterized radical environmentalist communities.

Activists who worked to link environmentalism with other causes during the late 1990s were significantly influenced by the presence of anarchists at forest action camps in the Northwest. Their concerns were also shaped by the emergence of anarchism at the World Trade Organization (WTO) protests in Seattle in 1999, as well as around the Occupy movement of 2009. At the same time, radical environmentalists were involved with Seattle and Occupy, suggesting that anarchism and radical environmentalism have had a symbiotic relationship, influencing each other in important ways. According to Tsolkas, "While Earth First! (EF!) has never considered itself to be explicitly anarchist, it has always had a connection to the antiauthoritarian counterculture and has operated in an anarchistic fashion since its inception . . . it has arguably maintained one of the most consistent and long-running networks for activists and revolutionaries of an anarchist persuasion with the broader goal of overturning all socially constructed hierarchies."[91] The anarchist influence in environmental and animal rights circles meant that social justice concerns were increasingly foregrounded in the early twenty-first century.

Late twentieth-century anarchism in the United States did not become publically visible in the mainstream news media until the 1999 Seattle protests against the World Trade Organization. Since then, the number of Americans, especially younger Americans, identifying with anarchism has risen.[92] Activists are exposed to anarchism through college organizations, friends, infoshops, Food Not Bombs, or at protests and in hardcore music scenes. When he was in college, Marten, a former activist with the Buffalo Field Campaign, became involved with a cross-section of loosely anarchist groups. A decade earlier, he was exposed to punk rock at age ten when his uncle took him to a Rancid concert. He became a vegetarian around age twelve after driving through stockyards on a family trip. Marten recalls that his father, an attorney, often complained about how flawed the justice system was. His father also gave him Edward Abbey's fictionalized account of eco-saboteurs, *The Monkey Wrench Gang*, when he was a teenager. At college, Marten met "freegans" while dumpstering, was involved with the campus vegetarian/vegan society and Students Against Sweatshops, and read anarcho-syndicalist works and the writings of anarcho-primitivist writers John Zerzan and Kevin Tucker.[93] For Marten, all of these experiences validated "turning it all down as an appropriate response."[94]

The new anarchism that attracted Marten was built on classical anarchism of the nineteenth and early twentieth centuries, but was also influenced by a host of other factors, including radical feminism and the Zapatista rebellion in Mexico in 1994. Classical anarchism began to take shape as a coherent political philosophy within "the left wing of socialism," according to Russian anarchist Peter Kropotkin.[95] The anarchist slogan "No gods, no masters" expressed the view that socialism was not critical enough of the state and institutional power. Classical anarchists like Kropotkin (1842–1921) and Gustav Landauer (1870–1919) were concerned with capitalism and the suffering caused by the Industrial Revolution. From the 1880s through the Red Scare of the 1920s and the Spanish Revolution of the 1930s, large numbers of anarchists were politically active in the United States and Europe. Anarchist thought and practice spread from the United States to South America and Africa. It was expressed through a variety of experiments, including communal living, federations, free schools, workers councils, local currencies, and mutual aid societies.[96]

Repression in the United States and by Communist governments in other countries, not to mention the rise of Nazism in Germany, resulted in most anarchist leaders being killed or disappearing by the 1940s. For these reasons anarchism became "a ghost of itself," according to anarchist writer Cindy Milstein.[97] In the United States during World War II some anarchist ideas were "resuscitated" and influenced the Beat movement of the 1950s, expressed through the poetry of Alan Ginsberg, Diane di Prima, and other Beat poets.[98]

The reemergence of anarchism in the United States came about through the 1960s counterculture and the New Left of the 1960s and 1970s. It was also shaped by the following: radical feminism and gay rights movements; the Situationists (1962–1972) who advocated playful disruptions of the everyday; social ecologist Murray Bookchin's (1921–2006) writings linking social and ecological crises; the West German Autonomen's creation of communal free spaces and a masked black bloc in demonstrations in the 1980s; and the Zapatista rebellion in 1994.[99] Anarchist thought and practice played a role in various movements that developed after the 1960s, including radical feminism and gay rights, but especially the antinuclear movement.

In addition to anarchism, divergent forms of feminism, including anarcha-feminism, ecofeminism, and feminist spirituality, were important factors in shaping the direct action antinuclear movement of the 1970s and 1980s.[100] In addition to North American protests, women played an important role in the United Kingdom, especially at Greenham Common Women's Peace Camp, a protest against nuclear weapons at a site in Berkshire, England, that ran for nineteen years.[101] In many ways, the feminist movement was at the center of 1970s radicalism and was instrumental in creating a set of self-empowerment organizations and practices, such as health collectives and rape crisis centers run by women. Feminist activists also founded women's studies programs at colleges and universities that would influence generations of young women and other participants in the antinuclear movement and environmentalism.[102]

The nonviolent direct action movement that coalesced around antinuclear activism in the 1970s and 1980s is the most direct link between the countercultural and protest movements of the 1960s and radical eco-activism of the 1990s. The antinuclear movement specialized in road blockades as well as other forms of protest and drew together feminism, anarchism, environmentalism, nonviolent direct action, theatrical protest elements, and in some instances, both Christian and contemporary Pagan spiritual currents. In the antinuclear movement, Quaker consensus decision making converged with anarchist organizing tactics such as affinity groups.[103] These practices, spread nationally by the antinuclear movement, carried on through twenty-first-century anticapitalist, environmental, and animal rights protests.

The Clamshell Alliance was the most influential expression of anarchist, environmentalist, and feminist countercultural tendencies in the 1970s. Clamshell was formed in 1976 to protest the construction of a nuclear power plant near Seabrook, New Hampshire. Clamshell was founded by Quakers and antiwar activists, some of whom had been involved in the civil rights movement. It picked up on anarchist counter-cultural tendencies from the 1960s, as well as Gandhian nonviolence from the civil rights movement, and Quaker commitments to consensus and community building.[104] Clamshell's commitment to feminism encouraged women to take on leadership roles more than earlier movements had done.[105]

The antinuclear movement in New England, Northern California, and elsewhere was often composed of "radical countercultural activists."[106] They had been politically active in the 1960s, but moved to rural areas by the early 1970s, as part of the back-to-the-land movement. They spread ideas and practices about small-scale communities, grassroots democracy, nonhierarchical decision making, pacifism, and anarchism. Clamshell and other antinuclear groups brought together this older generation of former antiwar activists and participants in the 1960s counterculture with young urban activists. Although Clamshell was short lived, it served as a powerful model for later direct action campaigns. In the couple years of its existence, Clamshell trained thousands of activists in consensus decision making and nonviolent direct action, practices that spread across the country to other antinuclear struggles.[107]

On the opposite coast from Clamshell, Abalone Alliance was one of the largest and most successful antinuclear campaigns. Abalone was formed in 1976 to protest the opening of the Diablo Canyon nuclear plant near San Luis Obispo, California. Like Clamshell, Abalone was composed of former peace activists as well as "radically ecologically oriented activists" from Northern California who had been part of the 1960s counterculture. Although Clamshell included prominent women leaders and a commitment to feminism and egalitarianism, Abalone was shaped by even stronger strains of feminism, environmentalism, and anarchism. "Anarcha-feminism," inspired by the work of anarchist writer Murray Bookchin and his book *Post-Scarcity Anarchism*, was particularly important in Abalone's development. The anarcha-feminists developed a movement culture that was very much like the culture of radical environmentalist gatherings of the 1990s and 2000s. They insisted that any anarchist revolutionary politics must also be feminist and sometimes referred to themselves as "ecowarriors." Abalone also promoted leaderless resistance, a characteristic of radical environmental activism in the 2000s.[108]

Like Abalone, twenty-first-century Food Not Bombs, infoshops, barter networks, tool lending libraries, community gardens, the DIY

(Do-It-Yourself) movement, and hardcore punk rock have been anarchist at heart. They have tended to be organized horizontally rather than vertically and have stressed grassroots communities and mutual aid. These anarchist expressions have perpetuated the stream of anarchist thought and practice running from the 1960s antiwar movement through the 1970s women's movement and the nonviolent direct action antinuclear movement of the 1970s and 1980s.

Radical environmentalists in Earth First! were part of this mix and some of them were significantly influenced by the anarchist Wobblies (International Workers of the World).[109] Activist Panagioti Tsolkas claims that the journal *Green Anarchy* (2001–2008) "reshaped" Earth First!: "The GA movement and its magazine contributed significantly to developing the theory that surrounded EF!'s basic tenets." The green anarchy movement was one of many "frequent crossovers" between Earth First! and the anarchist movement that led to young activists moving beyond the tactics of mainstream environmental groups.[110] For all these reasons, by the end of the 1990s, anarchism had become the most influential political view among radical activists who linked environmental and nonhuman animal issues with social justice concerns and critiques of capitalism and the state.

THE NEW ANARCHISM IN PRACTICE

In addition to the 1999 World Trade Organization protests in Seattle and the 2011 Occupy movement, Food Not Bombs and street medics are two examples of anarchist networks that have played a role at radical environmentalist protests and gatherings. Several activists I interviewed were involved with Food Not Bombs, an anarchist organization that helped organize the logistics of the Seattle protests.[111] Since 1980 when it was founded by anarchists in Cambridge, Massachusetts, Food Not Bombs has spread across the United States, feeding homeless people and protesters with vegan food from dumpsters and food banks. A mainstay at Occupy and other protests as well as some Earth First! gatherings, Food Not Bombs also helped arrange food for displaced people after Hurricane Katrina.[112] During Occupy Wall Street, Food Not Bombs, along with other anarchist mutual aid organizations, provided support for protesters. The Food Not Bombs Boston chapter, for example, served hot meals every day at the Occupy Boston encampment.[113]

Some activists became involved with radical environmentalism and animal rights activism through Food Not Bombs and other anarchist projects. In 2014 I spoke with Rabbit, an activist and *Earth First! Journal* editor, about his experience working with Food Not Bombs. Rabbit grew up in Los Angeles and was active in animal rights protests after graduating from high school. He was a part-time activist at first, what he called a "weekend warrior," joining protests against Huntingdon Life Sciences. While in college at California State University, Long Beach, he volunteered with Food Not Bombs for four years. It was not until this period of his life that Rabbit came to a realization: "It shouldn't have taken me twenty-three years to realize that if there's food in a dumpster and there's hungry people, that I can give it to them, but because of the way I was raised in society, it took me that long to realize." As well as being involved with Food Not Bombs, Occupy, and animal rights demonstrations, Rabbit spent a year working on homesteads and organic farms, and visited the Tar Sands Blockade in Texas. After college, he volunteered as a canvasser and fundraiser for Greenpeace following the 2010 Gulf of Mexico BP oil spill.[114] Like other activists, he traveled through these networks of affiliation, many of which were shaped by anarchism, before he became involved with Earth First!

Food Not Bombs is one of many direct links between radical environmental/animal rights activism and the Occupy movement. Like a number of young activists I met, Rabbit also credits Occupy with having a significant influence on his and others' radicalism: "It got a lot of people off their asses, many people who had never protested. Since then I've done nothing but activism and know so many people for whom that is the way it is." For Rabbit, Occupy was an "awesome way for people to learn skills: how to march, how to chant. I learned how to break into foreclosed homes and open up squats." Aaron, another Earth First! activist previously involved with Occupy, had worked on the 2008 Obama campaign as a teenager. He was disillusioned by what he saw as "Obama selling out," which led him to radicalism. Although he was in college, he would go to class during the day and then spend the night with the Occupy encampment at a park in his Midwestern college town. After his time with Occupy, Aaron became active in Earth First! and involved with the 2012 Tar Sands Blockade in Texas.[115]

In a similar fashion to Food Not Bombs volunteers, anarchist street medics serve protests like those of the Occupy movement and Earth First!, as well as helping in disaster-stricken areas. They also have links to earlier streams of radicalism. Street medics originated in the civil rights and antiwar movements of the 1960s and were also involved with the American Indian Movement in the 1970s.[116] Many of the early twenty-first-century street medic collectives formed to meet a need felt during the 1999 Seattle protests.[117] Some medics have formal medical training and are nurses, physicians, or EMTs (Emergency Medical Technicians) but others are lay people who had been through street medic training. Street medics ran a training I participated in at the Wild Roots, Feral Futures gathering, and they staffed the medic tent and supported a protest action at an Earth First! Rendezvous I attended. But they also traveled to New Orleans to volunteer their services after Hurricane Katrina and to Haiti after the 2010 earthquake. Others worked in free community clinics in large U.S. cities. In 2015, some street medic collectives supported antiracism protests in Ferguson and St. Louis, Missouri.[118] Activists circulate through these various anarchist sites of learning and practice, sharing information and connecting each other to like-minded communities.

In all of these examples—Food Not Bombs, street medics, Occupy, Seattle—anarchism serves as a worldview that allows radical activists to create meaning out of their lives by linking activist practices to a broader movement for social and political change. Environmental activism in the late twentieth century was shaped by the confluence of anarchism and deep ecology just as animal rights was shaped by anarchism and critiques of anthropocentrism. But religious and spiritual movements also played a part, even while most anarchists were suspicious of institutional religious expressions and particularly of Christianity.

YOUTH MOVEMENTS AND AMERICAN RELIGION SINCE THE 1960S

So how might we situate religion within this story of youth-led direct action movements since the 1960s? Because adolescents are no longer children but not yet adults, their religious commitments are usually not fully formed, which allows them to be open to new ways of understanding the world. Moreover, young people feature prominently in a number of developments on the post–World War II American religious landscape, such as the growth of Asian religions, new religious movements, evangelicalism, and the rising ranks of the religiously unaffiliated at the beginning of the twenty-first century.[119]

Like many new religions, animal rights and environmental organizations sometimes actively court young people, as PETA does with its "PETA 2," targeted at teenagers and billed as "the largest animal rights group in the world."[120] Late twentieth-century animal rights activist

Henry Spira urged his fellow activists to reach out to the young: "Our Coalition must connect with young people while they are still sorting out their values."[121] Conversion to new religions as well as to political and social movements like animal rights typically occurs during teenage and college years. One possible reason for this may be because teenagers are able to think abstractly and multidimensionally, calling into question received truths. However, because of "the yielding of the certainty of childhood," they are not yet seen as fully formed adults.[122] They are perceived as both vulnerable *and* potentially powerful because of their transitional status, unpredictable as they leave childhood behind and decide who they want to be, not necessarily following the dictates of their parents or other adults.[123]

Because of this liminal position of being both powerful and vulnerable, young Americans have been seen as innocents at risk *and* as potential converts in the context of new religious phenomena. Puritan minister Jonathan Edwards, for instance, was particularly concerned about the salvation of young adults. During revivals of the Great Awakening, the majority of conversions were young men and women, a fourth of them in their teens.[124] Moreover, three out of four converts in nineteenth-century evangelical revivals were young women.[125]

In the 1970s, young adults were again imagined as both spiritually powerful and defenseless, sometimes posing a threat to other youth and to social stability. During the 1960s and 1970s, transplanted Asian religions and new religious movements gained popularity among a generation of youth open to spiritual experimentation. However, youth interest in these new religions was countered by the anticult movement of the 1970s.[126] Young converts were seen by many American adults, often including their parents, as victims of so-called cults, such as new religions like Krishna Consciousness, the Unification Church, and contemporary Paganism.

For new religions like contemporary Paganism, an umbrella terms that includes Witches and Druids, youth interest was a boon. While teenage religious experimentation was magical for the youth who found it, these occult traditions were also the target of a satanic rumor panic of the 1970s and 1980s. This perpetuated a sense that youth were "at risk" and reified societal stereotypes of "dark teens." Young Pagans rarely followed their parents' or neighbors' religious identities, whether atheist or Christian, and so their beliefs and practices tended to be either demonized or trivialized.[127]

Contemporary Paganism has a parallel history with radical environmentalism. Both emerged in the wake of the 1960s counterculture and focused on the Earth, attracting young Americans throughout the last few decades of the twentieth century. In addition to the new anarchism, late modern youth culture, and deep ecology, Paganism is another important factor in creating a context in which radical activism could thrive at the turn of the millennium.[128] Paganism has had a significant influence on radical environmentalism, especially Earth First!, although less so on animal rights. In the United Kingdom Pagans have been involved with antinuclear and antiroads activism, though less visibly in the United States.[129]

Contemporary Pagan involvement with anarchist movements and direct action has its origins in the antinuclear movement of the 1970s and 1980s. Pagans, especially Witches, participated in Abalone Alliance protests against the Diablo Canyon nuclear power plant. Reclaiming, a well-known collective of Witches that was founded in San Francisco, joined Abalone's campaign. They held rituals in jail and at protests, even though by no means all protesters were Pagan. Contemporary Pagans were also active in the Livermore Action Group (LAG) protesting nuclear weapons development at Lawrence Livermore Laboratory in California between 1981–1984. LAG was feminist, anarchist, ecologically concerned, and included significant groups of both Christians and Pagans working together against nuclear arms. The influential feminist Witch and writer Starhawk participated in LAG, Abalone, and Earth First! protests. In her activism and writing, feminism, Paganism, and radical environmentalism are intertwined concerns.[130]

Contemporary Pagans tend to look to the past for inspiration and wisdom. They are engaged in reviving and reimagining pre-Christian indigenous traditions of Europe.[131] Like activists, Pagans are often critical of Christianity, especially its role in the colonization of indigenous people and repression of their spiritual traditions. Pagans view the natural world as sacred; for many of them the earth itself is the body of a goddess. Most Pagans create rituals to mark the changing of the seasons, such as Spring Equinox and Summer Solstice. Many Pagan rituals involve the natural elements of water, fire, air, and earth and orient ritual space around the four cardinal directions of east, west, north, and south. Pagan teachings emphasize the interconnectedness of all things and celebrate the ways in which humans and the natural world are part of a web of life.[132]

In the late twentieth century, teenagers accounted in part for the growing popularity of Paganism, especially within Wicca and Witchcraft. Silver RavenWolf's *Teen Witch: Wicca for a New Generation*, published in 1998, sold over 200,000 copies.[133] A number of activists who corresponded with me from prison were involved with or interested in Paganism when they were teenagers. Jeff "Free" Luers was one of them. In 2001, Luers was sentenced to twenty-two years and eight months in prison for setting fire to three SUVs at a car dealership as a protest against global warming.[134] As a teenager growing up in Southern California, he communicated with nature spirits as well as trees, even though he knew that outside his circle of like-minded friends, "the idea is so foreign. And yet it is totally acceptable to talk and pray to a totally invisible god."[135] According to Luers, these earlier experiences set the stage for his conversion to activism a few years later.[136]

Some contemporary Pagans emphasize ecological connections more than others. The Church of All Worlds (CAW) is one of the oldest Pagan organizations in the United States. It was founded in 1968 by Oberon (Tim) Zell-Ravenheart and teaches that Gaia is a living entity in which humans are connected to the "web of life."[137] Historian of Wicca Chas Clifton argues that "Gaian Nature," a phrase he borrows from Zell-Ravenheart's 1970 article on "deep ecology," is a common variety of contemporary Paganism. Pagans who follow this type of Paganism are likely "to speak of the spirit of nature and, as heirs of the Romantic Movement, to see humanity as suffering from its spiritual divorce from nature."[138] Like radical environmentalists, these Pagans look to childhood, nature, and the past, especially the pre-Christian past, for truth and inspiration. The Church of All Worlds also has a historical connection to Earth First! According to activist Darryl Cherney, during the 1990s Earth First!ers went to CAW's Northern California nature sanctuary, Annwfn, for gatherings and spiritual restoration.[139]

At various radical environmental events, I met activists who were involved with Paganism to some degree. Some had been to "Free Witchcamp" or to Radical Faerie gatherings (Radical Faeries integrate Paganism, queer culture, anarchism, and radical environmentalism). Free Witchcamp is a gathering for activists with rituals and workshops inspired by Reclaiming Witch Camps. Some Reclaiming members were active in the environmental movement of the 1980s and 1990s, including Earth First! actions.[140]

The influence of contemporary Pagans had become less visible by the time I was conducting fieldwork. There were no community-wide Pagan rituals held at any of Earth First! Rendezvous I attended, even though many individuals I met expressed Pagan leanings. Paganism, like anarchism, has helped to shape the radical milieu in which many activists place themselves, even though it is often an implicit and unacknowledged contributing factor in activist commitments. Like anarchism, Paganism offers an alternative to more widespread American religious traditions such as Christianity that most activists have rejected.

Because of their anarchist leanings, activists may practice a more implicit Paganism instead of participating in established Pagan communities such as Wiccan covens or Druid groves. Currant, an activist I corresponded with while she was serving a prison sentence for her role in ELF actions, briefly experimented with Paganism as a teenager. She suggested to me that contemporary Pagan elements in radical environmentalism "are more cultural than religious." As she sees it, there is a widespread "reverence for nature" among radical environmentalists, including practices such as "keeping a special stone from a favorite wild place, maybe placing it on a shelf as a kind of altar." For Currant, Paganism serves as "a cultural replacement for Western rationalism and Christianity," a view shared by many activists I encountered, unless they were opposed to all religions, which is also common.[141]

As an implicit radical activist worldview, Paganism offers activists a way of thinking about the cycles of time and seasons without referring to the Gregorian calendar. The *Earth First! Journal* releases its issues in accordance with the cycle of seasonal festivals followed by many Pagans and called the Wheel of the Year, which revolves around the solstices, equinoxes, and four cross-quarter holidays (October 31: Samhain, February 2: Brigid, May 1: Beltane, and August 1: Lughnasadh). Pagan elements appear in animal rights communiqués dated with Pagan holidays and in the *Earth First! Journal*. The practice of using Pagan holidays as date markers was continued by the ELF. The ELF's first American communiqué in 1997 was dated "Beltane."[142]

Radical environmentalism and animal rights have inherited a creative tension between the anarchistic distrust of religion and an attraction to worldviews like Paganism that place spiritual value on the lives of other species and the Earth. For some anarchist-identified activists, the solution is to make spirituality this-worldly and material. Instead of sharing a contemporary Pagan view of immanence in which divine energy flows through everything, in which gods and goddesses are trees or our bodies, these activists see trees and nonhuman animals as inherently sacred. If they are gods and goddesses, that is because of their "tree-ness" or "rock-ness," not the presence of a divine power. In this way, activists who hold such a view—in contrast to those who are more theologically "Pagan"—are aligned with the growing trend of Americans, young Americans in particular, who claim to be "spiritual but not religious."

Looking back on youth-driven political and religious trends in the second half of the twentieth century helps provide historical context for the emergence of radical activism. By the end of the twentieth century, the proportion of young Americans identifying with a particular religious tradition had declined, as had high school students' weekly attendance at religious services.[143] In the opening decades of the twenty-first century, American youth experienced the greatest shift in religious disaffiliation, according to a survey of over 35,000 Americans conducted by the PEW Research Center in 2014.[144] Radical activism is one of many possible sites where moral beliefs and spiritual values take shape and are expressed outside religious institutions.[145] Twenty-first-century activism came about largely due to the shifting landscape of American religiosity as well as various historical forces tempered by twentieth-century youth culture. However, activists' personal pasts are as important as these historical contexts for tracking the development of their commitments. In the next chapter, I trace the ways in which activists draw from and shape narratives about childhood experiences in nature and with nonhuman animals. Attention to activists' narratives about childhood memories and the identities they have forged from these memories reveals much about the inner histories of their commitment to activism.

CHAPTER 3

Childhood Landscapes of Wonder and Awe

To articulate the past historically does not mean
to recognize it the way it really was, but to seize hold
of a memory as it flashes up at a moment of danger.

—Walter Benjamin

A child's world is fresh and new and beautiful, full of wonder
and excitement. It is our misfortune that for most of us
that clear-eyed vision, that true instinct for what is beautiful
and awe-inspiring, is dimmed and even lost before we reach
adulthood.

—Rachel Carson, *The Sense of Wonder*

Adults follow paths. Children explore. Adults are content
to walk the same way, hundreds of times, or thousands;
perhaps it never occurs to adults to step off the paths.

—Neil Gaiman, *The Ocean at the End of the Lane*

I sat with Maia, a friend of one of my students, under a large pine tree, talking about the experiences early in her life that set her on the path to radical eco-activism. During high school, Maia had become troubled by what was happening in her Southern California desert community. As she watched, more and more tract homes were being built in the open spaces she had loved as a child, places where she had called wild animals her friends. One summer night, Maia and her boyfriend climbed the fence of a construction site for a new housing development under construction on desert tortoise habitat. The teenage saboteurs put Karo syrup and tampons into the gas tanks of bulldozers on the site and pulled up survey stakes. Maia described to me how exhilarated she felt when they snuck back over the fence. She marked that night as a "tipping point," after which she was committed to radical environmentalism. Looking back a few years later when she was no longer involved with direct action, she saw this period of her life as one of spiritual seeking through action, as she blended the moral values of her upbringing among Jehovah's Witnesses with contemporary Pagan and environmentalist views of the natural world as sacred.

For many Americans, Maia's ecotage is an extreme choice, while for others she is a poster child for youthful resistance to suburban sprawl. Actions like hers and those of other young activists I interviewed have been called amoral and antisocial by the news media and law enforcement agencies.[1] But the young activists I spoke with were some of the most sensitive and thoughtfully moral people I have ever met. They were much less willing than most of us to compromise their values, striving to be consistent with their ideals in which all life, human as well as other-than-human, should be respected. Many of them created through memories a childhood world that offers an ideal future, one in which humans learn to listen to other species and live with them in ways that do not put human needs and desires first.

When I asked activists like Maia how they became committed to activism, almost all of them cited teenage or college years as pivotal times in their becoming activists. However, they also emphasized the ways in which experiences when they were younger had already inclined them towards activism. I explored with them the nature of these early experiences by asking them to identify what characteristics of their childhood made them particularly likely to become activists. In this way, I may have guided a certain kind of remembering by my interest in childhood experience. But the stories that emerged in our conversations are closely echoed by other activist accounts of childhood experience I came across online and in print.[2] This chapter explores the landscape of childhood as it is configured in activist narratives. I understand landscapes to be active in these encounters with children, rather than stages upon which children grew into their identities. Children work on the landscape as it works on them, calling each other into being.[3] These experiences and memories later affected activists' willingness to take extreme actions on behalf of the more-than-human world. At the same time, their activist commitments as young adults shaped the ways they remembered the past and the values with which they imbued the childhood landscape.

For Maia and other activists, activism takes place in the context of inner histories composed of memories, childhood experiences, and family background, as well as constructed narratives. However, activists' childhood memories of wonder in nature are *bittersweet*: on the one hand they remember nature as a special place in which they developed close relationships to trees and animals; on the other, many of them grieved for disturbed and desecrated places in nature. Grief and loss became for them the *dark side of wonder*. Because the boundaries between child self and nonhuman other were porous, loss of the other or its degradation were even more disturbing. Activists' remembered childhood worlds of wonder held pain and suffering when beloved childhood places were lost to roads, new houses, and shopping malls.

INNER HISTORIES

Maia, like other teenage eco-saboteurs, had a sense of herself as a spiritual person with high moral standards. She grew up in a family of Jehovah's Witnesses in a small town in Southern California. Even though as an adolescent she began questioning her family's religious beliefs, she still credits them with instilling in her a strong "moral compass." She suspects her parents allowed her more freedom than other Witness kids she knew. Her mother nurtured Maia's creativity and inspired her desire "to create a more loving world."[4] Her family did not celebrate holidays or own a television and encouraged her to read books and play outside, where she developed a sense of closeness to desert creatures. She made water holes in the desert for her animal friends, lining the holes with foil so the water would not drain out. Maia not only tried to care for wild animals but also developed close relationships with domestic ones. She recalled becoming deeply attached to a neighbor's cow, whom she named Daisy, and being heartbroken when Daisy was eventually slaughtered. Because of this traumatic loss of a friend, Maia became a vegetarian at age five. In her view, being vegetarian, caring for animals, and spending time outdoors set the stage for her later activism.

Maia's story resonates with others I was told during fieldwork or read in other sources. These are stories of co-becoming with nonhuman others and experiencing the pain and suffering of those others. While some activists told me they were "born that way," most of them describe coming of age in a world of influences, human and other-than-human. They ended up at protests and action camps, they explained, because of the early histories that led them to activism. Although many people have similar experiences, activists' narratives of childhood emphasize experiences in nature as *unusually powerful and formative*. For some activists, childhood experiences even model the world they want to live in. In these ways, childhood landscapes and animal friendships become models for appropriate ways to live with other species and serve as resources for adult actions.

At the same time, the gestures and bodily practices of protests construct as well as reveal a past in which the natural world is an emotionally significant aspect of activists' youth.[5] The remembered childhood landscape becomes an important space for activist identity formation and activists mimic childhood activities in later actions. In Maia's case, for example, there is a direct connection between action (protecting tortoise habitat) and childhood memory (putting out water for tortoises). In this way, activism not only becomes a rational choice for Maia and her activist counterparts, but a necessity driven by moral commitments dating to childhood.[6]

Activists cast off some aspects of their upbringing, such as the social goals and religious commitments of their parents, yet they are sometimes inspired by their parents' values. I am particularly interested in what activists remember from childhood and what they forget, what they embrace and what they reject, and what these stories tell us about activist understandings of the bonds they formed with the natural world as children that inform their later actions.

For Maia, the religion of her Jehovah's Witness parents became unacceptable as she grew older, yet she found the experience of growing up as a Witness useful. She was accustomed to being "different from the norm," so she easily embraced activism since she already knew how to "think outside the box." She borrowed from but reinterpreted the Witnesses' millennialism: "The time of the end may come, but why not do something now?" she decided when she became involved with direct action. She credited her parents for providing her with "a clear sense of right and wrong."[7]

When activists "convert" to environmental and animal rights causes, their conversion is not necessarily a distinct break as many scholars have argued.[8] Instead of a clear separation from the past, converts to activism find ways to reshape and reinterpret their pasts so that there are continuities as well as discontinuities. They take the features of their upbringing that suit their activist lifestyles and discard those that do not. When activists tell stories of the past, of special wild places and important relationships with humans and other species, they bring the past to life both in terms of what is rejected and what is brought forward from childhood.

By bringing childhood landscapes into the present when they share childhood stories in the context of direct actions, activists reconstitute the past and charge it with emotional meaning. As ritualized activity both set apart from daily life and rehearsed, protests engage the body and imagination, evoke memories, and express values. The physical experiences of climbing trees and making tree houses and the emotional urgency of the struggle to save these places link present to past in powerful ways.

Activists tend to reverse conventional thinking about the past as part of their refusal to submit to the norms of a society they have scorned. The father of the field of child development, Jean Piaget, opposed "primitive thinking" in children to the gradual development of "scientific objectivity." Piaget argued that "The child as enlightened scientist is assumed to outgrow the child as confused metaphysician."[9] But activists want the confused metaphysician back, and many of them blame scientific objectivity for the degradation of the environment. Their emphasis on intimate childhood relationships with nature and the personhood of trees and animals is the inverse of what they reject in the broader society. By celebrating and nurturing the "immanentist" views Piaget argued would decrease with age, activists practice a thoughtful kind of anthropomorphism, well aware they are challenging more dominant ways of thinking about other species.[10] Activists value the child's perspective and the so-called primitive instead of leaving them behind.[11] They deliberately look to childhood anthropomorphism and indigenous cultures' animistic relationships with the other-than-human world as ideal approaches to living with other species. In this way childhood may become for them not just a storehouse of experiences, but a way of thinking and being in the world.

It is not that unusual in the early twenty-first century for people of all ages to treat pets like human beings and to imagine nature as alive and full of power. However, activists as a group tend to foreground these approaches more than most Americans. For this reason, childhood experience might be seen as an important facet of the spiritual orientation of many radical activists. For these activists, childhood experiences endow the landscape, its trees and animals, with meaning and value. The following sections explore some of the ways in which this dynamic kind of remembering and reenchanting of the natural world takes place within activists' accounts of their pasts. In stories of how they became involved with direct action, the following themes from childhood play an important role: experiences of self extending into landscape; child self merging with nonhuman other; free play outside; and cross-species relationship/communication/kinship, often involving the personification of particular animals and special trees. These themes work together to create the contours of childhood memory that shape and are shaped by activist commitments.[12]

LANDSCAPES OF CHILDHOOD MEMORY

As children like Maia actively work on the world around them—woods and deserts—they prepare themselves for the adult work of acting on larger social and political worlds.[13] Their work on the landscape models a relationship they revisit later in life as activists when they identify with the suffering of forests and build platforms in trees to block logging and construction crews. As they become familiar with the ecosystems where they go to sabotage housing developments or interfere with mountain lion hunting, as they name particular trees they sit in, activists' emotions become embedded in the landscape and the other species that inhabit it, just as they did in childhood.

In their childhood stories, activists' inner landscapes of the self come to be reflected in the contours of the outer landscape, as the self extends out beyond the boundaries of their bodies into the bodies of trees, animals, deserts, and lakes.[14] As they explore deserts and woods near their homes or camp in mountains with their families, they become themselves in the company of human and nonhuman others. When children explore the landscape—making paths, finding climbing routes in trees, damming small creeks—they externalize their sense of self into the spaces around them at the same time they internalize the outer landscape.[15] In these ways, they act on the natural world while it acts on them; they actively shape the landscape, and in the process become intimate with it. This dynamic of co-becoming and intimacy often comes to characterize direct actions as well.

Eighty feet up in the Piney Woods near Winnsboro, Texas, a hundred miles east of Dallas, activists posed for a photo in a tree village composed of a series of ropes, tarps, platforms, and walkways. Some of them stood above a banner hanging from the tree village that read "You Shall Not Pass," illustrated with a painting of a giant hand in a "stop" gesture. On September 24, 2012, eight activists climbed into the tree village of "Middle Earth," which is the name they gave to the forest where energy giant TransCanada was clearing land for a pipeline to carry Tar Sands oil from Alberta, Canada, to ports on the Gulf of Mexico. A reporter from the *Texas Observer* who visited the village described it as follows: "Their world is confined to the 4-by-6-foot platforms and the ropes connecting them. They're able to zipline between platforms, but the structures only offer enough room to sit or lay. If they want to stretch their legs, they use a catwalk—nicknamed "Helm's Deep"—that extends 100 feet across the tree village's northern boundary."[16] The tree village in Middle Earth lasted for eighty-five days before it was dismantled after pipeline construction was rerouted around it.

Middle Earth's tree village was established by a group of activists and local landowners who created the Tar Sands Blockade, a series of actions to resist pipeline construction across eastern Texas. In addition to building a tree village to block construction crews, activists locked down to and stood in front of bulldozers, locked themselves inside pieces of pipe, and held rallies to proclaim solidarity with their grandchildren, the "grandchildren of the trees here," and indigenous people of Alberta whose lands were being despoiled by Tar Sands extraction. According to *Blockadia Rising*, a documentary film about the campaign, the area to be cleared for the pipeline included some of the oldest trees in Texas. The area was also home to armadillos, cougars, bobcats, white-tailed deer, tree frogs, catfish, luna moths, an endangered woodpecker, and many other species.[17] As one activist put it, "being here has motivated me to keep being here. Look around. This place is beautiful." "We need to break people's hearts this winter," insisted Peaceful Uprising director Henia Belalia, one of the organizers of the blockade who was interviewed in the film. Belalia is referring to the powerful love many activists feel for wild places and the vulnerable positions they put themselves in to draw attention to the devastation caused by plowing down forests.[18] To break people's hearts, activists create an identification of their own vulnerable bodies with the land, to induce in others the same love they feel for wild places.

Tree-sits like Tar Sands Blockade's tree village Middle Earth—named after J. R. R. Tolkien's enchanted world of monstrous wolves and eagles, wizards and elves, shapeshifting bears and tree-like beings—reflect childhood experiences as well as the influence of popular culture. When activists like the Tar Sands blockaders climb into platforms hundreds of feet up in trees, some of them draw on memories of childhood places and experiences with other beings, as well as skills and strategies learned in action camps and workshops. The inner histories they bring with them include memories of multispecies landscapes in which they became intimately connected with trees and animals.[19] Ritualized actions such as creating sacred space at forest action camps and chaining themselves to blockades to prevent logging shape and reinforce activists' memories of earlier relationships to nature. A place becomes important to them because it has been inscribed by emotionally intense encounters with human and other-than-human beings.[20] In the context of direct actions like Tar Sands Blockade's tree village, beloved landscapes and memories surface in and are constructed by the process of sharing stories and being involved with direct actions. These memories, then, contribute to activists' powerful experiences of the places they inhabit when they build and live in tree villages and other blockades.[21]

I met Lakes, an activist and direct action trainer from Michigan who was at Tar Sands Blockade, at an Earth First! Rendezvous. I ran into her by chance at an antifracking march two years later, and we arranged to talk by phone. I called her at home in Michigan while she was busy tanning a deerskin someone had given her. Lakes described to me how she grew up playing outdoors near her suburban Detroit home. As a child she spent many hours on the water, sailing with her family on a lake near their home that was "a really big refuge" for her, and she felt an "intense love for it."[22] In a similar fashion, Tush, an activist from Indiana whom I also met at an Earth First! Rendezvous, grew up outdoors in a suburb of Indianapolis. She had "a drawer full of play clothes" and remembers she and her brother were outside "all the time." As a source for her adult work to "connect with and preserve the world," Tush sees the importance of her childhood in this way: "I grew up with a sort of ecologically-minded worldview, or at the very least an imagination that was based on playing in the woods. I grew up in the country, on an apple orchard, and spent most of my time climbing trees and playing in creeks. . . . I try to live my life thinking about everything being sacred."[23]

As activists like Tush remember it, something precious was generated from their experience in the landscape as children: a worldview that imbued woods and creeks with value. In her study of "childscapes," writer Jay Griffiths describes this generative process as one by which landscapes are "kindling children," as children's identities and values emerge from their experiences outdoors.[24] In Griffiths's view, nature plays an active role in these experiences, rather than simply being a stage upon which children explored and acted.[25] Tush *became* an activist within the woods where she played, "kindled" by the places she loved. Her ideas about what is sacred came about from these direct encounters.

Hammock and banner on road blockade at fracking site. Photo: Marcellus Shale Earth First! Used with permission.

For Tush, being comfortable and familiar with tree climbing from childhood was an asset when she became an activist. She was not dizzy or afraid of heights when she was trained by other activists to climb trees: "For me, trees represented a sort of refuge, even if they didn't house a treehouse or fort. There was a book that I used to read . . . a children's book, about some kids who made this amazing tree fort inside the branches of a willow tree—they even put on a circus inside!—and I would hang out in the willow tree in my family's front yard and pretend about that sometimes."[26] However, because activists may feel comfortable in tree-sits that are reminiscent of childhood, the dangers posed by them, such as falling, may seem less real. Moreover, threats do not always come from outside, but can be imposed by the challenging personal commitments activists make to trees and nonhuman animals. It is activists who believe forests and animals are relying on them, regardless of what the forests and animals think. Family members, friends, lovers, and children (for the few who have them) are left to suffer when activists are imprisoned, injured, or die for their causes. Activists acting for the animals and for the wild do not necessarily put their human commitments first.

Activist accounts of childhood suggest a number of reasons why they sometimes prioritize other species over their own. Their stories reveal why they develop and hold onto a sense of porous boundaries between species, why they empathize, identify with, and talk to trees and animals. When researchers ask children what it means to live in harmony with nature, a variety of conceptions emerge. Many children describe having direct, "sensorial" experiences in nature, while others emphasize "relational" aspects that might involve talking to trees and animals.[27] Activists' early identities are formed at the same time that they are learning the world around them through their senses and in relationship to nonhuman others.[28] As poet Gary Snyder observes in *The Practice of the Wild*, "the childhood landscape is learned on foot, and a map is inscribed in the mind—trails and pathways and groves—going out wider and farther." This mapping of self in relationship to nature and nonhuman animals is expressed in a variety of ways; friends and family may even be features of the map.

Animal rights activist Rod Coronado has been involved in many direct actions on behalf of animals, including sabotaging whaling ships and damaging fur farms and animal research laboratories. In 2006, he was sentenced to eight months in prison for interfering with a mountain lion hunt in Arizona's Coronado National Forest by spreading false scent trails with mountain lion urine and springing traps. Coronado believes his childhood and family background were the basis for his later activism, creating in him mind maps like those described by Snyder. Coronado's parents introduced him to wilderness areas through camping and fishing trips in California's Sierra Nevada, even though he grew up in the San Jose suburbs. In a biography of Coronado, journalist Dean Kuipers suggests these childhood trips to the woods became an essential aspect of Coronado's sense of self: "By the time he was a teenager, parts of the Western Sierra were hardwired in his memory." Kuipers explains Coronado's identification with nature this way: "He saw that he was connected to something bigger, a wholeness, and that even the yard back home was a version of that wholeness. The wilderness became part of his self, a bigger Self; it felt personal and close."[29] According to Coronado, in addition to family camping and fishing trips, he read books about tracking and wild foods and looked for edible plants while camping, trying "to imagine what it was like for the people who lived here a long time ago."[30] Later he drew on these childhood wilderness experiences to understand the proper relationship between humans and nature. In all these ways, Coronado's sense of identity was inextricably related to wild places and animals on a larger scale, extending out of childhood relationships to encompass whales in the North Atlantic and mountain lions in the Arizona desert.

WONDER AND THE ACTIVIST SELF

Activists like Coronado bring a wonder-filled attitude to the places they gather, an attitude many of them date to childhood. For activists, wonder is not always a rare experience, but more of an orientation towards the world, a way of perceiving and being attentive to the lives of other species. The ecological child of memory embodies values that activists aspire to: intimacy and empathy with other species and a sense of wonder in regard to the natural world.[31] In this way, wonder is not inherent in nature, but rather discovered by children who may feel wonder and awe, but are also conditioned by the imaginative frameworks they bring outdoors with them that are derived from books, films, and adult companions.

In *The Sense of Wonder* (1956), biologist Rachel Carson describes the kind of wonder activists recall experiencing as children. She advocates getting children out in nature and nurturing their delight in it because "a child's world is fresh and new and beautiful."[32] Children, she believes, immediately accept "a world of elemental things, fearing neither the song of the wind nor the darkness nor the roaring surf."[33] Carson suggests parents allow children to get muddy and stay up late in order to immerse them in the more-than-human world. She introduces her nephew to sea creatures on the shore and takes him out at night to marvel at the stars: "the memory of such a scene, photographed year after year by his child's mind, would mean more to him in manhood than the sleep he was losing."[34] She hopes the experience of wonder will stay with him and help shape the adult he will become.

Like many radical environmentalists, Carson balances her critique of the destruction of nature with pleasure and enjoyment in it. As environmental ethicist Lisa Sideris argues, Carson's work models a kind of environmentalism tempered by "the narrowed perception of fear and the expansive vision of wonder . . . at natural processes, as well as fear of the consequences of tampering with and destroying those processes." As Sideris sees it, both have "an important role to play in the environmental movement."[35] For many activists, childhood wonder carried into adult action is all that redeems their sorrow over environmental destruction and apocalyptic expectations of societal and environmental collapse. Activist childhood memories embody this tension between wonder and sorrow, hope and loss.

Action camps and environmentalist gatherings re-create both aspects—wonder and sorrow—of the landscape of childhood memory. They offer safe space, intimacy with nature, a sense of family and kinship, and adult activities like tree climbing that are reminiscent of childhood play. They also focus on environmental devastation and the suffering of other species caused by human activities. Gatherings like the Earth First! Round River Rendezvous usually include singing and playing music around campfires, craft activities like making banners, talent shows, skinny dipping, mud wrestling, and tree climbing (with gear and ropes). Earth First!'s 2013 Round River Rendezvous was held in a decommissioned remote campsite in the Smoky Mountains of North Carolina. Ropes strung in the branches to create climbing areas and tented workshop spaces with names like "Red Fox" lent an aura of playfulness to the serious business of organizing an antifracking direct action.

Of course action camps and gatherings are not childhood landscapes; they harbor risk and danger as well. While they may be reminiscent of childhood spaces and childhood play, they take place in a context in which bodily harm, arrest, imprisonment, and even death are a reality. Invoking childhood experiences is a way of downplaying these risks. The deaths of activists such as David Chain, who was killed by a logger felling trees where Chain was protesting, underline the perils involved with pursuits reminiscent of childhood. Chain was involved in the high-profile "Redwood Wars" of the 1990s when activists in Northern California argued with loggers, built tree-sits, and did everything they could to stop the felling of old-growth redwoods.[36] In images of tree-sits, some activists are smiling and seem to be enjoying a playful existence in the treetops, laughing as they elude climbers sent to extract them. But anger and fear also permeate these spaces, making them seem a far cry from childhood sanctuaries. The documentary film *Blockadia Rising* shows trees in Middle Earth being cut down by chainsaws and bulldozers and falling just twenty feet away from activists looking on fearfully from their treetop perches.

Tar Sands Blockade's Middle Earth is a reminder that childhood stories, like environmental actions, include sadness and destruction as well as wonder and solace. Filmmaker Garrett Graham portrays good and evil images invoked in environmentalist campaigns in stark relief in his film about the Tar Sands Blockade actions. Graham recalls, "We would often compare ourselves to the Ewoks of *Return of the Jedi* or the Ents of *Lord of the Rings*. I wanted to show images that even a child could understand." At the same time that activists in the tree village maintained a playful attitude with jokes about Ewoks and Ents, TransCanada monitored them all day and night to try to prevent resupplying—food and water being sent up to the tree village by a system of pulleys—in the hopes of starving them out. The company also shone spotlights on the tree-sit throughout the night, making it difficult for activists to sleep.[37]

In order to create a contrast between heroic activists and an evil corporation, Graham includes "Mordor-like" images—referring to Tolkien's dark and devastated land inhabited by the dark lord Sauron and his terrifying armies—of the desolate landscape of Tar Sands extraction because, "I wanted my film to revolve around this repeating visual metaphor. People understand those images. Luckily, the Tar Sands already look like Mordor, so all I had to do was make sure that I took the time to record the forest before and after the destruction as well as recording the machinery in action."[38] Invoking Tolkien's epic battle between good and evil suggests activists view their struggle as one of larger-than-life proportions. For them, evil is not embodied by one being like Tolkien's Sauron. Instead, it exudes from the greed and shortsightedness of global capitalism, in this case exemplified by a transnational corporation. Innocence and wonder at the tree village were accompanied by the language of struggle and battle imagery. As an activist Graham interviewed put it, climate justice is "the struggle of our time," so being for the wild means being against those who are seen as threatening wild creatures and wild places. In Graham's film, activists choose the unspoiled forest that is Middle Earth and reminiscent of the landscape of childhood, while they opt out of a civilization that requires Mordor-like destruction.

Wonder towards nature is nurtured and reinforced by plant walks and other nature-appreciation-type workshops at radical environmentalist gatherings. "Fauna Cabala," a column in the *Earth First! Journal*, has featured stories on mating tortoises, wombat castles, and other esoteric aspects of animal life.[39] Taking delight in the banana slugs at a tree-sit in California's redwood forests or cautiously observing a copperhead snake at a gathering in North Carolina's Smoky Mountains allows activists to reconnect with childhood. By invoking a child-like wonder and awe, activist stories and actions imbue nature with qualities that make it worth saving.

Since a prominent theme in radical activists' childhood stories is the contrast between wonder in nature, which they want to save, and discontent with civilization, which they have come to despise, they might

Tar Sands pipeline construction near Tar Sands blockade, Winnsboro, Texas. Photo: John Fiege. Used with permission.

be expected to completely reject the worlds of their parents. Yet this is often not the case. In addition to special places and animals, activists' childhood stories feature family members and other adults who inspired their appreciation for the natural world.[40] In particular, they often identify parents and grandparents as significant influences on their moral development and love for nature, while at the same time rejecting family religious traditions and political views.[41] In their childhood stories, radical environmentalists and animal rights activists identify the influence of family camping trips and parents or grandparents who instilled in them a sense of wonder and appreciation for nature.

Eileen McDavid, the mother of Eric McDavid, an activist who was sentenced in 2008 to over nineteen years in prison for "conspiracy to damage or destroy property by fire and an explosive," made a public statement about how family influenced the love of nature that lay behind McDavid's activist commitments. "When Eric was growing up we never missed an opportunity to camp and hike together," she recalled. As Eric McDavid grew older, the family also "worked together building on our property and . . . in our vegetable garden." His mother identifies family heritage as an important aspect of McDavid's identity: "Eric has a love for animals and nature, like his father, mother, and grandfathers before him who were farmers and taught the value of all living things."[42]

In a similar fashion, Rod Coronado attributes his values to the spiritual orientations of his Yoeme and Yaqui heritage through his grandmothers as well as to his parents who took him camping: "my dominant moral influence came from both of my grandmothers. But more than being taught the beliefs I identify with today, I believe I was born with them and allowed to nurture rather than neglect them like many men."[43] Like many other activists, Coronado believes he was born with empathy for other species. Yet he gives his parents and grandparents credit for shaping his inborn tendencies into commitments. He remembers what was special about spending time with his father in California's Sierra Nevada mountains:

> We would get up before dawn and go out into these remote lakes in the Sierras and just spend hours sitting "fishing" and watching the life all around us come awake. We didn't have to talk and my Dad taught me what the fish liked, the conditions, how on full moons they could see well enough to feed at night, things like that, how to "listen" to what was going on around us. Then we'd eat what we caught and it was good, it was a union with nature unlike the connection with my food that I had back in town where my Mom shopped at Safeway.[44]

In activists' accounts, a sense of being born with certain beliefs, or "always having been this way" is then supported by time spent outdoors with families and mentors. Through his father's example, Coronado learned to watch and know how fish would react, to be aware of the life around him, experience a close connection to the sources of his food, and establish a contrast to life "back in town."

If the childhood landscape has already been mapped onto the child's body, if the child's sensory world has been infused with the smells and sounds of the woods and orchards where they played, if their sense of being shapers of the world and shaped by it has created an identity inseparable from other species, then family members who accompany children in their discovery of the natural world further affirm these aspects of childhood experience. Adult mentors who model wonder and awe at the natural world become important figures in childhood memories that inform later orientations towards nature."[45] Lakes credits her Lutheran family for her earliest awareness of environmental problems. "They weren't radical at all," she acknowledges, but when she was sailing with her family, her parents complained about motorboats polluting the lake. She believes that given her "intense love" for the lake, her family helped set her on the path towards activism.[46] Here Lakes both distances herself from her family—they were not radical and she is—and at the same time recognizes the environmental awareness they instilled in her.

Not all activists characterize their families as "not radical." Some activists were influenced by the general orientation of parents who embraced unconventional lifestyles and consciously rejected urban and suburban life in favor of the woods. Currant, an activist I corresponded with while she was serving a prison sentence for her role in Earth Liberation Front (ELF) actions, told me her parents' love of nature set the precedent for her activism. Currant's parents were part of the 1970s back-to-the-land movement that emerged from the counterculture of the 1960s. They left their home in New York City and bought eight acres in rural Montana to build a house in the forest. Currant noticed how her choices reflected those of her parents: "They had rejected the culture of their parents. There is some consistency in values through the three generations—regard for nature, strong moral compass, innate instinct to always 'do the right thing,' a certain willingness to buck convention. My parents took these values and wanted to actually live them, but to do so needed to make a break from the lifestyle they were raised in. I continued this pattern." Becoming familiar with the woods and river outside her house and being aware of her parents' lifestyle choices made her amenable to activism early on.[47] Like her parents, she did not follow a path typical of many of her peers. By adolescence Currant had continued a pattern established by her parents, taking it a step further with her uncompromising stance on environmental issues.

KITH AND KIN

Even those activists whose parents were important in shaping their relationships with the more-than-human world credit nonhuman kin as well for influencing the course of their lives. Like the woods they explored, nonhuman animals activists befriended in childhood were active agents in shaping activists' commitments. Jeff Luers, the first environmental activist in the United States to receive a significant prison sentence for property destruction (twenty-two years), recalls his delight at conversing with his dog "by thought at a very young age. My parents used to marvel at my ability with animals. I've always felt that connection."[48] Luers felt close to animals as a child, communicating with wild animals as well as his dog: "I can remember being able to pet and carry a wild raccoon that would attack anyone else."[49]

Similar memories of childhood relationships with animals also play a significant role in prominent animal rights activists' life stories. Paul Watson, a founding member of Greenpeace, founder of the Sea Shepherd Conservation Society, and star of the Animal Planet television series *Whale Wars*, says he was "an eco-warrior before puberty."[50] Growing up in a fishing town in New Brunswick, Canada, he was a sensitive child who was appalled by the realities of fishing. Watson befriended a wild beaver he called Bucky and spent much of his time alone destroying animal traps (after Bucky was killed by one), becoming a "hit man for the Kindness Club."[51] Activists like Watson take a protective and proactive role early in their lives because of close friendships with nonhuman animals. It is in part because of these relationships that they feel compelled to challenge the boundary between species and a hierarchy that relegates other animals to subservient roles.

Activists become activists in a multispecies world when animal friends cause them to shift their understanding of humans' place in the world. Nonhuman animals from their pasts may even take on a talismanic quality that gains significance and meaning over time. Julia Butterfly Hill spent 738 days on a platform in an ancient 180-foot California redwood called Luna in the late 1990s to protect it from loggers. Hill locates the origins of her activism in a childhood experience with a particular butterfly that landed on her when she was six or seven. She believes that "butterflies have always come to me during times of need, sometimes in reality and other times in visions or dreams."[52] She internalized the lesson of the butterfly and her later acceptance of redwood trees as persons with rights came about in part because of this earlier experience. Not surprisingly, when she first arrived in Northern California and encountered coastal redwoods, she took "Butterfly" as her forest name. As Julia Butterfly she brought her childhood encounter into the forest and to the news media. She identified with and conveyed to the public the close connection between child self and butterfly, tree-sitter and tree. Images of Julia Butterfly in Luna spread through news outlets and celebrities like musicians Bonnie Raitt and Joan Baez climbed into Luna to speak with her. Hill introduced them to her friend Luna while they were visiting.[53] In this way, Hill became a public figure in a campaign to save redwoods and at the same time publicized new possibilities for relating to other species.

Hill's two-year tree-sit in Luna attracted a lot of media attention, not only for her unusual dedication, but also because of the extent to which she personified the tree Luna and imagined what the tree's life was like. As Hill's tree-sit lengthened through the seasons, Luna's value grew as more supporters rallied to her cause. Children, too, tend to make contact with nature through personalized, *individual* species and places, particular trees, animals, and bodies of water, rather than nature in the abstract. They tend to be attracted to "the near and small," as Hill was to the butterfly.[54] They often personify and name trees and animals, relating to them through the language of kinship and friendship. Kinship and friendship relations with other species are among the defining features of the remembered childhood landscape.[55] By naming other species as Hill did, children more easily imaginatively identify with their lives.[56]

Many activists emphasize their bonds with other creatures as being formative and exceptional.[57] In their childhood stories, empathy for nonhuman animals is a quality they are born with or cultivated while they were growing up. They reacted differently to nonhuman animals than other children around them, especially in school. Lindy, an animal rights activist, remembers her deepest friendships were always with animals. As a child she was "obsessed" with animals. Her mother told her that "my first word was not 'mommy' or 'daddy'; it was 'cat.'" At seventeen, Lindy refused to dissect a live frog in her high school biology class. She smuggled the frog out of the lab and drove it to a nearby pond: "I hid her in my coat pocket and drove her up to Fern Dell, a man-made pond at Griffith Park in Los Angeles. While I am sure she, herself, is long since deceased, I entertain the fantasy that some of her distant descendants are still hopping around up there."[58] In activists' narratives, episodes like this are evidence of being born with a special compassion for nonhuman animals that prefigures adult commitments.

Some activists also stopped eating meat at a young age because of their unique sensitivity to nonhuman animal suffering.[59] Tush was a child with an early awareness of animal slaughter and a certainty that meat eating was wrong: "I think the first time that environmental sensitivity became political for me was when I was eleven or twelve and became a vegetarian. My brother was trying to raise a pet pig (Sherman was her name) and when I made the connection that eventually she would be sold and eaten, I said 'nope! I'm not gonna have any part in that,' and gave up meat. I was probably really militant and annoying about it for at least a few years."[60] In this account, Tush is a nascent activist, already making choices that put her at odds with her family and peers.

Awareness at a young age of nonhuman animal deaths and suffering suggests another way in which activists' memories of childhood are not always idyllic. Wonder and awe may characterize some aspects of childhood experience, but others—a slaughterhouse—evoke horror. Activists who as children had close relationships with nonhuman animals were vulnerable to the pain and suffering of these friends.

Activists' biographical accounts, then, identify many continuities with childhood experiences, especially when as adults they continue to challenge boundaries between species that privilege humans. Compassion for nonhuman animals—frogs, dogs, pigs, cows—and a sense of what other creatures' lives are like call into question human exceptionalism. Jay Griffiths argues that the boundary between human and nonhuman animals is especially porous during childhood: "In childhood, the boundary is quivering . . . The world creeps in through the portal of our senses, there is a paw scraping at the gate and our transgression is not a sin but an act of kinetic accomplishment."[61] These other worlds do more than "creep in"; experiences of being enmeshed with them as children leads to developing empathy and compassion later on. As Griffiths puts it, "faithful to anthropomorphism until they are ridiculed out of it, children nurture a relationship with the animal world whereby they become party to other sensitivities, to other stories and a diversity of viewpoints."[62] Activists shamelessly anthropomorphize. They imagine the ways in which landscapes and animals they identify with are affected by logging and resource extraction or hunting and food production.

When activists describe their bonds with places and animals as emotionally significant, it is the emotion of love as well as wonder that particularly motivates them. Those beings whom they love and resonate with emotionally become sacred to them.[63] As a teenager, Canadian activist Rebecca Rubin swore off meat after watching a video of animals being slaughtered and confined under terrible conditions. Like other young activists, the empathic response that connected her childhood love for animals with the suffering she watched and found unbearable drove her to act rather than to turn away. Journalist Sandro Contenta tells the story of Rubin's dedication to animals in his coverage of her trial and sentencing:

> A deep love of animals had become a story about the rise and fall of an eco-saboteur . . . Her affinity for animals was evident at an early age. As a child her favourite books were *Charlotte's Web* and *Beautiful Joe*, both of which concern threatened or abused creatures. She dreamed of being a veterinarian but changed her mind when she discovered the training involved "cruelty to animals," as she put it. She always had pets—cats, dogs, a rabbit—went camping with the family and spent summers at her grandparents' lakeside cottage in B.C. At 16 she became a vegetarian; at 18 a vegan.

In February 2014, Rubin was sentenced to five years in prison for five ELF arsons. In a letter to the judge before her sentencing, Rubin explained her thinking during the years she was involved with illegal direct action: "Animals and the natural world have always been for me a source of profound joy, wonder and solace, and their mistreatment and destruction a source of indescribable pain."[64] Rubin felt that she had no choice but to act to relieve their suffering and her own pain on their behalf. She assembled firebombs for a covert direct action at a Bureau of Land Management's (BLM) facility for wild horses in Oregon, which held horses before sending them off to a slaughterhouse. During the action she opened gates to release the horses while other activists set devices that destroyed the facility without harming anyone, horse or human. After the action, the group issued a communiqué accusing the BLM of "hypocrisy and genocide against the horse nation."[65]

The ability to think of animals as other nations may come about in part because of empathy and intimate childhood experience with nonhuman animals.[66] But at the same time it also entails distancing and the recognition that animals' worlds are their own. They remain opaque and impenetrable to us even when we recognize what we share with them. The mystery we sense when faced with their self-sufficient lives is a different kind of wonder than that evoked by feelings of kinship. From this perspective, difference, not sameness, shapes the desire to protect nature.[67] A child might not be aware of this difference, but adult activists are. Many activists share the view of animals as other *nations*, echoing the famous words of naturalist Henry Beston (1888–1968): "They are not brethren, they are not underlings; they are other nations, caught with ourselves in the net of life and time."[68] In this way, the influence of other species on activists' developing commitments is a result of both identification and differentiation. Identification is more characteristic of childhood experience, while awareness of animals as other nations emerges later when young adults revisit childhood experiences in the context of direct action.

MEMORY AND DEVOTION

As activists name and become acquainted with particular trees and animals and their identities are formed within these relations of kinship and friendship, they begin to generalize from the particular to the general. They extend the community of value that is deserving of love and protection beyond precious places and animal friends. Julia Butterfly

Hill's dedication to redwood forests in general was a result of her deepening relationship with a particular redwood tree, Luna. For Hill, Luna came to represent all redwoods and old-growth forests, just as Maia's slaughtered friend Daisy the cow signified all cows that become meals. Over time, wilderness or animals in general become valuable to activists in the same ways familiar places and animals were beloved in childhood.[69]

Perhaps more important than what actually happened during activists' childhoods is the context in which their remembering takes place. The contours of remembered childhood landscapes are as likely to reveal the values of adult activists as the experiences of the children they were. Daniel Schacter and other psychologists who study memory remind us that memories are not a video replay of the past, but shaped by the contours of the present context in which we remember. Our present circumstances distort our remembrance of the past. Emotionally intense experiences from the past are likely to return when we reexperience similar moods. In this way, activists' wonder and empathy with suffering in the present may trigger memories of similar past events, perhaps making these past events more important than they originally were. For these reasons, memories are unreliable as factual accounts, but they powerfully convey the emotional content of past experiences.[70]

For activists, remembering often occurs in the context of protest rites and environmentalist gatherings set apart from the broader society. In these contexts the lives of nonhuman others, the creation of sacred space, mass extinction, climate change, environmental degradation, and human oppression of nonhuman animals are central preoccupations. In addition, action camps are often in forests or farmland, places that might feel familiar to activists who roamed outside when they were children, places that seem likely to bring forth memories of being outdoors. Adult feelings of responsibility for trees and animals may shape the ways in which childhood relationships with them are remembered, confirming the importance of these relationships.

Because memories of childhood involve active self-construction, they do not necessarily reveal the immediate experience of children playing outdoors. Remembering beloved places and animals, then, means creating as well as recalling affective bonds with nonhuman others. Remembering and telling childhood stories are ways of *uncovering* ecological identity as well as actively creating stories of childhood connections to trees and animals.[71] Action camps and tree-sits in the woods during which activist bodies touch tree bark for hours, sleep under the stars, and listen to the creatures of the woods conjure up particular images and relationships from the past. This conjured past is thick with the smell and feeling of trees and earth, once vivid to and valued by the remembered childhood self, just as to the adult remembering. The present illuminates the past in particular ways, shining light on those scenes in which the ecological child was taking shape.

THE ENCLOSURE OF CHILDREN

The free play that is emphasized in some activists' memories of ecological childhoods has been declining in the United States and other Western countries over the last few decades. A number of scholars and journalists bemoan the enclosure of childhood that is largely responsible for this diminishment. By the beginning of the twenty-first century, children have been increasingly shut in and constantly supervised, abandoned lots and ditches where they once explored have been paved over, wild places have become more scarce, and children's access to these places has been circumscribed by safety concerns.[72] By the twenty-first century, American children's increasingly solitary and sedentary play had resulted in a decrease in unstructured or autonomous play outdoors.[73] Such a shift entailed substituting contact with an abstracted and distant nature, mediated through devices such as televisions, for direct contact with the natural world.[74]

Loss of direct contact with nature and the increasing tendency to enclose children in safe settings has profoundly negative effects on children's developing sense of the nonhuman world as something of *value*. In what biologist Robert Michael Pyle describes as an "extinction of experience," children in the last decades of the twentieth century became "morally depleted" by the shrinking opportunity for unsupervised outdoor play in which they come to know other species.[75] From this perspective, children who are kept enclosed are less likely to be committed to the natural world, to see it as animated with life and deeply connected with their own lives. Activists' stories pick up on this sense of loss and nostalgia for a childhood experience of nature untrammeled by pavement and excessive concern for safety and control. They may contrast their own experiences playing outdoors to other Americans' tendency to control children and enclose childhood.

Unlike many other children, many activists' remembered ecological child self was free to play outside in an imagined world of his or her own making. Crow, an activist who was sentenced to eight years in prison for an arson at a fast-food establishment when he was twenty, located the roots of his activist commitments in a childhood spent in free play in nature. In his letters to me from prison, he emphasized the ideal part of his childhood: "On sunny days and snowy days or basically whenever we could get out we were biking around the neighborhood, catching snakes and turtles in criks, hanging out and playing in vacant lots, climbing trees." Crow explained to me that his belief in "earth mother" and his "communion with fresh air" developed during his free play outdoors as a child. He came to "see earth mother in all things, Her body making up everything in this infinite universe, so the only real 'law' I follow is treating all things natural, sacred."[76] Crow did not share his family's strict Christian values, but developed his sense of identity apart from them. He felt at home in the landscape and attached to it in ways that would later affect his actions as a young adult who felt kinship with other species but alienated from American society.

In contrast to trends that diminish children's contact with nature, Crow and other activists recall their own play in gardens, woods, or creeks, as well as "the unlimited, undefined, untamed places," including derelict and abandoned lots and ditches in urban areas.[77] Their stories tend to emphasize being outside unsupervised, not in playgrounds and schools, which they remember as more structured and controlled. Allowing children to spend most of their time in shopping malls or urban environments, Crow told me, is "the root of the problem with Americans' attitudes towards environmental issues."[78] In his correspondence with me, Crow insisted that other American children were less fortunate because they did not experience the same freedom he enjoyed as a child roaming freely outdoors.

Some activists were influenced by parents who urged them outside, while others recall deciding for themselves: "I made a choice while young that I wouldn't submit . . . [to] the super-entertainment of technology," explains Crow.[79] He chose unstructured over structured play, and being outdoors over sitting inside in front of a television. In Crow's childhood narrative, early rejection of a controlled and enclosed childhood marked the beginning of an anarchist and environmentalist trajectory that would eventually make action against the corporate food industry seem appropriate.

Activist critiques of American child raising are expressed in tandem with campaigns against American lifestyles and values that have resulted in environmental degradation. In their childhood narratives, activists resist the diminished opportunities for American children to connect with outdoors places. During forest campaigns they also reclaim childhood free play outdoors. At gatherings and action camps in remote wilderness areas, they can easily re-create a world liberated from television and other indoor entertainment.

In contrast to stories that emphasize continuity between adult identity and a childhood spent in nature, some activists describe an opposite kind of childhood experience. In these stories their wild selves were domesticated during childhood and only later, as young adult activists, did they rediscover a connection with nature. Kite, an activist involved with the Buffalo Field Campaign, grew up in a large city and "didn't see vegetables growing until I was about 12. There was a trailer park just north of the city that my family would go to on the weekends and in the summer, and it had a scraggly little forest and an artificial pond." He discovered "the real world at a much later age" and realized that he "had been held prisoner by the television and consumer world until that point."[80] An antilogging activist named Skunk remembers that his parents used guilt "to control or train me during my domestication." He bemoans the effects of civilization on children, "their minds imprisoned, their thoughts convicted in schools."[81] Skunk and Kite were not proto-activists during childhood, but rather the opposite: their childhood experience was characterized by oppression and domestication. In their view, domestication—of children, animals, forests—is the central problem of civilization that must be challenged. Activists believe rewilding human beings and ecosystems together is important. For them, the free-roaming child, like the adult activist dedicated to trees and ecosystems, overcomes an estrangement from nature that is symptomatic of society's ills.[82]

NATURE AS REFUGE AND ABODE OF GODS AND SPIRITS

Along with attraction *to* woods or waterways, activists remember they sought nature as a place to escape *from* society or family. In memory as children, and later as adults, they approached nature as a sanctuary where they were free to discover a place of their own, imagining woods and fields as a world separate from the family home. As they grow older, children recognize, as an elementary student put it in a survey of children's attitudes towards nature, "The woods are my home and our house is my parents' house."[83] This sense of separation is especially important if their parents' house is not a safe place.

Activists who recall being neglected and abused children, who escaped to the bushes in their yards or the company of animal friends, find themselves in forest action camps, away from a civilization they also experience as abusive. Minnow, one of the organizers of Earth First!'s 2013 North Carolina Round River Rendezvous, explained the origins of her strong feelings about the natural world in this way: "My love of and sense of belonging to nature comes from a paradox. There were nature lovers in my family and my family was abusive. Many abused children, lucky enough to have nature as a resource, find comfort and cohesion in their place in it."[84] The woods near their homes provided them with protection from frightening family situations and nonhuman animal friends offered them solace.

Older children and adolescents in particular may feel closer to nature than to their homes, more themselves in nature than with their families, especially if their families are abusive, as in Minnow's case. The opposition between home and nature (woods, backyard, forts in the bushes, empty lots, creeks) becomes part of the process of separating out one's own identity from the family whole and making a lake or woods a place of security and comfort. Throughout his life, Rod Coronado sought out the company of wild animals for comfort: "When I have been sad or troubled, I have gone out into the wilds and they have come to me like old friends and said, 'We're here whenever you need us.'"[85] Later in their lives activists act in turn to protect those who protected them. Activists who have found solace and self in the woods and with nonhuman animals feel a sense of duty to reciprocate by interfering with animal hunts or preventing bulldozers from destroying trees.

While nature provides sanctuary from an inhospitable world, it also offers spiritual alternatives to religions activists find lacking. If activists inherited moral guidelines, lifestyle choices, and spiritual orientations from their families, they transformed and adapted these beliefs and practices in their own ways. Most activists I met grew up at least nominally Christian or Jewish, but left behind their religious upbringing, usually as teenagers. Lindy explained that she was raised Jewish, but now blames "the Judao-Christian [sic] ideology for promulgating anthropocentrism and speciesism."[86] At a young age, Jeff Luers questioned what he saw as Christian "dogma." Although Luers's parents were "non-practicing Christians" and generally open minded, he attended youth programs at a local Baptist church, which eventually led to his rejection of Christianity: "It became so ridiculously authoritarian and anyone who refused the precepts of God was condemned to hell."[87] Luers refused to obey "precepts" and decided that Christianity was too rigid for him. Christianity

and some other religious traditions are associated with what many activists see as a similarly authoritarian and meaningless civilization that
domesticates children and wild places.

When describing their path to direct action, activists recall a growing
disillusionment with Christian families and the rites they were required
to participate in as children. Crow grew up in a "strict Christian home,
in which participation in church services and functions was mandatory. . . . As expected, any other beliefs were 'Satan's' traps." But Crow
sought out alternatives to his parents' religious views and "questioned
their dogma at an early age."[88] Activists like Crow often disparage mainstream religious rituals while explaining their preference for choices such
as contemporary Paganism, Buddhism, or atheism. Sparrow, an Earth
First! activist in California, was raised as a Christian and attended Baptist and Nazarene schools until age sixteen, at which point he "rejected
the notion of a male super-ghost and an eternal lake of fire, and became
decidedly atheist."[89] But even "atheist" activists are not opposed to all
forms of spirituality.

In contrast to what they understand to be hierarchical religions of
transcendence, most activists hold up the natural world as alive with
spirit and meaning. If becoming adult Americans means leaving behind
a sense of nature as sacred, then again, they choose childhood as the
model for more appropriate relationships with other life forms. Crow
believes the divine is located in childhood: "I don't feel as I've grown
older that I've subjected myself to this conditioning and so can still tie
into that magic by immersing myself into the interconnection of life."[90]
For Crow, childhood embodies a Pagan and animist orientation towards
the world, a way of being that is usually replaced with a disenchanted
view of nature not conducive to environmental commitment. Crow and
other activists refuse to reject an animistic understanding of the world
for a disenchanted one. As religious studies scholar Graham Harvey
puts it, "Animists are people who recognise that the world is full of
persons, only some of whom are human, and that life is always lived in
relationship with others."[91] Animists like Crow want to reclaim animism as a worldview to live by rather than outgrow.

While many activists have no label for their spiritual and moral orientation, some call themselves "Pagan" and locate the origins of their
Pagan identity in childhood. For them, reclaiming childhood animism is
a way of remembering the past and constructing a future in which the
landscape is enchanted, its trees and animals active agents and persons
with spiritual and political worth. Tush lived in an enchanted landscape

inhabited by animal friends and fairies. She would bake tiny cookies and leave them "in special spots for faeries or other spirits that I felt a connection with."[92] Jeff Luers describes himself as "a pagan and an animist," who believes that "all life is interconnected, that it is this connection that allows life to flourish. The web of life keeps the earth in balance and creates a symbiotic relationship between us and our planet."[93] ELF activist Crow, for instance, felt a deep connection to his Celtic Pagan heritage, the earth, and all animals, especially birds.[94]

In the process of leaving behind their religious upbringing, radical activists often link anarchism and atheism as twin alternatives to American democracy and institutional religion. Most animal rights activists and some radical environmentalists also turn to veganism, rejecting meat eating for ethical and political reasons. As a T-shirt I noticed at the 2009 Earth First! Rendezvous put it: "no God, no religion, no state, no leaders."

Peter Young voiced a similar sentiment: "My actions are motivated not by celestial command, but by a deep reverence for life and contempt for the abuse of power."[95] It is this reverence for life that links the biographies of many young activists. Young, a self-described "atheist" who became a vegan at seventeen and was active with animal rights groups after graduating from high school, grew up in a Christian, suburban Southern California household. As a teenager he began to question the social values around him:

> Living in an upper middle class suburb, one is raised to live life along a certain course and with certain values . . . I was about 15 when I realized that I did not have to wear the clothes that everyone else was wearing . . . Once this lie—that you had to conform to be accepted—was unmasked as an empty threat, everything I'd been taught came into question . . . From there I began to question everything from what I was eating to television to politics to the "American dream."[96]

Young and other activists challenge many aspects of the so-called American dream of material success, refuse to adhere to Christian values, and commit themselves to anarchism, animal rights, environmentalism, and animism as meaningful alternatives to the worldviews of their parents.

MEMORY AND MOURNING

Childhood memories are double-sided for some activists: on the one hand they remember nature as a *special place* they explored and in which they developed close relationships to trees, animals, and human mentors; on the other, many of them recall *disturbed* childhood places and exploited animals.[97] The first relationship is one of love and attachment, the second of grief and loss. If a child's sense of self is extended into a landscape made sacred, then the loss of that landscape or its radical transformation into a clear-cut slope or a parking lot is a cause for grief. The flip side of love for a forest or orchard and the important role it plays in one's memories of childhood is grief over its loss. If particular trees in the landscape have been named, have become friends, then the loss is even greater. The shock of seeing a housing development where there was once a field spurs activists into action. They react because a world they knew intimately has been altered by a different reality, that of bulldozers and cement mixers.[98] In Maia's case, she reacted to the reality of what she saw happening during high school, as new developments destroyed the wild, open spaces she had roamed as a child. What she equated with childhood, she explained, had disappeared and become "unrecognizable."

Mourning for lost and desecrated landscapes provides a powerful incentive for the direct actions activists are willing to take to prevent further devastation. When Josh Harper, who was sentenced to three years under the Conspiracy to Violate the Animal Enterprise Protection Act because of his role in the animal rights organization SHAC (Stop Huntington Animal Cruelty), was nine years old, his family moved from San Diego, California, to Eugene, Oregon: "Seeing the juxtaposition between a sprawling hideous southern California city and a small tree-filled Oregon city was shocking to me ... As I got older some of the places I had fallen in love with began getting paved over, clearcut, or polluted. That was all the motivation I needed to adopt a militant outlook on the need for wilderness defense or more appropriately, offense."[99] Harper's memory of lost landscapes of childhood that once centered and gave meaning to his world inspired his militancy. Memories may become even more powerful when, as in these cases, activists' sense of a lost and beloved childhood landscape is placed in the context of global tragedies of deforestation, climate change, and mass extinctions.

Activists grieve for childhood places that have disappeared or been desecrated. For many of them, childhood intimacy with nature is how humans are meant to live, and the return to childhood through remembering and sharing childhood stories is a return to an idealized relationship. This kind of mourning for lost places and childhood play with animal friends may also exemplify an increasingly common narrative of loss and childhood that began in the 1890s. This narrative portrays children as preserving an idealized preindustrial past through their free play in nature and is characterized by the following assumptions: (1) nature is inherently a good place with a positive influence on human behavior and (2) children have a *special* need for nature, especially as developing environmentalists.[100] In activist narratives of the past, the child self models appropriate orientations to nature. Whether located in childhood experience or in the imagination, the ecological child self sets the stage for activist imaginings of what the future should look like.

Important memories of the past involving experiences in nature that surface in the context of current activism are often couched within a sacred framework in which the world is active and enchanted, just like the preindustrial past and the childhood landscape left behind.[101] Enchanted landscapes, talking animals, and forests of transformation lost to adult rationalism become the focus of activist desire. Crow explained to me his regret that as most people leave childhood behind, their "connection to the world of 'magic' severs little by little—they may and do encounter nature, but they don't any longer feel interconnected with it and it becomes abstract to them." For Crow, a childhood orientation of wonder toward nature unfortunately gives way to the "goggles of technological society and 'rational thinking.'"[102] He believes we become alienated from nature as outdoor places are no longer special, tree and animal names are forgotten.

CORPORATE YOUTH CULTURE AND THE GODS OF NATURE

Changes in how scholars and activists alike view children's relationships with animals and nature are emblematic of larger cultural shifts that can be traced through visual media, especially film and television. Although anthropomorphic representations of animals and trees have been common in children's print and visual culture for many decades, in the later twentieth century they acquired a kind of sacred power, as animals transcended their roles as human-like characters. For instance, Beatrix Potter's *The Tale of Peter Rabbit* (1902) features human-like animal characters still living their roles in nature, while in contrast, in the United States characters like Donald Duck (created by Walt Disney in 1934) humanized animals and placed them in human settings. Both of these examples are substantially different from literary and film images of animals and trees in the latter half of the twentieth and early twenty-first century, in which animals are gods (Hiyao Miyazaki's 2002 film *Spirited Away*), talking trees (the Ents in *The Lord of the Rings* fiction trilogy by J.R.R. Tolkien, published in the 1950s, and the films based on Tolkien's books), shapeshifting humans (*Harry Potter* books and films from the 1990s and 2000s), or human souls (*The Golden Compass* books and film, also from the 1990s and 2000s). In these instances, animals possess human qualities and yet go beyond human experience and understanding or transgress the human–nonhuman animal boundary. Japanese culture developed significantly different views from those prevalent in the United States about the relationship between humans and nonhuman animals, especially the possibility of souls crossing the human-nonhuman animal boundary, as seen in *Spirited Away*.[103] However, the new anthropomorphism and animism and the popularity in the United States of Miyazaki's animated features and other similar films indicate that in the twenty-first century, Americans are increasingly open to and interested in such boundary crossing.

Young people's experiences of co-becoming activists with trees and nonhuman animals reflect similarly transgressive moments in popular films as well. In *Ecologies of the Moving Image*, environmental studies scholar Adrian Ivakhiv observes that Disney's films—*Bambi* in particular—helped to shape environmentalist sensibilities that emerged in the 1960s. What he calls the "biomorphism" in *Bambi* (1942) produces "a sensuous texture of what appears to be life" and "blurs boundaries between humans and living or lifelike non-humans."[104] Boundary crossing in Disney's animated animal films (Ivakhiv also references the 2006 film *Happy Feet*) can be a matter of "anthropomorphic projection" or "objective biological kinship," but it typically focuses on similarity. In the case of *Happy Feet*, humans and penguins are on different sides of the boundary, but are thought to be similar. However, the boundary between them remains stable rather than in flux.

In contrast, Japanese animator Miyazaki's *Spirited Away*, an animated feature about a river spirit clogged with pollution who shapeshifts into both boy and dragon, was released by Walt Disney in the United States. It exemplifies young Americans' willingness to consider boundary crossing in which the boundary between human and nonhuman other is not as stable. In the process of shape-shifting, human and animal are intertwined and the boundary between them blurs. Although it was released in only 151 North American theatres, *Spirited Away* still grossed over $5.5 million.[105] Miyazaki's film depicts close relationships between humans and nonhuman animals and between humans and an enchanted natural world, a world in which magical powers and experiences are available to children.

I am not arguing for a direct cause and effect relationship, but rather the ways in which corporate media have contributed to and also express a cultural milieu in which particular notions about nature as sacred have emerged in the United States in the late twentieth and early twenty-first centuries.[106] Films about "gods" of nature illustrate the animating/anthropomorphizing trend because they feature hybrid forms and boundary crossing between species, including the human desire to be in another's (in this case a nonhuman animal's) skin as a kind of transcendence.[107]

WILD PLACES IN THEIR HEARTS

Not all activists had the childhood experiences I have described, even though these kinds of narratives are common. But many of them describe a shift from love of nature to an imperative to protect forests and nonhuman animals. This is not always a smooth and carefree transition; it may involve feelings of being an outsider or episodes of depression and withdrawal from society during teenage and early adult years. As teenagers, activists often reach a tipping point after which they are transformed into "earth warriors." For those who grew up playing outdoors, immersing themselves in forest action camps is a return to childhood experience. Childhood experiences in nature or with nonhuman animals may then be reimagined when activists find themselves deeply involved in a forest campaign or animal liberation action. For those who were raised in urban settings and experienced little free play in nature, their commitment may be made more powerful because of their awe when they first encounter redwoods or anger when they first see a wilderness devastated by mining or logging.

How then do activists deal with the dual nature of wonder: that it is accompanied by loss? For many activists, focusing on childhood experiences of wonder in nature as a model for the future necessitates an undoing of civilization as we know it. Reclaiming the personal past and cultural preindustrial past at the same time is the answer. If becoming adult Americans means leaving behind a sense of nature as sacred, then activists make a different choice. Activists embody the shift away from a developmental model that assumes children are "in the process of becoming rational" and will grow to reject talking with trees and

animals, feeding fairies, and other childhood acts activists see as formative in their childhood and desirable in their adult worlds.[108] They advocate a kind of "strategic animism," to borrow political scientist Jane
Bennett's concept.[109]

Activists' emphasis on childhood is not simply about childhood
experiences in nature and with animal friends; it constitutes a distinctive way of thinking, which in turn gives protests distinctive qualities.
Boundaries between people and nonhuman animals, between the past
and the present—all the dichotomies so fundamental to "adult" ration-
ality—become fluid for activists. In this way, the invocation of childhood as the basis for adult behavior articulates alternative ways of
knowing and being that become fundamental in activists' worlds.[110]

My account in this chapter of activist remembering has moved in and
out of what might be considered the real facts of childhood and the
memories we construct of the past. But the contours of these stories matter; they inform activists' understandings of how to think about and live
with the other-than-human. The truths in this chapter are intersubjective: the narratives I elicited from activists and the memories they elicited
from me of my own childhood roaming among trees and nonhuman
animals brought forth each other. In the same way activists want to live
in the imagined and remembered childhood world of wonder, I see in this
world the promise of another way of being with other species. But this
way of being is not without peril. Although activists I interviewed came
from different class backgrounds, the majority were not people of color,
and so these childhood worlds may be permeated by unexamined privilege and power. In addition, an idealized and romanticized childhood in
nature may efface the risks of being alone in the woods or having porous
boundaries with creatures destined for slaughter. Porous boundaries
between human self and other species can be dangerous. Violence done
to landscapes and nonhuman animal bodies is felt deeply by activists.
Childhood encounters with frogs fated to be dissected, calves destined
for the slaughterhouse, and desert habitats bulldozed for new houses are
experiences of tragedy and violation. However, it is these memories of
both wonder and suffering that provide powerful resources for adult
imaginings of other ways to live in a multispecies world.

Activist gatherings and action camps offer the opportunity for activists to discover and create "wild places in their hearts" and to project
their hearts into the wild.[111] Gatherings bring activists into settings reminiscent of childhood and may even allow them to re-create childhood
landscapes they did *not* experience, if they were kept indoors or grew

up on city streets. In the ritualized context of gatherings and protests, activists revisit childhood and affirm commitments made during conversion to environmentalism or animal rights. These ritualized actions—the rite of passage of conversion and rites of protest—configure memory into narratives that form the basis for activist lives and commitments. In the next two chapters, I explore the ways in which activists' ritualized conversion experiences and protest actions produce commitments in two very different contexts: forest action camps and urban hardcore punk rock scenes

CHAPTER 4

Into the Forest

Wherever you turn your eyes the world can shine
like transfiguration. You don't have to bring a thing
to it except a little willingness to see. Only, who would
have the courage to see it?
—Marilynne Robinson

People *exploit* what they have merely concluded to be
of value, but they *defend* what they love.
—Wendell Berry

In the early morning hours of June 16, 2000, twenty-one-year-old Jeffrey "Free" Luers and his friend "Critter" Marshall crept up to the Romania car dealership in Eugene, Oregon. They checked to make sure no one was around the car lot or in the buildings nearby before starting a fire that inflicted over $30,000 damage to three SUVs. Later that morning, Luers and Marshall were pulled over for a missing headlight and were subsequently charged with the arson. Luers was arraigned on nine felony counts, including arson and attempted arson. Other counts were later added, and in 2001 he was sentenced to twenty-two years and eight months in prison. Although depicted as an "ecoterrorist leader" in the news media and put on special watch in prison for being politically dangerous, Luers insists his actions were born of love. Because of his frustration over global warming and especially the U.S. role in climate change, Luers felt compelled to act in a way he hoped would bring attention to greenhouse gas emissions. In a statement at his sentencing hearing he explained: "You can judge my actions, but you can't judge my heart. It cannot be said that I'm unfeeling or uncaring. My heart is filled with love and compassion. I fight to protect life, all life, not to take it . . . My actions, whether or not you believe them to be misguided . . . stem from the love I have in my heart."[1]

In "How I Became an Eco-Warrior," an essay written in 2003, Luers explains how his actions were inspired by his close relationship with a particular tree. His first foray into forest activism occurred in 1998 when he was nineteen and made his way out to Oregon's Willamette Forest in the Cascade Mountains with some other "fuck-ups, gutter punks and anarchists, run of the mill, crusty squatter punks" to participate in a campaign to save an old-growth forest.[2] What came to be known as Red Cloud Thunder and the Fall Creek tree-sit was a loose-knit organization of tree-sitters protesting a timber sale in Willamette Forest, in which ninety-six acres of centuries-old Douglas Fir, Western Hemlock, and Red Cedar were scheduled to be cut in the Clark Timber Sale.

Some of the activists involved with Red Cloud Thunder were veterans of an earlier campaign at Warner Creek, also in Oregon's Cascade Mountains, that lasted for eleven months in 1995–1996. The protest ended when U.S. president Bill Clinton canceled a timber sale. The Warner Creek campaign was a watershed moment in two ways: it highlighted anarchism and popularized the practice of long-term tree-sits. Although tree-sitting had taken place in the northwestern United States throughout the 1980s, these earlier actions tended to be short lived. Longer-running tree-sits caused delays that often allowed environmental organizations the time they needed to work through other channels to prevent timber sales in environmentally sensitive areas.[3] In the case of Fall Creek, while tree-sitters were preventing trees from being cut down, a coalition of environmental groups brought a lawsuit against the U.S. Forest Service for failing to complete required wildlife surveys in the area.[4]

Jeff Luers's encounter with the forest and his feeling of belonging in it would be transformative in a number of ways. On his first visit to the forest, his friends returned to town, since none of them had appropriate gear for wet, chilly weather. Luers stayed on alone. A storm blew in and he soon realized how unprepared he was:

As I shivered around my pathetic fire the temperature dropped even further. The sleet had turned to full on snow. For the first time in my life I wondered if maybe I wouldn't make it through the night. I knew that I needed to stay awake, not so much because I was worried about my body temperature, but I was worried about the storm and my tarp. To pass the time I talked with my favorite tree. I spoke out loud to hear my voice, but I was speaking with my heart. Now, for some people this may sound crazy, to me I've spoken with trees and animals all my life. I'd never gotten an answer until that night.

Luers felt the tree ask why he was scared: "It was like this sensational feeling like instinct . . . If you pay attention a whole new world opens up." He explained to the tree how unprepared he was to make it through the storm and they talked together for a while. He discovered that "the forest understood why I was there, that I was there to protect it. I understood that within this forest I would be safe."[5]

Later that month, Luers climbed into the young tree he called "Happy," as trees nearby them were cut down. Activists focused on saving the ones they could and delaying loggers' progress as much as possible. During his days and nights in the forest, Luers' relationship with Happy shifted and the boundary between his body and the tree's body became fluid. He began to feel the tree's grief and pain as his own. His close relationship with Happy occurred within the context of his memories of childhood and being a teenage Pagan communicating with trees and other nature spirits. But no other tree before Happy had talked back to him. In this way, he brought an inner history with him to the forest, in which childhood experience, and especially adolescence, helped shape the present.

> I sat cross-legged, my back against Happy, and I began to meditate. I forgot that there was a plywood platform below me. I forgot that I was a single entity. I felt the roots of Happy like they were my own. I breathed the air like it was a part of me. I felt connected to everything around me. I reached out to Momma Earth and I felt her take my hand. I could feel the flow of life around me. I felt so in tune with the ebb and flow of the natural cycles. I asked Her what it felt like to have humanity forget so much, and attack her every day like a cancer. I told her I needed to know, I needed to feel it. . . . She granted my request. My body began to pour sweat. I felt the most severe pain all over, spasms wracked my body. Tears ran down my face. I could feel every factory dumping toxins into the air, water, and land. I could feel every strip-mine, every clearcut, every toxic dump and nuclear waste site. I felt my body being suffocated by concrete. I could feel every awful thing our "civilized" way of life inflicts on the natural world. The feeling only lasted a second, but it will stay with me for the rest of my life. . . . My life changed that day. I made a vow to give my life to the struggle for freedom and liberation, for all life, human, animal, and earth. We are all interconnected, we are all made of the same living matter, and we all call this planet home. I vowed to defend my home, I vowed to stand in defense of Mother Earth.[6]

Two years later, Luers put his promise into action at the Romania car dealership.

The emotions that motivate radical activists, especially love, develop through powerful, embodied experiences that involve sensitivity to the feelings of forests and the softening of boundaries between human and tree bodies. Forests mark the boundary both literally and metaphorically between what forest activists reject and everything they hold dear. As sites at the edges of civilization, forests often serve as places of radical change in activist life trajectories. In many activists' narratives, forests are transformative places that lie beyond the bounds of ordinary life and yet become like "home."[7]

Like Luers, most activists remember becoming increasingly disaffected with American ideals during their adolescence and young adulthood, as they grew more and more critical of capitalism, consumerism, private property, and Christianity. For many of them, rejecting aspects of American society and embracing a community of forest kin went hand in hand. As they became further separated from relationships in society outside their circle of friends, their lives expanded to include increasingly close relationships with nonhuman species and other activists.

The arc of many activists' conversion to direct action begins with leaving society behind for the forest. Not all of them completely isolate themselves from other social contexts, but activist communities and the more-than-human world become more vitally central to their lives once they spend time in forest action camps. Forests, of course, are not their only way into the activist world. They may undergo similar transformations during campaigns against mountaintop removal in West Virginia or mountain lion hunting in Arizona. Regardless of their way in, in most cases they enter spaces in which humans are largely absent, with the exception of other activists. Environmentalist action camps and clandestine animal rights actions make participants into "activists" by separating them from the outside world and bringing them into a community with distinct practices like tree-sitting or animal releases, and beliefs such as deep ecology and biocentrism. They often leave forest action camps or night-time animal liberation actions forever altered and committed to fighting "for the wild" and "for the animals."

Ritualized protest activities such as creating sacred space at forest action camps, sitting in treetops or tripods, and chaining themselves to blockades to prevent logging both construct and reinforce activists' earlier memories of emotional and physical identification with trees or nature more generally. These experiences transform young men and women into activists and confirm their commitments to direct action in a process that functions like a rite of passage.

This chapter explores the dynamics of becoming forest activists through ritualized protest practices. Some activists' accounts involve looking back on these experiences years later from a prison cell, while I heard others within hours or days of the experiences. I am concerned here in particular in the ways in which *emotional* and *embodied* experiences are linked to being in the forest and participating in protests. Ritual protest actions such as tree climbing and tree-sitting exist in dynamic relationship to activists' emotional and embodied experiences: they create and shape each other.

From the mid-1980s, and especially through the 1990s, radical environmentalism was nearly synonymous with forest activism, as young activists from across the country were drawn to forest tree-sits and anti-logging campaigns, especially on the West Coast of the United States.[8] Other campaigns, such as anti–coal mining actions, also took place during this period, but did not attract the same amount of publicity or numbers of young people. Forest activists' tactics such as tree-sitting and media outreach were honed in the struggle to save the redwoods and other old growth forests in Northern California and the Pacific Northwest.

According to activist Ron Huber, an Earth First!er named "Doug Fir" was the first tree-sitter. He climbed into a Douglas Fir tree and unfurled a banner reading "Don't Cut Us Down," identifying with the tree's perspective.[9] In Huber's view, "to occupy a wild canopy community at risk, to unite one's survival to it, is a powerful act . . . Unsurprisingly, given *Homo Sapiens* arboreal ancestry, living for a time as part of a canopy community seems to trigger a rewilding reflex that forever changes a person's relationship with Nature."[10] Huber's perspective identifies two central themes that form part of tree-sitting's legacy: activists' sense of being at home in the forest and experiences that bring about an identification between their lives and the lives of other forest species.

PLACE MAKING AND THE EMOTIONAL LIVES OF YOUNG ACTIVISTS

Ritualized actions like tree-sits may trigger memories of childhood love for the natural world and grief over its destruction. Because powerful bonds with trees and animals are often formed during childhood and adolescence, nature becomes inextricably connected with activists' self-identity that is also developing during these years. Such bonds are characterized by love for other species that biologist Edward O. Wilson calls "biophilia . . . the urge to affiliate with other forms of life." For Wilson, this urge is largely innate and "unfolds in the predictable fantasies and responses of individuals from early childhood onward."[11] In *Biophilia*,

Wilson desribes growing up in the woods of the northern Florida pan-handle. As a teenager, he liked to hunt and catch snakes. During one of his expeditions into the woods, he caught a huge water moccasin. The snake suddenly twisted in his hands and gained control of the situation; Wilson had to quickly throw it into the brush to avoid being bitten. He remembers this experience as formative, an encounter that inspired awe and bound him even more closely to the woods and its creatures.

Wilson's biological explanation of emotional attachment to nature emphasizes neurological causes and the universality of biophilia, but tends to downplay the importance of social and cultural contexts.[12] Even his own account of roaming the Florida woods suggests that folklore shaped his experience with snakes as much as the biological urge to affiliate with other life forms.[13] Activists' accounts of becoming committed to activism suggest some of the ways culture affects love for other life forms. For activists, biophilia becomes manifest through a sequence of unique life experiences that result in their presence on the front lines of campaigns to save wild beings and places. Their commitments to the more-than-human world may be rooted in childhood but develop over time, shaped especially by cultural forces that act on activists' lives as teenagers.[14]

In activists' stories of their teenage years, special places outdoors become increasingly identified as *socially* significant, and their attachment to these places comes about in part because of experiences with friends and family that occur in them. Like Jeff Luers, many young activists first travel to action camps and forest protests with friends or lovers. The geographies activists carry in their embodied memories link important transitions in their lives to specific places in which these transitions took place.[15] Experiences with family and friends in the outdoors are more likely to be integrated into teenagers' self-identity. In this way, a place becomes meaningful because the relationship between the people who experienced that place together was important. Places experienced in the company of others may facilitate the passage from childhood to young adulthood in a number of ways. This includes expanding kinship relations between human and nonhuman species that developed during childhood.[16]

I corresponded with Jeff Luers while he was serving time in prison for the Romania car dealership arson. He told me that his teenage encounters with trees were significant not only because he was able to communicate with the trees themselves, but also because of the close bonds he developed with friends in the context of his connection to trees. Luers identified himself as a Pagan teenager: "Many of my closest friends in high school embraced the occult. It was not uncommon for us to practice magic or talk to trees. We saw the underlying spirit in things. I became very in tune with the energy around me." Because his friends were also Pagans, if he mentioned he had a great talk with a tree, "I didn't get laughed at." By his late teens he was communicating with animals, trees and nature spirits: "I've talked to trees nearly all my life. . . . the hardest part about being a pagan is overcoming all you have been taught. I mean people think I'm crazy when I say I can talk to some trees."[17] Being with like-minded friends in nature encouraged Luers to take his relationships with trees and animals more seriously and created memories linking beliefs about the spiritual presence of trees with social experiences.

Teenagers' visits to special places may include significant others such as adult mentors or teenage friends, but they may also be solitary experiences that are important to adolescents' developing sense of self. Teenagers wander farther afield than younger children, seeking out ways to escape adult supervision. Places to be alone may become significant, as teenagers tend to prefer relatively wild and undeveloped landscapes when they need to get away from school and family pressures (if those landscapes are available to them).[18] Both being alone *and* hanging out with friends—human and nonhuman—become central to teenagers' developing sense of self.

While some activists are inspired by childhood experiences playing in the woods, seeking sanctuary in special outdoors places, talking to trees, and camping, others experience the wild for the first time when they travel to forests and action camps. For this reason, their first encounter with forests may be even more life changing. Darryl Cherney grew up in New York City where "there was no environment to save" and first encountered redwoods on a cross-country trip with his family at age fourteen: "Being a lifelong Manhattanite whose exposure to vegetation tended to be limited to salad bars, the giants made, as they had on generations of others, a life-altering impression."[19] He dreamed of one day living in the redwoods. In 1985 in his late twenties, he decided he was fed up with life in New York City, so he packed up and headed west.

Daniel McGowan, an Earth Liberation Front (ELF) activist who was sentenced to seven years in prison for two arsons (with a terrorist enhancement), also grew up in New York City. When he moved out west in 1998 and visited old-growth forests, he had "never seen trees like that before." But it was not just trees that had a considerable effect on McGowan. He was shocked by "the arrogance" of clearcut logging, felt that the trees were "just butchered," and wondered why he and his friends were being "so gentle" with their activism. After years of letter writing for environmental causes, McGowan became involved with the ELF because, "when you see things you love being destroyed, you just want to destroy." For McGowan, letter writing was activism at a distance that no longer seemed tenable after his face-to-face encounter with Western forests. He had been in the presence of ancient trees and witnessed the devastation caused by logging. In this case, both awe when confronted with ancient forests and grief at their destruction became motivating factors that galvanized him to more radical action.[20]

Activists like McGowan who gravitated to West Coast forests and action camps join a centuries-long history of westward migration that resulted, at least in part, in the devastation of the forests they now seek to save. This is a history activists want to change by bringing a stop to logging and resource extraction and then rewilding damaged places.

THE MEANINGS OF FORESTS

The association of radical environmentalism with stereotypes of "tree-huggers" is shaped by the ways in which forests have been configured in the Western imagination.[21] The identification of activists with trees by mainstream news media and other observers constitutes both activists and forests as other, opposed to civilized behavior. Tree-hugging activists, like trees, are treated as unruly.[22] Activists tend to accept and even promote this characterization, opposing their intimate relationships with trees to the view of forests as resources to be exploited or wilderness to be tamed. As Robert Pogue Harrison argues in *Forests: The Shadow of Civilization*, "the governing institutions of the West—religion, law, family, city—originally established themselves in opposition to the forests."[23] In a sense, then, civilization has its source in and emerges from this opposition. The views European colonizers brought with them to North America included fear of the wild as well as the desire to claim what the wilderness promised, such as animal furs and spiritual opportunities.[24] From Harrison's perspective it is fear of the otherness of the wild that has most shaped our attitude towards forests.

This "forest phobia" is best exemplified for Harrison in Jean Paul Sartre's description of threatening trees and vegetation in *Nausea*. In *Nausea*, cities are under siege, giving way to encroaching forests. Sartre's protagonist Roquentin describes the ravenous vegetation waiting outside cities to take over: "It is waiting . . . Once the city is dead, the

Boar with power plant by Max Jurcak. Used with permission.

vegetation will cover it, will climb over the stones, grip them, search them, make them burst with its long pincers; it will blind the holes and let its green powers hang over everything."[25] What Sartre's character fears is what activists hope for: a rewilding of the planet. Instead of an evil wilderness against which civilization is constituted, for activists forests become the opposite: a locus of truth and meaning.

Americans' ambivalent relationship with forests has ranged between these two registers of meaning, represented best in this context by resource extraction companies on the one hand and radical activists on the other. Most Americans are somewhere in between, enjoying their beautiful redwood decks as well as family vacations in protected redwood groves. When Jeff Luers felt the forest's grief and suffering, he situated himself within a particular orientation to nature and way of being with trees.

Two types of thinking about trees in particular represent more general attitudes towards wilderness in North American history. These different perspectives are reflected in the work of two famous American writers. Poet Walt Whitman's "Song of the Redwood Tree" (1900) begins with the poet mourning the departing nature spirits as the tree is cut down. By the end of the poem, however, he ends up promoting progress and manifest destiny. In Whitman's poem, the tree appears as "an abstraction" rather than an individual with a distinctive history and appearance. In fact, Whitman had never been to California and had never seen a redwood.[26] While activists share Whitman's mourning over logging, they disavow rather than embrace progress.

In contrast to Whitman's perspective, Henry David Thoreau (1817–1862) writes in *Walden* about the landscape he knew intimately. He notices the small changes in the trees around him and encounters them as particular beings with individual identities. Like Jeff Luers, Thoreau imagines trees as divinities: "Do behold the King in his glory, King Sequoia . . . Some time ago I left all for Sequoia and have been and am at his feet; fasting and praying for light, for is he not the greatest light in the woods, in the world? . . . The King tree and I have sworn eternal love."[27] This kind of love and devotion toward intimately known trees characterizes activists' attitudes towards trees as well.

Most activists identify with the lineage of Thoreau; they approve of his rejection of taxation and adopt civil disobedience as a strategy. They also share Thoreau's sense of kinship with a natural world that in many ways remains beyond human understanding.[28] Like Thoreau, activists want to be altered by nature. They even want to claim wildness as *self*, not other, as something within them to be nurtured and expressed as they become wild creatures of the forests during tree-sits.

GOING FERAL

Activists' journeys into forests that come to feel like home have unexpected and sometimes dangerous consequences. Activists may act on behalf of the wild, have a sense of kinship with wild species, and feel the forest to be a place of sanctuary and belonging, but they are also at risk there.

In 1998, twenty-four-year-old activist David "Gypsy" Chain was killed by a redwood tree felled by an irate logger in the area where Chain and other Earth First! activists were trying to prevent clear-cutting of old-growth redwoods. Chain first encountered redwoods after he left his childhood home in Pasadena, Texas, and headed for California with his girlfriend, Stephanie Kirby. According to journalist Jeff Goodell, Pasadena is "a flat, hard landscape of oil refineries, toxic fumes and dying bayous. Huge freighters drift up the ship canal nearby. The air tastes metallic. Take one breath and you understand why this area has one of the highest cancer rates in America."[29] Goodell argues that Chain spent his life trying to leave Pasadena far behind. It was in part the contrast of the forest to Pasadena that made the forest so appealing. Chain was no typical Texan, according to his family and friends. He became a vegetarian in high school and after graduating, he moved to Austin, where he got to know Kirby. She remembers, "He disagreed with consumer society and ignorant people who had no feelings for where their food came from or how their lifestyles affected the earth."[30] When Chain first met her, Kirby had been traveling around the country and had fallen in love with Humboldt County, California, and its giant coastal redwoods. When their relationship fell apart in California, Chain sought out a group of Earth First!ers involved in actions to stop logging in redwood groves. These actions were focused around an area called Headwaters that became famous in the 1990s during the "Redwood Wars."[31]

The morning of Chain's death, a small group of Earth First!ers set out from their camp, hoping to draw attention to an infraction of California law. Maxxam, the multinational corporation controlling Pacific Lumber Company, was logging in the habitat of the endangered marbled murrelet, a seabird that nests in coastal redwoods. Chain and other activists planned to confront the logging crews directly to let them know Maxxam was logging illegally. As the Earth First!ers tried to talk with A. E. Ammons, one of the loggers, Ammons grew angry and threatened to fell a tree on them, so the activists backed off. Later that day, they decided to try again to prevent Ammons from cutting down trees, reminding themselves they had a chance to save at least one big tree that day. As they approached the logger a second time, they made a lot of noise so he would stop sawing and they yelled out "Don't cut the tree." Then they heard the tree crack and start to fall. Although everyone else scrambled to get out of the way, the tree hit Chain and killed him instantly.[32]

When activists like Chain travel to forests to join tree-sits and blockades, they leave society behind for causes so compelling, they are willing to risk their lives. Among the trees, activists' internal journeys mirror their physical journeys from cities and suburbs to the wilderness. In forests, young adults' transformation into activists is what anthropologists Tim Ingold and Gisli Palsson call a "biosocial becoming."[33] David Chain became an activist over a period of years with a variety of other beings, human and other-than-human. His process of becoming an activist began early on: he spent time outdoors as a child, distanced himself from American consumerism as a young adult, became involved with Kirby, traveled West, entered redwood forests, climbed into trees, and became part of an activist community. In a similar fashion, Jeff Luers became an activist because of his teenage years as a Pagan who spoke with trees, his experiences in the forest with the tree Happy and other forest beings, and because of the influence of other activists.

Luers's trajectory of movement and growth involved moving away from the Southern California suburbs of his childhood into the anarchist communities and old-growth forests of Oregon. Chain's process of becoming an activist was a similar kind of journey, in his case away from a Texas landscape of oil refineries to a redwood forest.

Forests effect physical as well as moral changes in activists like Chain, who express what is happening to them internally through their outward appearance and bodily gestures. When activists climb into trees, they enter a world populated by birds, flying squirrels, and other species they are less likely to encounter on the ground. Journalist Patrick Beach describes climbers' ascent into this arboreal world in his book about Chain: "Sometimes climbers begin to feel different when the forest floor gives way as they climb. They become aware of birds and other wildlife. The ground begins to lose definition. . . . The majesty of the giants and their function as living habitat is better grasped from 180 feet looking down than from the ground looking up."[34] When activists climb into trees and live on platforms high in tree canopies for many days, distinctions between human body and tree bark become unclear. They acquire what philosopher and cultural ecologist David Abram describes as a different kind of perception, characterized by reciprocity with the other-than-human, touching the forest and being touched by it.[35] Moreover, the process by which activists become activists often involves the blurring of boundaries between human and nonhuman bodies, so that self and other are no longer distinctly separate beings.

Activists who are involved with tree-sits and other action camps often cannot bathe frequently and travel lightly with few clothes. They may look and smell more like forests than civilization. After a year and a half in the redwood tree Luna, Julia Butterfly Hill described the ways in which her body was transformed: "The tree had become part of me, or I her. I had grown a thick new muscle on the outer sides of my feet from gripping as I climbed and wrapping them around branches. . . . My fingers were stained brown from the bark and green from the lichen. Bits of Luna had been ground underneath my fingernails, while sap, with its embedded bits of bark and duff, speckled my arms and hands and feet. People even said that I smelled sweet, like a redwood."[36] When they live in tree-sits for extended periods of time during ongoing campaigns, activists experience their bodies becoming part of the place where they are living, whether or not they are native to that place. Their transformations might be disturbing to outside observers, but to activists, they are badges of kinship and co-becoming.[37]

"Looking Down" at Tar Sands Blockade tree village. Photo: John Fiege. Used with permission.

Activists may appear shockingly different when they emerge from the forest and return to civilization. As suggested by Hill's account, signs of the transformation that fuels their resistance are evident on their bodies. Activist Joan Dunning describes one of the first meetings she attended to learn about clear-cutting in redwood groves. "Who were these children?" she wondered as she looked around the room. "What is the message with the dreadlocks? Feral . . . Like goats or cats gone wild. . . I was surrounded by nose-ringed, dreadlocked, baggy-clothed young people . . . ."[38] Activists cultivate this kind of ferality because it links them to their forest kin and to nonhuman animals, as Dunning suggests.

When David Chain returned home from the forest after his first experience at a tree-sit a few years before his death, his family was shocked by the change in his appearance and attitude. His dreadlocks were "woven with beads and trinkets," and he had "a thick beard." His sister Bridgett thought "He looked like a forest creature." And something had changed inside him as well: "He arrived sparkly eyed, with a kind of presence that wasn't there before," said his long-time friend Chris Martin, "It was like he had finally figured out exactly what he wanted to do with his life."[39]

Chain's appearance and manner reflected the conversion he had undergone. The forest and its inhabitants, including other activists, had become his community, so he embodied these new commitments. In a similar fashion, when Jim Hindle left a tree-sit to visit some old friends he had not seen for a while, they were taken aback by his appearance. He was clearly "not the same person who'd said goodbye three months back. I'd more or less worn the same outer layers ever since, and they were covered in layers of woodland dirt and the green that rubbed off of the trees."[40] In these ways, activists often appear to friends and families as altered, hybrid beings, as wild as they are human. Their transformation enables them to see and experience something about the wild that other people who retain their separate humanness might not.

Acted on by trees, forest animals, and activist friends, in the process of remaking the forest as a site of meaning, activists remake themselves as creatures that belong there. Like Julia Butterfly Hill's bark-stained fingers, the forest gets under activists' skin and in their hair; they are claimed by it. They express their commitment to nonhumans with their bodies and go by "forest names" to highlight their identification with other species. During my fieldwork I met Nettle, Earthworm, Thrush, Magpie, Burdock, Rabbit, Turtle, Grasshopper, and many others.

Nettle, a former *Earth First! Journal* editor, told me the story of how she came by her name. When she lived at the Bilston Glen tree-sit in Scotland, she and other inhabitants of the Glen often foraged for wild foods. Stinging nettle grew all around the area, so Nettle and her friends drank a lot of nettle tea and experimented with different ways of cooking nettles. At the time, she was going to a nearby herbal school where she learned stinging nettle could be used to treat arthritis and similar ailments. She began treating her tendonitis by swatting herself with stinging nettle and found that this treatment helped keep her pain-free. She had become obsessed with stinging nettle. After she had been working at the *Earth First! Journal* for a while, a co-worker asked if she wanted "Nettle" to be her "biocentric name" for her email at the Journal, and she did: "It was my power plant, my healing plant . . . a strong metaphor for myself: I can be a healer for someone, or I can be a thorn in their side."[41] As Nettle came to know her namesake, her identity and well-being were shaped by her relationship to the plant. In this and other ways, activists draw closer to other species, rejecting anything that smacks of civilization and reversing the taming of the wild by humans. Unlike forms of colonization they critique, activists *choose* to be taken over by the wild.

Tattoos are another way activists embody their affinity with the non-human world. Although not all activists have them, tattoos are common, especially among younger activists. They often figure in activists' narratives of commitment, as I discovered on a visit to the Earth First! Journal collective in Lake Worth, Florida. In a backyard full of tropical plants, I interviewed some members of the Earth First! Journal collective. As our conversations roamed over different topics, I asked about the meanings of their tattoos. Rabbit, one of the editors, pointed out his newest tattoo: a rabbit in a cage, "to remind me of no matter how much fun I'm having, there are still things in cages."[42] Onion, another Journal editor has an anarchy bomb tattoo: "not like in a violent way but what we have inside ourselves, recognizing our own power, cause once you do that, no one's going to give you power." Nettle decided to get a tattoo of a "spiral of life . . . an ongoing, never ending symbol, my paganism." For Nettle, the tattoo is a reminder that "we are all divine, no hierarchy between individuals, plants and animals."[43] Onion also has tattoos of the faces of historical figures that are significant to him, including Gandhi, Martin Luther King Jr., and Emma Goldman.[44] The smell of campfires on one's skin or the mustiness of tree bark from long days spent in a redwood canopy are temporary transformations of the body. Tattoos suggest a more permanent identification with activist causes.

Activists' bodies may express their resistance to domestication as well as their desire to remake themselves in the image of the wild (or the revolutionary). Roddy is a British activist in Jay Griffiths's fictionalized account of the 1990s Newbury bypass protest in England. He was first drawn to join the antiroads movement when he saw activists in the road looking out of place in his suburban neighborhood: "there they were, mud after my own heart, partners in grime . . . They sat in the earth to stop a road being built through beauty." Roddy leaves his parents' house and joins the protesters. He builds a treehouse in an oak and makes a hammock in its branches, spending many days in the oak and trying to think like a tree.

Over time, Roddy notices some changes: "My senses are quickened to changes of weather and season, and I feel enlivened in the animal department of myself. Trees are living things to live in, houses are not alive. It becomes a relationship. I wouldn't go so far as to call it my commonlaw tree, but you live close to it, and you feel its moods, you get its bark on your clothes, its moss under your fingernails and you wear its leaves in your hair." As a child, Roddy wanted to be a bird and so it is in the tree, in contrast to being inside his parents' home, that he feels free: "I am satisfying my nesting instinct," he says.[45] From his treetop perch, he experiences freedom as a gift from nature, "for living here has brought down the fences, has repealed the enclosures between my inner landscape and the woodlands outside me. I am nature and it is me. Inside me is all outdoors." Because of this affinity, Roddy becomes committed to the woods: "I love this place . . . I have never felt an emotion quite like this, this impassioned altruism, needing both love and hate, love running savage to protect what it loves. Love like a waterfall with rocks of fury behind it."[46] After living in the tree-sit, Roddy's "inner landscape" is no longer separate from the woods around him.

The physical changes activists undergo, viscerally felt, are part of a powerfully transformative vision of the human. For many activists, going feral requires both an undoing of civilization and a rewilding of self.[47] Their human bodies and spirits are made over by their encounters with wild beings and places. Rewilding of the human self in a community of other species is first and foremost a reaction against domestication, which activists see as a social ill linked to capitalism and consumerism. Avalon, an ELF activist who committed suicide while in prison awaiting sentencing for environmental sabotage, railed against domestication and "even preached against domesticated pets and houseplants, explaining that humans could never fulfill the true desires of cats and ferns."[48] In "How Do We Go Wild," activist Wolfi Landstreicher hopes for the eventual "overturning of domestication" and advocates a positive vision of the future as well, which is "wildness—especially as an aim for individuals to achieve in revolt against domestication and civilization. . ."[49] Activists want to uncivilize themselves by reestablishing deeper connections with other, wild species. Living more intimately with plants and other animals is an antidote to the alienation they feel in the broader society and the pessimism many of them have about the future of life on Earth.

The anonymous author of "Born Caged," an article in a zine I picked up at an Earth First! gathering, explains it this way: "I was born in prison. I grew up in prison. . . . I first became aware of my status as a prisoner in high school. Subjected to thousands of hours of confinement, sitting at a desk, monitored and surrounded by walls . . . I forged countless passes and then I would walk along the still-wild streambanks. I began to sense that if school was prison, then my suburban neighborhood was the prison yard . . . My rambling walks gave me a taste of freedom, a taste of my kinship with critters other than leashed dogs, potted plants and manicured lawns."[50] Here the wild does not have to be far removed from the domestic; it may even exist alongside suburban neighborhoods.

In his rant against domestication, an activist named Skunk bemoans the effects of civilization on young people who have "their minds imprisoned, their thoughts convicted in schools."[51] For him, "the real world lies beneath the asphalt, just as our true selves lie buried under all the lies we were taught about who we are."[52] As a bumper sticker I saw at the Earth First! 2013 Round River Rendezvous gathering warns, "You Were Wild Once, Don't Let Them Tame You." But going feral is more than an undoing of civilization, it is a rewilding of the planet in which the fate of human lives is unimportant to many activists.

In a reversal of the long history of Western views of forests described by Robert Pogue Harrison, activists welcome the demise of human civilization and its colonization by nonhuman animals and vegetation. The anonymous author of a zine called "Down With Empire, Up with the Spring" notices the wild everywhere, not just in forests: "Wildness is everywhere, from the grass between the paving slabs to the high mountains—they should all be defended." Even small ruptures of wild plants in suburbs and cities are to be celebrated. In "Keep Vacant Lots Vacant," Tree Bark, an activist from Philadelphia, rejoices in "neglected" feral places in the city: "I can't wait until my whole city is neglected and taken over by 'weeds.'" He sees weeds as "scabs . . . growing over the open wound of industrial civilization . . . quit picking at them!"[53] From this perspective, the conquest of cities by weeds is exactly what is needed.

Because activists embrace a world beyond the human and try to overcome the kind of rationalism that measures a forest's worth in board feet, they want cities to decay at the same time that forests thrive. In the zine *feral: a journal towards wildness*, the narrator of the poem, "Ned Ludd was Right," describes city buildings as "ugly monstrosities of steel and glass and concrete, overpowering in their hugeness and sterility." He dreams they are in ruins, "being eaten by a forest."[54] In "Coastal Remains," a similar vision of the future, "warrior poet" Sean Carr dreams of "creeper vines reaching over concrete/of trees to shadow the shore/and gulls to roost in the apexes/of mansions long abandoned beside the sea."[55] Since many activists see humans as the most destructive invasive species, they celebrate the incursion of other species into the human-made world.

Just as activists blur species boundaries by becoming wild, wild animals and trees take on human-like agency in activist culture. Activist art

True Cost of Coal animal activists by Beehive Design Collective. Licensed under Creative Commons 2.0.

and news reporting emphasizes the agency of other species, celebrating stories of wild animals attacking humans or domesticated animals escaping their lives of captivity in factory farms or circuses. For instance, *Satya* magazine featured a round-up of stories called "Sharks Bite Back: Direct Action by Animals Around the World" that showed "animals taking matters into their own hands."[56]

Activist poetry too, often envisions nonhuman animals revolting against everything humans have made, working alongside activists to dismantle civilization. In the poem "Swamp Anarchists," Karen Coulter identifies with animal revenge:

the swamp anarchist tribes/have their own cultural responses—armadillos infiltrate suburbia/ dig up the lawns/ alligators prow the canals/ into posh wealthy manor backtards/ snatching up pets and small children/ for dinner . . . We Earth First!ers practice our own rewilding/ climbing cypress trees, talking strategy/ then ascend into public attention/ with a tree-sit to show the last/ 700 acres of natural intact forest/ in eastern Palm Beach County/ that Scripps corporation plans to turn into/ a biotechnology nightmare city.[57]

Many examples of activist art work depict animals getting the better of their enemies, such as logging companies and animal testing labs. In one *Earth First! Journal* illustration, two wolves stand on top of an overturned bulldozer, howling into the wind.[58] On the cover of another *Earth First! Journal* issue, animals sabotage a bulldozer and block a road being constructed through a forest. Two raccoons are rolling away a tire, a bear is taking something apart with tools as a badger holds a flashlight, a hawk flies into the fray with a wrench, and a mountain lion and lynx are working with a blowtorch. Behind them, vehicles on a logging road are going up in flames. While activists find these kinds of images inspiring, outside observers might see them as clear proof that activists are misanthropic, celebrating property destruction and alligators dining on children.

Activists advocate aggressively defending ruptures of wildness and speeding along the process of rewilding. Rabbit urges other activists to "take the wild back" and offers some examples: "people taking back the forests with pickaxes and barricades; taking back the billboards with spray paint and kerosene . . . They're bursting open cages with chants and sledgehammers." He imagines the delight of wild things at these human actions: "The rivers yearn for jackhammers and dynamite. Birds soar and sing for the end of industry."[59] By projecting their own delight at rewilding efforts onto birds and rivers, activists emphasize what they imagine to be a shared cross-species desire: to undo human projects that control and civilize the wild. Birds and rivers, then, become like activists, just as activists want to become more like birds and rivers, rejoicing in cross-species kinship.

In these visions of undomestication and animal activism, forests hold the promise of two possible futures: a rewilded world of awe-inspiring redwoods and streams full of salmon spawning, or ugly clearcuts and silt-filled rivers. As Julia Butterfly Hill sees it, the two possibilities are "magnificence and devastation."[60] These opposing visions of the future, one dark and the other hopeful, run throughout activist art work, media releases, poetry, and other writings. In one of these possible futures we might live in interdependent relationships with other species, treating them as our equals. In the other, we destroy and dominate other species and their habitats, hastening extinction rates and the disappearance of wild places.

THE FOREST AS HOME AND PLACE OF BELONGING

Activists are motivated to bring their version of the future into being in part because their identities have been fundamentally shaped by interactions with other species. In the redwood forests of Northern California and old-growth forests in Oregon and Washington where so many protests have taken place, the many species shaping activist commitments include salamanders, bald eagles, bears, salmon, marbled murrelets, spotted owls, mycorrhizal fungi, banana slugs, loggers, marijuana growers, forest rangers, the Klamath and other local Indian tribes, human consumers of forest products, and countless others activists come to know or are influenced by while they live in the woods. In the context of these various relationships, activists reject any sense of human exceptionalism and embrace their own place in the wild, where they have come to feel at home.[61]

Jim Hindle left behind college and his middle-class family to participate in antiroad protests in England during the 1990s, a life that seemed to him more real than other available options for a young person: "I couldn't trust myself to work at university, doing something I had no passion for, and I couldn't jump on the wagon of partying as much as possible; another distraction from the very real problems we were all faced with but which nobody wanted to acknowledge, never mind do something about."[62] Hindle knew the woods he was living in were destined to be cut down, even though the protesters did their best to delay the inevitable. Still, the months-long blockade became his home, the first place he had come to live as an independent adult: "Our common purpose bound us together as a true tribe—not merely making the right noises, but acting together with our hearts."[63] Being part of a community at action camps intensifies many activists' sense of separation from the world outside where they often do not feel at home. As one activist explained it, gatherings like the Earth First! Rendezvous and Feral Futures are for many "a place of rest and healing from the outside world."[64]

When they embrace rewilding the planet and themselves, activists' experience in forests among like-minded others confirms a path they were already on. Rachel was a recent college graduate who had "no clue" why her life "felt so empty." She left her home in Ohio and headed west, stopping in New Mexico where, for the first time, she lived off the land. She was "fed, comforted, soulfully nourished by beings" she had "overlooked as a suburban kid raised on television screens and shopping malls." She participated in various radical environmental gatherings and action camps in Montana and the Pacific Northwest where she "learned to climb trees, came to love sleeping outside, met plants that offered healing guidance." The end result of these experiences was that she "felt more in myself than I had my entire life . . . Enamored with the darkness, in love with the wild." Leaving her middle-class suburban home behind, she discovered, "the wild is not a place to be afraid of, but to revere and cherish."[65]

When activists come to feel at home in their forest abodes, they believe other forest-dwelling species respond to them in kind. For Rachel, plants that offered guidance helped her to feel comfortable in the forest. British activist Jim Hindle became so used to the wind in the trees at a road blockade that the silence that fell when he entered a building seemed strange. At night in the forest camp, he felt "there was only a thin skin between us and the outer world."[66] He belonged in that forest: "It was as if everything suddenly fitted into place . . . Everything was working out exactly as it should, and to be rooted in this place, to have a sense of place within it, made everything seem whole." Hindle and other road blockaders believed the land also responded to them: "It was as though the hills were waking up with us and years of separation between us and the Land were falling away like an old skin."[67] Jeff Luers had a similar realization after he "stayed to protect what I now considered my forest, and my home." He too noticed his relationship to the forest had changed, so that when he hiked around, "birds didn't treat me as an intruder."[68]

When they travel to forest action camps, many activists experience a sense of malleability and openness that allows both forests *and* activist communities to work on them. Maia explained to me during our interview that she was "looking to be part of something" when she first traveled to the redwood forests of northern California. The grandfather of a high school friend was involved with an Earth First! tree-sit, so after graduation, the two friends traveled to Humboldt County, California, where they helped support tree-sits by making food supply runs. Maia remembers that her "brain was ready to be molded" by the older and more experienced Earth First!ers.[69]

Elizabeth Marie Egan felt accepted by both the trees and the human action camp community when she joined her first tree-sit at age eighteen. She was involved with the Minnehaha Free State and Four Oaks Spiritual Encampment in Minneapolis, established in 1998 to block construction of an interstate bypass to the Minneapolis airport. When Egan joined the camp, she felt "overwhelmed by a sense of welcome." She recalls how "those first hours in the tree expanded my understanding of the entire ecosystem. These net-nest tree-sits can envelop a person wholly. It is the closest I've felt to being in a womb since Mama. . . . The Free State ripped open my heart and enabled me to see clearly the immense possibilities of action."[70] Egan remembers just as clearly how devastated she felt when she returned a few weeks later after leaving to attend her college classes to find the tree that had welcomed her cut down.

In a logical extension of the view that they belong in the trees, activists do not see themselves as intruders on federal, state, and private land even when they are accused of trespassing, although they do acknowledge they are settlers in the homelands of particular indigenous cultures. The police who come to arrest them and the loggers who are forced to stop work are the ones who have no right to be in the forest. A tree-sitter named Julia explains it this way: "I have seen the panicked look in the eyes of the cops as night settles into the forest and they begin to no longer feel in their element. I had a similar feeling when I stepped into the Eureka courthouse for the first time."[71] For activists who have lived for weeks or months in the woods, being at the heart of civilization—in a courtroom, for instance—is a disorienting and alienating experience, just as they imagine the woods at night must be for police officers or security guards assigned to watch them. Activists are at home in the woods, even if their presence is illegal. As they see it, these other humans who have a legal right to be there are the intruders.

Some activists endow forests with explicitly spiritual meanings in order to further distinguish them from a disenchanted world. When Julia Butterfly Hill, whose father was an itinerant preacher, first visited the redwoods, she was awed by the redwoods' grandeur: "When I entered the great majestic cathedral of the redwood forest for the first time . . . my spirit knew it had found what it was searching for. I dropped to my knees and began to cry, because I was so overwhelmed by the wisdom, energy, and spirituality housed in this holiest of temples."[72] Because of experiences like this, activists come to see trees as sacred beings that should be treated at the very least as close family members, and for some, even as deities.[73] Jeff Luers remembers the awe he felt on first encountering stands of old-growth trees, "Standing before them is a humbling experience . . . like standing before a God or Goddess."[74] Although most activists value forests for their intrinsic worth, others go further in seeing them as the abode of spiritual beings, whose violation they are all the more determined to prevent.

Even forest action camps themselves, like the forests they exist to protect, can become sacred spaces for activists. Activist Tre Arrow was

Wild Roots Feral Futures entrance. Photo: author.

involved with a tree-sit and action camp in Mt. Hood National Forest in 2000. In his story on Arrow, *Rolling Stone* journalist Randall Sullivan describes the scene he came upon: "Like just about everyone who spent time there, Tre experienced life in the resistance camp as a sort of perpetual religious service conducted in an evergreen cathedral, a place where people discovered spirits in the morning fog and raptures in the afternoon sun. For them, the raid on the camp [by federal agents] was not just an assault on a political action, but the desecration of a sacred site."[75] David Chain's fellow activists in Northern California engaged in ritual practices to enchant their forest action camp. As journalist Jeff Goodell observed, "It isn't unusual to be walking in the woods near an Earth First! camp and come across a small altar built at the foot of a redwood, or to find a volunteer with his or her head bowed, engaged in silent communication with a tree."[76]

My journeys to the Earth First! Rendezvous and other gatherings underscored the importance of these sites' special, even sacred, identity apart from the outside world. I had the distinct impression of leaving civilization behind because the gatherings were located at remote sites, usually a long drive from major highways or towns. These gathering spaces are cloaked in mystery and possibility: people's lives are changed there. But being isolated in the wilderness at a gathering or action camp can be dangerous as well as exciting. Gatherings I attended were threatened by both a forest fire (near the 2013 Wild Roots, Feral Futures in

Colorado) and flooding (at the 2013 Earth First! Rendezvous in North Carolina). When I helped at the medic tent at an Earth First! Rendezvous, participants came in with bee stings, poison ivy reactions, and a number of other ailments and wounds. The apparent absence of human control at these remote sites lent power to the feeling of being in a separate space away from ordinary life.

Action camps and gatherings sometimes visibly announce their role as special spaces in the midst of forests. In this way, being at home in the forest does not necessarily mean blending in with the forest, but instead, creating a human-identified space. Activists at Red Cloud Thunder Fall Creek tree-sit arranged river rocks at the site in the form of the Celtic sign for the sun, strung a maypole with a ribbon, and hung a large cloth banner with the name "Red Cloud Thunder" between two trees. Two of the trees activists lived in were named Kali-Ma after the Hindu goddess and Yggdrasil for the world tree of Norse mythology.[77] Banners, religious references, and trees named for gods and goddesses enhance the meaning of otherwise practical and mundane aspects of action camps. In this way, action camps become spaces in the forest shaped by *human* action (decorating) and human understanding (naming). They also have an impact on the forest, bringing food, creating waste, and trampling plants where blockades are built or workshops and circles are held. Becoming feral and blurring the boundary between human and other than human do not erase the human, but they are aspirational gestures of attunement to other ways of thinking and being.

CIRCLES OF KINSHIP

While activists value wild beings and places for themselves, they also relate to them as kin who can be drawn into relationship with human beings. When they become closer to the lives of forest species and make temporary homes in "evergreen cathedrals" they tend to describe trees and animals in kinship terms. In his poem "Mountain Justice," Proteus describes the affinity with nonhuman others that activists experience in this way: "our roots/the roots that grip these mountainsides./We connect the earth and sky/when we reach our arms wide/and embrace Creation like kin./The same water that courses through these mountains/flows in my veins."[78] This kind of understanding of other species as kin increases activists' motivation to act on behalf of their relations. As one panelist reflected on the ethic of "No Compromise" during a workshop I attended on deep ecology and biocentrism at the Round River Rendezvous in

2013, "If every tree of the forest is kin, you can't just get rid of some kin; that's your sister."[79] In his 1986 song, "Earth First!" Darryl Cherney urges listeners to take action: "Our sisters and brothers are dying every day/While we drink our coffee and look the other way." For many activists, looking the other way is not an option because of the identification they experience with tree and animal kin.

These kinship relationships are reinforced by ritualized protest actions in which activists protect the kin they love and mourn those they lose. Because nonhuman species are their "brothers and sisters," activists grieve for fallen trees as if they were close friends.[80] According to Patrick Beach, at Northern California tree-sits, "Whenever a tree would fall, the protesters would yell out, either in fear or to vocalize the tree's death wail—another bit of Earth First theatricality."[81] Julia Butterfly Hill describes what she experienced when trees fell around Luna: "Each time a chainsaw cut through those trees, I felt it cut through me as well. It was like watching my family being killed. And just as we lose a part of ourselves with the passing of a family member or friends, so did I lose a part of myself with each friend."[82] Rod Coronado voiced similar sentiments about kinship with nonhumans: "Over the last ten years I have placed myself between the hunter and the hunted, the vivisector and the victim, the furrier and the furbearer, and the whaler and the whale. These are my people, my constituency."[83] For activists like Hill and Coronado, then, the loss and suffering of nonhuman family members is experienced as the loss and suffering of a human friend, brother, or sister.

During tree-sits, the more a tree is experienced as a person, the closer and more committed the relationship between tree and activist.[84] Reporters and celebrities were drawn to the story of Julia Butterfly Hill's two-year tree-sit in part because of what was seen as Hill's unusual dedication, but also because of the extent to which Hill personified the tree, Luna.[85]

When activists describe trees they have known, they endow them with agency and personality that make their presence, and thus their loss, more vivid. Jamie McGuinn describes getting acquainted with the trees around him during a tree-sit: "When I was in this tree called Ursus, a cedar in Oregon, I could sit up on the platform and look out and see the other trees in the grove . . . The Doug firs were the sentinels, like guards of the forest, tall and stout and straight. And the hemlocks, they all had these tops bent over, and they were the more emotional, poet types. Cedars were really strong and sturdy. They were the protectors of the forest . . . You don't see that from the ground." When the wind blew he thought it sounded like they were talking to each other.[86] Through this kind of personification, activists make clear their understanding of the moral status of other species and shore up their sense that they are acting as their brother and sister trees would want them to.

Personification of trees also suggests a dynamic tension between intimacy and distance. Activists endow trees with souls and human-like characteristics, but they also see them as beautiful biological mechanisms that have their own agendas. Trees are human-like kin, yet they remain mysterious beings living in tree worlds we cannot hope to know. These tree worlds have meanings for trees and other species that lie beyond the human, meanings that do not revolve around human existence and human understanding. What is important for activists is creating bonds of love and responsibility across the differences between humans and other species.

By personifying trees and nonhuman animals and treating them as valued presences in the world, activists contradict assumptions about human superiority. They approach redwoods and salmon as wise and ancient beings that have much to teach us humans. As one of the Headwaters forest activists that writer and activist Joan Dunning interviewed sees it, "the salmon were here before the land, before the forest. They have been here sixty million years. They swam over Headwaters when it was still under the ocean." In this way, activist bodies in trees become sites of learning about how to relate to other species. In a tribute to "Lady Oak," in a zine I picked up at the 2013 Earth First! Rendezvous, the unnamed author describes "communing with this being" and what she learned from this oak tree that "called" to her:

> I moved to her elevation and region. . . . So I am here learning her lesson. I came here quite concerned with her presence but quickly learned reverie. I learned she grows at a specific elevation as a gateway to ascension. I had been bashful with my relationship with the forest for some time. I felt inadequate coming from concrete to abyss. I tend to be bulky and cumbersome in the midst of such natural grace. I desire acclimation and reciprocation in wild places though. So I have bowed to her. I ask for her guidance . . . Sometimes we are welcomed to cross boundaries and we learn.[87]

Instead of mastering nature, for this anonymous author the point is to practice humility, to feel "bashful" rather than in control, and to cross boundaries when welcomed to do so.

When activists speak and act on behalf of nonhuman beings, they also draw attention to how these others have shaped their commitments. As "accidental activist" Joan Dunning describes it, the forest called her to join the struggle to save the redwoods: "The forest has chosen all of us who are involved in its protection. It has tapped us on the shoulder, tapped our souls and engaged us."[88] And it is not just the forest that calls people to action, according to Dunning: "For each of us, regardless of where we live, there is a river, a mountain range, a beach, a whale, a peregrine, a gnatcatcher, that, if we merely give our time as a witness to loss, will gradually unite the veins of its existence with our own, will ground us by putting us in touch with what is wild and speechless, will empower us when we speak out in defense of the powerless."[89] Activists approach forest species, hoping to learn from them, but they are also approached by these species.

RITES OF IDENTIFICATION AND MIMICRY

Crossing species boundaries and viscerally experiencing the suffering of nonhuman others are central points of connection between radical environmentalism and animal rights. Animal rights activists also perform rites of identification and kinship with other beings that are suffering at the hands of humans. In a 2013 video, "Suffering is Suffering: Live Human Branding," Iowa animal activists perform a branding on one of their own, "in solidarity with animal suffering and exploitation."

The video opens with a quote from philosopher Jeremy Bentham (1748–1832) that is often invoked by animal rights activists: "The question is not, 'Can they reason?' nor 'Can they talk?' but 'Can they suffer?'"[90] In this protest the suffering body of an activist representing a calf is the central focus. In the video, a nearly naked young woman is chained and put in a cart with a cover over it. Three masked activists dressed in black drag her out, wrap heavy chains around her neck, hands, and feet, and shave off her long reddish-brown hair. They brand her, then put her in the back of a windowless truck with "269 Life" emblazoned on it. The reference in the protest is to 269 Life, an organization named for a calf with the tag #269 and started by three Israeli activists to promote awareness of animal suffering in agribusiness. "We are all 269," reads the caption on the branding video. By branding the calf's number on their bodies, these activists identify with "the victims of the animal holocaust all around the world, remembering to never forget." Here pain becomes a distinct medium of acting in the world on behalf of nonhuman others. It is a way into their experience, which we can feel more easily as our own through the lived reality of pain in the bodies of the activist-ritualists. Kinship relations are created and expressed when activists and nonhuman animals are wounded together. 269 Life is one of many examples of the global context for American radical activism, in which campaigns and techniques move across global media flows.[91] These protests are intended to work on viewers watching the video anywhere in the world, making them vicariously experience the pain and suffering of activists who take the place of nonhuman animals.

This kind of identification occurs in many types of protests, even when there is no direct reference to other species' suffering, as there is in the branding video. After watching a sixteen-year-old girl pepper-sprayed by police officers at a 1997 nonviolent demonstration at Pacific Lumber Company's headquarters in Northern California, Joan Dunning explains why protesters refused to move when the police asked them to: "They cannot leave because they are the trees that cannot choose new forests. They are the salamanders who cannot hike to new watersheds. They are the marbled murrelets circling in search of trees that no longer exist. They are the salmon who return home to creeks filled with mud."[92] In this view, the activists' actions should be what nonhumans would do if they could: "We must do for them what we believe they would do for themselves . . . They would burn down research facilities, and kill animal researchers . . . they would form an underground of saboteurs to disrupt the machinery of the vast human killing machine called society."[93] Rites of self-inflicted pain and endangerment work to seal activists' pact with the other-than-human world. Through their own vulnerability in these acts of mimicry, activists experience other species' vulnerability. In so doing, they hope their sacrifice and utter helplessness, the image of their pain that is also the pain of other beings, will change those who witness their sacrifice.

Environmental and animal rights activists not only substitute human bodies for the bodies of trees or nonhuman animals, but they also sometimes dress as other animals during campaigns. For example, PETA (People for the Ethical Treatment of Animals) activists may wear animal costumes during protests, such as those against Kentucky Fried Chicken for inhumane treatment of chickens.[94] At the same time that they mimic other species, activists engage in what communications scholar Kevin DeLuca calls "disidentification" with accepted social values of progress and the dominion of human over nature.[95] Activists dressed as chickens are not simply performing, they are trying to get onlookers to identify with the chickens' perspective, to call into question human dominion over other species. By identifying with nonhuman animals, they also disidentify with the humans causing these animals' suffering.

By these acts of identification and disidentification, activists try to create images and stories designed to elicit compassion and care in those who see and hear them. Most forest actions that try to delay logging and draw attention to endangered old-growth forests involve positioning human bodies between loggers and trees, so logging cannot occur without hurting or killing activists. Activists' positions have to be precarious to be effective, even though they do their best to follow safety procedures in order to prevent accidents. Tree-sits are inherently unsafe in order to work effectively as a tactic to keep police officers or company workers from easily removing them. Such risky tactics heighten suspense and increase the affinity between activists and those they are acting for. At the same time, they express activists' disidentification with other social values, such as profit and progress.

In these ritualized protest actions, young people become activists with many other agencies in all the ways I have suggested, including when they are pepper-sprayed or handcuffed by police and photographed by reporters. They even see images of their own vulnerability and suffering on behalf of others in online news reports later, images that confirm their activist identities. For tree-sitters, the ritual stage includes material objects like the platforms they live on and the ropes they are attached to, as well as the representations of protests that circulate online and in print. Loggers and police officers who yell at and cajole them, or are friendly and give them granola bars, also shape their activist identities. All of these beings and things make activists into activists. In return, activists bring into being in public and visible ways the plight of the forest, its old-growth trees, marbled murrelets, and other creatures.

RUPTURAL PERFORMANCES

Animal rights activists in the branding video and forest activists being pepper-sprayed, lying on the ground in front of bulldozers, or hanging precariously from redwood canopies put themselves in the path of danger. They participate in and orchestrate performances meant to skew assumptions about what and who is of value. These protests are interventions, ruptures in the social order that call into question our notions of who belongs in society. Such protests/performances interrupt the everyday, taken-for-granted world.[96]

Anti–mountaintop removal activists risk arrest at EPA headquarters. Photo: Chris Eichler. Licensed under Creative Commons 2.0.

Forest activists reconfigure public space by preventing loggers from doing their jobs. They turn public (and sometimes private) lands into spaces of resistance and confrontation. Activists transform the meaning and significance of public spaces when they challenge capitalism and multinational oil companies at the Tar Sands protests, and the U.S. forest service and timber companies at forest tree-sits. These protests suggest new understandings of democracy by arguing for the rights of nonhumans to be seen and heard. At protests, what philosopher Hannah Arendt calls a "space of appearance" comes into being when activists make animal and tree bodies present in public space.[97] In the case of environmental activism, the bodies that compose the space of appearance include the redwood tree referenced by a protester whose eyes are being pepper-sprayed during a demonstration at a logging company and the endangered northern spotted owl mentioned by activists lying hand-cuffed on the ground in front of a bulldozer.

So how do these other bodies—nonhuman animal bodies, tree bodies—participate in new kinds of publics? Other-than-human bodies are typically excluded from society and from public space; their concerns are not represented in most legal and political forums. Bodies that have been invisible in public discourse become visible at protests through the

Dancing on equipment at fracking site. Photo: Marcellus Shale Earth First! Used with permission.

grief, anger, and sacrifices of activists. Grief and self-sacrificial acts make spotted owls, salmon, rivers, and trees present as the objects of grieving and sacrifice. Protestors lying in the dirt and pine needles of a logging road in front of a logging truck reference the destruction of trees carried out by the road, destruction they are trying to prevent.

But protests and demonstrations do more than produce a space of appearance; they seize spaces permeated by corporate and state power. By their actions, protesters disrupt the relationship between such spaces and those who control of them. At Earth First!'s 2013 Round River Rendezvous, while police officers were busy attending to an activist on a tripod blocking the road into a fracking chemical plant, another activist locked down to a fire truck brought in to remove the activist on the tripod. In this way, the fire truck, intended to dismantle the protest action, became part of the action. In a similar fashion, activists use logging roads to access old-growth forest that would otherwise be much harder to reach, turning timber company routes into stages for action. They also overturn and lock themselves to bulldozers and trucks that would otherwise be clearing trees. Trucks and bulldozers become part of the protest, remade by activists into tools of resistance rather than destruction. In these and other ways, forest protests bring an alternate space of politics into being, if only temporarily.[98]

STRATEGIES OF INTIMACY AND OPPOSITION

In the process of becoming activists with other-than-human species and risking injury on their behalf, activists engage in a number of practices of intimacy and opposition that complicate their commitments. They construct oppositions between the environmentally destructive practices of civilization and the redemptive promise of "the wild." By siding with the wild, activists emphasize *similarity* between themselves and other species and *differences* from other humans, such as loggers. Activists often dehumanize loggers and law enforcement since they are identified as being on the side of civilization against the wild. This has not always been the case in radical environmentalism, and some activists have worked hard to cross boundaries with loggers and police, but oppositional practice and rhetoric are more common. In the courtroom, many activists are not remorseful at sentencing hearings, but reiterate their dedication to "the wild" and visions of a future in which animals and plants take back the planet.

At the same time, activists often disregard the fact that they share with police officers the capacity for empathy. Just as activists identify with the suffering of trees and other animals, police officers and loggers must identify with activists' vulnerability and suffering for a protest to "work." Tree-sits and other actions take place *because* activists are counting on police and loggers to avoid injuring them. Activists assume their adversaries have empathy for other humans even if they do not for nonhumans.[99]

On the other hand, precisely because of the precariousness of activist bodies living in treetops or perched on tripods, activist protest rituals are sometimes dismissed as the antics of homeless "hippies" or "eco-terrorists" in the media and by local communities. This tends to further an oppositional divide that activists sometimes play into. Their crusading fervor is not lost on loggers whose jobs are at stake, often eliciting aggressive and angry responses in turn and hatred for the creatures activists are trying to protect, as in the bumper sticker "Shoot an Owl, Save a Logger."[100] For these reasons, protests vary in effectiveness at constructing new understandings of relationships between human and nonhuman bodies.

By disrupting the hierarchical classification of beings as they do during rituals of protest, activists create new oppositions and hierarchies as they open up some kinship boundaries and close others. Going into the forest becomes a rite of passage into a multispecies community in which activists separate from everything identified with civilization, the world outside the forest. Their experiences in the forest initiate them into a new community of kin they dedicate their lives to. Their new status is emblazoned on their bodies with tattoos or forest names. Rewilding themselves by disidentifying with dominant social values and aligning themselves with the lives of forest creatures, they seek to become like the wild. In doing so, they embody an identity that is the inverse of what most young American adults are expected to become. Every time they go into a forest, they are remade as activists. In these ways, tree-sits and action camps have functioned as powerful sites of transformation for many activists, but they are only one of many paths to activism. Young activists in the 1990s also became activists in a very different context: the urban hardcore punk rock scene. In a similar fashion but in a very different context, bands and fans disidentified with broader cultural norms and identified with the suffering of other species and the degradation of the environment.

CHAPTER 5

"Liberation's Crusade Has Begun"

Hare Krishna Hardcore Youth and Animal Rights Activism

Meat eating flesh eating think about it
so callous to this crime we commit
always stuffing our face with no sympathy
what a selfish, hardened society so
No More
—Youth of Today

satanic ritual: set the corpse upon the table. cosmetic religion:
hide your horns if you are able. killer of the animal. only a
demon could dine on the flesh of the dead. each hair on the
back of each cow is a birth you'll spend in hell.

—108

On a dark and foggy night in 1997, after a long drive down a deserted road forty-five miles north of Seattle, nineteen-year-old Peter Young and his companion hid their car. Dressed entirely in black with socks over their shoes, they approached sheds housing "thousands of mink on death row." As they entered the cages, Young realized "we were laying our eyes on those animals for whom we had stood outside fur stores with signs, slipped fliers into coat pockets in department stores, and hung slogan-embossed banners from rooftops. Thousands of mink, four to a cage . . . Their eyes spoke of helplessness, fear and betrayal." In the two months after that night, Young visited over thirty fur farms, confronted "8-foot tall mountains of mink carcasses" and "animals separated from a chance of life by only a latch on a cage . . . In time we would no longer just look those animals in the eye only then to turn away."[1] In October 1997, a rash of mink releases took place across the Midwestern United States as part of Operation Bite Back, a campaign spearheaded by the Animal Liberation Front (ALF). Operation Bite Back had several phases, beginning in the early 1990s. In one two-week period in 1997, activists cut fences, opened cages, released mink and other fur farm animals, and destroyed breeding records from six farms.[2] In 2005 Peter Young was arrested after seven years of being wanted by the FBI for his role in these actions and was sentenced to two years in federal prison for "Animal Enterprise Terrorism."

Like radical environmentalists fighting for the wild, radical animal rights activists see themselves as "freedom fighters" at the forefront of a revolutionary movement. For law enforcement agencies, fur farmers, medical research organizations, and so on, animal rights activists are dangerous and amoral. However, on animal rights and radical environmentalist websites, at protest marches and gatherings, imprisoned activists' numerous supporters praised them as martyrs, warriors, and heroes. At his sentencing in 2005 for freeing mink from a mink farm, Peter Young was unrepentant:

> This is the customary time when the defendant expresses regret for the crimes they committed, so let me do that because I am not without my regrets. I am here today to be sentenced for my participation in releasing mink from six fur farms. I regret it was only six. I'm also here today to be sentenced for my participation in the freeing of 8000 mink from those farms. I regret it was only 8000. It is my understanding of those six farms, only two of them have since shut down. More than anything, I regret my restraint, because whatever damage we did to those businesses, if those farms were left standing, and if one animal was left behind, then it wasn't enough.

Like most other activists who are unapologetic for committing acts they believe are morally defensible, Young reverses the accusations against him by casting fur farmers as the real criminals:

> I don't wish to validate this proceeding by begging for mercy or appealing to the conscience of the court, because I know if this system had a conscience I would not be here, and in my place would be the butchers, vivisectors, and fur farmers of the world. Just as I remain unbowed before this court—who would see me imprisoned for an act of conscience—I will also deny the fur farmers in the room the pleasure of seeing me bow down before them. To the people here whose sheds I may have visited in 1997. Let me tell you directly for the first time, it was a pleasure to raid your farms, and to free those animals you held captive. It is to those animals I answer to, not you or this

court. I will forever mark those nights on your property as the most reward-
ing experience of my life . . . Let me thank everyone in the courtroom who
came to support me today. It is my last wish before prison that each of you
drive to a nearby fur farm tonight, tear down its fence and open every cage.
That's all.[3]

In a similar fashion to forest activists, animal rights activists identify
with nonhuman species and distance themselves from those who do not
recognize the rights of the other-than-human world. Animal rights
activists, too, become activists by undergoing a rite of passage away
from a society they reject. They become committed to a community that
defines itself by its difference. For a number of activists in the 1990s,
this rite of passage took place through the hardcore punk rock music
scene. The music and their peers in the scene, as well as other factors
like childhood experiences, moved these activists to identify with nonhuman animals and disidentify with more broadly accepted norms of
treating other species. Like forest activists, their transformation came
about in a space removed from everyday life, in a subculture that gave
them different values and ways of being in the world. They too experienced the pain and suffering of nonhuman beings as their own.

How do animal rights activists like Young get to the point where they
no longer turn away from the pain and suffering of other animals? The
majority of animal rights activists sentenced in the United States during
the late 1990s and early 2000s were self-described atheists. However, in
many cases their passionate and deeply held beliefs about the inviolability
of nonhuman life informed their actions. The majority of animal activists
who served or were serving prison sentences in the late twentieth and
early twenty-first century were involved with hardcore punk rock music.

In this musical subculture, a number of prominent bands advocated
for animal rights and supported vegan or vegetarian lifestyles. This subculture, and especially a movement within it called straightedge, was
directly responsible for nurturing activist tendencies among some of its
young participants. These bands and fans promoted the view that other
species' lives are sacred and merit protection. It was because of the
beliefs nurtured in this subcultural setting that many activists rejected
dominant American values and decided to act "for the animals." Many
of the themes that emerged in hardcore punk rock and straightedge
scenes played a significant role in shaping radical activist cultures in the
late 1990s and early 2000s. In addition to animal rights, punk culture's
DIY (Do-It-Yourself) mindset encouraged many anarchists to get
involved in autonomous self-sufficient communities, creating what

anthropologist David Graeber describes as urban "anarchist landscapes" of communal households, coffee shops, infoshops, and community gardens.[4]

Hardcore/straightedge culture, often accompanied by anarchist leanings, worked on activists to generate an internal revolution that resulted in commitment to animal liberation. This internal conversion experience often mirrored their outward rebellion and took a variety of forms. For Peter Young, it came about through emotions elicited by the intensity of hardcore music and lyrics about the suffering of nonhuman animals. In the lives of other radical animal rights activists, internal changes brought about by watching documentaries about seal hunts or fur farms worked in tandem with their experiences in hardcore to bring about a radical transformation. For some activists, aural experiences in hardcore scenes affirmed at a visceral level their desire for a world devoid of animal suffering.[5] Being in straightedge cultural spaces, like being in forest action camps, brought about a similar kind of transformation in which activists set themselves apart from other Americans and expanded their circle of kinship to include other species.

THE NEW WATERSHED OF HUMAN–NONHUMAN ANIMAL RELATIONSHIPS

Operation Bite Back activists like Young represent the radical wing of a much broader cultural shift in understanding the proper relationship between humans and other animal species at the beginning of the twenty-first century. The ALF, which has garnered the majority of media attention for acts of sabotage and animal releases, attracted new adherents in the United States as a change in attitudes about nonhuman animals was gaining momentum during the 1980s and 1990s.[6] Emerging commitments to animal rights in youth subcultures were also influenced by Hinduism and other religious views about the sacredness of life. These developments coincided with broader cultural changes in the West, especially in the United States, concerning the place of nonhuman animals in society and humans' responsibilities towards other species.[7] As I argue in Chapter 2, this trend converges with and is influenced by other cultural shifts that have occurred since the 1960s.

Growing awareness of the conditions of nonhuman animals' lives and concern for their welfare has come about in part because of research into animal emotions in the field of cognitive ethology, among other factors.[8] New ways of "anthropomorphizing" are exemplified by a number of cultural trends in the late twentieth and early twenty-first centuries: the growing animal rights movement; increasing facilities for pet memorials; the National Geographic channel's "Crittercam," which supposedly shows the world through animals' eyes; and the language of companion animals and dog culture.[9] A good example of shifting cultural attitudes towards activism on behalf of animals is the *Whale Wars* television series featuring Sea Shepherd, a prominent animal rights group, which premiered in 2008 on the cable network Animal Planet. Books like *The Emotional Lives of Animals* (2007) and *Hope for Animals and Their World* (2009) by animal behaviorists Marc Bekoff and Jane Goodall respectively, who were once criticized by their colleagues for "anthropomorphizing" their data, are enjoying renewed and widespread interest.[10]

Animal rights activists have also aggressively promoted changes in thinking about and acting towards nonhuman animals by renegotiating the taken-for-granted boundary between human and nonhuman animals. Sociologist Elizabeth Cherry argues that animal rights activists use strategies like "universalization" to shift the symbolic boundary between human and nonhuman animal so that the boundary becomes blurred and problematized by campaigns such as "Meat is murder." Slaughtering animals for food is generally not considered "murder" by most Americans. But activists call into question this assumption because they believe other animals have the same moral status as humans. In a way, this is a different strategy from approaching nonhuman animals as other nations, unlike us. Nonhuman animals are like us in in contexts where their moral status is important.

A "SYMBIOTIC RELATIONSHIP": RADICAL ANIMAL
LIBERATION AND AMERICAN HARDCORE

Within this context of new understandings of the relationship between humans and other animals at the end of the twentieth century, the ALF attracted young American hardcore music fans committed to animal liberation. Walter Bond, an ALF activist, was sentenced to a total of twelve years and four months in 2011 for arsons at the Sheepskin Factory in Denver, Colorado; the Tandy Leather Factory in Salt Lake City, Utah; and the Tiburon Restaurant in Sandy, Utah, which sold foie gras. Bond sees the relationship between hardcore and animal rights this way: "the A.L.F. and Vegan Edge [a form of hardcore] have always had a very symbiotic relationship. . . .Throughout the 90s, Hardline bands like Vegan Reich, Raid and Green Rage got the youth focused like a laser beam on radical and fanatical Animal Liberation activism by blending the best elements of the struggles for Earth, Animals, antiracism and anticapitalism with the seriousness and purity ethic of the fundamentalist."[11] This "symbiotic relationship" has its roots in the late 1980s and early 1990s when the Animal Liberation Movement arrived in the United States from England and hardcore fans in Washington, DC, and New York became straightedge vegetarians and vegans.

Hardcore, a faster, more intense version of punk, began in the 1980s on the East Coast and in Southern California. According to hardcore promoter Steven Blush, the movement was "something alienated kids created . . . born of a doomed ideal of middle-class utopia . . . Punk juiced their nihilism."[12] Paul Rachman's 2006 film *American Hardcore: The History of American Punk Rock 1980–1986* frames the first wave of hardcore in the 1980s in the context of rebellion against the Reagan years. For Rachman, hardcore was young Americans' reaction to social and political conservatism. Hardcore bands, largely composed of young adults, many of them still in high school, tended to ignore the mainstream music industry. They were not looking for radio play or lucrative record contracts. Like the ALF, this music scene was underground, grassroots, anarchist, and very much focused on DIY.

Numerous hardcore bands maintained the political edge, apocalyptic tones, and fiercely independent spirit of original punk bands like the Sex Pistols and the Clash, but focused their message on protesting cruelty to nonhuman animals.[13] Although some hardcore bands were simply rebelling against what they saw as lies about the American dream offered them in the Reagan years, others had more specific political platforms, especially anarchism.

The straightedge movement within hardcore emerged among young fans in music clubs from Washington, DC to Seattle in this context of antagonistic political commitment. In the early 1980s, straightedge became what Ibrahim Abraham calls "a subculture's subculture" in the East Coast hardcore/punk scene. Washington, DC, band Minor Threat's 1981 song "Straight Edge" promoted a drug-free lifestyle: "I've got better things to do/ Than sit around and fuck my head/ Hang out with the living dead/ Snort white shit up my nose/ Pass out at the shows.[14] The animal rights message intensified as many straightedgers became involved in social or political activism with Greenpeace, Amnesty International, and more clandestine groups like the ALF.[15]

Straightedge advocated vegetarianism or veganism and discouraged drug use, drinking, and promiscuous sex. Ray Cappo, who founded the bands Shelter and Youth of Today, remembers that "the straight edge scene gave me a society of like-minded individuals who appreciated punk energy, but didn't want to end up in the gutter."[16] In its rejection not only of alcohol and drugs but also of a corporate-driven meat industry, straightedge encouraged a lifestyle consistent with animal rights.

In straightedge, political views of capitalism and the animal industry overlapped with commitments to not drink, take drugs, or eat meat. Straightedgers contrasted their values and lifestyle not only to the broader society but also to other punk rock/hardcore youth. Straightedge tended to attract teenagers who did not fit into their high school's social milieu *or* heavy partying punk rock scenes. One musician for a hardcore band that played on a benefit compilation for imprisoned activist Peter Young in 2007 recalls why he was attracted to the straightedge scene: "I got involved with the punk and straight edge scene at age 13 . . . I had a keen awareness of how fucked up I was and knew, at an early age, that if I allowed myself to enter into the whole drinking/drug scene that it would be a pretty ugly thing."[17]

In some cities, such as Washington, DC, straightedge teenagers helped to move the punk/hardcore scene out of clubs and bars that sold alcohol and into other kinds of spaces, such as rented out VFW (Veterans of Foreign Wars) posts, as an alternative to bars and other venues rife with substance abuse.[18] In a letter to the zine *Maximum Rock'nRoll*, one straightedger criticizes nonstraightedge punks: "You pump your money into corporations that kill people, pollute the earth, do animal testing, make sexist ads, ruin families, cause drunk driving, alcoholism, and are responsible for child abuse, rape, and murder because people were under the influence, etc. How can you be all politically correct without being straight? It doesn't make sense."[19] From this perspective, straightedge offered and expressed a critique of punk, claiming to be *more* consistent with punk's anticapitalist, anarchist ideals.

The direct action wing of the animal rights movement provided an opportunity for some young straightedgers to act on their beliefs. At the same time, activists helped shape the straightedge scene as it spread across the United States in the 1990s. Teenagers who were attracted to the music learned about straightedge lifestyles and animal rights from friends in the scene or their favorite bands' lyrics. SHAC (Stop Huntington Animal Cruelty) activist Josh Harper discovered the straightedge band Minor Threat when he was fourteen and a friend gave him a copy of a Minor Threat record. Harper recalls, "When

I heard the lyrics on that album I felt like they were written just for me. I called myself straightedge for the next seven years."[20] Many hardcore bands active in the straightedge scene wrote protest songs including pleas for animal liberation. Peter Young credits the straightedge band Earth Crisis with

> raising my awareness and evolving my consciousness towards empathy for the plight of nonhuman animals. . . . Earth Crisis was a band that played abrasive Hardcore music and preached a militant animal liberation message, with lines such as 'Liberation's crusade has begun, your laws will have no meaning past the setting of the sun.' Their influence brought me to an understanding that this issue was much more urgent than I had allowed myself to admit.[21]

Here Young refers to a line from an Earth Crisis song, "Wrath of Sanity." Other Earth Crisis songs, such as "Ultramilitance" (1998) and "Biomachines" (from the 2000 album *Slither*) praised direct action and condemned vivisection.

Bands like Earth Crisis blended deep ecological beliefs with anarchism to criticize corporations and politicians for exploiting the environment and nonhuman animals. In 2009 Earth Crisis made a public service announcement for PETA (People for the Ethical Treatment of Animals) with a quote from singer Karl Buechner: "Veganism is the essence of compassion and peaceful living. Animals are living creatures who have the right to live in peace."[22] Many Earth Crisis songs describe the abuse of animals and the destruction of the environment. In "Biomachines," the band takes on vivisection: "Horrific cruelty inflicted, demons in white coats leer down at their prey. . . Helpless beings brutalized by madmen, trained to deny that they're even alive . . . Behold the dawn of the biomachines. Monstrosities brought into being. Behind the walls of laboratories, crimes go unseen."[23] Earth Crisis made a point of not letting these hidden activities "go unseen," and many of the band's fans were inspired to take up the cause as well.

Perhaps more than any other band, Earth Crisis expresses an apocalyptic worldview prevalent among radical activists in which human beings are responsible for a hell on earth that is rapidly drawing to a disastrous culmination. In "Biomachines" and other songs about cultural decline, Earth Crisis is clear about where they think blame lies (scientific experimentation on nonhuman animals) and what the solution is (veganism). In this way, bands like Earth Crisis politicized hardcore and advocated different moral guidelines for their listeners, guidelines that sometimes came into conflict with American laws.

Many straightedge bands' song lyrics included prescriptions for change as well as critiques of speciesism, and urged their listeners to act. Tears of Gaia, a straightedge band that listed animal rights prisoners on its MySpace page, describes its mission as follows:

As activists our greatest influences are the injustices that we have experienced first hand by the shadow of oppression. We have seen the deforestation and the vanishing of the Earth's natural habitats, we have seen living sentient beings caged, confined, cut, slaughtered, poisoned, burned, and we have also seen that any resistance to these atrocities are met with extreme repression. We all live to fight another day but we must never forget our comrades who have been captured or killed by this system that seems bent on devouring everything beautiful in this world leaving only the crude stench of its rotting carcass to lay testament.[24]

Tears of Gaia links their concerns about animals to environmental issues such as deforestation, locating themselves on the side of the wild and the animals, against the "system."

At the same time that this political emphasis in hardcore was taking shape, some bands expressed a spiritual message that promoted respect for all life forms and advocated action. According to Peter Young, it was not simply the hardcore/straightedge music scene, but particularly Krishna Conscious hardcore, or "Krishnacore," bands advocating vegetarianism, that influenced his commitment to animal rights.[25] By imbuing hardcore music with ancient spiritual teachings, Krishnacore offered straightedge youth a religious framework for their animal rights commitments. These bands placed animal rights in the context of a spiritual struggle and promoted specific ideas about humans' moral duty to the nonhuman world.

The International Society for Krishna Consciousness (ISKCON) is a new religious movement founded by Bhaktivedanta Swami Prabupada (1896–1977) in 1965 and based on Hindu traditions of his native India. It continues to be practiced in temples and households from India to California.[26] For the most part, it was hardcore band members, not activists, who became devotees and frequented temples. Most band members did not participate in illegal actions even if they sang about them. Activists inspired to vandalize animal testing laboratories or free mink from mink farm cages were carrying out the messages of their favorite band's lyrics and adopting their moral guidelines, if not their religious identification.

Krishnacore and other religious forms of punk rock preaching social change might seem to contradict punk's history, which since its origins in the 1970s has had a reputation for being antireligious and anarchistic.[27]

After all, the foundational British punk band the Sex Pistols' 1976 song "Anarchy in the U.K." insists, "I am an antichrist/I am an anarchist."[28] But punk rock has not been simply an apolitical free-for-all; many punk bands have taken political and moral stances.

In his study of punk philosophy, Craig O'Hara argues that punk has been mischaracterized as mindlessly violent and that punk rebellion is not an end in itself but often "turns into a force for education and personal change."[29] This transformational aspect of punk is the strand that most influenced straightedge or vegan hardcore. According to O'Hara, "Vegetarianism and animal rights are two subjects which were first popularized by the European punk community. English bands . . . often included in their records information and images on the horrors of animal use and abuse. Politically minded punks have viewed our treatment of animals as another of the many existing forms of oppression."[30] But it was not only politics that provided a larger context for the music. Almost from the beginnings of punk rock, there were those musicians and fans who did not divorce their music from their spiritual practice, even though they were a minority. Over time these spiritual leanings also contributed to awareness of animal rights issues.

Even during the early years of punk in the 1970s, some punk rock musicians were becoming interested in Hinduism. For instance, Poly Styrene of the English band X-Ray Spex joined ISKCON after a "mystical breakdown/vision in 1978.[31] But it was not until the advent of American hardcore in the late 1980s and 1990s that Krishna Consciousness became a significant influence on a number of American hardcore bands.[32] Over time, the hardcore scene became more diverse and incorporated other kinds of religious influences, such as Islam. But Krishna Consciousness continued to have a significant impact on hardcore, both in the United States and internationally, through the beginning of the twenty-first century.[33]

For some hardcore bands and straightedge youth, religious affiliation became another way to embrace oppositional identities and critique other hardcore punk bands and fans. One of the first hardcore band members to adopt Krishna Consciousness and make the rejection of other punks' lifestyles explicit was John Joseph of the band Cro-Mags. Joseph was first exposed to Krishna Consciousness in New York City during the 1980s.[34] The Cro-Mags album *Age of Quarrel*, released in 1986, included the song "Do Unto Others," in which the band specifically addresses nonhuman animal suffering:

See these wars they're happening
And then you're asking why
But just stop by some slaughterhouse
And hear the animals cry
You missed the point it's over your head
I guess you'd rather be negative instead.

By telling audiences to get "the point," the Cro-Mags take a swipe at hardcore punk rock's reputation for being nihilistic. Musicians like Joseph discovered in Krishna Consciousness what they believed was a deeper calling.

In his memoir, *The Evolution of a Cro-Magnon*, Joseph describes his encounter with Krishna Consciousness in the 1980s. He started shopping at a Krishna Conscious health food store on the Lower East Side of Manhattan, attended yoga classes where he met devotees, and eventually became involved with an ISKCON temple.[35] As his religious commitments grew and shaped the band's message, Joseph realized, "That's the gift the Cro-Mags had to offer the world . . . an alternative, an answer, and the only reason we had that was because of Srila Prabhupada and the message of the Vedas. If we didn't we were just like every other knucklehead band singing about chicks, drugs, or how tough we are."[36] Like other Krishnacore musicians, Joseph saw spirituality-infused hardcore as going beyond what secular hardcore could attain, by creating a positive and more spiritually meaningful world.

Krishnacore offered another way for straightedge punk rockers to reject the status quo and claim alternative identities. Norman Brannon, who played briefly with Shelter, observes that "the Hare Krishnas, who took aim at historically atheistic punk precepts, muscled their way into the scene—and perhaps more stunningly, actually went on to cultivate hundreds of followers. I latched on to that trend, most likely because a kid with a Kinko's card hadn't invented it."[37] Sociologist Ross Haenfler describes the impact Shelter had on him when he was a straightedge teenager: "These guys were so cool. Not only did they not drink, use drugs, eat meat, or have sex, they 'adopted' a religion many people considered to be a cult. It was like they were giving the entire 'normal' world the middle finger and laughing all the way to enlightenment."[38] According to Ray Cappo (Raghunath das), one of the earliest influential Krishnacore musicians, both through his band Shelter (formed with John Porcell in 1991) and the record label Equal Vision that he started for devotee music, "the only way to go beyond Straight Edge is to take Krishna Consciousness."[39]

The ascetic ethic straightedgers lived by was "fertile ground" for the Krishna Consciousness movement, according to religious studies scholar James Wilson.[40] In addition to the daily practice of mantra meditation, initiated ISKCON members take four vows: no meat, fish, or eggs; no illicit sex; no intoxicants (including cigarettes, alcohol, and illegal drugs); and no gambling.[41] Journalist Erik Davis summarizes the ways in which these punk proselytizers brought together music and spiritual practice with a political edge: "Singer Ray Cappo is a *brahmana* (priest) and guitarist Porcell is a *brahmachariya* (renuncient student) who live in a Krishna temple housed in a former synagogue in downtown Brooklyn. *Mantra*, their latest album . . . includes vegetarian battle cries, attacks on sex and TV, and homages to self-realization and the Bhagavat-Gita."[42] Because Krishna Consciousness melded physical and spiritual purity, it was particularly attractive to those already living a straightedge lifestyle.

Since most straightedge youth were disillusioned with religious traditions like Christianity, Krishna Consciousness offered a spiritual practice more consistent with their values and life experiences. Vic DiCara, of the band 108, chose Krishna Consciousness as an alternative to other religious options. He read an interview with the Cro-Mags in *Thrasher* magazine and discovered that the band was involved with the "subversive" religion of Krishna Consciousness.[43] A friend gave him a book from a Cro-Mags show, and that book, one of the Upanishads, "blew my mind straight out of the back of my head. I sat up in bed night after night; tripping out on how amazing it was to be reading concrete, rational, logical explanations of spirituality. It was exactly what I couldn't find in the Bible."[44] Spiritual beliefs, then, like straightedge lifestyle choices, became ways for hardcore musicians to further embrace identities opposed to dominant social norms.

However, just as some punks were suspicious about religion, older ISKCON devotees were uneasy with tattooed punk youth showing up at their temples in the late 1980s and 1990s. Others saw an opportunity for religious outreach to a new generation. ISKCON's magazine, *Back to Godhead*, featured articles by writers who defended the new devotees. In "Bridging the Gap (Youth Outreach)," the anonymous author explains that punk musicians are serious devotees: "If the up-and-coming punk group Cro-Mags sounds like people you'd rather avoid, think again. The band's members, especially lead singer Harley, openly and strongly preach Krishna-conscious philosophy and behavior. . . . The famous Jadurani painting of Lord Nrsimhadeva killing Hiranyakasipu is on the cover of their latest LP, *Best Wishes* (with full credits to the Bhaktivedanta Book Trust)."[45] Other articles on Krishnacore published in *Back to Godhead* noted the Hindu content of album covers and the devotional commitment of young punk rockers.

Older members of the religion began to see young hardcore devotees as evidence of the spread of Krishna Consciousness among a new generation of youth. Ravindra Svarupa dasa, a member of ISKCON's Governing Board, enthusiastically described the impact of a Shelter concert he attended in Reading, Pennsylvania:

> By 9 P.M. the club is packed, maybe 500 kids crowding this industrial loft of 150 feet by 40 above an auto parts warehouse. . . . As I pause at the entrance to put in ear plugs, Ekendra dasa, Shelter's drummer, sees me and offers obeisances . . . In the area before the stage—the pit, it's called—a tight crush of kids carry on what looks like a contained riot, complete with occasional flying bodies. Here, in calmer mid-club, boys and girls crowd at round tables, most of them scarfing down huge helpings of Krsna prasadam on paper plates. . . . Everywhere I see the new Shelter T-shirt—on the front Ananta Sesa in full color torches the universe, while the back enjoins: "Self-Realization—Not Sense Gratification." A vision of these shirts filling the halls of American high schools gives me delight.[46]

During the show, Svarupa dasa begins to understand that he is witnessing a renaissance of Krishna Consciousness among 1990s youth that reminds him of its initial popularity with 1960s and 1970s youth: "Twenty-five years ago Krsna Consciousness first spread in America through a network of youth who were particularly open to its message—'hippies' to the outsiders, 'freaks' to the in. Now history's repeating itself, with variations. Here is another youthful social protest movement, originally called 'straightedge.'" For Svarupa dasa, the link between these two youth movements is clear; straightedge youth signal a new countercultural movement that promises to expand the reach of Krishna Consciousness.

Caught up in the excitement of the event, he joins Shelter onstage to lead *kirtan* (devotional chanting). Before he begins, the owner of the club hosting the show jumps up on stage and takes the microphone to tell the crowd he and his wife have decided to stop eating meat:

> We've been thinking about it, but finally something happened. I was driving behind a truck that was hauling baby pigs to the slaughterhouse in Lancaster. And the pigs were happy! I mean, their pink noses were all sticking out in a row through the slats, and they were just enjoying the air, and they were happy! They didn't know they were going to be slaughtered. They just thought they were going for a nice ride. And that was it! I made up my mind! No more meat![47]

As this scene suggests, Shelter and other Krishnacore bands helped to focus straightedge/hardcore youth not only on spiritual practice, but also on animal rights. In the space of a hardcore show, music and spirituality came together to bring about lifestyle changes in some participants, resulting in new attitudes towards nonhuman animals as well as straightedge youth.

The Shelter concert in Pennsylvania is one of many examples of the ways in which Krishnacore bands proselytized to crowds of young straightedge fans. These tended to be young men, who made up the majority of the hardcore population in the early 1990s. For instance, Vic DiCara's band Inside Out toured with Shelter on the "Traveling Circus Krishna Tour" during the summer of 1990. He recalls that "There were more Hare Krishnas on that tour than there were people in bands." The tour was fronted by a Greyhound bus converted into a temple on wheels, which DiCara recalls was "home to a stern looking 50 year old Swami and more than a half a dozen teenage boys and men with shaved heads and orange robes."[48] DiCara wrote an article for ISKCON's *Back to Godhead* magazine, describing the receptiveness of hardcore youth to ISKCON's message:

> As we traveled around the country, it became obvious that Krishna consciousness had become a major force in hardcore. Imagine four hundred teenagers, most wearing tulasi [beads] on their necks, paying like five or ten dollars apiece to come listen to a bunch of Hare Krishnas. It's a far cry from getting ignored on the street corner. Nor is it sheer numbers alone that's impressive. Have you ever been approached in a parking lot by five enthusiastic kids who spontaneously want to know how to offer their food to Lord Krishna and where they can get japa beads?[49]

The traveling temple was an interesting hybrid of missionary outreach and hardcore concert tour. It also marked the wider reach of vegetarianism and animal rights into hardcore scenes across the country and the beginning of a decade that would see animal rights activism grow among a generation of young adults.

The traveling temple and its ritual activities not only expressed the coming together of hardcore and Krishna Consciousness, but also created possibilities for their mutual influence in the lives of devotees. For Krishnacore band members, much of their spiritual practice came to be focused on trying to harmonize these two very different worlds. One of the ways to bring them together was to explicitly recognize what Krishna Consciousness brought to the straightedge scene. 108's song "Holy Name" (1994) explains succinctly why hardcore punk rock rebellion is not sufficient to change society or individual consciousness and why young punks are attracted to Krishna Consciousness and to the practice of chanting the name of Krishna:

This is the weapon of real revolution
This is the fire of the final rebellion
Politics, that ain't gonna solve this
Sociologist, your plan is useless

Without the heart being changed
You won't do nothing but re-arrange
The deranged situation
Of human exploitation
And that is why I imply.

This is the weapon of the real revolution
Unlock the coils
The clamped around your spiritual frame
By crying out the holyname

From this perspective, a change of heart is what is called for to create a real revolution. This kind of inner transformation facilitated by Krishna Consciousness pushed some youth to engage in animal liberation actions that expressed their heart change.

"BHAJANS FOR THE 90S"

Young ISKCON devotees in the 1970s were known for proselytizing in airports, but young devotees of the 1990s expressed their religious identities publicly through hardcore. They infused the hardcore scene, especially on the East Coast, with religious meaning and purpose. Krishnacore musicians like the members of 108 thought of themselves as "spiritual beings" playing music, not musicians simply inserting religion into their band. Their music became a key aspect of their devotional practice. From Cro-Mag John Joseph's perspective, the notion of playing music as spiritual expression originates in the Vedas: "Not everyone is meant to live in a temple. There's the kshatriyas who were meant to be warriors. I would chant and meditate before I went onstage, and get into this mystical-type warrior mentality."[50] Similarly John Porcell of Shelter sees his musical practice as "doing *bhajans* [Indian devotional songs] for the 90s . . . Onstage, I'm meditating on the lyrics. Five hundred years ago, when these traditional *bhajans* were written by the great *acharyas* [learned men], the mood was the same, except they used old drums and cymbals."[51] By expressing their spiritual commitments through music, musicians like Porcell situated themselves within an ancient tradition of beliefs and practices that could still speak to contemporary youth.

An important aspect of band members' spiritual orientation that influenced their young straightedge fans was a general commitment to the sacredness of life. Although vegetarianism and veganism were not a significant presence in straightedge at first and animal rights did not become a focus until the end of the 1980s, the movement's rejection of drugs or drinking made these next steps logical ones. Ross Haenfler credits Youth of Today's 1988 song "No More" for launching vegetarian straightedge:

> Meat eating flesh eating think about it
> so callous to this crime we commit
> always stuffing our face with no sympathy
> what a selfish, hardened society so
> No More
> just looking out for myself
> when the price paid is the life of something else,
> No More
> i won't participate.[52]

As the straightedge scene grew through the 1990s, many bands wrote songs deploring animal testing, factory farming, and meat eating in general, as in 108's song "Killer of the Soul" from the album *Threefold Misery* (1996):

> satanic ritual: set the corpse upon the table. cosmetic religion: hide your horns if you are able. killer of the animal. only a demon could dine on the flesh of the dead. each hair on the back of each cow is a birth you'll spend in hell. || the killer of the soul (whomever he may be) shall be forced to the darkest regions (embrace your decisions) in the darkest regions of hell. || self killing ritual: set the bottle upon the table. cosmetic ignorance: kill the pain if you are able. killer of the animal within; liquid poison to wash your brain. drown in your misery. your life becomes hell. || the killer of the soul (whomever he may be) shall be forced to the darkest regions (embrace your decisions) in the darkest regions of hell. || i won't kill my soul.

The song describes the haunting effects of karma and reincarnation due to meat eating, thus infusing the music with a specific ethical view about the consequences of one's lifestyle choices.

Krishnacore bands placed human and nonhuman animals in the same karmic wheel of *samsara* (the endless cycle of birth, death, and rebirth), subject to the laws of reincarnation in which actions and experiences in each lifetime affect and are affected by other lifetimes. Like forest activists who expanded the circle of kinship because of their experiences sharing emotions and bodies with other species, Krishnacore bands saw human and nonhuman animals as kin on the level of the soul. Killing them or causing them pain results in negative karma and rebirth in, as 108's lyrics for "Killer of the Soul" describe it, "the darkest region of hell."

Straightedge youth of the 1990s who were inspired by the lyrics and lifestyles of Krishnacore bands that urged animal liberation are the most recent activists to be influenced by Hindu beliefs. However, Hinduism has a history in the West of attracting disaffected youth and providing them with powerful tools to critique society and construct new visions of how the world should be. The influence of Hinduism, and especially Indian vegetarianism, on Western youth has been tied to radical political and animal rights activism for centuries.[53] Radical vegetarians who preached animal rights were active during the French Revolution and in seventeenth- and eighteenth-century revolutionary politics in Great Britain. In *The Bloodless Revolution: A Cultural History of Vegetarianism from 1600 to Modern Times*, historian Tristram Stuart argues that in the 1600s and 1700s, "the impact of Indian vegetarianism vitally influenced a shift away from the Bible's mandate of unlimited dominion."[54] One of Stuart's most colorful examples is John Oswald, a Scottish friend of Thomas Paine, who adopted Hindu beliefs after traveling in India in his early twenties and promoted "the philosophy of militant vegetarianism."[55] Oswald was active in the French Revolution and, like other revolutionary leaders of the time, united radical politics and animal rights.

Radical youth activism influenced by Hinduism played a part in the social and political protests of the late 1960s as well. Over half of the early Krishna Consciousness converts were anti–Vietnam War activists. Krishna conscious youth had their own political party and chanted at antiwar rallies during the late 1960s. However, a shift away from politics took place during the late 1960s and 1970s, resulting in many young devotees turning inward. They began to prioritize self-discovery and self-transformation over changing the world. In response, some of their contemporaries criticized Krishna Consciousness and other new religious movements for depoliticizing 1960s activists.[56] In the 1990s, the influence of Krishna Consciousness on hardcore subculture again gave spiritual meaning to political activism and attracted similar charges of depoliticization within hardcore's anarchist-tinged communities.

UTOPIAN SABOTEURS

While Krishna Consciousness provided spiritual motivation for hard-core youth's activism, it also situated animal issues in an apocalyptic narrative about impending doom. Activists' expectations of decline par-allel Krishna Consciousness millennial beliefs about the "Age of Quar-rel" or Kali Yuga. As sociologist Robert T. Wood suggests in his study of straightedge, Krishna Consciousness may have gained momentum in the 1990s in part because of the belief in the Kali Yuga, an evil age preceding the end of humanity: "The Kali Yuga concept may be highly appealing to some straightedge youth who perceive a world plagued with addic-tion, sense pleasure, and the murder of animals for human consump-tion."[57] Certainly many straightedge bands shared the sense that meat eating and abuse of animals were signs of an evil age that needed to come to an end.

The lyrics of Krishnacore bands provoked the hope and rage of young activists who came to see animal industries as symptomatic of the Kali Yuga, if they were Krishna Conscious, or the downfall of civi-lization, if they were not. Song lyrics describing animal suffering, like those of Earth Crisis's "Behind the Wire," fueled their urgency to act: "Imprisoned behind the wire, the doomed await their end./Tangled corpses fill the pits, starved, shot, or poisoned./To the horrors the world turns away from the suffering in apathy./A blind eye to the victim's pain that they choose not to see." For many fans who later became activists, hardcore lyrics may have been their first encounter with images of a slaughterhouse or lab animal that they could not get out of their head. These images triggered their anger towards societal disregard for the horrors of vivisection and the suffering of animals in factory farming.

Peter Young recalls that he thought about caged and slaughtered ani-mals every waking moment. This obsession gave him a kind of "death-wish" because he was impatient to act. He remembers, "What made the Hardcore scene so powerful and drove so many people to activism is that for a lot of people it gave the plight of animals a sense of urgency for the first time. That sense of urgency is the crucial element that sepa-rates passive vegetarian from militant vegan."[58] The emotional urgency of the music and the intensity of being in a crowd of fans and musicians also helped facilitate activist commitments. The straightedge/hardcore scene brought about or gave fuel to the commitment of activists like Young by providing a way of life and a course of action to channel their anger over humans' brutal treatment of other animals.

This course of action was furthered by the inscription of a moral vision on their bodies through straightedge lifestyle choices and practices of purification that marked their separation from society. Several activists explained to me that their lack of apathy and their clear-headedness in planning actions came about because of their straightedge lifestyle. As Josh Harper put it, "being sober allowed me to see the world for what it really was."[59] Inspired by Krishnacore bands, straightedge kids focused on change at the most basic level of the body. As personal transformation became the basis for acting in the world, changing society had to be grounded in transforming oneself. The band Strife's song "Force of Change" (1997) illustrates the notion of social change through personal lifestyle practices: "Resistance in a time of mass destruction/Makes the few who walk the straight edge/A growing force of change/Committed, though gripped by the plague of a nation/Consumed by its intoxication and confined by crippling greed/In my rage/I walk the path of true change/Commitment sworn in the name/of those who will walk the straight edge/convictions held to my grave."[60] Eschewing animal products became part of this mode of self-purification for many straightedgers and thus an important step towards revolutionizing society.

Spiritual and straightedge commitments were also inscribed on the body with tattoos. Tattoos like John Joseph's of Vishnu on his back and the omnipresent "Xs" represented devotion and inner purity brought about by avoiding intoxicants and meat. Krishna Conscious and straightedge musicians wore their beliefs on their bodies for fans to see and emulate. These visual reminders of spiritual commitment and a straightedge lifestyle helped create a music scene that embodied aspirations for a future free of animal suffering.

HETEROTOPIAS: SUBCULTURAL SPACES

Straightedge subcultures shaped by Krishna Conscious beliefs and bands that pushed for radical social change and animal rights constructed a space in which activist identities could be forged. They created a set of practices that allowed young adults to challenge the world around them and to transform themselves, if they chose to. Few hardcore youth were regularly attending ISKCON temples, but at shows, the aura of the temple helped infuse the hardcore scene with moral purpose. The prohibitions of straightedge, often strictly enforced through peer pressure, become a way to set one's own community apart from others and to establish guidelines for living a moral life. Subcultural spaces like straightedge exposed young adults to unfamiliar way of thinking about nonhuman animals—the inversion of how they were brought up to think of animals—and contested human dominion over other species.[61] Like radical environmentalists who entered the forest, found a sense of belonging in treetops and actions camps, and became activists in a multispecies community, so too were animal rights activists made in the urban hardcore/straightedge community.

For many hardcore youth, experiences living and acting in these spaces led to their conversion to activism in a kind of anti–rite of passage. Craig Rosebraugh describes himself as a patriotic high school student from a middle-class family who wanted to become a professional soccer player and a successful businessman. His "rebellious phase" began when he graduated from high school and moved out of his parents' house: "It started with skateboarding, an activity that led to my involvement with the rebellious subculture of punk rock music . . . Many of the people I met had taken to this subculture as a political act of rebellion against a society that did not appear to provide a just and inclusive future for them."[62] As young straightedgers moved away from their parents' homes, they often joined communities of other rebellious youth who were making different lifestyle choices than their high school peers, such as becoming vegan.

Darius Fullmer, one of the SHAC 7, who was sentenced to a year in prison for running an inflammatory anti–animal testing website and released in 2007, wrote me from prison, explaining that he had always been an "iconoclast":

> I was never interested in drinking, drugs, or smoking, and at a certain point stopped eating animals. I did, however, feel somewhat isolated in my lifestyle. . . . I came upon the hardcore scene quite by chance. A classmate who I did not know personally was silk-screening t-shirts for the hardcore band Shelter in our art class . . . In the hardcore scene, and particularly in the straightedge element of that scene, I found acceptance for what had been a lonely lifestyle. This was crucial as it allowed me the confidence to grow and begin to make my voice heard.[63]

For Fullmer, becoming an active participant in the straightedge community overcame his sense of being isolated. Realizing other youth shared his frustration with society helped further his commitment to activism.

For many of these young adults, conversion to straightedge and activism may include living in vegan households and attending music shows with like-minded friends who may also be participating in animal rights protests. At shows, it is common to find a table filled with literature on veganism and animal rights next to a table with the band's CDs and T-shirts.[64] In these ways, the subcultural space of straightedge with its vegan bands, political commentary on contemporary society, dumpster diving, and vegan food contributes to a sense of radical difference.

Straightedge/hardcore youth extended the reach of their urban scene to rural mink farms. Just as their bodies were wound up at hardcore shows, they were adrenalin fueled for night actions against fur farmers. Even property destruction, such as arson and graffiti, typical of many ALF actions, had parallels in punk rock and hardcore. As Craig O'Hara explains, "violence to property has been an active part of both the pacifist and non-pacifist Punks' activities."[65] In this and other ways, some participants in the hardcore scene took the fury and anger of the music and the intensity of the shows into illegal animal liberation actions.

THE "TIPPING POINT": CONVERSION STORIES

Within these aural spaces, activists' conversion came about when they reached a tipping point that made action mandatory. In an interview for *Total Destruction: straightedge fanzine against the ruling order*, Peter Young attests that "the music made the difference . . . the vegan straightedge scene is directly responsible for the course my life has taken. . . . All praise and credit is given to this movement for providing the spark that ignited an internal revolution in me many years ago. One from which I would never recover." In the same interview, Young recalled the moment that marked his commitment to animal liberation: "I was skating the streets of Seattle, listening to Raid [a vegan straightedge band], and something in me broke . . . The fate that would have awaited myself and the animals had I continued as an inactive vegan stood to be far more horrific than prison. Hardcore taught me urgency. It taught me anger, and it taught me to point fingers."[66] The internal revolution that was Young's conversion to activism came about from the convergence of bodily experience, song lyrics, and a community of like-minded young people he found in straightedge. In the process of listening to the music, the driving intensity of hardcore brought about his rite of passage into activism that had been a long time coming.

When they look back on the paths they took to animal rights, activists construct narratives that make sense of their actions within a worldview that values nonhuman life. Young was raised Christian in a suburban home but had a skeptical bent: "I have always been motivated primarily by logic and reason, and even at the age of 5 or 6 found myself picking apart and defeating most arguments for the existence of a god. I'm quite certain my belief in Santa Claus outlived my belief in the Bible."[67] He recalls moving away from the values of his suburban community when he was a teenager: "the catalyst that set all this off for me was the punk rock and hardcore scene."[68] Young's internal revolution began at a young age with doubting Christian doctrines and values. Like other activists, he remembers the most remarkable changes occurring during his teenage years, when he began questioning everything.

Radical activists' claim to a higher morality goes hand in hand with rejection of "truth" as it had been defined for them.[69] Dedication to their cause in the face of legal restrictions and the threat of prison time is a test of their sincerity. Moreover, activists regularly refer to each other as "warriors" or "freedom fighters" who adopt new worldviews and identities out of frustration with their previously held values.[70] From the point of conversion on, activists' inner transformations are expressed through outward actions.

For many activists, conversion is influenced by internal factors (inner histories), as well as subcultural spaces. In order to understand diverse commitments to animal rights, it is essential to examine the various ways in which these commitments take shape during childhood, adolescence, and college years. Young people experiment with and craft identities that may inform their attitudes towards nonhuman animals for the rest of their lives. The aural and moral worlds of youth subcultures like straightedge have played a significant role in setting these youth on their course towards radical animal rights and environmental activism. Youth subcultures from which animal rights activists emerge have complicated relationships to both religion and politics. Radical animal rights activists may be atheists and anarchists as they claim, but their radical commitments and utopian rhetoric have been shaped in a context of religious fervor about vegetarianism and beliefs about the sacredness of life.

American law enforcement and the news media are not the only ones who demonize or trivialize the commitments of young radical activists and disregard their moral values and utopian ideals. Movements like straightedge are often described by scholars as subcultures having little or no impact on the broader culture beyond shaping musical tastes and personal lifestyles.[71] One trend in youth culture studies is to point to the gap between affect and ideology and to criticize the "apathy" of subcul-

Animal Liberation Front activists with beagles. Photo: Stock photo from Alamy.

tural youth, such as punk rockers. As cultural historian Greil Marcus puts it in his analysis of punk rock and related movements, the "performing spaces" of punk rock are where "revolution goes to die . . . where the shout of what should be is absorbed into the spectacle of what is."[72] The influence of straightedge on animal liberationists in the 1990s suggests that rage-filled music and confrontational youth subcultures are not always accompanied by youth apathy.

However, animal rights activists are not monolithic as a group nor are Krishnacore youth as a subculture. In fact, their communities are characterized by many rifts and tensions. There are significant fractures within both hardcore and animal rights movements. Within the animal rights movement there are varying attitudes towards the straightedge punk scene and the militancy of activists nurtured by this scene. For this reason, both the animal rights and straightedge movements are much more diverse than they might at first appear.

One of the most significant tensions within the broader animal rights movement concerns radical activists and their tactics, such as arson, which is often condemned by more mainstream animal rights advocates. Arson and other acts of property destruction are sometimes blamed on the youthfulness and punk rock subcultural affiliation of ALF activists and other underground groups. Animal advocate and lawyer Lee Hall, for instance, disparages what she sees as the trendiness of "the latest countercultural niche in a world entirely apart from the banalities of home life: metal bands, tattoos and body-piercings, being locked together inside Neiman Marcus to protest fur . . . and being initiated into an activists' circle by going on night surveillance trips."[73] Hall goes on to compare animal rights extremism to the Ku Klux Klan and describes a demonstration in Oxford, England, in which activists carried a banner proclaiming "Vegetarians Against ALF." On the other hand, young punk activists have not always felt welcome among mainstream activists. Craig Rosebraugh felt "out of place—a punk rocker in a fairly conservative animal rights group."[74] Like many others, Rosebraugh supported the ALF because ALF tactics seemed conducive to making changes come about more quickly and thus ending animal suffering sooner.

Another point of conflict within radical animal rights and hardcore is the issue of abortion. Some of the most religiously committed members of these disproportionately young white male movements have been adamantly pro-life, not a position typically linked to punk rock or to animal rights organizations. This position may be shaped by the same Hindu worldview that endows nonhuman animals with souls and sacred value, or by other religious worldviews that have spread through hardcore. Committed Hindus are not the only ones challenging abortion rights. In 1990, Vegan Reich, led by singer Sean Muttaqi who had converted to Islam, released a seven-inch single accompanied by a "Hardline Manifesto" that argued for a radical commitment "rooted in one ethic (the sacredness of innocent life)."[75] Hardline created a rift within straightedge between those who took the sacredness of life to include unborn humans, and others who prioritized a woman's right to choose.

At the same time, Vegan Reich was accused of being antigay.[76] The Hardline movement within straightedge became controversial among straightedgers who were more accepting of reproductive choices and sexual orientation. But Hardline also supported the increasing emphasis within hardcore on animal rights. For Muttaqi, for instance, radical activism is always justified: "I am in complete support of all animal liberation activity, whether violent or not. This is not to say that I believe in indiscriminate acts of violence, aimed at the common person on the street . . . But against the institutions built on exploitation and the individual merchants of death."[77] The issue of abortion brings into sharper focus one of many rifts in communities and subcultures activists participate in. These spaces of opposition to broader social and cultural norms, then, function as sites of belonging as well as contested spaces of meaning around tactics, gender issues, inclusivity, and ethnic diversity, tensions I explore further in the next chapter.

CHAPTER 6

Circles of Community, Strategies of Inclusion

I don't understand how all of these white people can run into the forest making up and practicing their rituals when we can't even go into our sacred forest and practice our rituals!

—Sabitaj Mahal

Anarchists and revolutionaries . . . are faced with the same dilemma: whether to try to create an alternative culture of their own, or to concentrate on alliance work, supporting the struggles of those who suffer most under the existing system. . . . To put it crudely: they have to choose whether to focus on their own alienation or others' oppression.

—David Graeber, *Direct Action: An Ethnography*

As the summer rain poured down on our makeshift tarp and straw bale seats and flooded the workshop area, we tried to keep our feet and gear out of the rising water. Struggling to hear each other over the rain, participants delegated with planning chants for an upcoming antifracking protest argued about the wording of a particular chant. When we began to practice the chant, which included the phrase, "our land," one participant interrupted and argued that we should not claim the land as "ours" since it was stolen from Native Americans. This led to a debate about who could rightfully claim the land on which the protest would be held and how the wording might be changed to be less objectionable. Throughout this annual, weeklong gathering, an Earth First! Round River Rendezvous held at a campground in the Smoky Mountains of North Carolina, much attention was given to "anti-oppression work" and "indigenous solidarity." Those who wanted to spend more time focusing on trees, endangered species, and watersheds were in the minority. They did occasionally speak up to remind others that the gathering was called "Earth First!"

What does it mean to put the Earth first in a movement that increasingly links the devastation of the natural world and the treatment of nonhuman animals to other forms of abuse and oppression? In the first decades of the twenty-first century, radical activists in the United States struggle to be all things to all beings, human and other than human. They have been on the forefront of efforts across radical communities to be welcoming to all people, especially to people of color and those who are gender nonconforming. In so doing, they call into question boundaries between insiders and outsiders, crafting a movement that aims to be radically inclusive, but continually, in practice, leaves someone out. In this chapter I focus on how tensions around activist commitments and community ideals, especially on who is included and who is excluded, emerge and are worked on through ritualized activities at activist gatherings and action camps.

Activists' commitments to human and nonhuman worlds are expressed, challenged, negotiated, and constituted through spatial practices. It is through these often intense conflicts and negotiations that participants may become even more invested in activist communities and in the wild. At the same time, conflicts can put off some activists who decide not to return to gatherings and protests because they felt unwelcome. I want to look at the ways in which activist communities are constructed through spatial practices and boundary making, including the integration of critique into new ritualized actions.

WELCOME HOME

As we left the interstate, panoramic views of the mountains outside Asheville, North Carolina, soon gave way to mixed farmland and forest. Small farms and modest ranch houses were occasionally carved into the borders along forested land, but we had the feeling of leaving civilization behind. My three passengers had come to the mountains from cities and had never been to the area before. I picked up Redtail and Lode in Knoxville and Tree Frog in Asheville, in order to share my rental car and have some company on my journey to the Earth First! Rendezvous. Redtail and Lode were students at the University of Minnesota where Lode was involved with a campaign against an iron mine and Redtail was working on an art education degree. Tree Frog attended a small college in Oregon and was studying international environmental relations.

The sky grew dark and rain fell in torrents as we pulled off a small rural road onto an even smaller gravel one and continued driving a few more miles into the forest. We finally spotted the entrance to the gathering, staffed by cheery but soggy greeters who explained where to park and camp and gave us welcome packets that included an "anti-oppression policy" and a "consent policy." If there was a "Home" banner like the one at the previous year's Rendezvous, I did not see it, but I was immediately flooded with memories of being part of an intense temporary community at the earlier gatherings I had attended. At a gathering in a forested realm removed from society, activists work hard to create a world more in line with their ideals. While it did not feel exactly like home to me, the gathering as a utopian place apart from ordinary life still held out compelling possibilities for living in another way.

We drove deeper into the forest, leaving the greeters to welcome the next travelers and to watch for police and hostile neighbors, so they could warn others with the walkie-talkies they carried. We parked and sat in the car to wait out the pelting rain, breaking out our snack food to share and worrying about the weather. Little did we know how relentless the rain would be throughout the week, flooding all community areas and forcing some campers to head home early, including two of my traveling companions. They had only brought garbage bags and flimsy tents for protection. Finally the rain let up and Tree Frog and I found a spot to set up our tents on high ground above the creek that ran through the campground. Redtail and Lode slept in the car. Evening was falling and some neighbors across the campground road began playing banjo and guitar. I knew dinner would soon be served in the community kitchen, so I pulled out the bags of rice and potatoes I had brought to donate and headed to the center of camp.

At the kitchen, campers were chatting in small groups, greeting old friends with hearty hugs, or sitting alone to carve a piece of wood, sew a patch on a jacket, or play music. Kitchen helpers were busy setting out the food made of dumpstered and donated ingredients. Dinner that night consisted of a stew with potatoes, lentils, broccoli, and cauliflower, served over rice with a topping of onions, apples, and squash cooked in butter and accompanied by a chopped salad of lettuce, cabbage, and carrots. We were all hungry and grateful for the hot food and company. I sat down on an old railroad tie under the rain tarp that covered our dining area and struck up a conversation about the weather with those sitting next to me. After dinner another downpour began, so I hurried back to my campsite and gratefully crawled into my water-proof tent where I read by flashlight while listening to the rain and worrying about the rising creek nearby.

I woke to the sounds of a tuba, as Kindling, an activist from New York City I had met at a previous Rendezvous, walked through the muddy campground in rubber boots playing taps on his tuba and shouting "Wake up campers, so we can smash capitalism!" After a quick breakfast of sourdough pancakes with fruit compote and potatoes sautéed in garlic and herbs, Morning Circle was called. Morning Circle is the most important time for making announcements, working out grievances, sharing information, and learning about what workshops will be held that day.

This Morning Circle began with an apology. Local organizers had neglected to include in the welcome packet any information about the indigenous people who originally lived in the land we were on. The participants who were upset saw this omission as the perpetuation of a colonial mindset that ignored the tragic history of Native Americans. One activist had googled information on her laptop the day before and read to the assembled circle about the Cherokee people who once lived in what was now designated the Pisgah National Forest. The organizers promised to put right their mistake by printing a new set of welcome packets including information on local indigenous cultures and their history. Discussion followed about the need for activists to work towards "decolonization," and everyone was encouraged to attend workshops on indigenous solidarity.

After this discussion and its temporary resolution, the business of Morning Circle continued. Campers offering workshops that day gave brief descriptions of what they were planning. Organizers provided information about the medic tent and latrines ("shitters" to gathering participants), so newcomers would be oriented to essential safety information. The medic team issued warnings about ticks, copperhead snakes, and poison ivy. Expert climbers from the Earth First! Climbers Guild announced climbing trainings for all levels, as well as trainings specifically for women and transgender campers. Everyone was asked to volunteer for meal preparation, dishwashing, digging and maintaining the latrines, working at the medic tent or on twenty-four-hour security, and staffing the front gate. After over an hour, Morning Circle disbanded and we headed off to our workshops, trainings, and volunteer shifts.

Anyone new to the Rendezvous will leave Morning Circle with the impression that this temporary community reflects the ideals of radical activism, in which everyone participates in all aspects of a self-policing, inclusive anarchist community. Campers are encouraged to take full responsibility for being in the activist tribe by examining their own assumptions about gender and race and avoiding oppressive behavior. The organizers' intention is also for participants to take new skills and knowledge back to their home communities and relationships, thus spreading social change.

For many activists, cultural spaces like the Rendezvous offer values and practices that are the inverse of most American social institutions and political bodies. There are no apparent hierarchies or leaders and few rules, decisions are made by consensus, gender identity and sexual orientation are fluid, and status is conferred on those who have skills, knowledge, and experience, not money or material goods. Activists practice what anthropologist David Graeber calls "living utopianism . . . the idea that radical alternatives are possible and that one can begin to create them in the present."[1] For many activists, Earth First! Rendezvous and other similar gatherings, tree-sits, and other action camps are about bringing utopian ideals into the here and now. They aim to be the lived utopias of everyday activist communities.

Gatherings and action camps offer anarchist alternatives to social institutions and behavior outside activist communities. Such alternatives include self-policing, such as "call-outs" for abusive and oppressive behavior, as well as aspects of anarchist DIY (Do-It-Yourself) culture such as medical self-care and mental health self-care. Earth First!'s 2015 Rendezvous, for instance, included a "Mad Camp" for participants

> self-identifying as neurologically diverse folks within the Earth First! movement. Here we will share about our experiences with mental health, hardships and moments of clarity. We will brainstorm ways to support each other, while working to dismantle industrial civilization, overthrow capitalism, banish racism and smash patriarchy. Our intentions with creating a camp specifically for those of us challenged by mental health is to provide a sober space where folks can relax, host workshops and discussions specific to the camp, play games, and more![2]

In this and other ways, activist spaces aspire to be radically inclusive of participants who might not be welcomed in other kinds of social spaces, or in the case of Mad Camp, might be institutionalized.

Like the Rendezvous, action camps such as antiroad blockades create a sense of belonging to an alternative community that stands in contrast to the broader society. From the bumper stickers in the parking area to the names people introduce themselves with and the way they dress, activists challenge American norms. They celebrate difference and dissent in their appearance and names, as well as their consumer and political choices. Activists often use forest names instead of their legal names. These names provide anonymity and may be arbitrary, playful, or accompanied by stories about how they were acquired. They may reveal something about the nature of one's commitment to activism or affinity for a particular species. Names are one of numerous markers of belonging to an alternative community of radicals.

PRIMITIVE SKILLS AND THE PRIMAL PAST

To live in an action camp or a week-long gathering is to experience, for a time, another way of life. In 1986, Earth First! co-founder Dave Foreman told a reporter that "Earth First! is made up of people who are really trying to get back to their roots as a tribal civilization."[3] Being part of a "tribe" means not only creating models of what future communities might look like, but also invoking an ideal, preindustrial past that offers resources for contemporary environmental crises. The imagined past is communal, egalitarian, and characterized by living in harmony with other species. According to the anonymous author of the zine *Insurrectionary Ecology*, activists should actively work to "build a social culture that ranges from voluntary simplicity to 'radical hedonism' (do as you will but let it harm none, including the lives of other species) that is based on a natural wildness—a 'joie de vivre.' . . . It must include connecting people, and re-enchanting people . . . with the natural world."[4] Rewilding and reenchantment are twin tools for reclaiming a simpler past, a past that models possibilities for a different kind of future.

Environmentalist gatherings like the Earth First! Rendezvous and Wild Roots, Feral Futures look to lifestyles of the past as rich resources for the future, and in doing so link their interests to the larger "primitive skills" movement.[5] The 2013 Wild Roots, Feral Futures was advertised as an opportunity to "Visualize Vast Wilderness, Actualize Industrial Collapse." In preparation for civilization's collapse and in the interest of creating possibilities for a different future, Wild Roots, Feral Futures featured workshops on blacksmithing, salve making, felt making, and hide stretching, in this case with possum and badger road kill.

Rewilding and primitive skills belong to a broad movement of people who seek alternative ways of living in the postindustrial West. A site called Rewild.com explains that rewilders are dedicated to "creating new cultures inspired by ancestral lifeways." Most participants in the primitive skills movement hope to adapt ancient skills like metal working, hide tanning, hunting, and gathering wild foods to contemporary life. Their models vary from Paleolithic cave dwellers and Native Americans to medieval blacksmiths and basket makers. Their aim is to live with the smallest possible environmental footprint. Wild Roots participant Christina Wulf explains that sharing with other activists "individual epiphanies—some moment, imprinted on us, when the wonder of the wild became manifest," helped her to see that environmental activism is not so much revolutionary "as it is a reconnection. Tracing our human bloodlines back a brief genetic distance, a handful of centuries, we can re-learn how to live on this earth in balance with breathing forests and all their inhabitants."[6] For activists like Wulf, reconnecting to what they see as an ancestral past is the best way forward.

In these ways, activists invoke a past that is both genetic (Wulf's reference to "bloodlines") and cultural. When they refer to "tradition" and "ancestral ways," they emphasize *continuity* with an imagined primitive past. F. Fox, who participated in a campaign in Minnesota and Wisconsin called "Real Hunters Don't Kill Wolves," describes what "real tradition" means in contrast to the "tradition" that justifies killing wolves: "'White' Americans have lost their indigenous knowledge . . . all humans came from distinct Earth-based cultures that knew how to live in balance with the creatures around them. There were codes and ethics surrounding whom to kill, whom to eat."[7] Reclaiming tribal existence then, refers to both the human tribe or family and the larger family of kin, including the nonhuman world. Activists argue that returning to ancestral ways we have lost can create meaningful and sustainable futures. They believe these ways of being in the world will either bring about hoped-for change or provide models of how to live after the collapse of civilization.

Of course not all activists see everything about the past as ideal, even if they want to. As Minnow, one of the 2013 Rendezvous organizers wistfully put it, "I'm one of those people who thinks it would be nice to be part of an indigenous population that lived on land bases for thousands of years without destroying the land or themselves. At the same time I recognize that they had struggles and illnesses and mortality."[8] For this reason, many activists embrace the past cautiously, reminding each other that the challenges of the present require other resources as well. The organizers of the 2013 Rendezvous suggested to participants that "no amount of romanticization can return us to the distant past . . . There are no more frontiers, no more outside to escape to. There is no 'back to the land,' despite the remaining few wild places. The past should serve as a root, not as an anchor, to our analysis and our dreams. A home in your heart is a weapon in your hand, and our connection to this past and the land are both home and that weapon. May it serve us well."⁹ In this sense contemporary activists differentiate their agenda from earlier back-to-the-land movements; they do not necessarily expect "the wild" to redeem them. Activists, then, are ambivalent about the past they so often invoke: it promises possibilities for the future but has perilous limitations.

As sites of tribal community, gatherings and action camps work hard to create a sense of unity and at the same time accommodate participants from diverse backgrounds and identities. According to one participant who wrote a message on "Rewild Resist," Wild Roots, Feral Future's blog, "WRFF attracts a variety of people: college students, older hippies, drifters, radical faeries, liberals, anarchists, socialists, families with small children, musicians, train hoppers, activists, conservationists, farmers, and those who refuse to be categorized."

Yet ironically, gatherings are often characterized by an atmosphere of sameness and conformity some participants find off-putting. At first glance, a Rendezvous or action camp in the early 2000s is visibly different from the world outside. There is an activist "look" that is common, even if everyone does not embody it. Dreadlocks, asymmetrical hair or partially shaved heads, multiple piercings and tattoos, faded black and brown clothing, bags and packs with patches, comfortable and well-worn boots, shorts or utiliskirts with combat boots, bandannas, and necklaces made of objects on black or rawhide cord were common attire at the gatherings I attended. The style is ragged and irreverent, part punk rock, part vagabond wanderer. Of course not everyone stands out in this way: other gathering participants were dressed in jeans and flannel shirts or rock-climbing pants and sun hats.

During direct actions, dress is one marker that distinguishes between eco-warriors and their enemies, such as police officers in uniform. As the anarchist Free Association collective puts it in *Moments of Excess: Movements, Protests and Everyday Life*, their study of activism, "the way people look, talk, and hold their bodies can reflect a certain commonality and can help spread recognition of a shared antagonism."¹⁰ Dressing differently than a fashionable young American in the outside world marks participants with particular political and social identities, but can make those who do not conform feel excluded from the tribe.

Some participants in the Earth First! Rendezvous and Wild Roots, Feral Futures told me they felt uncomfortable at first until they got to know people at the gatherings. At her first Earth First! Rendezvous, Lakes felt a bit uncomfortable initially when she encountered what she thought of as a kind of "West Coast cliquishness." "There is a look," she noted, adding that it is less common in the Midwest where she was living to wear dreadlocks and patches when everyone is too busy working at "normal jobs." Lakes also found her Christian commitments to be at odds with other activists' religious views or lack thereof. A participant at Wild Roots, Feral Futures who was Christian "didn't share that with most of the people at Feral Futures for fear of their reactions."[11] For those who feel part of the crowd, group conformity is an embracing of what makes them ostracized outside activist spaces. For others, feeling included in these supposedly inclusive spaces is a challenge. What are the meanings, then, that activist communities give to concepts of "home" and "tribe" and who decides what the criteria for belonging are?

WAYFARING AND HOMECOMING

Understandings of home and tribe are dynamic in the lives of many young activists who have often rejected notions of home that characterized their upbringing. Free states are a prime example of how action camps and gatherings become the location of tribe and community for many participants. A free state rejects the ownership of land by private individuals or the government. At the 1998 Minnehaha Free State in Minneapolis a banner read: "To all who enter here, you are walking on holy ground."[12] The Minnehaha Free State was established by a coalition of groups, including Earth First! and the American Indian Movement, to protect four oak trees and a freshwater spring sacred to the Mendota Mdewakanton Dakota from a proposed road expansion. Activists called the protest area a "liberated zone." They created treesits, chained themselves to sleeping dragons, u-locked themselves to tripods, and moved into houses that were in the path of the highway. The Free State was also known as the Four Oaks Spiritual Encampment and included tipis, a sacred fire, and a sweatlodge.

The Free State had an explicitly spiritual identity, in part because of the presence of Native American activists who conducted sweatlodges and created sacred fires. Tlingit activist Elizabeth Marie Egan remembers the protest as "times of deep ecology" and "times of sacred ceremony." She claims "Spirit" became "the glue that held the Free State together."[13] Some activists lived in the Minnehaha Free State for the entire eighteen months, until police forced them out with pepper spray and other aggressive tactics.

Like other road blockades, free states reconfigure public space (and sometimes private property) by claiming it on behalf of both human and other-than-human constituencies. These sites become what theorist Hakim Bey calls temporary autonomous zones (TAZ) that make possible the anarchist practice of creating new communities and ties of interdependence "on the spot."[14] Ritualized protest actions and sacred spaces like sweatlodges and sacred fires create alternate meanings for woodlands destined to become roadways or floor boards. Participants in free states and other activist gatherings also become different kinds of citizens. Instead of identifying as residents of Minneapolis or citizens of the United States, activists insist on alternate ways of positioning themselves in relation to larger political bodies.

In the United States, "free states" were among the first attempts by activists to create communities lasting longer than a weekend. The *Earth First! Direct Action Manual"* explains that free states range from "small shanty towns of tents" to "quasi-sophisticated villages with living and cooking shelters and elaborate blockades." The goal of these camps is to ensure a continuous presence of activists to keep police officers or park service employees from destroying the blockades. A few years before Minnehaha, the Cascadia Free State in Oregon (1995–1996) became "a blockader's playground" in which activists experimented with a range of different techniques inspired by British and Australian antiroad movements. The blockade provided an elaborate "base camp" from which activists could launch a long-term campaign against "the Earth rapers."

> The heart of the blockade was the main tipi village guarded by a fort-like pole wall, complete with watch tower, cat walk, draw bridge and moat. There was a pole hut built further up on the road with several other livable structures. Scores of trenches were dug into the road and culverts were pulled and plugged to wash it out. A wooden bridge allowed people to pass over one of the biggest trenches (which was as big as a school bus). Rock and wood debris walls and artistic obstacles were built up and down the road as well.
>
> There were two tripods on the blockade, as well as one bipod. Several steel barrels were fitted around the forest service gate and filled with concrete . . . There were three sleeping dragons in the road, one covered by a steel fire door which had an arm-hole cut through it . . . A concrete crawl space with lockdown positions, known as 'the dog house' was built into a large rock and wood debris pile.[15]

Earth First! Elliott Forest Free State blockade. Photo: Margaret Killjoy. Licensed under
Creative Commons 2.0.

As a reporter for the *Eugene Weekly* put it, "The activists began to lose
their identities as Americans and pledge their allegiance to Cascadia—
their bioregion, home of the ancient pines and dizzying stars, wherein
all people could become wild again. They dubbed the blockade Cascadia Free State and themselves Cascadia Forest Defenders."[16] Techniques honed at Cascadia then spread to other forest campaigns in the
Western United States.

   Although some blockades last for years and others fall apart after a
few weeks, at a free state, "home" comes to mean being at home in the
woods as well as belonging to a community of like-minded people. Activist Jim Flynn, who participated in the Warner Creek blockade, remembers that activists there settled in to create a more permanent community:
"people went up to the woods and declared that Cascadia is our land,
and we're not going home, because *this is our home*."[17] Gambit described
a similar desire at the 2009 short-lived Elliott Free State to create "our
own pirate country out in the woods."[18] Free states create utopian spaces
for the future, experimenting with ways to unify their diverse communities and, at the same time, develop new tactics of obstruction.

   The sense of home and family that activists experience at free states
and other gatherings to some extent also reflects how they live outside

of the gathering or action camp. Activists range from those living largely itinerant lifestyles to those deeply rooted in a single community or eco-system. Marten, who attended Wild Roots, Feral Futures in 2015, observed that while a large number of traveling youth were present, many at the gathering "were also focused on community projects, such as intentional living communities, queer and ecologically minded farms/homesteads."[19] Gatherings and action camps may function as both ideal communities apart from *and* in continuity with daily life elsewhere when that life is also outside the norm. Activists bring with them skills and knowledge from their home communities and return to their home communities with new skills and knowledge gained in camp.

After graduating from college with a degree in philosophy, Lakes attended her first Earth First! Rendezvous in Montana. Her account suggests some of the ways in which activists at first experience belonging to a gathering community at a national event like the Rendezvous as a place apart from daily life and then later develop continuity between gatherings and their home communities. Lakes was quickly drawn into the Rendezvous, even though she felt a bit out of place at first, because she "hadn't heard people talking like that before." She had never experienced living biocentrically, using consensus, or sharing food and drink in a big communal kitchen. She attended an herbalism workshop and was thrilled with the new information she acquired. The beauty of the Rendezvous site in Montana's Lolo National Forest awed her when she went, "waltzing by the bonfire overlooking a beautiful vista." At the end of the Rendezvous she participated in her first action in Helena, Montana.

For the end-of-Rendezvous action, activists occupied the state capitol building in Helena. One of them reported, "During the occupation, we turned the capital rotunda into a 'No Coal Exports' camp with facilitated workshops, skill shares and, of course, choir practice." One of the occupiers played ragtime on piano while everyone else danced: "it was hilarious," remembers Lakes.[20] During the occupation, for a time, alternate ways of being, including skill sharing and singing in a government building, were put into practice. For Lakes, all of these experiences suggested new ways of being in the world that she could take home with her.

Lakes's commitment to more active involvement with environmental campaigns had solidified by the time she left the Rendezvous. She was already inclined towards a different kind of relationship to the nonhuman world as well as to other humans from a childhood spent in the outdoors with friends and family. Now she felt fully committed to activism as a *lifestyle* to be expressed locally as well as at actions away from home.

After the Rendezvous, she worked for the *Earth First! Journal*, helped with climbing training at the Tar Sands Blockade in Texas, became involved with the Michigan Coalition Against Tar Sands, and started an Earth First! chapter in Michigan to fight fracking. Over time her main priorities became wilderness advocacy, especially for roadless areas, and supporting the rights of indigenous people. At the time of our interview, she lived in a communal household that other activists travelled through and in which organizing for actions sometimes took place. The housemates also went dumpster diving and practiced preserving food. When I spoke with her on the phone, Lakes was in the process of tanning a roadkill deer hide. Although still involved with direct action, she is also rooted in place in Michigan where she grew up roaming outdoors and loving bodies of water, where Nordhouse Dune and Sleeping Bear Dune are her special places she visits for "spiritual cleansing." Like many other activists, her daily lifestyle involves both putting in place an anarchist community and strengthening bonds with particular landscapes.

In contrast, some young traveling activists who participate in gatherings and protests have adopted a lifestyle that is not rooted in particular places. Nomadic youth hitchhike and hop trains, busk and dumpster-dive to eat, own as little as possible, and live off the waste of consumer America. Even early Earth First!ers like co-founder Dave Foreman came from "rootless backgrounds," according to journalist Susan Zakin, and found "a tribe" with compatible activists.[21] Marten, an activist who attended Wild Roots, Feral Futures in 2015, estimated "over half of the people present traveled at least half the year; many spoke of the hardships of finding communities that were healthy and functional, and the struggle of finding housing and food while on the road." However, Marten also noted, "many people talked about the importance of nomadism in their lives. Freedom of movement and unrestricted travel seemed to be a goal for many people at Feral Futures."[22] Homeless youth drifted through Wild Roots, Feral Futures and Earth First! Rendezvous, climbed into the trees during the Redwood Wars, and joined the Warner Creek blockade. Some older activists at forest actions were dismayed at the influx of "homeless youth" with no skills or knowledge.[23] But many of them acquired skills along the way and took on important roles during actions.

Lily and Johnny were the young hitchhikers I stopped for on my way to Wild Roots, Feral Futures. Their only possessions were small, well-worn backpacks, a ten-gallon bucket of dog food for their dog Pearl, canned goods, and a ukulele and washboard for busking and jamming with friends. Johnny left home at sixteen and had been on the road for over seven years. He lived a vagabond existence, train-hopping across the country, teaching other kids how to hop trains, and picking up random work when he needed it. He visited his mother in New Mexico occasionally, but otherwise was mostly on the move. Lily had recently joined him after dropping out of the prestigious Chicago Art Institute.

Lily and Johnny are part of a network of feral youth, many of them homeless by choice, fed up with capitalism and the materialistic goals of their generation. Kaleb, once a wandering youth, describes his years as a traveler: "Being a traveling kid is a pretty feral existence . . . the whole time my goal also was to learn more about living as naturally as I could, without having to purchase food or clothing. It had a dramatic effect on my view of the world when I suddenly went out and every day had to find somewhere to sleep and food to eat."[24] Gatherings and action camps offer food and company for traveling youth, as well as workshops that provide them with an alternative education. Wilderness protection is not necessarily their central concern, at least not at first.

For settled activists like Lakes and travelers like Kaleb, "living naturally" has different meanings. Both try to reduce their environmental impact by dumpstering or processing roadkill and both model their lives on earlier cultures. Unlike Lakes, who usually had a paying job in her community, young travelers have the least possible involvement in consumer capitalist society. David Graeber observes that teenage and young adult travelers who are runaways or living lives of voluntary homelessness "set a kind of romantic standard for autonomous existence—dumpster-diving food, refusing paid employment—that represents one possible ideal for those wishing to establish an existence outside the logic of capitalism."[25] Because of their rootless existence, they are free to sit in trees and lock down in road blockades for indeterminate lengths of time. These feral youth represent the convergence of activist communities and anarchist youth itinerancy.

While some activists model their primitivist impulses on cultures that harbor deep knowledge of the places in which they dwell, others identify with a global activist community focused more intensely on fighting patterns of consumer capitalism.[26] In order to be globally involved as well as locally identified, activists travel to protest spaces around the world. These include climate camps in the United Kingdom and the years-long airport protest village La Paz in France.[27] Climate camps, road blockades, tree villages, and free states transform temporary gatherings into less temporary communities. Global flows of information, experiences, and skills are shared across these various gathering spaces through the movement of individuals, zines and other printed materials, and accounts published online.

Some activists have fluid lives distinctly different from others' rootedness in place, though they all tend to be connected through social networks. They may aspire to preindustrial lifestyles in some areas of their lives, but they remain active participants in networks of the larger environmental, animal rights, and antiglobalization movements. Many of them have online access even if they are homeless and use computers at a local library to check on activist campaigns in France or Australia. Lily, one of the traveling youth I met on the way to Wild Roots, Feral Futures, had a tablet she used for email. Temporary communities at gatherings and protest spaces are always connected to larger networks of others working for social change. Where people come from and where they go after the Rendezvous suggests an extensive web of associations and interests that affect and are affected by what happens at gatherings and actions.

Exchanges of people and information enrich a community by bringing in new skills and ideas, some more welcome than others. The influx of activists associated with Occupy, an urban phenomenon, created tensions, but at the same time directly connected the Earth First! community to urban anticapitalist struggles. Protest rites and community practices from urban street battles have been transposed onto the woodland settings of antiextraction and antilogging campaigns. For instance, at Wild Roots, Feral Futures, a street medic training combined wilderness first responder techniques with medic practices honed in street battles with police. Sharing alternative medical and decision-making structures and tactics across international protest spaces is another way in which activists are creating the world they want to bring into being. But how to go about doing so is fraught with tensions as well as possibilities in these communities.

EARTH FIRST OR ANTIOPPRESSION?

While environmentalist gatherings, free states, and other action camps are intended to be all-inclusive, to facilitate and embody community ideals, in practice they often fall short of these goals. Establishing a place apart from a society many participants have rejected shores up the boundary between activist community and outside world. Activists want to "Subvert the Dominant Paradigm," as an Earth First! bumper sticker proclaims. However, within gatherings and action camps, living out a new paradigm is a challenge. Activists carry past experiences and inner histories with them into these spaces, including histories of abuse, harassment, oppression, trauma, and mental illness.

Green Mountain Earth First!, the organizers of the 2016 Round River Rendezvous, addressed this dilemma in publicity for the Rendezvous: "We recognize that the same violence that permeates our relationships with the Earth permeates our relationships with each other and ourselves. Eco-liberation = Biocentrism + Deep Ecology + Anti-Oppression + Solidarity! We cannot confront the forces destroying the earth without confronting the systems of power destroying subsistence cultures and exploiting people of color and other oppressed groups around the planet."[28] Rather than providing blank slates to be created anew as green anarchists, participants' experiences reveal deep fissures within environmental and animal rights movements, especially along lines of gender and ethnicity.

Sexism and racism have been the main points of tension in activist attempts to create utopian, egalitarian communities. People of color, trans people, queer people, differently abled people, and cis women have often felt marginalized in radical environmentalism. The issue of their marginalization in "EF's white-cis-hetero-dominant existence," as one critic put it, surfaced repeatedly at Earth First! gatherings and other radical environmentalist events I heard about or attended over the years I was conducting research.

In a "Reportback" from the 2016 Earth First! Round River Rendezvous, "Dirty Rack," of the "Gay Oogle Camp" describes a number of examples of marginalization. For instance, the "queer square dance" scheduled as part of the program, included gendered language like "ladies" and "gents." For the authors of the Reportback, this was an example of gathering organizers trying to be "queer-inclusive" and failing, in part because they were not truly "queer-centric." The problem of inclusivity, according to the Reportback, is that it gets activists off the hook too easily. They can feel self-satisfied without doing the harder work of checking to make sure the people they are trying to include feel comfortable in the spaces they are creating.[29]

Earth First!'s male founders dominated leadership in its early years. Earth First! in the 1980s is typically characterized by activists I met in the 2000s and 2010s as full of raucous, macho energy and focused overwhelmingly on saving forests and watersheds without addressing sexism and racism. However, renowned women activists have been involved with radical environmentalism since the 1980s. Judi Bari was one of the most notable early female leaders on the West Coast. She was instrumental in engaging Earth First! in larger struggles concerning social inequalities perpetuated by capitalism. From her perspective, "to define our movement as being concerned with 'wilderness only,' as Earth First! did in the 1980s, is self-defeating. You cannot seriously address the destruction of wilderness without addressing the society that is destroying it."[30] For a number of reasons, the animal rights movement has included more women, dating to its nineteenth-century origins in the United States, but male participants have been prominent in radical animal rights groups like the ALF and Sea Shepherd.

Gender issues involve some of the most charged discussions in activist communities. Activist gatherings typically include consent policies and spaces clearly set aside for participants who have felt marginalized or unsafe in the larger activist community, namely, transgender and female participants. In the late 1990s and early 2000s, many activists were influenced by gender studies courses they took in college as well as anarchists' broader critique of capitalism and related social ills. Activist communities began to put more emphasis on intersectionality: the intersection of interrelated forms of oppression.[31] While such concerns were present in Earth First!'s early years, they became more pronounced in the 1990s and 2000s. As one activist put it, "A shit-hole society with old-growth trees is just that, a shit-hole society."[32]

Activist communities addressed gender issues through a variety of strategies of inclusion and exclusion, with mixed results. Marten was frustrated by practices of inclusivity he encountered at the 2015 Wild Roots, Feral Futures because "almost the entirety of the effort to create a nonoppressive space focused on relatively recent niches of the queer/trans scene and on race; this, combined with the recent practice of people claiming that it's not their obligation to educate those with privilege, creates a space that is unwelcoming for those outside the radical/social justice milieu." According to Marten, strategies to include the concerns of multiple interest groups may make others who do not identify with these groups feel unwelcome. Such strategies also tend to exclude participants who are new to radical communities and unfamiliar with anti-oppression language. As a result, Marten noticed that "folks new to radical culture [were] afraid to speak, or sometimes even participate in workshops and community activities."[33] But attempts to address oppressive behavior have been a long time coming in the view of other activists.

Creating safer spaces and "calling out" oppressive and abusive behavior are strategies of direct action *within* direct action communities. Kiera Loki Anderson explains the importance of "calling out" in this way: "Direct action-style tactics like call-outs are necessary to challenge the entrenched and widespread oppression that marginalized activists face in supposedly 'radical' activist communities." Through interviews with activists who were involved in forest defense actions in the early 2000s, Anderson discovered numerous examples of women who had experienced sexist behavior and sexual assault by other activists. These incidents took place in activist communal houses and at action camps that were intended to be safe spaces set apart from societal ills like sexual violence.[34]

Activist communities have responded in diverse ways to accusations of unsafe and abusive behavior. Sometimes the victim has been blamed or vilified and sometimes the accused has been exiled from the action camp. Creating safe spaces within activist gatherings is a common strategy for addressing gender issues and bringing them into the open where they can be shared and worked on. A "Trans and Womyn's Circle" at one gathering I attended involved passing around a "talking stick," allowing each participant to talk about experiences of oppression or abuse. We were also encouraged to express frustration with activist communities for failing to live up to their egalitarian and inclusive ideals. The "talking stick" passed around this circle was a wrench, symbolizing "monkey wrenching," a long-standing Earth First! tactic used since the group's founding in the 1980s.[35] This symbol is taken from Edward Abbey's book *The Monkey Wrench Gang* (1975), which describes the antics of eco-saboteurs. The wrench represents sabotage of machinery as well as putting a wrench in the system, here the system of oppressive gender relations.

At this circle and throughout the Rendezvous and other gatherings I attended, much discussion focused on white, cis men (assigned male at birth and male-identified) dominating actions and leadership roles. As Mercurious observes in "The Challenging Male Supremacy Debacle," "without a culture of anti-oppression, i.e. a culture of actively working interpersonally on our oppressive behavior, the ghost of hierarchy still lingers strong—specifically 'environmentalism trumps social justice,' creating a myopic focus on ecodefense."[36] The repercussions of the Trans and Womyn's Talking Circle I attended were felt even after the circle had ended. Many of those who had participated in the circle spoke out within the larger Rendezvous community, calling attention to "patriarchal behavior" and asking men to work on "dismantling patriarchy."

Men's circles responding to concerns about patriarchy and oppression resulted in often contentious and painful discussions, as activist men attempted to work on challenging their own unexamined male privilege. Mercurious's "ghost of hierarchy" is one of many examples of the impact participants' inner histories can have on their involvement in activist communities. Participants' attitudes and behaviors learned through years of socialization in the other, outside world do not vanish on entering the utopian space of a gathering or free state.

At the 2013 Earth First! Rendezvous, many participants mentioned memories of the previous year's debate about sexist behavior. Throughout the week leading up to the protest action at the end of the gathering, conflicts and tensions surfaced around who should be included in the movement and in what way. On many occasions during the gathering, a transgender person would express feeling excluded and a female-identified person would confront cis men about dominating conversations. In response, antioppression workshops, workshops on "challenging patriarchy," and indigenous solidarity organizing were common at radical environmentalist gatherings during my fieldwork.

These workshops took place alongside and sometimes in tension with workshops on nonviolent tactics, tree identification, wolf reintroduction, and mountaintop removal, more traditional Earth First! topics related to deep ecology and direct action. Marten was dismayed that at Wild Roots, Feral Futures "it felt that the majority of time and energy at the gathering was devoted to discussing what could be categorized as 'anti-oppression' concepts and practices." For him, too much emphasis was "placed on how people in radical communities interact with each other, especially in terms of the language we use . . . Noticeably absent from this vision was any meaningful discussion of ecology, especially our relationships to other animals."[37] Many older and some younger radical environmentalists express frustration that the focus is being taken away from wild places and wild beings. Those who want the earth to come "first," may find antioppression concerns a distraction from what they see as more urgent work.

Throughout gatherings and during actions, activists' inner histories of racism and sexism emerge in and are shaped by ritualized contexts in which grieving for the other-than-human world takes place. Because activists come to gatherings from a wide range of backgrounds and experiences, some bring childhood memories of being in the woods with them and arrive fresh from forest tree-sits or antiextraction campaigns. Others bring experiences in urban straightedge or anarchist communities. Stories of deep connection to nature are often accompanied by accounts of personal abuse and trauma such as rape, domestic abuse, childhood sexual abuse, homophobia, sexual harassment, and hate crimes. Such experiences are often shared openly in the context of environmental struggles.

Inner histories composed of memories and emotions from the past that participants bring with them to gatherings and protests, then, shape their experience of the tension between working for the wild and against oppression. Activists' creation of the gathering or action camp as a place apart from and set in contrast to the outside world also influences how these issues are experienced. Memories of deep connections to place or personal suffering, as well as the nature of their conversion to radical environmentalism, shape the heightened emotional responses (weeping, yelling, and self-described "breakdowns") that characterize conflicts over "Earth first or antioppression."

DECOLONIZING THE MOVEMENT

In addition to gender, among the most emotionally charged issues are those involving Native Americans and other people of color. Radical activist events that try to embody an ideal egalitarian and inclusive society apart from a capitalist America founded on stolen land are concerned with racism both within and outside radical movements.

At Wild Roots, Feral Futures 2012, campers decorated with body paint, wearing masks, and carrying torches marched through camp and gathered around a fire. They called the four directions and the rain and made wishes. They declared, "To the earth, to the sky, to the earth," and then "After some hoots and hollers, the circle broke and people drummed, sang, danced, got naked, drank whiskey, smoked and howled into the night." A Diné (Navajo) family who had come to the gathering to talk about their local campaign and to learn tree climbing left quietly after the ritual, "upset and offended" according to one of the participants I spoke with.[38]

The following day, people of color at the gathering discussed the offending ritual: "I don't understand how all of these white people can run into the forest making up and practicing their rituals when we can't even go into our sacred forest and practice our rituals!" objected Sabitaj Mahal, who identifies as a woman of color.[39] Mahal recalled a friend's warning: "'Have fun hanging out with those primmies.' What he meant was, 'Good luck with those white dudes and their shitty politics in the woods.'" Mahal explained that her friend was "poking fun" at those who "fetishize so-called primitive societies that have been colonized and exploited by white people" and who simultaneously neglect "to unpack their own relationships to institutions of oppression—ultimately emulating and enforcing the systems they say they're against."[40] She went to the gathering anyway because she wanted to learn basic skills such as "firemaking, shelter building and plant identification." She complained that she came away from the gathering having learned more about oppressive behavior within radical communities.

When I attended Wild Roots, Feral Futures the following year, the Solstice celebration was subdued and informal. Participants intentionally tried not to replicate the previous year's controversial event. But once again there were conflicts over cultural appropriation of Native traditions. This happened the day before I arrived and was explained to me by a couple of different people who had witnessed what happened. A Lakota man who had come to the gathering to lead a workshop noticed a medicine wheel made out of rocks at the site and was offended. He launched into an angry speech about white people who have no awareness of their own heritage and steal Native people's traditions. He ended up leaving the gathering.

In his wake, ongoing discussions about this incident took place throughout the week and some participants called for decolonizing the gathering. According to activist Derrick Jensen, founder of the organization Deep Green Resistance, "decolonization" is "the process of breaking your identity with and loyalty to this culture—industrial capitalism, and more broadly civilization—and remembering your identification with and loyalty to the real physical world, including the land where you live."[41] In private conversations with Wild Roots participants I heard a variety of perspectives on the incident. Some felt critics were being overdramatic and shrugged off their own responsibility: "They weren't my ancestors!" They had expected the desire to be "in solidarity" with indigenous people would be welcomed, but instead they were lectured for their white privilege and profiting off colonialism. This was not why they came to the gathering, I heard some say: "Why is guilt like this productive?" one person asked me, "Let's move on."

Throughout the various gatherings I attended, organizers and other participants attempted to address the accusation that radical environmentalists are perpetuating colonialism. There was much talk about the need for decolonization and indigenous solidarity work within radical communities. On numerous occasions at an Earth First! Rendezvous, participants insisted on acknowledging that our activities were taking place on stolen lands and agonized over the movement's failure to build bridges with Native American causes. At the 2013 North Carolina Rendezvous these issues emerged in the chanting workshop over the language of "our land," as well as with concerns over the omission of information about indigenous people of the area in the welcome packet. At other gatherings I attended, organizers were also criticized for getting a permit from the Forest Service, but not from the people indigenous to the area. Although they are dedicated advocates for indigenous solidarity, in practice, activist communities struggle over how to work with Native Americans without at best being unwelcome and at worst perpetuating colonialism.

For activist communities like Earth First!, decolonization is a rigorous and ongoing process that may be a distraction from, but is also fundamentally entwined with, wilderness defense. "All us parties affected by the same Invader need to build stronger alliances," observes activist Rod Coronado.[42] In a workshop I attended on Black Mesa, the largest strip mine in the United States, Turtle told us she had been working with the Diné/Navajo people against the mine for sixteen years: "Why they aren't here is a story we should all know."[43] Turtle identified several issues that had created problems for Earth First!ers trying to support Native people at Black Mesa. First, "they just came in and wanted to lock down—not what the Navajo wanted." They acted as if they were "more indigenous than the Natives." When offered ham and beans, some refused to eat it. This attitude perpetuates the problem, she argued, so activists need to "break your vegan edge." Rod Coronado insists that building bridges between animal rights and indigenous movements can begin with "not being so fucking judgmental of people who eat animals. Long before there was an animal rights movement, there were indigenous people defending the earth and her animals with their lives. And they still are!"[44] Here, a softening of boundaries occurs, when supporting the concerns of other humans takes precedence over identification with nonhuman animals.

The other obstacle to Native American participation that came up in discussions during workshops and in my informal conversations with activists was alcohol. Activists concerned with why more Native Americans were not joining cause with them frequently brought up the issue of drinking in activist communities. Turtle explained that because of the presence of alcohol she "would never bring Diné youth to an Earth First! gathering." Drinking and drugs have become increasingly controversial at Earth First! events, in part out of the desire to create a welcoming environment for Native activists. But participants in recovery are also a factor, as is the presence of animal rights activists influenced by the 1990s straightedge punk rock scene, in which drinking and drugs were vilified. In 2015, the Earth First! Organizers' Conference, held near Santa Barbara, California, was alcohol-free.

In addition to concerns about alcohol and dietary choices, "white privilege" continually comes up as an issue when activists try to include people of color in their communities. Many of the experiences prized by activists, such as serving time in prison for animal and environmental causes or living off dumpstered food, have negative connotations for some people of color. In workshops I attended on "decolonizing" environmentalism, white privilege was examined—often in the form of ritualized confession—and denounced. In one workshop, a presenter who identified as a person of color criticized "that non-violent shit" as well as anarchist beliefs about no national borders or governments. She observed that such beliefs deny the sovereignty of Indian nations. She also identified permaculture and homesteading as problematic since they are further invasions of stolen land. Finally, as an indigenous person from a poor family, she was offended by activists who were proud of doing prison time or being homeless. In an Earth First! Rendezvous workshop, one participant described a protest at which "one of the Native guys got angry at the Earth First!ers for protecting trees: 'Trees can grow back,' he said, 'it's the land and people to be worried about.'" These examples suggest some of the points of tension between those who prioritize solidarity with indigenous people and others who want to hold firm to the "no compromise in defense of Mother Earth" that expresses Earth First!ers' deep sense of kinship with trees and other species.

Such controversies within activist communities are not new in the history of Earth First! even though they have taken on a heightened emotional intensity in the first decades of the twenty-first century. Shortly after Earth First!'s founding in the 1980s, critiques of racism and misogyny surfaced, as well as differences over whether humans should reproduce, how to integrate animal rights advocates, vegans, and vegetarians into a community that also includes staunch meat eaters, and what to do about "crystal-gazing" New Agers.[45]

By the late 1980s, Earth First! founder Dave Foreman and other early Earth First! leaders distanced themselves from a movement they believed was no longer putting Earth first, but was overly populated by "leftist, anarchist, humanist, class struggle types."[46] As they face many endings in an era of climate change and extinction, some activists continue to emphasize the need to prioritize saving the biosphere over all other issues. All problems are trivial, Paul Watson argues, "compared to the one most important issue: the escalating diminishment of *global biodiversity*."[47] But participants at Earth First! gatherings who see social issues as inextricably linked with environmental degradation challenge the biocentric paradigm that has guided the movement. Many of the younger activists I communicated with entered radical environmentalism at what one of them described as a time of transition from "the Dave Foreman 'rednecks for wilderness'-era to the black clad anarchist street punks of later years."[48]

Conflicts over issues concerning transgender people and people of color and tensions around patriarchal and misogynist behavior sharpen and soften boundaries within radical environmental and animal rights movements. Inclusivity does not come about automatically, but necessitates constantly shifting positions about what are appropriate stances and actions. At the gatherings I attended in the 2010s, disagreements over violent property destruction like arson might be heated, but did not usually result in exclusion from the community. Arguing that transgender identity is a social construction, on the other hand, might result in being ostracized from activist communities.

Because of the rise of transgender awareness and activism in the 2010s, transphobia has been added to the list of issues radical environmentalists call attention to within their communities.[49] Derrick Jensen and Lierre Keith, well-known biocentric activists and founders of the organization Deep Green Resistance, sparked heated discussions in activist communities by their stance on transgender issues. In an editorial statement, the *Earth First! Journal* editorial collective explained why the *Journal* would no longer include pieces written by members of Keith's and Jensen's Deep Green Resistance organization: "In light of DGR's continued assault on trans people, with language and analysis that denies the struggles of trans-people and even goes so far as to deny the value, worth and power of their existence in radical movements, labeling trans people as somehow 'not real,' or as Post-Modern manifestations of individualism, the *Earth First! Journal* collective will no longer print or in any way promote DGR material."[50] Anyone suggesting limits on immigration and reproduction for ecological reasons might get a similar response in the second decade of the twenty-first century.

Clearly who and what is included and excluded has shifted over the more than thirty decades of radical environmental and animal rights activism's history in the United States.

SOFTENING AND SHARPENING THE BOUNDS OF INCLUSION

Spatial and ritual practices at gatherings and protests reveal some of the ways in which activists are negotiating these internal conflicts and issues. In response to criticism that the Summer Solstice ritual at Wild Roots, Feral Futures was culturally offensive, the following day a "fishbowl" was designed to help facilitate understanding of and education about the legacy of colonialism for Native Americans. Anyone who identified as a person of color could join the inner circle of the fishbowl. An inner circle of seven people then voiced concerns about cultural appropriation and related issues. Some began to cry as they described traumatic experiences. Everyone else—about forty people—composed an outer circle that listened and then asked questions after everyone in the inner circle was finished and a longer discussion ensued.[51]

At gatherings, boundaries are drawn and safer spaces created, but these boundaries are constantly being transgressed, safer spaces violated. When conflicts emerge, a common response has been to establish "trans and women circles" and "safer spaces" for people of color. In this way, activists may experience identity and community differently in small, separate spaces than in the greater gathering community.

Sometimes these small safe spaces even become institutionalized, as was the case with the Trans and Women's Action Camp (TWAC) that developed from separate spaces within gatherings to stand-alone gatherings open only to women and transgender people. The first stand-alone women's and transgender gathering was a response by a group of transgender and female participants to what they saw as patriarchal norms and transphobia in Earth First![52] This may have been the first camp to explicitly exclude cis men, but momentum for creating safe spaces had been growing over the previous decade.[53]

At Fall Creek tree-sit in 1996 some women started their own camp in response to incidents of sexual assault at the blockade. These first separate camps were associated with forest defense, but were not yet called TWAC. According to Widdow of TWAC Cascadia, TWAC was "founded in the early 2000s by West Coast forest defenders and anarchists" because of "uneven distribution of 'hard skills' (blockades, climbing, rigging, etc.) in the Cascadia Earth Defense scene in the early 2000s."[54] TWAC was organized at the site of the Straw Devil timber sale in Oregon in 2004 and then took place as a weekend campout before the Earth First! Rendezvous in Indiana in 2005. Following this model, a designated TWAC was held again four years later at an Earth First! Rendezvous in 2009, a few days before the Rendezvous, but at the same site. Since then, a number of regional spin-offs have developed. In 2014, action camps were held by Bay Area TWAC, TWAC Maine, and TWAC Northwest.

I attended a TWAC in the Sierra Nevada Mountains, a much smaller gathering than the Earth First! Rendezvous, but with a similar design. Organizers and participants emphasized training for direct action and attention to concerns about diversity and oppression. I did not observe any workshops on deep ecology, the local ecosystem, or wildlife protection campaigns. In Internet publicity for the camp, organizers described their intentions as follows:

> TWAC is an action camp for folks who identify as female and/or trans, trans women, trans men, gender queer, gender variant, two-spirited and agender to build community, heal and strengthen our cultures of resistance. Our focus will be on developing skills for climbing, blockading, flash-mobbin' and making art for protest as well as having safer and mind-expanding workshops and discussions about diversity, anti-oppression, intersectionality, transphobia, transmisogyny, environmental justice, and direct action.

In addition to these activities and concerns, many TWAC gatherings have ended in actions protesting logging or resource extraction, even though this was not the case the year I attended.[55]

Even within TWAC, a separate space from the broader radical environmental movement, conflicts emerge, notably about transphobia, white privilege, and exclusion of people of color. Even though TWAC offers a safe space by excluding cis men and supports female and transgender activists taking leadership roles at actions, nevertheless, these gatherings may not be experienced by every participant as being as inclusive as they are intended to be. Transgender participants and people of color experience oppressive behavior even in spaces carved out for them.

At one radical environmentalist gathering for women and trans-identified people, I participated in a decolonization workshop organized in response to people of color who felt they were being treated in oppressive ways. Two separate circles were created in different parts of the camp: one for "white folks," which I joined, and another for people of color that included participants who identified with their Native

American, Mexican American, and Asian American heritage. The white circle discussed various ways participants benefited from white privilege and what efforts they were making in their lives to overcome the legacy of colonialism and their privilege.

Like most circles I participated in at environmentalist gatherings, the emphasis was on making sure everyone was heard and that no one dominated the conversation. This was done by either going around the circle and speaking one by one or by one person "taking stack" and being responsible for keeping track of who wanted to speak next. In the white circle, some participants resisted the opposition between oppressed people of color and white oppressors. Some of us argued that class is as important as ethnic background and is often invisible. It seemed to me this was an issue that could only be safely raised in a "white-only" space, which suggests silencing can certainly go both ways. The white circle also discussed how we might better support people of color in struggles for social justice, and at the same time include them in the environmental movement in ways that did not perpetuate colonialism.

After over an hour of discussion, the two groups came back together to share what they had learned and to imagine together some ways in which future gatherings could be more inclusive and further the work of decolonizing radical environmentalism. In response to these kinds of ritualized processes, activist communities try to be proactive. A flyer for a TWAC Cascadia gathering made the group's priorities explicit. It invited prospective campers to: "Join us in the Woods of Occupied Coast Salish Territories" and listed these features:

- Direct action skills
- Disability justice
- Critical anti-oppression
- Environmental justice
- No cis men, everyone else[56]

The organizers further explained, "We aspire to tease apart the many intricacies of conflict and experiences rooted in oppression" and they urged participants to be more aware of their own assumptions: "Gender comes in many forms. Don't push yr gender expectations onto other people. Some women have beards. Some men menstruate. Some butch dykes wear pink. Some trans folks don't take hormones. Some people have a gender outside the binary." Moreover, they cautioned campers against simple oppositions: "Leave the misandry at home: Men are part of TWAC and always have been. It is ok to vent about men in yr life but blaming all men or all cis men for oppression ignores how cis women and trans people perpetuate oppression as well. Use appropriate language. If you mean all men say men. If you mean cis white men say cis white men."

Regardless of these priorities, the organizers acknowledged in their welcome packet that creating "an environment free of oppression" is impossible because they "recognize that we live in a pretty thoroughly fucked up world." Campers bring complicated personal histories and biases with them.

One strategic response to conflict at gatherings and action camps is a *defensive* move, a retreat into smaller "safer" spaces within the larger community for those feeling oppressed or marginalized by other activists. For example, the Earth First! Rendezvous in the Smoky Mountains featured a "chill space" for people of color and a special area set aside for a trans and women's tree-climbing camp. As one Earth First!er admitted during a Rendezvous Morning Circle: there are only "safer spaces": the boundary of the gathering itself, with guards at the front gate twenty-four hours a day, spaces set aside for trans and women's circles, camps and tree-climbing, and then spaces within those spaces for people of color. In addition, some gathering organizers differentiate "sober" from "rowdy" late night fires to address the needs of campers who are in recovery, as well as those who want to drink.

The practice of creating different levels of safe spaces in which safer and more intimate sharing can happen is seen as essential, even in preparing for large public protests. Clearly there is a tension here in drawing boundaries of separate spaces for women, trans-identified people, and people of color, fracturing the community into smaller "safer" spaces," when the goal for most activists is to build a broad and inclusive movement.

Activists also created spaces that reified the "normal" by separating into circles of ritualized self-examination in order for men to dismantle patriarchy and for "white" people to explore white privilege. As Nell put it in her analysis of gender hierarchy at the 2006 Rendezvous: "uneasy feelings about gender hierarchy . . . were never effectively communicated to the entire rondy, because discussions of "manarchists" (self-proclaimed anarchists behaving in patriarchal and oppressive ways) were relegated to smaller circles: the queer/trans circle, the wommin's circle, the patriarchy-in-the-movement workshop and the challenging oppression working group meeting."[57] The tension between the desire to create smaller safe spaces and the need to address oppressive behaviors with the entire gathering community is an ongoing concern.

For this reason, in contrast to separating into smaller, safer spaces, the other type of spatial strategy I witnessed at gatherings was an *offensive* move. This strategy brought open discussion about fraught issues into the largest public gathering spaces such as Morning Circles. In these gathering-wide spaces, activists told stories, made arguments, and brought about changes. An apology at one Morning Circle for not including information about indigenous people in the welcome packet was a public response to critique and conflict. Another example of more public, institutionalized responses is the practice of beginning workshops by asking each participant to give their preferred gender pronouns (as in "he," "she," or "they"). In this instance, notions of difference and inclusion are expressed and heard, allowing participants to self-identify and avoid everyone having to guess gender identity by the way people present themselves.

On the other hand, this practice can be off-putting for those unfamiliar with it. I had never heard of identifying one's preferred pronouns before attending my first Rendezvous in 2009. What did I identify with that day? Was there something wrong with being an essentialized "she" rather than a "they"? For me this practice at first felt awkward, like a forced essentialism that did not capture how I thought of myself as a pronoun or otherwise. On the other hand, it made me realize how gender nonconforming or transgender people must feel when categorized as a "she" or "he" they are not, simply because of physical characteristics.

In contrast to creating boundaries around safer spaces by differentiating people, one way boundaries are softened is through role playing. This practice is most common in direct action trainings in which ritualized responses require identification with a vilified group such as police officers. In workshops geared towards end-of-gathering actions, activists take turns playing police officers or angry workers who have arrived at work to find their office doors blockaded. For instance, during a role-play on "de-escalation" I participated in, one activist played a Texas Republican who could not understand why anyone would fight against American oil self-sufficiency. She entered into the mind of the Republican to try to understand and act out a very different perspective. In this way, role playing involved overcoming distances between activist and enemy. Without compassion for the police officer's or worker's perspective, nonviolent civil disobedience (which this training was about) is not as effective.

Other strategies to address oppressive and oppositional relationships include working as allies with specific communities. Such efforts try to avoid further marginalizing the concerns of female and transgender participants and people of color. Solidarity work with Native Americans is common because their struggles often involve environmental issues and endangered species, as well as concerns for sacred sites and land use. Regardless of the many tensions existing between non-Native activists and Native people, numerous stories in the *Earth First! Journal* and among activists I spoke with attest to successful collaboration.

Radical environmentalist involvement with Black Mesa is one of many examples of solidarity with Native American campaigns, even though non-Natives' support has been controversial.[58] In 2013, I was handed a flyer inviting activists to support the Black Mesa struggle: "For non-indigenous defenders of mountains and earth this is an opportunity to work with and for Native Americans most impacted by colonialism and corporate sponsored environmental injustices on the front lines on their terms." In a similar expression of solidarity with indigenous causes, Earth First! activists in Minneapolis joined a coalition of Anishinaabeg people trying to prevent wolf hunting. Although the Earth First!ers acknowledged they are "of European heritage, as are the wolf killers," one of them invoked their ancestral past in another way: "Some kind of fundamental agreement is being broken, an understanding that goes back past Jesus, past Rome, back to a time when our ancestors lived side by side with the wolves of old Europe."[59] In these acts of solidarity, white activists disidentify with other white Americans and try to usher in a less oppressive society that challenges the legacies of colonialism.

Radical activists partner with other organizations and movements with which they have common cause. In the *Earth First! Journal*, at gathering workshops, and during the annual Earth First! Rendezvous "Bioregional Roundup," activists share stories of working in support of or in coalition with a wide range of groups, including Catholics as well as Native Americans. An activist who was at the Tar Sands Blockade in Texas described to me his surprise at a local Baptist church that opened its doors and welcomed Tar Sands activists. The pastor was a former anti–nuclear power activist and gave a sermon supporting direct action and civil disobedience. As the blockade went on, several activists lived with people from the congregation.[60] Some activists at the 2013 Rendezvous also attended "Witness Wednesdays," organized by the National Association for the Advancement of Colored People (NAACP) in Raleigh, North Carolina. These examples complicate the anti-Christian rhetoric so common among activists. In practice, then, religious as well as ethnic and class boundaries are crossed or blurred.

Activists fighting mountaintop removal in Appalachia provide another example of coalition building and cooperation with local communities. Following in the tradition of Judi Bari and other Earth First!ers who tried to forge common cause with loggers in Northern California, the Radical Action for Mountain People's Survival campaign in rural West Virginia addresses local communities directly on its website: "As predominately outsiders in these communities, we are in a position of privilege. Our work here is guided by local residents whom themselves may not walk onto a mine site, but do support direct action in the coalfields. In solidarity, we offer our resources, our networks, our time, our bodies, and our personal freedom to this struggle."[61] In a similar fashion, activists with Rising Tide, a group founded by Earth First!ers, shut down the port of Vancouver, Washington in 2013, in solidarity with the International Longshore and Warehouse Union that was fighting a new oil terminal.[62]

In the lived reality around these issues, boundaries between activists and their supposed enemies are broken down in some cases and shored up in others. What I witnessed repeatedly was a contrast between these dynamics in two kinds of ritual/social space: the gathering and the protest site. The first was the space of a gathering like Wild Roots, Feral Futures or the Earth First! Rendezvous, hidden away in the woods with no cameras in sight, no cell phone reception, and a clear emphasis on creating a utopian space apart from the broader society. When participants who come from different backgrounds with different inner histories converge at gatherings, they think they know who the other is, and *then they come up against the other within their own movement*. Their comrades are the ones they accuse of sexist behavior or oppressive language.

In addition to the two responses to conflicts that result in either creating separate spaces or reshaping the larger collective space of the gathering, I want to draw attention to the contrast between days-long gatherings in the woods and public protests. On the last day of the 2013 Rendezvous, everyone departed before dawn in a long caravan of cars heading towards an undisclosed protest site. Leaving the forest behind, our destination was a manufacturing plant for chemicals used in hydrofracking. Workers arrived that day to find both entrances to the plant blocked by two activists sitting in tripods. Activists on the ground who were chanting, drumming, dancing, waving banners, and otherwise supporting the tripod sitters were no longer discussing inner differences

Facing off at Dakota Access Pipeline protest. Photo: Patrick Clayton. Used with permission.

within the collective whole. They were focused on the "enemy": a dozen police cars with officers carrying guns and plastic handcuffs.

After hours of standing around or talking with an Earth First! police liaison, the officers started arresting people and there was confusion over what areas were safe for those who wanted to avoid arrest. Some people moved across the road from the action and others left the site completely as soon as the officers began handcuffing people. We all felt the escalation and our fear and anticipation grew, after hours of waiting around for something to happen. There was a lot of anger in our group about how unnecessarily rough the arrests had been, especially when officers grabbed one activist by the hair and pushed her down, even though she was not resisting.

When activists bring their memories and emotions to gatherings and protests, when their stories are told on blogs, in circles, or to me in interviews and letters, typically binary oppositions are established. The "wild" is everything of value and the "Other" is police officers, civilization, Christianity, the logging or oil companies that destroy wild places, or patriarchy and sexist men. At public protests, no one criticized chants or called for creating separate spaces for those feeling silenced or oppressed. Drama and danger, heightened emotions, and a sense of collective identity prevailed. Everyone was unified against the police and fracking chemical plant owners. As one anarchist activist explained, regardless of "all the rules about how to use your body as an activist . . . resisting together is more important than any of the rules."[63] Resisting together in public protest spaces tends to dissolve differences that are more apparent in activist-only sites like remote gatherings or small action camps.

With these and other oppositional practices, activists define their struggle in the context of a war against civilization and all who represent its interests. They bond with each other across their differences in order to work together towards common goals. These strategies at public protests or during clandestine actions *conceal* inner conflicts at the same time that they are shaped by those same conflicts.

The two tripod sitters at the antifracking action were not cis men: no accident at the end of a gathering that had focused on dismantling patriarchy. The social dynamics that emerged in workshops and gathering circles, in contrast to protests, suggest the importance of tracking how rituals and social relations change when networks of actors move across various kinds of spaces. Different boundaries are drawn and different kinds of boundary-crossing happen in the hidden, private spaces of forest gatherings than in public protest spaces. Radical environmentalists intend to create radically inclusive communities that extend boundaries to a large network of species and humans. Yet in practice these rituals exclude in at least two ways. Even when they try to be explicitly inclusive of people of color and transgender people, they are experienced by some participants as exclusionary. Moreover, gatherings and protests always explicitly exclude radical environmentalists' others: capitalism, corporate America, law enforcement officers, oil company workers. These enemies are always positioned in contrast and opposition to "the wild," to "Mother Earth," pagan religions, and indigenous communities.

Although I wanted to linger, I drove away from the 2013 Earth First! Rendezvous and back to my nonactivist life. I wrote the following in my field notes: "We enjoyed the intimacy of strangers so common at activist gatherings, a shared experience together. In a beautiful wilderness setting we talked about what's wrong with the world out there, tried to address the parts of the outside world we have brought with us and tried to create new kinds of relationships, learn new skills. Some people leave for Rainbow, others leave for the Tar Sands Blockade in Utah. I can see why moving from one event to another, from one activist space to the next would be attractive." Gatherings and actions do more than "attract"; they offer rare opportunities to connect deeply with other beings, critique social ills, engage in self-criticism and self-transformation, learn concrete skills, create the kinds of communities we want to live in, and engage body and soul in direct actions geared towards change. The sense of being part of a shared struggle is generated both from working together over internal conflicts and from facing off against the enemy. Both experiences occur in the context of a sense of urgency in the face of mass extinctions and impending planetary disaster. In this way, activist gatherings and action camps offer glimpses of a future we are far from achieving any time soon, a vision fueled by grief for a world that was once and could still be.

CHAPTER 7

Rites of Grief and Mourning

We are living in the age of extinction
Coral bleaching, glaciers melting
Biodiversity has had its day
Mass extinction is underway
Natural balance for millions of years
Has been disrupted since the advent of gears
Worldwide science has its fears
Created by man, If denied by man,
will soon cause the collapse of man
—Black Hole of Calcutta, "Age of Extinction"

Again and again, we need to ask: What does it mean to bring
an abrupt ending to *this* particular way of life? What does
this loss mean inside its specific multispecies communities?
How are "we" called into responsibility *here and now*, and
how will we take up that call?
—Thom van Dooren, *Flight Ways: Life and Loss*
    at the Edge of Extinction

In the damp, leafy Allegheny Forest of western Pennsylvania, I was taking advantage of a break in the rain to browse in the "distro" area (tables
where numerous zines, graphic designs, bumper stickers, and buttons
are for sale or free) across the road from my campsite at Earth First!'s
2012 Round River Rendezvous. Amid copies of the *Earth First! Journal*,
buttons, bumper stickers, zines on deep ecology, herbal medicine, anarchist thought, and memoirs of actions, was a simple 4 x 6 woodcut print.
The downcast profile of a young woman with a braid and brimmed cap
is turned toward a highway with a dotted line down the middle. Splayed

out on the highway are two animals that look like a coyote and fox, roadkill lying helpless and abandoned, dead on the road. A caption over their bodies reads, "sometimes the grief is too hard to bear," and the heading in larger letters below the image is "WELDSCHMERZ" (world-pain). The image moved me, and I took a copy from the stack. Every time I look at it, I feel the grief and shame the destruction caused by roadways brings and the emotion behind activists' anticivilization comments, as well as the reason some of them eat roadkill.

The image I found on the distro table draws attention to the everyday destruction of other species, endangered or not, by human activities. In this and many other instances, activists draw attention to the hidden costs of contemporary life and reveal the motivating emotions behind their anticivilization rhetoric: empathy, love, grief. Like the woman in the image, they choose to turn towards what is unbearable, putting grief into words and actions.[1] This means not only paying attention to the everyday destruction of other species, but also to mass extinction. The print took an intimate moment of one activist's encounter with dead animals to suggest a more powerful grief about the impact of human life on the lives of other species with which we share the planet. Radical environmental and animal rights activists mourn for nonhuman others in a variety of ways that both express their kinship with these others and strengthen their commitments to radical causes. In the context of activism, grief is an overwhelming sense of loss and sadness, often felt viscerally in one's body for the bodies of others who are suffering or have died. Grief is a central influence in conversion and commitment to activism. It is both an expression of deeply felt kinship bonds with other species and a significant factor in creating those bonds.[2]

In this chapter I explore the role of grief in environmental and animal rights activism within an apocalyptic context in which activists are engaged in a war "for the wild" and "for the animals" that involves martyrdom and self-sacrifice. Childhood memories of mourning for destroyed places, experiences of watching trees fall, kinship with trees and animals, the irate lyrics of hard core/straightedge music about animal abuse and environmental devastation, struggles within activist communities to work on antioppression in the context of animal and earth activism, all shape activist mourning for vanishing forests and suffering animals.

The presence of intimate others (trees, nonhuman animals) in childhood memories and forest action camps and the experience of meeting the eyes of mink in cages before liberating them, go hand in hand with a powerful sense of loss over their absence/death. Grief and mourning for these losses take place inwardly through the emotions activists feel, as well as outwardly through action. Activists' actions as well as their inner histories both express and constitute grief at protests. Their very participation in protests is part of an ongoing process of remembering the dead and disappearing, including those who are intimately known or the more abstract dead of the "Sixth Extinction."[3]

In the Sixth Extinction, exacerbated by climate change, about 40 percent of all amphibians and a quarter of all mammals are considered endangered, among a host of other endangered species. In this extinction, "humans are the asteroid," to borrow Elizabeth Kolbert's phrase, and are likely to have catastrophic effects on many different species, not unlike the extinction of dinosaurs at the end of the Cretaceous period that was caused by an asteroid.[4] Most environmental and animal rights protests reference some kind of loss, including extinctions. "Scratch an environmentalist and you'll find loss," insists activist Joan Dunning.[5] For this reason, protests themselves might be understood as rites of mourning, as they are so often motivated by loss and grief, as well as love and anger. They function as a cry for what has been lost as well as a call to action.

Activists' mourning comes about because they situate themselves in particular biosocial networks of empathy and love in which the loss of nonhuman others is deeply felt.[6] Activists criticize other humans for policing the boundary of difference between ourselves and nonhumans, allowing us to ignore the impact of mass extinction.[7] Our failure to mourn comes from our inability to bridge the difference between human self and animal other, our inability to understand and feel our connections and kinship with other species. In contrast, many activists experience an extreme sensitivity to deaths in the other-than-human world, the deaths of those beings they have come to know as kin.

Dead comrades, trees they lived in, and animals whose eyes they met behind the bars of cages, as well endangered and extinct species, come to matter to activists in all the ways I have described in earlier chapters. By risking their own safety at protests, by sacrificing for beloved others, activists become vulnerable bodies just like those nonhuman animals and trees they are trying to protect are also vulnerable. At the same time, through protests, activists draw attention to losses and the suffering of nonhuman others referenced by their self-sacrificial actions. In this way, protests work as ritual practices to express loss at the same time that they constitute the meaning of that loss.

PERPETUAL MOURNING

"I feel like I'm in perpetual mourning," Earth Liberation Front (ELF) activist Daniel McGowan, who was sentenced to seven years in prison for two arsons (with a terrorist enhancement), tells the filmmakers of *If a Tree Falls*. This is a common sentiment among activists who track and circulate information about the loss of individual animals and trees as well as entire ecosystems and species. They cannot turn away from thoughts of species death and destruction and they cannot ignore the losses they are implicated in.[8] For animal rights activist Keith Mann, "the way animals are treated is like a wound I have that won't heal."[9] Activists' actions and their sense of urgency, then, might be seen as the direct consequences of this kind of perpetual wound and perpetual mourning.

For this reason, they often credit loss and grief for their radicalization. Animal rights activist Josh Harper served three years for his participation in the Stop Huntington Animal Cruelty (SHAC) campaign. He wrote to me from prison that although his views and actions were influenced by "anti-civilization" and feminist theories as well as hardcore punk rock, they were also fundamentally shaped by loss. When Harper was young, he did not consciously choose activism as a path, but "reacted passionately to the abuse and destruction" he saw around him, especially the desecration of childhood places where he remembers boating, camping, and hiking. After witnessing these places being logged and paved over, he became more militant about wilderness defense.[10] Like Harper, many activists describe grief over the destruction of beloved places as a source of commitment to activism. They bemoan what biologist Robert Michael Pyle calls "the extinction of experience."[11] The inhabitants of Harper's neighborhood a generation later will not have these places to enjoy that he remembers from childhood, only pavement. In addition to valuing other species for themselves, activists also imagine the experiences other people will not have because of the places and species vanished from the Earth.

In 2000, long before the SHAC indictments, Josh Harper was on a boat off the Olympic Peninsula in the Pacific Northwest trying to stop a Makah whale hunt.[12] His boat was boarded by the Coast Guard and he was issued a subpoena to appear at a Grand Jury investigation. The Grand Jury was investigating Animal Liberation Front (ALF) and ELF actions he had vocally supported, although there was no evidence that

Old growth clearcut in Oregon. Photo: Francis Eatherington. Licensed under Creative Commons 2.0.

he was involved in any of these actions. Harper refused to cooperate with the Grand Jury and explained why: "First and foremost, this world is dying. All that is beautiful about the world is being destroyed and paved over. The animals are being either killed or turned into machines for human consumption."[13] Harper's story suggests the ways in which childhood memories of beloved and destroyed places and ongoing awareness of environmental devastation and the suffering of other animals motivates activists. The contrast between a beloved wild landscape and the parking lot it becomes, or a wild mink and the fate of its caged brethren, is what makes activists "keep fighting."

In a letter to the *Earth First! Journal*, an activist named Kris describes how loss of a special landscape was directly responsible for his becoming involved with direct action. Kris lived at the end of a dead-end street surrounded by woods until a lumber yard came in with trucks, chainsaws, and bulldozers and "destroyed every thing . . . I went to my window to stare into the lush, dark green of the beautiful woods as I had done all my life . . . this time their [*sic*] was only bare dirt." Kris wept and then decided, "NOW YOU KNOW WHAT TO DO WITH YOUR

LIFE."[14] Transformation of a wild landscape into something alien effects a transformation *within* activists. Activists' transformations result in a turning towards, rather than away from, the deaths and suffering of nonhuman others. Activists feel compelled to make their predicaments visible and act through tree-sits, blockades, and animal liberation to prevent further losses.

Activists' grief is the flip side of their love for and identification with nonhuman others. They react to the visual absence of those others' or visible signs of the damage done to them. For Kris and Harper, the damage was to places they had lived in for years. But for many activists, the desecration of forests where they have come to protest, among trees they have come to know, even just for a few weeks, creates a similar sense of loss. Marrow recalls a tree-sit eviction in which "there came a machine that 'prepared' (destroyed) the ground for the cherry picker." Another activist locked himself to a branch with a lockbox and Marrow was sitting behind him to support him when "I heard chainsaws and the first tree falling to the ground." It was a tree in which Marrow had been constructing a treehouse, a "200 year-old oak, which I had totally fallen in love with." Knowing the tree personally made the eviction much worse: "It sounds horrible when a tree is hitting the ground. It is the moment when you realize it is too late—that you cannot make this unhappen—and that the tree, which you know so well and which has become your friend, is now dead."[15]

In his account of the antiroad protests in England, Jim Hindle remembers the destruction of an action camp and tree-sit he had been involved with, as well as the deaths of trees he had come to know: "Every time a tree went down, it fell to the sound of women screaming . . . it was a kind of keening, a cry that left no one in doubt that this was the death of a friend."[16] For Marrow and Hindle, the loss of tree friends is even worse because of their sense of responsibility. They were unable to make tree deaths "unhappen," which makes them even more determined to prevent further losses.

For activists who sought to protect the trees they once were, stumps and clear-cuts become *images of absence* and of failed responsibility. Hindle's book about antiroad protests includes images of tree-sitters in lone trees in the centers of clear-cuts, activists sorting through huge piles of brush after an eviction, and activists sitting in bulldozed sites that had been their camps, looking "homeless and traumatized."[17] After one eviction, Hindle approached the remains of a tree that protesters had named "Granny Ash": "The stumps of the tree were fat and raw and seemed to cry out to me in shock. Hours ago they'd been the root of an incredible, living thing and now they stood there; white and garish. Testament to fresh amputation. This place had been beautiful last night and now it was a swamp of carnage."[18] Activists experience such raw "amputations" as wounds to their own flesh, identifying with the trees that have died.

Clear-cuts are particularly striking examples of devastation and loss for activists who have become familiar with particular forests or individual trees. Joan Dunning walked into the forest with some other activists to visit Julia Butterfly Hill after trees had been cut down around Luna: "I almost tripped over Molly, collapsed on a stump. The rest of us had either never seen the forest that had once surrounded Luna, or else had already revisited the area after the helicopter logging. Only Molly was being hit with the brutal reality of before and after. She had her face down, and was unmoving, except for her sobbing."[19] Eric McDavid, who served ten years in prison for his participation in planning ELF actions, recalls the shock of walking into a clear-cut: "it was like walking upon an open wound, 1 which i was experiencing in my own body, destruction that is often hidden from us."[20] This kind of visible loss, viscerally felt, is the inverse of what environmental humanities scholar Thom van Dooren calls "the dull edge of extinction," in which what is lost is less visible because the disappearance of species has taken place over such a long stretch of time. These activists experience the sharp edge of extinction. They have intimate knowledge of the devastation of forests, the deaths of trees they have known and animals whose habitats have been destroyed.

HOW PROTESTS MAKE LOSS AND GRIEF VISIBLE

Activists depict absence, suffering, destruction and loss through artwork, photos, videos, and written descriptions. They bring public attention to what is otherwise hidden: the hunting of predators like mountain lions and wolves, the killing of seals and whales in remote places, and the abuse of beagles and primates in research facilities. They rally support through the outrage provoked by videos of seal slaughter and experimentation on beagles in laboratories or images of clear-cuts and land bulldozed for oil pipeline construction. Media exposés, undercover videos of animal abuse, videos of activists being beaten or pepper-sprayed, these are all strategies in the struggle to shape public opinion. These strategies make logging companies and animal researchers into evil-doers and eco-warriors into saviors of animals and the wild. Activists aim to disrupt and shift public perceptions of logging and animal testing by making the victims of these practices visible as objects of grief.

For many activists, grief about clear-cuts and roadkill functions as what photographer Chris Jordan calls "a powerful doorway." While Jordan hopes his "Midway" photographs of dead baby albatrosses full of plastic detritus from Midway Atoll will arouse grief in the viewer, so too do activists hope to affect others with their actions that make losses and suffering visible.[21] From their perspective, civilization stands on the often invisible foundations of coal, oil, and gas. Moving up from those invisible depths, "you pass through a jumble of supporting horrors: battery chicken sheds; industrial abattoirs; burning forests; beam-trawled ocean floors; dynamited reefs; hollowed-out mountains; wasted soil. Finally, on top of all these unseen layers, you reach the well-tended surface."[22] Activists insist that we ask what other, hidden, suffering makes our lives possible.

Although Julia Butterfly Hill saved the redwood tree Luna through her highly publicized two-year tree-sit, about a year after she came down from the tree, someone vandalized Luna, chainsawing a big gash in her side. Because of Hill's and Luna's previous fame, the story was covered by major news outlets.[23] Hill was bereft when she learned of the damage: "Luna is the greatest teacher and best friend I have ever had. I gave two years of my life to ensure that she could live and die naturally. But two years is nothing compared to the thousand years she has lived, providing shelter, moisture and oxygen to forest inhabitants. It kills me that the last 3% of the ancient redwoods are being desecrated. I feel this vicious attack on Luna as surely as if the chainsaw was going through me."[24]

Hill grieved for Luna and held a healing ritual for her friend. She treated her with a mixture of herbs and clay, packing clay into the gash. A "medical team" of forest ecologists stabilized the tree with steel cables and braces since the damage would not kill it, but would make it more vulnerable to toppling over in a storm.[25] In a poem called "Luna's Cut," Hill writes:

> I heard today . . .
> Luna's been cut. . . .
> The pain I feel right now that threatens to rip me apart
> is the pain I feel every time I see an Ancient Elder cut . . .
> the pain I feel every time another species goes extinct . . .
> Chainsaws to sacred beings.
> When do we begin to look at where this DIS-EASE begins?
> In the disconnection from the sacred . . .
> In the disconnection from the heart.

The person who ripped metal into Luna's flesh
is just as ripped apart inside as Luna now is,
as I now am,
as is the world.
May the tears that pour out from the depths of my soul
cleanse the sadness of any who would wish to react in rage.
The person who so viciously attacked Luna
has enough anger for the world.[26]

Luna survived the attack, but Hill is reminded by her injury that other species continue to go extinct. By attracting news media attention to her grief over Luna's wound and her attempts to heal the tree, Hill demanded that suffering and loss of other species be made visible. For Hill, the act of the individual who wounded Luna exemplifies greater destructive acts committed by humans against other species.

MOURNING THE INTIMATE DEAD AND DISTANT EXTINCTIONS

Julia Butterfly Hill's concern for Luna's wound, Josh Harper's witnessing of a beloved wild place paved over, and Jim Hindle's encounter with the stumps of former tree friends are on one end of the spectrum of activists' sense of loss: close-up and personal. But entire species that are threatened and endangered become important to activists too, just like the trees and animals they have known as close friends.[27] There is a clear connection between the demise of places and beings activists have loved and their more general sense that "the world is dying." For activists, campaigns to save specific places such as old-growth redwood groves are important not only in and of themselves, but also because they are small battles in a larger war against the onslaught of development around the world. In a poem entitled "New Chimney Farm Bedtime Stories," poet Gary Lawless sees it this way:

This morning the field
is full of trucks,
tractor trailers with
pieces of a house soon
to stand where last year
there was forest.
This morning the turtle who
spent the week laying eggs
in the sand beside the road
lies crushed on the pavement,

eyes open, still breathing and
just yards down the road,
the squirrel has already died.
These are the first signs.
We leave the earth a cleared place,
spaces where the woods were,
spaces where the turtles were,
what becomes of the world
with us in it.[28]

For Lawless, these local signs tell us of greater tragedies caused by humans and the likely outcome for a world with us in it.

To understand our "clearing" of the world, activists invoke scientific research, especially on habitat destruction and extinction rates. In 2010, the *Earth First! Journal* dedicated two pages to a "Species Obituary," although the author, Aguamala, notes, "much larger lists exist, none can ever be complete. The roll call of species sacrificed on the altar of industrial civilization grows by at least six organisms every hour." The obituary includes birds, moths, toads, flowers, and mammals, among others. Seven species are highlighted with information about specific conditions caused by humans that led to their extinction: loss of habitat and breeding sites, hunting and poaching, toxoplasmosis carried by feral cats, pollution, and overfishing. Aguamala observes that "a part of all living beauty and inspiration dies with" the Alala crow, and the extinction of the Holdridge's Toad in 2007 "leaves a hole of sorrow."[29] For most activists, imagining extinction comes easily, in part because of first-hand experience of the loss of beings and places they cared for whose disappearance is visible and viscerally felt. And so the call to action comes from the silencing of species and the vanishing of forests both nearby and far away. As activist Christopher Manes put it, radical environmentalism "begins at the end, the end of the world as we know it."[30]

Because of humans' role in all that has been lost, radical activists do not tend to promote the survival of the human species and have often been accused of being misanthropic. Poet Jane McGarry laments our role in the disappearance of other species in *Earth First! Journal*'s "Warrior Poets Society" section:

. . . the ivory bill is alive
some small scrap population
along Arkansas rivers . . .
amid the welter of gone and going species
birds crustaceans insects spiders salamanders
orchids sandworts meadow voles milkweed butterflies

amid the flood of dead and dying creatures
the tsunami of extinction
triggered by the earthquake of us.[31]

For many activists, then, because of the "earthquake of us," the survival
of humanity is not a priority when compared to saving wild spaces and
other species. In Paul Watson's account of his struggle against the
bloody baby seal slaughter for fur in Canada, he predicts that "humanity is doomed." Moreover, Watson adds, the world will be a "nicer"
place without us.[32] Shame, guilt, and grief over the impact of humans on
other species often result in activists imagining and even celebrating a
"world without us."

When they recognize the broader implications of local losses, activists
are motivated by what writer Martin Amis has called "species shame."
Although Amis's context is the terrorist attacks that brought down the
World Trade Center towers in New York City on September 11, 2001,
"species shame" seems an apt phrase. It captures what activists like the
band Torch Runner on an Earth First! music compilation (2013) express
in their song "Feeding": "we have failed/ in a world that would have
been better off never knowing us." In the song "Manufacturing Greed"
(2013), the band Landbridge gives voice to the hopelessness many activists feel: "crushed by the weight of a wretched system/ it is not us, but
what we have created/ that is the disease// competitors in the race to our
total end/ worshipers of death/ in profit we trust/ until our final breath."
One Northern California activist felt guilty that he had watched a thou-
sand-year-old redwood being cut down and did nothing to stop it:
"Every time I pass the stump, I touch it, put my hands on it, and sit down
for a while and renew my vows to the forest."[33] Shame and "survivor
guilt," then, provide more reasons to act, to counter the environmental
devastation our species is responsible for.[34]

As a result, although most activists are not misanthropic, many of
them believe a drastic human population reduction is necessary and
emphasize the importance of not having children.[35] They sometimes
engage in shaming other activists who decide to have children, since
population growth is linked to many other problems, such as habitat
loss and energy consumption. In a letter protesting Earth First! Journal
articles on "Rad Babies" and "Birth First," Geddon argues that "Breed-
ers are the selfish individuals that are sperm or egg donors for the next
generation of human parasites."[36] Geddon advocates sterilization and
adoption for those who want to be parents, and his views are not
uncommon. As suggested by the article on "Rad Babies," other activists

have a more positive attitude towards human beings and human reproduction and believe humans can learn to live in harmony with other species and more lightly on the land.

EARTH WARRIORS

The desire, born of grief and species shame, to slow the decimation of biodiversity is often promoted with the language of warfare. Activists side with the wild against civilization and help the collapse of modern human economies along, while at the same time trying to save animals and the wild. *Collapse* has two meanings for activists, either the decimation of ecosystems and climate change that must be prevented, even though it may be inevitable, or the decline of civilization as we know it that they believe *is* inevitable. Former antiroads activist and writer Paul Kingsnorth clarifies this distinction in a debate on "Hope in the Age of Collapse": "The modern human economy is an engine of mass destruction. Its ravaging of all nonhuman life is not incidental; it seems to be a requirement of the program." For Kingsnorth, it is this economy and the culture that supports it that are hopeless, but nevertheless, "Standing up in whatever small way we can to protect beauty and wildness from our appetites is a worthy cause."[37] For many of the activists I spoke to, this is the cause to which they are dedicated. Being "for the wild" and "for the animals" means protecting animals and wilderness from human appetites while society collapses around them.

When they urge others to join their cause and explain their motivations, activists tend to divide the world into a battle between good and evil. In forest action camps and hardcore punk rock music scenes, as I have shown, civilization and its agents are the enemies. "Earth warriors" fight on the side of ecosystems, nonhuman animals, and indigenous people, and against the forces of "civilization": sealers, multinational corporations, greed, police, and "snitches" (activists who have taken plea bargains and informed on other activists to reduce their prison sentences).

Earth First! co-founder Dave Foreman argued in 1989 that "We are involved in the most sacred crusade ever waged on earth."[38] In a zine, "Down With Empire, Up with the Spring" I picked up at Earth First!'s Round River Rendezvous, the anonymous author insists, "At the beginning of the 21st century we all have to choose sides. Do we remain on the side of industrial civilization or do we stand with struggling peoples in defense of our earth?"[39] In an anonymous ELF communiqué entitled "Beltane" the "elves" refer to themselves as "the burning rage of this dying planet." Because "the planet is dying," they justify their actions as part of a war to save it: "The war of greed ravages the earth and species die out every day. . . . We have to show the enemy that we are serious about defending what is sacred. Together we have teeth and claws to match our dreams."[40] Activists like the ELF, who are frequently labeled "terrorists," attack the enemy, the "real terrorists": oil and logging companies and governments they believe are at the beck and call of corporate interests who allow delicate ecosystems to be laid waste.

By defending what is sacred against the enemy, activists engage in "crusades" and "battles" that involve clear notions of good and evil, heaven and hell. For activists, heaven is the wild, while hell is, as one zine describes it, "industrial civilization ploughing onwards."[41] By emphasizing the opposition between the two, activists highlight the urgency of their cause. "I have been to heaven," Paul Watson explains, describing his experiences on the pristine ice that serves as a nursery for baby seals. But Watson's paradise is invaded by seal hunters with clubs who are "conscripted by Lucifer" and "whose faces and hands drip red with the blood of the innocent."[42] The slaughter of seals transforms heaven into an "annual baptism in blood" through which he must "trod the darkened killing field of the north."[43]

In the midst of this "Hades" Watson recalls, "I have stood on the heaving ice . . . and I have sworn by all the righteous passion in my heart that the madness would be vanquished. But the enemy is all-powerful. . . . Armoured by the philosophy of dominion, all killing is sanctioned."[44] For most activists, few of whom are practicing Christians, Jews, or Muslims, heaven, hell, good, and evil are metaphors. Nonetheless, to describe the dire environmental crises of the late twentieth and early twenty-first centuries, they turn to the language of biblical traditions and the cultural power of rhetoric about holy war.

Radical environmentalists and animal rights activists appropriate the language of revolution and warfare from religion and political movements in order to rally their supporters and give themselves courage. They also draw on this language to distinguish themselves from mainstream environmentalists whom they believe are too willing to compromise. Darryl Cherney told me that a quip he made in an interview on Earth Day, "I am not an environmentalist, I am an Earth Warrior," became a bumper sticker and popular slogan. But according to Cherney, this distinction goes back to the beginnings of Earth First!: "Earth First!, especially back in the day, thought of itself as a Warrior Society." Earth First!'s definition of the warrior, then and now, "is one who offers one's life for the greater good." For Cherney, being an Earth Warrior means acting on behalf of others in dire need:

> Even a cursory look at the actions of my comrades will display a willingness to take risks for the greater good . . . The Earth and its inhabitants are being slaughtered. This is no time for mucking around. But how, oh how, do we proceed? While that answer is open to experimentation, the spirit behind the answer for many of us is clear. And it includes, in large amount, the spirit of the warrior.[45]

So what does the spirit of the warrior entail? For many activists, the spirit of the warrior means being self-sacrificing, willing to risk injury in a tree-sit, or arrest for liberating captive animals.

In an essay called "Brave Hearts Forward," the "Western Wildlife Unit" calls on "brave-hearted warriors of all sexual persuasions, races, religions and beliefs" to join their struggle. It is these warriors, assert the author(s), who provide inspiration: "In our darkest moments we have seen others take on the warrior path and the light at the end of the tunnel is growing into a brilliant blaze fed by the spirits of young warriors who are the hope of millions of oppressed animals and our wounded mother earth."[46] From this perspective, other methods of stopping animal suffering and environmental degradation are slower and less effective. The "hope of the millions," then, must come from these "young warriors." Jeff Luers explains what it means to him to be a warrior:

> There comes a point where if you are paying attention, you become aware of all the wrongs and injustices around you . . . You have to decide if you are willing to be part of something larger than yourself. And you have to decide if you are willing to fight for it. . . . If your answer is "yes," then it is time to pick up your spear, draw a line in the ground, and say: "You have come this far and you shall come no further. I have a voice and I will use it. I will speak for the voiceless, and if you will not hear my words then you will feel my actions."[47]

For activists like Luers who have decided to draw a line, acting means being willing to endure long prison sentences or risk dying during dangerous actions. Because of their grief and shame over the loss of species and suffering of nonhuman animals, activists believe self-sacrifice and martyrdom are required to defend the Earth and its creatures.

Martyrdom can mean enduring prison time or living undercover; it can also mean risking serious injury. The sentiment of a bumper sticker I saw at an Earth First! Rendezvous is not uncommon: "Live Wild or Die Tryin'." In a struggle with some angry sealers as he was trying to prevent

them from clubbing seal pups to death, Paul Watson yelled, "Hoka hey!
. . . It was a Lakota war cry that I had learned so many years before
while under fire from U.S. forces at Wounded Knee . . . I faced death
then, and I would do so here with the same resolve as any true warrior
before me. 'Hoka hey, It is a good day to die.'" Watson, Luers, and other
activists who put their bodies between seals and seal hunters, trees and
bulldozers, know they are at risk. They assume loggers and law enforcement will not want to kill them, but they can never be sure.

One way activists make sense of their warrior role is by identifying
with diverse revolutionary movements and leaders ranging from the
Black Panthers to Gandhi. When they face off against their enemies in a
struggle to defend other species, activists invoke freedom fighters and
revolutionaries who fought for their own species in other eras or countries. Rod Coronado put it this way as he prepared to enter prison for
the beginning of a four-year sentence: "We are all Subcommandante
Marcos, Crazy Horse and the ALF. Never, ever should we forget that in
order to achieve the peace and liberation we strive for, some sacrifice
must occur . . . It is with total love that I say goodbye to my earth
mother for a little while to enter the concrete and steel prisons the U.S.
Government reserves for its discontent citizens."[48] Coronado urges
activists to turn to other animals as well as leaders of revolutionary
movements. He tells them, "Pray to the powers of earth for guidance—
stealth of Cougar, night sight of Owl, like lightning, the power to strike
your enemies suddenly and return home safely."[49] These figures, human
and nonhuman, are sources of inspiration for activists, offering different
models of action and sacrifice.

Identifying with other animals and other heroes can be a significant
source of strength during risky actions. In a detailed account of a coyote
release in the zine *Memories of Freedom*, activists convey their commitment to being on the side of animals. This account suggests how they
come to take on their role as warriors who must move between worlds,
drawing from the models of coyote brethren as well as human heroes.
In their role as warriors for the Earth and animals, they deeply empathize with their nonhuman kin whose lives are at stake.

The target for the coyote action was the U.S. Department of Agriculture's Animal Damage Control (ADC) Predator Research Facility in Mil-
lville, Utah, which tests eradication methods such as lethal traps and poisons on coyotes and other nonhuman animals. ALF investigators and
other animal rights activists discovered a variety of methods developed at
the ADC and used on coyotes and other species, including "M-44 sodium

cyanide charges, steel-jaw traps, aerial shooting, neck snares, cage traps, burning and smoking out dens, spotlight shooting, shotgunning, leg and foot snares, and a variety of poisons which frequently kill thousands of 'non-target' species" as well.[50] In "The Last Bite: Animal Damaged Control," an article in the zine *Memories of Freedom*, an anonymous author tells the story of an ALF action against the research facility.

Activists watched the facility for days, then they held a full moon council during which they decided: "the path would be war." They sent out "moles . . . recruiting warriors for this massive attack." Some of them dressed like hikers and camped out in the hills above, watching researchers and students come and go. Each night they listened to wild coyotes howl nearby and the responses from eighty captive coyotes inside the facility: "The first time these songs penetrated the hearts of the hidden warriors, tears of sadness and rage would cloud their vision through binoculars as they pledged to avenge the dying coyotes in the pens below."

During long nights of watching and planning, they began to feel "personally connected to the coyotes in the pens," some of whom they watched being fed poisoned food. Impatient to do something about the coyotes' dire circumstances, they finally felt confident they had enough information to pull off a successful action. On October 24, 1992, ten warriors came together. Some wore camouflage gear and ski masks. Those who would be drivers were dressed as "normally" as possible, looking like regular citizens, not outlaws. They had radios and police scanners, maps, and cash. Two of the camouflaged activists carried incendiary devices and tools in their packs.

On the night of the action, on a nearby university campus, two bicyclists parked near the primary predator researcher's office, which they entered through a window. They gathered books, files, and other combustibles, placing them near an incendiary device, which they set with a timer. At the same time, several activists approached the coyote pens with bolt-cutters, while others went into the labs and assembled desk drawers and a pile of traps, which they placed near a second incendiary device. As the five activists cut fences, "coyotes in groups of twos and threes could be seen escaping the pens and racing to freedom." After the release, "six warriors quietly padded down the same path they had entered as the star-filled sky was filled with the songs of coyotes disappearing into the mountain wilderness." While they had identified with the coyotes trapped in the pens, they also imagined how the coyotes might have looked on them: "Running from the torture chambers . . . the escaping coyotes saw not six human figures trotting down a mountain path, but six wild coyote warriors who had not forgotten their four-legged brother and sisters." Throughout the planning and the action itself, these activists drew on feelings of kinship and identification to carry out the vandalism they hoped would end the suffering of their coyote kin.

The two incendiary devices went off in the early morning hours after the activists' night work, destroying over half of the lab. The rest was eventually demolished, although the researchers later rebuilt and continued their research. Most of the coyotes, however, were not recovered. Days later, at "a remote hideout victory campfire," the activists fed computer discs they had taken from the lab into the fire: "Once more the ALF had proven that what could not be accomplished with years of protest, could be achieved with a handful of brave-hearted warriors."[51] This action was claimed as part of ALF's "Operation Bite Back," a series of animal releases at fur farms and other animal liberation actions in the 1990s.[52] The predator research facilities, like Paul Watson's description of bloodied ice where seal slaughters take place, are centers of evil for activists: "torture chambers" and "concentration camps," while escape into the wild is liberation from evil. The coyotes escaped the ADC facility with its traps and poisons—"a bastion of environmental and animal destruction"—for "the star-filled sky" and "mountain wilderness."

By conducting themselves like coyotes and feeling the misery of coyotes in their cages, activists highlight the arbitrariness of the species boundary and remake their kinship with other animals. This remaking of activists into coyote kin renders these actions successful on one level, even when the concrete goals of the action or protest are not achieved. These actions function as initiatory rites of passage for those who are joining an action for the first time, or for those who have participated in many actions, as rites of affirmation that kinship relationships matter. In this instance, an animal release is a ritualized act in response to grief over animal suffering, specifically targeting scientific research.

During actions like the coyote release, activists skirt the bounds of two worlds—the wild and civilization. Not only do they find strength in identifying with wild animals, but they also draw on the tools and strategies of their enemies. They aspire to belong to the wild, and reject science, progress, capitalism, and consumerism. But ingredients for fire bombs and tools for sabotaging heavy equipment are made possible by the civilization they reject.

After witnessing the suffering of coyotes for the benefit of livestock raised for human consumption, which the many of them who are vegans and vegetarians are against in the first place, ALF warriors felt justified in damaging the ADC research facility. However, other animal rights activists distance themselves from ALF and ELF tactics and argue that legal, or at least nonviolent, approaches should be used to stop animal suffering. Animal rights activists agree they are engaged in a struggle for justice for nonhuman animals. They agree this war has high stakes, as unbearable suffering and species extinction take place every day, but they differ on what are the most effective and appropriate tactics.

EVERY TOOL IN THE TOOLBOX

Radical environmentalists and animal rights activists have a range of positions on what constitutes violence and nonviolence. They also distinguish between violent rhetoric and actual violence towards things or people.[53] Stances on property destruction and arson shift and vary within activist communities and individual activists' lifetimes. When Craig Rosebraugh stepped down after four years as the ELF's spokesperson (1997–2001), he voiced his increasing discomfort with ELF's "acts of psychological intimidation" as one of the reasons for his resignation. Nevertheless, he still advocated an "every tool in the toolbox" approach, which is a common position for many activists, even when they themselves do not use all the tools.[54] In this way, they downplay divisive differences on what means are justified to achieve goals on which they mostly agree.

Not surprisingly, activists' views differ from what many Americans, especially government agencies and property owners, would consider violence. In their study of the animal rights movement, sociologists Jasper and Nelkin call the more radical elements of the animal rights movement "fundamentalists." On the other hand, ethicist Gary L. Francione, codirector of Rutgers University Animal Rights Center, suggests that most animal rights activists are not extreme *enough*: "animal welfare reforms often conflict directly with the fundamental values of rights theory." For Francione and other ethicists who share his views, the rights attributed to nonhuman animals necessitate their liberation from oppressive situations: making cows more comfortable before they go to slaughter is not sufficient.[55] The tension between nonviolence and property destruction emerges within protests (arson, sabotage, rock throwing, and breaking windows are advocated by some and criticized by others) and also in relation to other movements activists emulate. Some aspire to the nonviolent resistance of Martin Luther King Jr. and the civil rights movement, while others prefer to emulate the more militant approach of the Mexican Zapatistas.

In rhetoric, if not always in practice, many radical environmental and animal rights activists prefer more confrontational figures that align with their sense of being involved in an urgent struggle. Malcolm X's dictum "by any means necessary" is often invoked by activists. They also draw inspiration from Spanish anarchists, the Palestinian Intifada, and the South African antiapartheid movement, among others.[56] SHAC activist Kevin Kjonaas argues that history has taught us "valuable lessons" about "guerilla tactics used in the overthrow of the South African apartheid government, how economic sabotage in the Boston Tea Party ignited our country's fight for independence." Kjonaas does not deny "violence" is involved, but insists that the use of violence as an appropriate tactic is "not done out of a love of causing destruction and harm." For Kjonaas and other activists, violence is often a last resort when other methods are too slow and forests and animals are dying.

The broader anarchist movement has significantly shaped attitudes about the use of force among radical animal rights and environmental activists. Property destruction during the Occupy Wall Street movement and at the 1999 WTO protests in Seattle was lauded by some but critiqued by others. While there are many pacifists among American anarchists, some anarchists are condescending toward and critical of pacifism, seeing it as something for "white liberals." From this perspective, nonviolence is a luxury for those who have privilege. As a POC (people of color) -identified leader of a workshop on decolonizing the environmentalist movement at an activist gathering I attended put it, "leave off with all the white non-violent shit." Regardless of their urgent words and the use of forceful symbols like Earth First!'s raised and closed fist, reminiscent of the Black Panthers, most activists do not engage violently with other humans, even when they have not committed themselves to nonviolence. However, they have no such qualms regarding property destruction.

For the majority of activists involved with Earth First!, the ELF, and the ALF, property destruction is justified when that property is harming nonhuman animals and ecosystems. As Rod Coronado, who later admitted being involved with the ALF ADC coyote liberation, puts it, "I've seen what goes on behind laboratory doors of places like Huntingdon Life Sciences and I'd be a hypocrite to say I wouldn't want to plant a bomb to stop it."[57] But the ALF and ELF, whose actions tend to be more militant than those of Earth First!, explicitly state that everything must be done to ensure no one is injured during the action. ALF's mission statement urges those planning actions to consider: "Danger to other sentient beings. Take into account humans as well as rodents you can't see. Realize that 'change' may upset a miniature ecosystem on which some beings may rely. Fires or bombs can kill mice and birds you didn't see."[58] For this reason, at the Vail, Colorado, arson, Bill Rodgers did not set fire to one of the buildings the saboteurs had planned to burn because a hunter was sleeping in it.[59]

Behind these justifications of property destruction is a critique of speciesism. For activists, the assumption that the rights of nonhumans are as important as those of humans is a key justification for acting with force. Rod Coronado suggests activists are hypocritical when they do not support ALF and ELF actions that involve property destruction. As he puts it, "In failing to support actions that cause no injury, except to life-destroying property, we fail to live up to our own belief in the rights of other species . . . the Earth and her threatened animal nations deserve the same level of defense that we support when human life is threatened."[60] The facts of their suffering and the attribution of rights to other species excuse damaging "life-destroying" property.

For most activists, private property is not a right, nor is it something passive. Laboratories, cages, and bulldozers are all *agents* of suffering. Animals and forests are innocent victims and inanimate things are the evil-doers. One ELF communiqué put it this way, "The ELF wholeheartedly condones the use of violence towards inanimate objects to prevent oppression, violence, and most of all to protect freedom."[61] Property is not seen as something value-free. From this perspective, a researcher's desk holding reams of paper describing studies made possible by the suffering of animals is a fair target.

Activists, then, rarely see strategic property destruction as "violence," though some make an exception for arson, which they believe can too easily get out of control. They tend to nuance the meaning of property destruction so it is either a kind of nonviolence or a special kind of violence, even "anti-violence." Paul Watson describes his confrontational tactics as "aggressive non-violence" in which damage is "permitted to inanimate objects used to kill sentient creatures."[62] Pattrice Jones explains that "many uses of force are not violent . . . Violence is unjustified or excessive injurious use of force." For her, "breaking locks, tearing down cages, disabling bulldozers, and other ways of interfering with property are *anti-violent* [my emphasis] activities. . . violence is never okay but force is sometimes necessary."[63] Actions are "anti-violent" when they prevent further violence. Even though he does not engage in property destruction, forest activist Sparrow agrees that "property destruction is not inherently 'violent'" if "no life is taken or physically harmed," which does not include the harm of losing one's research or the stress involved with having one's office burned down: "I'm talking about physical harm . . . it's hard to feel sorry for the animal torturer or gas-guzzling SUV salesman when there are innocent critters and people dying left and right, every day, for profit."[64] But not all activists agree that these ways of thinking about actions involving property destruction keep them from being violent.

On the other side of the issue of property destruction are those committed to nonviolence for whom destruction of offices and research facilities is seen as a violent act. These critics denounce such tactics as violent because they see them as counterproductive. They believe activists' strategies should be in line with their goal to bring into being a nonviolent society. In his essay, "How I Became an Eco-Warrior," Jeff Luers describes a conflict at the Fall Creek blockades when some activists decided to fight back after receiving violent treatment at the hands of road construction workers. These activists rejected "dogmatic adherence to 'non-violence,'" because "no matter what we were not going to let this forest fall." For this reason, "When the Freddies pulled their pepper spray, we pulled ours . . . Over the camp flew a banner, 'If trees fall, blood spills.'" For this language and the willingness to fight back they were denounced by some activists and supported by others.[65]

In a critique of home demonstrations in which animal rights activists protested vivisection outside researchers' homes, author Carol J. Adams acknowledges the urgency activists feel to prevent nonhuman animal suffering: "Their powerlessness seems to call us to use any means possible to stop their abuse." But for Adams acting out of urgency is "dangerous" because it causes us "to see everything in black and white."[66] Animal activist Lee Hall goes farther, condemning acts of intimidation and property destruction because they are "a gift to the state." These acts can more easily be labeled "ecoterrorism" than nonviolent civil disobedience. They seem to merit repressive laws and allow animal researchers and loggers to paint all activists as dangerous criminals.[67] For all these reasons, property destruction and inflammatory rhetoric remain controversial in activist communities where their ethics and strategic value are hotly contested.

Radical activists chafe against the terrorist label and criticize its presence in courtrooms and news media coverage of their actions. "We were 'eco-saboteurs,' not terrorists," insists Chelsea Gerlach, one of the ELF cell members responsible for the arson at Vail, Colorado.[68] When arguing against attempts by the FBI, prosecutors, and judges to depict them as terrorists and apply terrorist enhancements in their sentencing, activists are particularly troubled by the groups they are associated with, given that their actions did not injure anyone. Daniel McGowan was shocked during his sentencing when "the prosecutor said that our actions were analogous to the actions of the Ku Klux Klan. I pride myself on speaking out when I hear racist garbage."[69] As an activist with the Buffalo Field Campaign sees it, "People are going to prison for their entire lives for defending the earth when rapists get a few years for a violent crime against another human."[70] Chelsea Gerlach got involved with ELF around the time "a right-winger had just bombed the Oklahoma City building—killing 168 people—and anti-abortionists were murdering doctors. But the government characterized the ELF as a top domestic terrorism threat because we burned down unoccupied buildings in the middle of the night."[71] The disproportionate sentences they have received, often because of post-9/11 terrorism enhancements, add to activists' sense of injustice.[72]

It is not *they* who are the terrorists, activists argue, but those they fight against. In an *Earth First! Journal* story about pollution in Alberta, Canada, activists accused of being terrorists responded, "The real eco-terrorism is what is going up the stacks and into the water."[73] One slogan for the campaign against Maxxam during the "Redwood Wars" declared, "The eco-terrorists live in Texas," referring to Maxxam's corporate headquarters in Houston.[74] When Paul Watson was asked about ecoterrorism in an interview, he contended that "Eco-terrorism is a form of violence usually carried out by corporations. The Exxon Valdez was an eco-terrorist ship . . . Eco-terrorism is simply the terrorizing of the environment and living things within the ecosystems under assault . . . Therefore, the destruction of a whaling ship is counter-terrorism."[75] If their enemies are the real terrorists, then activists are heroes, preventing real terrorist acts by multinational corporations. As Crow asked during his sentencing, "Am I a terrorist or a patriot?" As patriots in a long tradition of American radicalism advocating illegal acts, from civil disobedience in the civil rights movement to property destruction in the antiwar movement, activists serve a moral imperative that often makes them into martyrs for their causes.

MARTYRS AND FALLEN WARRIORS

On March 28, 2013, 140 miles north of San Francisco near the small town of Willits, California, a twenty-four-year-old tree-sitter called "the Warbler," a local farmer who had lived for two months in "Liberty Ponderosa," a Ponderosa pine slated for demolition, announced the beginning of her hunger strike while some of her supporters wept. She sent all of her food down to the ground in buckets.[76] She told her supporters by cell phone: "I, Amanda Senseman (Warbler) am going on a hunger strike to protest the proposed Willits Bypass . . . I am witnessing the destruction of my home."[77] The construction of the bypass would fill in wetlands and in other ways have a significant impact on Little Lake Valley and its watershed, the habitat of migratory birds, salmon, steelhead, and tule elk, among others. A few weeks earlier, Senseman, sitting on a platform seventy feet up in the ponderosa pine, explained in an interview that while this area was her home, she was also there to protest bigger issues: "It's not just about these wetlands and this forest, it's happening everywhere. We are part of this fragile matrix of life, not above or outside it . . . asphalt does not harbor life."[78] Six days later she was extracted by four police officers in a cherry picker.

Like the precarious bodies in road blockades and tree-sits I described in Chapter 3, activists like Senseman use hunger strikes to draw attention to environmental and animal rights issues by sacrificing their own comfort and health. Their vulnerability also works on their fellow activists, who may be moved by such sacrifice to act in turn. For instance, solidarity actions have taken place for tree-sits like the Warbler's, for activists in prison, or to mark the anniversaries of activists' deaths.[79] Peril and sacrifice both express and generate grief in self-sacrificing activists and those in their communities who witness their sacrifices.

Extractions of tree-sitters and confrontations between activists and law enforcement enforce the feeling of being in a war-like situation in which heroes and enemies are polarized. As Moonshadow, a tree-sitter involved with a Vail, Colorado, blockade, describes it, "My removal from 80 feet up in the spruce tree was one of the scariest moments of my life. Trees fell within five feet of my platform. . . . After the feller-buncher downed all the trees close to me, the operator cut trees further away and dropped them right next to me."[80] According to multiple accounts, activists at the Tar Sands Blockade in Texas experienced harassment from security guards and workers. Aaron described to me how bulldozers approached the tree village. From up in the tree where he was sitting, he was terrified when they started cutting down trees nearby. He watched the area around the tree village become "militarized" with dozens of police officers carrying guns.[81]

While those in trees are particularly vulnerable, support crews on the ground are also subject to harassment. Earlier in the Tar Sands Blockade action, on the day after eight protesters climbed eighty feet up in trees and began occupying what would become a tree village, two protesters on the ground locked themselves to a piece of machinery that was being used by TransCanada to bulldoze the area. An activist watching what happened described it this way:

> Under the active encouragement from TransCanada local police employ torture tactics on both peaceful protestors. They twist and contort the tube that the blockaders had locked their arms into, cutting off circulation to their hands and cutting abrasions into their hands and forearms. Police discharge pepper spray into their lockdown tube, and the chemicals burn their already-open wounds. Despite the immense pain, our brave blockaders remain locked to the machinery for several hours—determined to stop this toxic tar sands pipeline. Both protestors are then tased by police officers [who are] congratulated on a "job well done" by TransCanada's senior supervisors. Shannon and Benjamin are eventually removed and arrested when it is clear that TransCanada is willing to do whatever it takes to increase pain levels to physically unbearable levels.[82]

Activists share tales of pain and harassment by law enforcement, loggers, hunters, and construction workers, which heightens their sense of being locked in a struggle with a dehumanized and dehumanizing enemy.

Activists' status as martyrs on the front lines of environmental and animal rights struggles is also enhanced when they do time in prison.[83] Imprisoned activists typically have a significant support system. Parents and relatives, as well as their activist families, make sure they have money for supplies, books, and whatever else they need. Some activists describe receiving piles of letters from supporters, many of whom they have never met. Activist gatherings often feature group letter writing to prisoners.[84] Because they are typically cast as political prisoners, they may be punished for "inciting terrorism" and put into solitary confinement. Vegan and vegetarian prisoners struggle to get their dietary needs met. On the other hand, some prisoners choose to go on hunger strikes in prison to continue acting for their causes. Barry Horne, an English animal rights activist, died in prison as a result of a hunger strike, further enhancing his role as a martyr sacrificed in the struggle for animal rights.

Horne undertook a series of hunger strikes, including one that lasted sixty-eight days, while serving an eighteen-year sentence for planting incendiary devices in stores that sold fur coats and leather products. The purpose of his hunger strike was to persuade the British government to hold a public inquiry on animal testing. In his account of Horne's hunger strike, activist Keith Mann explains Horne's motivation: "It was for him very much a war—a war in which the only victims are countless millions of animals undergoing horrific suffering . . . for Barry there was nothing greater he could do in the war than offer his life."[85] Other activists and supporters held candlelit vigils outside the prison, activists in other countries burned Union Jack flags in front of British embassies in solidarity, and eighteen other animal rights prisoners in the United Kingdom started solidarity fasts.[86]

Over time Horne's health deteriorated and he made a living will specifying that if he should lose consciousness, he not be kept alive.[87] At the beginning of his third hunger strike, Horne explained how the difficult decision to start another hunger strike was made for the animals: "the tortured dead cry out for justice, the cry of the living is for freedom . . . The animals have no one but us, we will not fail them." He began the third hunger strike on October 6, 1998, and ended the strike after 68 days in failing health. He died a year later of liver failure.[88]

Activists hope their sacrifices will make others pay attention to and value the causes they sacrificed for.[89] In an article written in response to the death of Earth First! activist Brad Will, the contemporary Pagan writer and activist Starhawk explains that martyrs are made, because " 'sacrifice' means to 'make sacred' . . . In an instant, that ordinary comrade you remember singing at the fire or arguing at the meeting, someone you might have been charmed or irritated by or attracted to, or not, someone who showed no mark of doom or prescience of what was to come, becomes uplifted into another realm, part symbol, part victim, locus of our deepest love and rage." It is that love and rage, she argues, that "can move us to action."[90] Activists who die for animals or forests not only make their own lives sacred, in Starhawk's sense, but also point to causes that are worth dying for. Just as vulnerable bodies hanging from treetops bring the endangered species they want to protect into public space, so too do hunger strikes like Horne's aim to highlight the ideals activists strive for.

LOYALTY AND BETRAYAL

On the evening of the Summer Solstice, 2005, William Rodgers, known as Avalon, a name he took from the book *The Mists of Avalon*, suffocated himself in his cell where he was awaiting sentencing. He left behind a note to his friends and supporters: "Certain human cultures have been waging war against the Earth for millennia. I chose to fight on the side of bears, mountain lions, skunks, bats, saguaros, cliff rose and all things wild. I am just the most recent casualty in that war. But tonight I have made my jail break—I am returning home, to the earth, to the place of my origins."[91] Rodgers was arrested and charged with one count of arson for his alleged role in an ELF arson at the National Wildlife Research Facility in Olympia, Washington. He was also suspected of participating in the $12 million fire at the ski resort in Vail, Colorado, in 1998. Rodgers had a long record of involvement with radical environmentalism since at least the early 1990s and thought of the United States as an "ecocidal empire."[92]

With his suicide, Rodgers moved into a pantheon of "fallen warriors" who are remembered around circles at activist gatherings and invoked as an inspiration for direct action.[93] In his suicide note, Rodgers echoed the words of labor union martyr Joe Hill who was executed in 1915: "Don't mourn, organize."[94] Some of his friends chalked "live wild" on a sidewalk in his honor.[95] Memorial services were held and actions were committed in his memory soon after Rodgers's death. According to Erica Ryberg, "During a nighttime memorial ceremony in which they remembered his warrior spirit, a picnic table burst into flames at a crucial moment. They put out the fire, blew out the remaining candles, and remembered Bill in the darkness he loved so well. Surrounded by the scent of Ponderosa pine and granite, his friends lingered a few moments more before gathering around the campfire to tell stories of Bill."[96] On the anniversary of his death in 2012, the liberation of twenty-eight beagles from a laboratory was dedicated to Rodgers.[97] As his friends wrote in an elegy, "Long Live Avalon," "Endless tears on this dark night, but no fading memories or forgotten names—it will go down in action!"[98]

Accidental deaths are also tragic opportunities for commemorative action. In April 2002, twenty-two-year-old Beth O'Brien fell to her death at the Eagle Creek tree-sit when she slipped while climbing a rope ladder between platforms, 150 feet up in "Truth," a four-hundred-year-old Douglas fir. As in the case of other activists' deaths, O'Brien's was made meaningful in the context of a holy war in which she was the latest casualty, a war her friends would continue to fight on her behalf.

According to one friend of O'Brien's, "At her funeral in Santa Rosa her father noted that right-wing talk-show host Rush Limbaugh had called her a 'Tree-sit suicide bomber.'" O'Brien's father was outraged and "called for us to take action."[99] Before taking action, Cascadia Forest Alliance held a memorial vigil at Mount Tabor Park in Portland that drew more than 200 people.[100] A few months later, Cascadia Forest Alliance activists returned to Mt. Hood to establish a tree-sit in another part of the forest they feared would be logged. A local newsweekly noted that O'Brien's presence was "reflected in renewed safety concerns and in the operation's name—Horehound, in honor of O'Brien's forest name.[101]

On the one-year anniversary of O'Brien's death, her friend Tristan linked her with other struggles by invoking a song from the 1980s about EL Salvador's FMLN guerillas: "The best ones have already gone/ Those that have fallen for our freedom/ Those that have fallen for our freedom." On the five-year anniversary of her death a remembrance appeared on Portland's Indymedia site: "Five Years Since Horehound Fell." An online post toasted her: "I lift a glass to her, pour some on the earth, and drink deeply," while another mentioned other activists who had died—David Chain and Avalon—as well: "they still live in our hearts, souls, and keeps the fire burning in our spirits . . . a howl goes up for all whenever i think about them and what they stood for."[102]

In addition to these gatherings, actions, and virtual memorials, O'Brien's memory was also carried on through material expressions of mourning. In 2015, O'Brien appeared in artist Kiera "Loki" Anderson's Earth First! memorial quilt, also known as the "Cascadia Tree-sitters Quilt" and designed to "commemorate twenty years of forest activism and honouring all the forest activists involved that are no longer with us." When Anderson brought the quilt to an Earth First! gathering and interviewed some activists about it, one of them explained its importance in this way: "The quilt connects me with the reason I'm angry, the reason I'm fighting and the reason why we've lost so much."[103]

On the night of another instance of memorializing, at another Earth First! gathering a year earlier, I made my way down a dark forest path at an Earth First! Round River Rendezvous. I was heading for the "Night to Howl," a bonfire set apart from the rest of the camp. Some participants sat on logs, while others stood at the edge of the circle, talking and laughing with their friends. One of the activists gathered at the fire asked us to remember fallen warriors. Those who had died, like Bill Rodgers and David Chain, were named and howled for. Those in prison, like Marius (formerly Marie) Mason were also honored. Endangered and extinct species were mentioned as well. We howled for each of them. Participants also sang songs and recited poetry. It was a night of mourning as well as celebration, as the community praised and commemorated its loyal fallen warriors.

Traveling to clear-cuts and other places where loss has happened to protest that loss and naming solidarity actions for dead activists are ways of keeping the memory of dead ones—trees, humans, nonhuman animals—alive. Inviting news media to cover protests also enables those losses to be remembered through images and stories circulated on the Internet and in print news sources. In these ways, the deaths of fellow activists as well as other species have a kind of afterlife, in which activists keep speaking to and talking to their beloved dead.[104] Through his suicide, Rodgers was making present the many nonhuman dead mentioned in his suicide note ("bears, mountain lions, skunks, bats, saguaros, cliff rose") to whom he had dedicated his life. His friends and other activists who admired him kept his memory alive by dedicating actions to him and continuing to tell his story. Fallen warriors, then, through public and shared commemoration, help to move the struggle forward. They are the loyal dead, who remain part of activist communities' work of mourning. Those who betray their comrades, on the other hand, cause rifts that cannot be healed in these ways; they are forgotten instead of remembered.

While Bill Rodgers used his death to call others to the fight "for the bats and whales," the dark side of his suicide was his feeling of being betrayed by those he trusted. Juxtaposed with stories of self-sacrifice and martyrdom, other stories circulate as well, of those who betrayed their friends, accepted plea bargains, or wore wires to help the FBI. In his decision to not cooperate with a Grand Jury, Josh Harper explains his reasoning: "as an anarchist I would never willingly cooperate with the grand jury system. . . . They can drag me to the grand jury room, but they can never make me speak."[105] When faced with sentences almost as long as their own lives and threatened by federal prosecutors, some activists do speak and agree to cooperate. When activists cooperate with the American legal system by implicating other activists, they become "snitches."

If fallen activists are memorialized and honored for their loyalty and sacrifice, snitches are seen as traitors and ostracized for their betrayal. To snitch in order to reduce one's sentences goes against the ideal of the self-sacrificing and loyal warrior that is so powerfully invoked in activist communities. Being committed to the wild and to animals means never informing on your activist friends. Great Grey Owl remembers a former friend who cooperated with prosecutors for a reduced sentence: "She's dead to us. I like to remember her as she was when she was one of us—when she was brave and fiery and dedicated."[106] Snitches, then, have gone over to the other side, against their own ideals: "I can't imagine being able to live with myself if I sold out my friends or betrayed the movement," writes Great Grey Owl; "the kind of cooperation we're seeing is a betrayal of everything these people believed when they became activists."[107] The issue here is not simply that snitches have betrayed their friends. Snitches also weaken a movement that relies on trust and noncooperation with the government. For their former comrades, such betrayal seems to call into question the seriousness of all activists' commitments.

Bill Rodgers' death exemplifies the difficulty many activists experience in balancing hope for change made possible by their actions and despair over extinction, nonhuman animal abuse, habitat loss, and the failings of their movement, in the case of snitches. Radical environmentalist rhetoric is characterized by this tension between hope and despair. Utopian visions of rewilding the world after industrial collapse and creating new communities compete with despair over the onslaught of destruction activists see around them.

APOCALYPTIC THINKING AND THE SEEDS OF CONTINGENT HOPE

The war for the wild and for the animals is made up of heroes and martyrs who risk their lives, are willing to spend years in prison, and never sacrifice their friends for their own self-interest. This war is imagined within an apocalyptic context that fuels some of the urgency activists feel. Since activists depict themselves as eco-warriors on the side of Nature in the battle for the future of Earth, their view of the future requires the destruction of everything they identify with the forces of evil.

Most activists both expect and hope for a collapse of civilization as we know it. They may desire the survival of small communities after the collapse, but many suspect there will be a devastating and chaotic period and that humans may not survive. Those I interviewed repeatedly told me that the end of civilization and perhaps the end of biotic life will come, if not in their lifetimes, then in the not too distant future. On an Earth First! compilation, the band Rizana characterizes the collapse this way: "ancient beauty covered in concrete, destroyed forests, theres nothing left to eat/ blow up the mountains, pollute the streams/ it takes more than dreams to fight the machine/ locked up our hearts sewn shut our eyes lookin' up to the smoke and charred skies." As Rabbit, a member of the *Earth First! Journal* collective put it, "if civilization as we know it collapses, probably the best case scenario, we're all going to die."[108]

For many activists, a collapse could mean one of two possible outcomes. In the first scenario ecosystems will be destroyed, the planet will die and so, too, will humans. In the second scenario, civilization will collapse, but the wild will continue in some form, regardless of what happens to humans, who may or may not survive. On the *No Compromise* CD, the band Oi Polloi sings, "there has to be another way . . . capitalism spread around the globe/ nightmare, pain and blood/ desert where trees grew/ pollution without end, destruction and death . . . we need another way." But most activists are not hopeful that contemporary human societies will find another way.

Activists' sense of hope in finding another way is fragile and contingent, especially next to their certainty about collapse.[109] Rabbit holds out this kind of contingent hope that some wild spaces will remain: "Rewilding can be as simple as tearing down a fence or creating a balance of an ecosystem by planting native plants, but the main thing is moving to where we can back off and let it do what it wants to do. . . . protecting what we have left that is wild is probably the most important thing we can do." Although most activists despair that civilization is doomed, they continue to act and advocate for the wild. Theirs is a hope in the intimate and immediate, the glimpse of a place reclaimed by weeds and wildflowers, the satisfaction of working side by side with friends to shut down a fracking site for a day, or to free dozens of coyote from a research facility.

Another source of hope for the future is in activists' attempts to create inclusive, egalitarian communities to replace hierarchical social structures that are in part responsible for exploiting forests and abusing nonhuman animals. Marten describes the kind of hopefulness he witnessed at Wild Roots, Feral Futures gathering that "seemed to lie in current social justice practices and concepts; primarily, this means recognizing the 'intersectionality' of struggles." Many people at the gathering believed that "meaningful" change could come about through radical anarchist and activist communities reshaping how humans live with each other as well as with the more than human world.[110] Hope, then, takes at least two forms among activists: hope for the end of industrial civilization and return of the wild and hope that human communities can be fundamentally transformed.

Radical environmentalism is characterized by a deep tension between apocalyptic doom and contingent hope.[111] This paradox leads to the call to act because, out of the rubble of civilization, perhaps something will

Earth First! Journal covers.

survive. Tar Sands activist Eamon Farrelly explains his determination to not give way to despair: "I'm a human being who still gives a fuck, and who hasn't been morally and spiritually crushed despite the best efforts of those who profit from the silence and complacency of the masses in the face of genocide. As a person of conscience and soul, I am not willing to stand by as the forests fall, as the waters run black, and as the least guilty among us are continually exploited and made to suffer the most."[112] The main source of hope for activists like Farrelly is that regardless of what happens to humans, the wild will survive, and perhaps with it, indigenous people, the "least guilty."

PRIMAL FUTURE

Because activists construct oppositions between the destructive practices of civilization and the liberating promise of "the wild," it is the wild that beckons from the primal future that activists envision.[113] Animal rights activist Peter Young argues that "The root of the problem is domestication." For this reason, his vision for the future is "a return to a harmonious relationship with our surroundings and the animals with whom we share this planet, one free of domination."[114]Activists' primal future is the opposite of a technological solution to environmental problems; it is a reaction against technology and a return to the past.

One aspect of this return to the past is rewilding, a way to address the ills of domestication. In the zine *reclaim, rewild: a vision for going feral & actualizing our wildest dreams*, Laurel and Skunk argue that "There's another way to live. . . . another, older world beneath the asphault of what's mistakenly referred to as the 'real world.' . . . Humans can belong as certainly as any forest, worm or wolf. The trouble is we've forgotten who we are, what we're for, and where we came from."[115] In the same zine, Griffin writes in "Human Domestication: Sickness of Separation," that "Each one of us is a wild animal suffering, isolated from our true livelihoods & homes in the arms of the true Mother . . . It is possible to become feral by overcoming the numbness of the civilized condition & become fully human."[116] To rewild means, among other things, rejecting domestication and uncovering a wilder self in order to "rejoin the community of nature."[117] Paradoxically, from this perspective becoming wild, becoming more like other animals, is the way to being more fully human.

Along with rewilding, many activists work towards a future in which small face-to-face communities either survive the collapse of civilization or are built from its rubble. Kite, an activist who worked with the Buffalo Field Campaign, is certain that civilization as we know it is coming to an end: "I look at the average North American and I'm certain they will consume us into chaos . . . Those of us willing to see what is going on are still a small minority with no real power to make changes." But this view, he explains, need not lead to despair. Instead, "I know a lot of other people who share my perspective. We can't stop civilization, we can't stop the coming collapse, but we can provide examples of community based survival, and a more sustainable relationship with the earth." He believes the only rational approach is a return to localized economies and community-based living, where the community includes other species.[118]

Because of these emphases on rewilding and learning from the past, radical activism increasingly overlaps with the broader primitive skills movement as well as both green anarchist apocalyptic views and more conservative survivalism.[119] However, unlike survivalism, activists' vision of a future after industrial collapse is one in which other species, not humans, are dominant. Rod Coronado holds a view of the future common among activists: "It's going to be a dark time," he wrote to me,

> but I think there will be pockets of people, nature and animals that will survive . . . We will rediscover the value of loving the world around us when our survival is inseparable from it. The intimate relationship we create with the natural world will reawaken a relationship with nature that will be a new enlightenment, one filled with new stories of our animal relations and prophecy and as we raise our children in this new world, the memory of consumerist worldviews will seem as crazy as our concepts of past societies who believed the earth was flat.[120]

Activist music, poetry, and art work clearly express these kinds of future visions in which going feral entails the undoing of civilization and rewilding of the planet. In the poem, "A Handful of Leaves," Sean Swain imagines the future as a return to the "Stone Age":

> A prayer for the children of the next Neolithic,
> That we leave to them
> A field of lilies where a Walmart once stood,
> Salmon upstream from the ruins of a dam,
> Kudzu vines embracing skeletons of skyscrapers,
> Cracked and overgrown ribbons of nameless super-
> Highways.
> A prayer for the children of the next Neolithic,
> That you may
> Lay entwined in fields of lilies,
> Sustain yourselves on sister salmon,
> Climb the vines of kudzu to shelter,
> Salt meat on the remains of the highway,
> And use this poem for kindling at sundown
> So you can spare a handful of leaves
> Where the gods write poetry of their own.[121]

Activists' response to grief and loss is a hoped-for future in which the wild and the animals take over the planet. If humans have a place in this future, it is as one among many other species; human exceptionalism must become a thing of the past. While a primal future may be predicated on societal collapse, for activists the end of industrialized civilization presents an opportunity to create something new out of the ashes.

As Julia Butterfly Hill sees it, "If we are strategic about it, we'll look at that collapse as compost, and we'll begin to build the beautiful garden we want."[122] Relearning and rewilding may involve a return to certain aspects of the past, but they are fundamentally about shaping the past into something new. For many activists, the vision of a rewilded planet remains their prayer for the future, a final rite that reverses the mourning of dying species, where mourning for a dead civilization is a celebration of the return and triumph of the wild.

Conclusion

As a participant who howled for those in prison and cried for the dead around a fire deep in the forest, listened to the moving tributes and heartfelt songs, laughed at the jokes and irreverence that accompanied grief and anger, I was immersed in the values and desires of activist communities. I experienced first-hand the transformation of my own childhood memories and relationships with other species in the context of activist gatherings and protests. The closeness I had always felt to trees and other animals took on new meaning and resonance. These relationships charged my desire to act as well: to cheer for the young activists in hammocks and tripods, to fear for their safety, to talk with police officers about what a leaderless movement meant, and to care for people seeking help at the medic tent. At gatherings and actions, I experienced the sense of shared struggle, grief over loss, and anger for what seemed so entirely wrong—cutting down old-growth forests, for instance, or torturing coyotes to test better ways of killing them.

Activists live in a world in which the lives of nonhuman others become as valuable as their own. They live with the reality of environmental destruction and animal deaths every day. What most of us keep at a distance is close up and personal for them. Surrounded by the stories and emotions of others who are similarly committed, despite their differences, it is hard to see things otherwise. What is the world we want our children and grandchildren to inherit? How can we turn away from the crises of other species and those of our own? What happens if we turn towards them? These questions are unavoidable in activists' worlds and vividly present in everything that happens. Gatherings, workshops, trainings, circles, and protests are all oriented towards insisting that the world can be otherwise, that there is a better way. It is these alternate ways of thinking and being in the world that give protests their distinctive qualities.

During protests, activists reconfigure their relationships with trees and nonhuman species as well as with other humans. Activists' experiences attest to the importance of childhood, memory, emotion, and ritual actions in shaping our relationships with these other species. Protest rites inscribe new meanings on activist bodies and articulate new visions of the future. They challenge the taken-for-granted order of things and suggest innovative approaches to being human with the more-than-human world. Through disruptive, ritualized performances in treetops and on logging roads, activists situate themselves within a multispecies community and make other things and beings sacred. Ritualized practices bind people together and bind humans to other species. At the same time, they may reveal rifts and construct oppositions, such as between "the wild" and "civilization." Nevertheless, activist communities hold out the possibility of a different kind of social understanding in which other species are foremost in our concerns both because they are inextricably linked with the lives of humans and because they have intrinsic value.

What to make of the "terrorism" label that so often frames public understandings of radical activism? There is clearly a gap between my account of activist communities and the ecoterrorism stereotypes circulated by American law enforcement agencies. I saw no evidence of any danger to other human beings posed by activists during my fieldwork despite the sometimes inflammatory rhetoric that emerges in activist contexts. Property destruction, of course, can cause pain to other humans, even if no physical injury occurs. Many activists do not value private property when they are faced with human and nonhuman animal suffering and environmental destruction. For this reason, some of them—not the majority—are likely to continue acts of sabotage that they believe will reduce suffering and destruction. For these activists, not to do so is morally wrong and flies in the face of our responsibilities to other species. Activists' confrontational and emotional behavior during protests can make them difficult and challenging to work with, but not dangerous. A common emphasis on nonviolent communication, respect for other people's boundaries, and a culture of consent, make life-threatening violence against humans unlikely.

However, activists are idealistic and, like most of us, do not always live up to their ideals. They sometimes fail to treat each other with respect or to get consent, and they sometimes make women, transgender and gender-nonconforming people, and people of color in their communities suffer. Activist communities aspire to create new and better ways of doing human relationships, but their communities, like the world outside their communities, remain fraught with inequality and oppressive behavior.

Radical activist culture tends to valorize pain and suffering, praising martyrs and fallen warriors. Scars on the landscape and on human bodies and psyches draw their attention. Pain and sacrifice do important work in activist communities by charging environmental and animal issues with meaning and inspiring commitments among activists. At the same time, activism is stressful and risky, so activist burn-out is common. While humor and joy permeate activist communities as well, they do not always go far enough to assuage helplessness and despair in the face of environmental devastation and overwhelming human and non-human animal suffering.

Radical activists are not outliers or outsiders, although they may perceive themselves that way. Their language of chosenness and their sense of moral responsibility in the face of powerful enemies are strategies and sensibilities in keeping with a long-standing American tradition of radical dissent. Moreover, their debates over the meaning of violence and nonviolence and who is included and excluded from social and political consideration reveal larger dynamics in the American public sphere in the early twenty-first century. Their concerns could not be more relevant as I write this conclusion in early 2017 and President Donald Trump has just taken office. Activists oppose almost every single point of President Trump's agenda, especially his disregard for environmental protection, gay rights, feminism, and indigenous rights. The issues activists raise will continue to be central concerns for Americans who similarly desire a more tolerant, inclusive, and sustainable society.

Many other Americans know that we cannot continue to live as we have been, that resources are limited and climate change is already affecting our communities. Practices such as mountaintop removal and oil pipeline construction risk the health and well-being of human and other-than-human communities. Corporate capitalism, greed, and an anything-goes-for-profit mentality are what activists oppose. Putting a stop to excessive consumption of natural resources and forcing us as a society to consider alternatives—these are goals that locate activists closer to a much broader constituency. The large numbers of people who participated in the Occupy movement or supported Occupy, the many who traveled to or donated money to the Standing Rock protests against the Dakota Access pipeline, those who supported Black Lives Matter, whether or not they were African American, the crowds of young people who rallied around Senator Bernie Sanders when he campaigned for the Democratic presidential nomination, and the outpouring of thousands protesting President Donald Trump's immigration ban as un-American are all cries for a more inclusive and sustainable society. Even the many white voters who turned out to vote Donald Trump into the presidency felt disenfranchised by the current political system and wanted "change."

Since at least the WTO protests in Seattle in 1999, there is a sense among many young Americans in particular that something is broken in American democracy and that economic structures and policies are a key aspect of that brokenness. This awareness is coupled with growing trends that value the natural world and nonhuman animals. Radical activism's concern for the intersectionality of oppressions, in particular, is likely to resonate with a broader audience as college campuses increasingly address transgender rights and prison populations surge, and as oil pipelines are approved for construction next to Native American sovereign lands. Issues involving the rights of nonhuman animals and the environment will continue to be linked with human rights and environmental justice issues, especially as the effects of climate change are tragically felt. If these activists are any indication, resistance to unbridled consumption that benefits a minority of Americans and takes precedence over the survival of the wild and the well-being of many humans will continue to grow.

AFTER-LIVES

Radical activism is exhausting and hazardous. For this reason and others it is not a long-term occupation for most activists. Yet even when they leave the front lines, they continue to be engaged with activities in continuity with their lives as activists.

Rod Coronado was released in 2008 and although he retreated from public protests for a few years, by 2015, he was back in action.[1] He founded the Wolf Patrol to monitor wolf hunting in Wisconsin. In an interview with Kevin Tucker for the green anarchist publication *Black and Green Review*, Coronado described the ambiguous role of being a monitor since he can no longer engage in illegal and more confrontational actions due to the conditions of his parole. He watched a hunter set a wolf trap and then Coronado placed a camera where it could film the captured wolf's suffering and trauma. But he could not do anything about the trap, legal in Wisconsin. As he drove back to camp, Coronado started thinking about the wolves in the area near the trap and worrying about one getting caught. He kept imagining the worst, that a wolf had caught the scent of the bait and was heading for the trap: "I started crying because I felt horrible. I consider myself a cousin to the wolf, he is my relative and I care about him. And here I was walking away from a threat placed specifically for him and all I could do was take pictures of his suffering . . . if I did more, I might go right back to prison."[2] If activism is the result of a youthful conversion, as it was in Coronado's case, what kinds of commitments, if any, occur over time?

This book has been concerned with youthful activists, the majority of those populating tree-sits, road blockades, and activist gatherings. Many of the activists I communicated with at the beginning of my research, such as Rod Coronado and Jeff Luers, are no longer involved with illegal activities, both because of legal agreements and because they have chosen to find other ways to put their commitments into practice. In 2015, this meant Coronado was dedicating his time to the Wolf Patrol. Even if they were no longer involved with direct action, almost all the activists I met or corresponded with were living out values consistent with those of their earlier activist identities.

Jeff Luers went back to college after being released from prison and received a degree in landscape architecture. He worked on a "Green Alley Project" in Eugene, Oregon, and forest restoration in Warner Creek, helping to conduct environmental impact surveys, arboreal surveys recording, photographing, and sampling red tree vole nests. He also identified native plant communities and performed select habitat treatments. He continued to speak out against the misapplication of the eco-terrorism label and the current state of radical environmentalism.

After serving forty months in prison, Lauren Gazzola of the SHAC 7 was listed as a staff member for the Center for Constitutional Rights in New York City in 2015. According to her bio on the organization's website, Gazzola "recently completed studies for an interdisciplinary M.A. in the 'Law, History, and Philosophy of Free Speech and the First Amendment,' through Antioch University. She serves on the Executive Committee of the New York City chapter of the National Lawyers Guild (NLG) and organizes with the NLG's Animal Rights Activism Committee."[3]

Chelsea Gerlach, on the other hand, was ostracized as a snitch and distanced herself from the radical activist community while in prison. While serving her sentence, she became interested in Buddhism. After being released she was in the news for her work as a DJ, raising money at an ecstatic dance event for her nephew who has cerebral palsy. In 2015, according to a news story about the dance event, she was a student at Portland State University and planning to pursue a graduate degree in divinity after finishing her BA. She explained the course her life had taken in this way: "During my prison time, I found spiritual practice to be a source of life, peace and positive transformation." As an activist, she remembered, "I was trying to change the world, basically by brute force, but I've learned that true change requires a change of heart, and that comes from within."[4] In this way, Gerlach also continued to express the values that shaped her earlier activism: compassion and concern for others, human and nonhuman.

For these activists and the many others I spoke with, their years of direct action were not a frivolous, youthful indulgence, but very much in continuity with their lives as older adults. The urgency they once felt to sacrifice their own health and safety for the other-than-human world usually shifted. With time, they settled into more socially acceptable jobs and became committed to stable lives with their partners and children. Even though they were no longer involved with putting their bodies on the line in tree-sits or animal releases, they continued to carry out their commitments for the wild and for the animals.

The distinctive kinds of thinking and being that emerge in and are constituted by activist ritualizing offer models for other ways of being in the world. But what it means to be "for the wild" and "for the animals" remains a charged debate. Over their lifetimes, activists are working out on the ground what it would look like to acknowledge the porous boundaries we share with other living beings and the Earth.

Notes

INTRODUCTION

1. Jeffrey St. Clair, "How Tre Arrow Became America's Most Wanted Environmental Terrorist," http://www.counterpunch.org/2009/08/28/how-tre-arrow-became-america-s-most-wanted-environmental-quot-terrorist-quot/ (accessed July 12, 2015).

2. Forest names are created for purposes of anonymity as well as identifying with nonhuman species. "My name is Emma Murphy-Ellis and I support Sabotage," accessed July 11, 2015, https://drstevebest.wordpress.com/2012/08/10/my-name-is-emma-murphy-ellis-and-i-support-sabotage/.

3. *Earth First! Journal*, Brigid 2014 (the editor's introduction to the issue was signed "For All the Wild Hearts").

4. Paul Joosee, "Elves, Environmentalism, and "Eco-terror": Leaderless Resistance and Media Coverage of the Earth Liberation Front," *Crime Media Culture* 8 (2012): 75–93.

5. Henry Schuster, "Domestic Terror: Who's Most Dangerous? Eco-terrorists Are Now Above Ultra-Right Extremists on the FBI Charts," CNN, July 29, 2015, http://www.cnn.com/2005/US/08/24/schuster.column/.

6. Evan Wright, "Swamp's Last Day on Earth," *Rolling Stone*, March 30, 2000, 44.

7. Will Potter, "The Green Scare." *Vermont Law Review* 33 (2009): 672.

8. Will Potter, *Green Is the New Red: An Insider's Account of a Social Movement Under Siege* (San Francisco: City Lights Books, 2011).

9. Nancy Lesko, *Act Your Age! A Cultural Construction of Adolescence* (New York: Routledge Farmer, 2001). Jeffrey Jensen Arnett calls the period of development between the late teens and early twenties "emerging adulthood," a phase of life characterized by profound change in industrialized countries in the late twentieth and early twenty-first centuries ("Emerging Adulthood:

A Theory of Development from the Late Teens Through the Twenties," *American Psychologist* (May 2000): 469–480.

10. See psychologist Lisa Miller's account of psychological research on the "surge" of "spiritual awareness" during adolescence: *The Spiritual Child: The New Science on Parenting for Health and Lifelong Thriving* (New York: Columbia Teachers College, 2015).

11. Sarah M. Pike, "Religion and Youth in American Culture," in *Children and Religion: A Methods Handbook*, ed. Susan B. Ridgely (New York: New York University Press, 2011). Notable exceptions include Lynn Schofield Clark, *From Angels to Aliens: Teenagers, the Media, and the Supernatural* (New York: Oxford University Press, 2005) and Eileen Luhr, *Witnessing Suburbia: Conservatives and Christian Youth Culture* (Berkeley: University of California Press, 2009).

12. For example Christian Smith, *Soul-Searching: The Religious and Spiritual Lives of American Teenagers* (New York: Oxford University Press, 2009). An exception is Helen Berger and Doug Ezzy, *Teenage Witches: Magical Youth and the Search for Self* (New Brunswick, NJ: Rutgers University Press, 2007).

13. Field notes, 2012 Round River Rendezvous.

14. See especially the introductory essay for the first issue of the journal *Environmental Humanities*: Deborah Bird Rose, Thom van Dooren, Matthew Chrulew, Stuart Cooke, Matthew Kearnes and Emily O'Gorman, "Thinking Through the Environment, Unsettling the Humanities," *Environmental Humanities* 1 (2012): 1.

15. Among other works: Bruno Latour, *Politics of Nature: How to Bring the Sciences Into Democracy*, translated by Catherine Porter (Cambridge, MA: Harvard University Press, 2004); Donna Haraway, *When Species Meet* (Minneapolis: University of Minnesota Press, 2008); Anna Tsing, "Unruly Edges: Mushrooms as Companion Species," *Environmental Humanities* 1 (2012): 141–54; Tim Ingold and Gisli Palsson, eds., *Biosocial Becomings: Integrating Social and Biological Anthropology* (Cambridge: Cambridge University Press, 2013); Nurit Bird-David, "'Animism' Revisited: Personhood, Environment, and Relational Epistemology," *Current Anthropology* 40 (1999): S67–S91; Graham Harvey, *Animism: Respecting the Living World* (New York: Columbia University Press, 2013); Jane Bennett, *Vibrant Matter: A Political Ecology of Things* (Durham, NC: Duke University Press, 2010); and Karen Barad, *Meeting the Universe Half-way: Quantum Physics and the Entanglement of Matter* (Durham, NC: Duke University Press, 2007).

16. This term appears in the work of Gilles Deleuze's and Félix Guattari's *A Thousand Plateaus* (Minneapolis: University of Minnesota Press, 1987), but my usage comes from Bruno Latour's Third Gifford Lecture, "A Secular Gaia," 2013, http://www.ed.ac.uk/arts-humanities-soc-sci/news-events/lectures/gifford-lectures/archive/series-2012–2013/bruno-latour/lecture-three.

17. See, for example, Mary Evelyn Tucker and John Berthrong, eds., *Confucianism and Ecology: The Interrelation of Heaven, Earth, and Humans* (Cambridge, MA: Harvard University Press, 1998); James Miller, *Daoism and the Quest for a Sustainable Future* (New York: Columbia University Press, 2017); Winona LaDuke, *All Our Relations: Native Struggles for Land and Life* (Boston: South End Press, 1999).

18. "Ecuador Adopts Rights of Nature Constitution," http://therightsofnature.org/ecuador-rights/.

19. http://www.bruno-latour.fr/sites/default/files/downloads/MIW-summary-GB.pdf.

20. See Damian Carrington, "The Anthropocene Epoch: Scientists Declare Dawn of Human-Influenced Age," *The Guardian*, August 29, 2016, https://www.theguardian.com/environment/2016/aug/29/declare-anthropocene-epoch-experts-urge-geological-congress-human-impact-earth.

21. Ingold and Palsson, *Biosocial Becomings*, 8.

22. Haraway, *When Species Meet*, 49. A number of other scholars have also influenced my thinking on these points: Anna Tsing ("Unruly Edges"), Deborah Bird Rose (*Wild Dog Dreaming: Love and Extinction* [Charlottesville: University of Virginia Press, 2011]); and Thom van Dooren (*Flight Ways: Life and Loss at the Edge of Extinction* [New York: Columbia University Press, 2014]).

23. http://rampscampaign.org. For a scholarly account of mountaintop removal activism see Joseph D. Witt, *Religion and Resistance in Appalachia: Faith and the Fight Against Mountaintop Removal Coal Mining* (Lexington, KY: University Press of Kentucky, 2016).

24. Catherine L. Albanese, *Nature Religion in America: From the Algonkian Indians to the New Age* (Chicago: University of Chicago Press, 1991).

25. Letter to author, June 3, 2007.

26. Robert Orsi, *Between Heaven and Earth: The Religious Worlds People Make and the Scholars Who Study Them* (Princeton, NJ: Princeton University Press, 2005), 2.

27. "The sacred" is a charged concept in the field of religious studies. See René Girard's study of the links between the sacred, sacrifice and violence in *Violence and the Sacred* (Baltimore, MD: Johns Hopkins University Press, 1979).

28. With my focus on conversion and extreme actions, there is some relevance here to issues of radicalization more generally, but most activists are on the political left with only a tiny minority voicing xenophobic comments, usually in the context of population control, a pressing environmental issue.

29. Timothy L. Ingalsbee, "Earth First!: Consciousness in Action in the Unfolding of a New-Social-Movement," PhD dissertation, University of Oregon, 1995, 142–43.

30. Albanese, *Nature Religion*.

31. Bron Taylor, *Dark Green Religion: Nature Spirituality and the Planetary Future* (Berkeley: University of California Press, 2009), 10.

32. Bron Taylor, "The Religion and Politics of Earth First!," *The Ecologist* 21 (November/December 1991): 260.

33. Rik Scarce, *Eco-Warriors: Understanding the Radical Environmental Movement* (New York: Left Coast Press, 2006),176.

34. Evan Berry, *Devoted to Nature: The Religious Roots of American Environmentalism* (Oakland: University of California Press, 2015) and Mark R. Stoll, *Inherit the Holy Mountain: Religion and the Rise of American Environmentalism* (Oxford: Oxford University Press, 2015). The study of religion and ecology grew considerably over the early decades of the twenty-first century, but it roots are in two foundational scholarly organizations that appeared in the

1990s and early 2000s: the Forum for Religion and Ecology begun by Mary Evelyn Tucker and John Grim and the International Society for the Study of Religion, Nature and Culture begun by Bron Taylor and others.

35. There are many fine histories of American environmentalism in this period, including Samuel P. Hays, *Beauty, Health, and Permanence: Environmental Politics in the United States, 1955–1985* (Cambridge: Cambridge University Press, 1987) and James Morton Turner, *The Promise of Wilderness: American Environmental Politics Since 1964* (Seattle: University of Washington Press, 2012).

36. Arne Naess, "The Shallow and the Deep, Long-Range Ecology Movement: A Summary," *Inquiry* 16 (1973): 95–100; George Sessions, ed., *Deep Ecology for the 21st Century* (Boston: Shambala, 1995).

37. Charles DeBenedetti, *An American Ordeal: The Antiwar Movement of the Vietnam Era* (Syracuse, NY: Syracuse University Press, 1990); Todd Gitlin, *The Sixties: Years of Hope, Days of Rage* (New York: Bantam Books, 1993); Flora Davis, *Moving the Mountain: The Women's Movement in America Since 1960* (New York: Simon & Schuster, 1991); Estelle Freedman, *No Turning Back: The History of Feminism and the Future of Women* (New York: Ballantine Books, 2003); and Michael Bronski, *A Queer History of the United States* (Boston: Beacon, 2012) are all good places to start.

38. Timothy L. Ingalsbee discusses the relationship between Paganism and Earth First! in *Earth First!*, 95–99. For an introduction to Neopaganism, see Sarah M. Pike, *New Age and Neopagan Religions in America* (New York: Columbia University Press, 2004). In an interview, Darryl Cherney told me that the influence of Paganism was an important factor in West Coast forest activism during the 1990s (interview by author, February 17, 2015).

39. Taylor, Bron, "Earthen Spirituality or Cultural Genocide?: Radical Environmentalism's Appropriation of Native American Spirituality," *Religion* 27 (1997): 183–215.

40. Cindy Milstein, *Anarchism and Its Aspirations* (Oakland: AK Press, 2010). See Jensen's and Zerzan's websites for more information: http://www.derrickjensen.org/work/books-dvds-cds/ and http://johnzerzan.net/. Kevin Tucker gives his definition of "green anarchy" on the anarchist Black and Green Press website: http://www.blackandgreenpress.org/p/what-is-green-anarchy.html.

41. http://earthfirstjournal.org/newswire/.

42. Interview by author, October 1, 2014.

43. Thanks to Ronald Grimes for suggesting I think of ritual, like history, as another kind of scholarly lens.

44. Here I have learned from anthropologist Tanya Luhrmann's discussion of the process of shifting beliefs as "interpretive drift" (*Persuasions of the Witch's Craft: Ritual Magic in Contemporary England* [Cambridge, MA: Harvard University Press, 1989], 312).

45. See Houseman's chapter on "Relationality" in *Theorizing Rituals, Volume I: Issues, Topics, Approaches, Concepts*, ed. Jens Kreinath, Jan Snoek, and Michael Stausberg (London: Brill, 2006), 413–28.

46. For example, Ronald Grimes describes ritual as "a way of partaking in an event" and Michael Houseman discusses "a ritual mode of participation"

(Houseman, "Refracting Ritual: An Upside-down Perspective on Ritual, Media and Conflict" in *Ritual, Media, and Conflict*, ed. Ronald Grimes, Ute Huesken, Udo Simon, and Eric Venbrux (New York: Oxford, 2011). Suzanne Langer argues that ritual provides an orientation or attitude towards and about the world (Roland Delattre, "Ritual Resourcefulness and Cultural Pluralism," *Soundings* 61 [1978]).

47. Kevin DeLuca, *Image Politics: The New Rhetoric of Environmental Activism* (New York: Guilford, 1999), 55.

48. Ronald Grimes, *Deeply Into the Bone: Re-Inventing Rites of Passage* (Berkeley: University of California Press, 2002), 103.

49. Ibid., 91 and 94.

50. Ibid., 98.

51. Animal rights activist Peter Young described his conversion with this term. Letter to author, March 24, 2006.

52. For further discussion of these issues see Sarah M. Pike, "Radical Animal Rights and Environmental Activism As Rites of Passage," in "The Denial of Ritual," a special issue of the *Journal of Ritual Studies* (July 2013): 35–45.

53. Field notes, 2009 Animal Rights Conference.

54. "America's Changing Religious Landscape," *PEW Research Center*, http://www.pewforum.org/2015/05/12/americas-changing-religious-landscape/ (accessed July 12, 2015). Sociologist Mark Chaves argues that "younger people are more likely than older people to say they have no religion" (Robert J. Bliwise, "Flagging Faith," *Duke Magazine* [November/December 2011], 45.

CHAPTER 1. FREEDOM AND INSURRECTION AROUND A FIRE

1. The quote "freedom and insurrection around a fire" comes from an announcement for the 2015 Earth First! Rendezvous in Vermont. http://www.campusactivism.org/displayevent-3266.htm (accessed June 15, 2015).

2. Mark Fischetti, "Groundwater Contamination May End the Gas-Fracking Boom," *Scientific American*, August 20, 2013, http://www.scientificamerican.com/article/groundwater-contamination-may-end-the-gas-fracking-boom/.

3. Susan Zakin, *Coyotes and Town Dogs: Earth First! and the Environmental Movement* (Tucson: University of Arizona Press, 1993), 7.

4. Ibid., 399.

5. Peter Young, *Animal Liberation Front: Complete Diary of Actions, the First 30 Years, 1979–2008* (N.p.: Warcry Communications, 2010).

6. Animal Liberation Front Credo, http://www.animalliberationfront.com/ALFront/alf_credo.htm (accessed July 14, 2015).

7. For an earlier study of radical eco-activism in the United States that is full of anecdotes about activists and stories of actions, see sociologist Rik Scarce, *Eco-Warriors: Understanding the Radical Environmental Movement* (New York: Left Coast Press, 2006).

8. Interview by author, December 22, 2014.

9. The year I attended, rumors were circulating that more mainstream groups, like People for the Ethical Treatment of Animals (PETA), had boycotted the conference because its organizers supported the ALF. For a perspective on

the tensions from someone critical of animal liberation, see this report from the Animal Rights 2008 conference: http://speakingofresearch.com/2008/08/18/report-animal-rights-conference-part-1/.

10. Rod Coronado, for example, is well known by Earth First!ers, but most of his actions have focused on the plight of nonhuman animals.

11. Paul Watson, interview by Lisa Louden, "Adore Animals," http://adoreanimals.com/articles/captain-paul-watson-saving-our-seas-part-2/ (accessed June 17, 2015).

12. http://supportblackmesa.org; http://forms.nomoredeaths.org/en/; http://rampscampaign.org (accessed June 17, 2015).

13. See performance theorist L.M. Bogad's *Tactical Performance: The Theory and Practice of Serious Play* (New York: Routledge, 2016) and Paul Joosee, "Leaderless Resistance and Ideological Inclusion: The Case of the Earth Liberation Front," *Terrorism and Political Violence* 19 (2007): 360.

14. Will Potter, *Green Is the New Red*.

15. Quote and description from Ayla Mullen, "Revolution in the American Living Room: Reflections on Growing Up in the Northwest Ancient Forest Campaign," *Earth First! Journal*, Litha 2016, 78.

16. Susan Phillipps, "Earth First Shuts Down Drilling Site in Moshannon State Forest," http://stateimpact.npr.org/pennsylvania/2012/07/08/earth-first-blocks-frackers-in-moshannon-state-forest/ (accessed June 9, 2015).

17. These creative combinations are often criticized as cultural appropriations, the complex dynamics of which I discuss in more detail in the context of contemporary Paganism in *Magical Selves, Earthly Bodies: Contemporary Pagans and the Search for Community* (Berkeley: University of California Press, 2001), 134–44.

18. Phillipps, "Earth First! Shuts Down Drilling Site."

19. Interview by author, July 24, 2013.

20. "Marcellus Earth First! Action," https://www.youtube.com/watch?v=x4sZnURgz6k (accessed June 12, 2015).

21. http://marcellusshaleearthfirst.org/2013/11/05/msef-drops-direct-pressure-on-frackers-in-williamsport-pa/ (accessed June 18, 2015).

22. http://marcellusshaleearthfirst.org/2014/04/05/breaking-good-college-students-spend-time-off-fighting-extraction/ (accessed June 15, 2015).

23. http://marcellusshaleearthfirst.org/2015/01/29/911/ (accessed June 12, 2015).

24. http://headwaterspreserve.org/headwaters-forest-campaign-history/ and http://www.tarsandsblockade.org.

25. Aaron, interview by author, July 24, 2013.

26. "A Successful Fracking Protest in Pennsylvania," *Utne Reader* (September/October 2012), http://www.utne.com/environment/fracking-protest-zmoz12so-zlin.aspx.

CHAPTER 2. AT THE TURN OF THE MILLENNIUM

1. Interview by author, October 1, 2015.

2. Van Gennep, *The Rites of Passage* (Chicago: University of Chicago Press, 1960).

3. The tree-sit began in 2002 to resist a highway being built through the Glen and was still in place in 2014.

4. Interview by author, October 1, 2015.

5. *Earth First! Journal*, Beltane 2009, 1.

6. Greenpeace is often criticized by radical activists for being too mainstream; nevertheless, at gatherings I met Earth First!ers who had been or were involved with Greenpeace.

7. http://forms.nomoredeaths.org/en/.

8. There are many examples, such as Jake Conroy's talk, "Purity Politics" at the International Animal Rights conference in 2015: https://www.youtube.com/watch?v=X5xUDgkBQVE.

9. Roderick Nash, *Wilderness and the American Mind* (New Haven, CT: Yale University Press, 1967) and Evan Berry, *Devoted to Nature: The Religious Roots of American Environmentalism* (Oakland: University of California Press, 2015).

10. Berry, *Devoted to Nature*, 151.

11. Bron Taylor, "Wilderness, Spirituality and Biodiversity in North America—Tracing an Environmental History from Occidental Roots to Earth Day," in *Wilderness in Mythology and Religion*, ed. Laura Feldt (Berlin: DeGruyter, 2012), 306–7.

12. Ingalsbee, "Earth First!"

13. Dorceta E. Taylor, *The Rise of the American Conservation Movement: Power, Privilege, and Environmental Protection* (Durham, NC: Duke University Press, 2016), 352–60.

14. Taylor, "Wilderness," 296.

15. Nash, *Wilderness*, 145.

16. See Berry's discussion of late nineteenth- and early twentieth-century nature enthusiasm as remedy for city life in *Devoted to Nature*, 129–33).

17. Bron R. Taylor, "The Tributaries of Radical Environmentalism," in *Journal for the Study of Radicalism*, 2 (2008): 41.

18. Ibid., 30.

19. Taylor discusses these figures in ibid., 41–45. White's article appeared in *Science* 155 (1967): 1203–7.

20. Dave Foreman, quoted in Stoll, *Inherit the Holy Mountain*, 190.

21. "Mother Nature's Army: Guerilla Warfare Comes to the American Forest," *Esquire*, February 1987, 100.

22. Quoted in Bron Taylor, "Earth and Nature-Based Spirituality (Part 1): From Deep Ecology to Radical Environmentalism," *Religion* 31 (2001): 175.

23. Ronald Bailey, *Eco-Scam: The False Prophets of Ecological Apocalypse* (New York: St. Martin's Press, 1993), 3 and 1.

24. Quoted in Taylor, "Tributaries," 37.

25. Ibid., 46.

26. Jessica Thornton, "Animal Rights, Imperialism, and Indigenous Hunting," Indian Country Today Media Network, April 18, 2013, Http://indiancountrytodaymedianetwork.com/2013/04/18/animal-rights-imperialism-and-indigenous-hunting (accessed July 28, 2015).

27. "Standing Rock Resistance," http://rampscampaign.org.

28. Harriet Ritvo, *The Animal Estate: The English and Other Creatures in the Victorian Age* (Cambridge, MA: Harvard University Press, 1987), 162.

29. Tristram Stuart, *The Bloodless Revolution: A Cultural History of Vegetarianism from 1600 to Modern Times* (New York: W. W. Norton, 2006), xx–xxi.

30. Diane L. Beers, *For the Prevention of Cruelty: the History and Legacy of Animal Rights Activism in the United States* (Athens: Ohio University Press, 2006), 20 and 92.

31. Richard W. Bulliet, *Hunters, Herders, and Hamburgers: The Past and Future of Human-Animal Relationships* (New York: Columbia University Press, 2005), 198.

32. Beers, *For the Prevention of Cruelty*, 4.

33. Ibid., 12.

34. *Earth First! Journal*, http://earthfirstjournal.org/about/.

35. *Earth First! Journal*, Eostar 2004, 7.

36. *Earth First! Journal*, Beltane 2007, 6.

37. Earth First! groups have been formed in Australia, Iceland, Ecuador, and the Philippines, among other places.

38. Julia Butterfly Hill, *The Legacy of Luna: The Story of a Tree, a Woman, and the Struggle to Save the Redwoods* (San Francisco: Harper San Francisco, 2000).

39. Portland Independent Media Center, http://portland.indymedia.org/en/2005/04/314898.shtml.

40. Graham Messick, "Burning Rage: Reports on Extremists Now Deemed Biggest Domestic Terror Threat," November 13, 2005, http://www.cbsnews.com/news/burning-rage/ (accessed June 15, 2015).

41. Donald Liddick, *Eco-Terrorism: Radical Environmental and Animal Liberation Movements* (Westport, CT: Praeger, 2006) 40.

42. "Eco-terrorism: Extremism in the Animal Rights and Environmental Movements," Anti-Defamation League, http://archive.adl.org/learn/ext_us/ecoterrorism.html (accessed July 1, 2013).

43. Many other scholars and activists have addressed the problems of violence in this movement and of labeling Young's kind of activism "terrorism." See Steven Best and Anthony J. Nocella, eds., *Terrorists or Freedom Fighters? Reflections on the Liberation of Animals* (New York: Lantern Books, 2004).

44. *Behind the Mask*, directed by Shannon Keith, (Uncaged Films, 2006), DVD.

45. For example, almost all the ALF and ELF activists I corresponded with in 2006–2008 who were serving prison sentences mentioned hardcore or straightedge as influences on their activism, including Peter Young, Rod Coronado, Josh Harper, and Darius Fullmer, among others.

46. See Robert T. Wood, *Straightedge Youth: Complexity and Contradictions of a Subculture* (Syracuse NY: Syracuse University Press, 2006) and Ross Haenfler, *Straightedge: Clean-Living Youth, Hard Core Punk, and Social Change* (New Brunswick, NJ: Rutgers University Press, 2006).

47. Letter to author, November 9, 2006.

48. Brad Knickerbocker, "Back Story: Eco-vigilantes: All in 'The Family?'" *Christian Science Monitor*, January 30, 2006, http://www.csmonitor.com/2006/0130/p20s01-sten.html (accessed July 31, 2015).

49. "Firestarter," McKenzie Funk, *Outside*, September 2007, 1.

50. Steven Mintz, *Huck's Raft: A History of American Childhood* (Cambridge, MA: Harvard University Press, 2004), 9 and 89.

51. Quoted in *Rethinking Youth*, eds. Johanna Wyn and Rob White (Melbourne: Allen and Unwin, 1997), 20.

52. William Reese, *The Origins of the American High School* (New Haven, CT: Yale University Press, 1995).

53. Jon Savage, *Teenage: The Creation of Youth Culture* (New York: Viking, 2007), 448–62.

54. Oded Heilbronner, "From a Culture *for* Youth to a Culture *of* Youth: Recent Trends in the Historiography of Western Youth Cultures," *Contemporary European History* 17 (2008): 577.

55. Grace Palladino, *Teenagers: An American History* (New York: Basic Books, 1996), 194–198 and Rob Latham, *Consuming Youth: Vampires, Cyborgs, and the Culture of Consumption* (Chicago: University of Chicago Press, 2002), 42.

56. Mintz, *Huck's Raft*, 282.

57. Palladino, *Teenagers*, 117–35.

58. Jacob R. Fishman and Fredric Solomon, "Youth and Social Action: An Introduction," in Anthony M. Orum, ed., *The Seeds of Politics: Youth and Politics in America* (Englewood Cliffs, NJ: Prentice-Hall, 1972), 249.

59. Christopher Lasch, *The New Radicalism in America 1889–1963: the Intellectual as a Social Type* (New York: W. W. Norton, 1997).

60. Anthony M. Orum, "Introduction," in Orum, *Seeds*, 1–14.

61. "Youth in the Civil Rights Movement," Library of Congress Civil Rights History Project, http://www.loc.gov/collections/civil-rights-history-project/articles-and-essays/youth-in-the-civil-rights-movement/ (accessed July 28, 2015).

62. "Interview with Allen Ginsburg and Margaret Mead," http://www .history.com/speeches/allen-ginsburg-on-the-beat-generation#allen-ginsburg-on-the-beat-generation.

63. Letter to author, November 20, 2006.

64. Originally called Weatherman, the name was changed to Weather Underground in 1970, so as not to be sexist (Bryan Burrough, *Days of Rage: America's Radical Underground, the FBI, and the Forgotten Age of Revolutionary Violence* [New York: Penguin, 2015], 159)

65. Lewis Feuer, "The Sources and Traits of Student Movements," in Orum, *Seeds*, 373.

66. Richard Flacks, "The Liberated Generation: An Exploration of the Roots of Student Protest," in Orum, *Seeds*, 259.

67. Raymond Aron, "Student Rebellion: Vision of the Future or Echo From the Past," in Orum, *Seeds*, 333.

68. Flacks, "Liberated," 354.

69. Bill Ayers, *Fugitive Days: A Memoir* (New York: Penguin, 2003), 198, Burrough, *Days of Rage*, 60.

70. Ayers, *Fugitive Days*, 146.

71. Ibid. Also see Dan Berger, *Outlaws of America: The Weather Underground and the Politics of Solidarity* (Oakland, CA: AK Press, 2006), 151.

72. Ayers, *Fugitive Days*, 241.

73. Ibid., 241.

74. Ibid., 296.

75. Burrough, *Days of Rage*, 157.

76. Panagioti Tsolkas, "No System But the Ecosystem: Earth First! and Anarchism," Institute for Anarchist Studies, March 31, 2015, http://anarchiststudies
.org/2015/03/31/no-system-but-the-ecosystem-earth-first-and-anarchism-by-
panagioti-tsolkas-1/ (accessed July 25, 2015).

77. Dan McKanan discusses a number of these development in *Prophetic Encounters: Religion and the American Radical Tradition* (Boston: Beacon Press, 2011), including Witchcraft and feminism on p. 245.

78. Daniel Berrigan, *The Trial of the Catonsville Nine* (New York: Fordham University Press, 2004 [first published by Beacon Press in 1970]), 34 and 81. For more information on the Berrigan brothers, see Murray Polner and Jim O'Grady, *Disarmed and Dangerous: The Radical Lives and Times of Daniel and Philip Berrigan* (New York, Basic Books, 1997).

79. Berrigan, *Catonsville Nine*, 48.

80. Berrigan, *Catonsville Nine*: protester George Mische mentions the "higher law" on 74 and Berrigan "our moral passion" on 114.

81. "Fighting to Win" (194–208) in Peter Singer, ed., *In Defense of Animals* (New York: Harper and Row, 1985), 197.

82. https://www.youtube.com/watch?v=X5xUDgkBQVE.

83. *Earth First! Journal*, Samhain/Yule 2007, 12.

84. http://www.shac7.com/hls.htm.

85. http://www.shac7.com/lauren/.

86. "Animal-Rights Activists Like Me Aren't Terrorists," http://otherwords
.org/animal-rights_activists_like_me_arent_terrorists/.

87. Lauren Gazzola, "From "Terrorism" to Activism: Moving from the Green Scare to Animal Rights," Common Dreams, July 31, 2015. http://www
.commondreams.org/views/2015/07/31/terrorism-activism-moving-green-
scare-animal-rights.

88. *Earth First! Journal*, Beltane 2007, 2–3.

89. Interview by author, February 17, 2015.

90. "No System But the Ecosystem," March 31, 2015, http://anarchiststudies
.org/2015/03/31/no-system-but-the-ecosystem-earth-first-and-anarchism-by-
panagioti-tsolkas-1/ (accessed July 15, 2015).

91. Ibid.

92. Milstein, *Anarchism and Its Aspirations*, 76. See also Ziga Vodovnik, *A Living Spirit of Revolt: the Infrapolitics of Anarchism* (Oakland, CA: PM Press, 2013).

93. See Zerzan's website at http://www.johnzerzan.net and the "Black and Green Network" Tucker founded at http://www.blackandgreenpress.org.

94. Interview by author, February 2, 2015.

95. Quoted in Milstein, *Anarchism*, 22.

96. Ibid., 82.

97. Ibid., 29.

98. Vodovnik, *Living Spirit*, 171.

99. Milstein, *Anarchism*, 82–87; Vodovnik, *Living Spirit*, 172–74.

100. One of many examples was Susan Griffin's ecofeminist book, *Woman and Nature: The Roaring Inside Her* (Berkeley, CA: Counterpoint Press, 2016 [1978]).

101. "19-year Greenham Common Campaign to End, " *The Guardian*, September 5, 2000, https://www.theguardian.com/uk/2000/sep/05/1.

102. McKanan, *Prophetic Encounters*, 242.

103. Epstein, *Political Protest and Cultural Revolution*, 174–75.

104. An important influence came from the Movement for a New Society (MNS), a Philadelphia-based organization founded in 1966 that had its roots in an earlier Quaker group active in the civil rights movement.

105. Epstein, *Political Protest and Cultural Revolution*, 52.

106. My discussion of these issues is indebted to Barbara Epstein's excellent book, *Political Protest and Cultural Revolution*.

107. Epstein discusses the origins of Clamshell's founders on 46–64 of *Political Protest and Cultural Revolution*.

108. In *Political Protest and Cultural Revolution*, Epstein discusses Abalone on 92–124, anarcha-feminists on 95–96, and the use of "ecowarriors" on 110.

109. Zakin, *Coyotes and Town Dogs*, 361.

110. Tsolkas, "No System."

111. "The Tenth Anniversary of the Battle of Seattle: Food Not Bombs Activists Organize a Protest to Block the WTO Meeting in Seattle in 1999," http://www.foodnotbombs.net/battle_of_seattle.html (accessed June 10, 2015).

112. "Common Ground Collective, Food Not Bombs and Occupy Movement Form Coalition to Help Isaac & Katrina Victims," August 31, 2012, http://interoccupy.net/blog/common-ground-collective-food-not-bombs-and-occupy-movement-form-coalition-to-help-isaac-katrina-victims/.

113. "Occupy Boston: Food for the Revolution!" September 29, 2011, http://fnbboston.org/2011/09/29/occupy-boston-food-for-the-revolution/ (accessed June 11, 2015).

114. Interview by author, October 1, 2015.

115. Interview by author, July 24, 2013. In *Occupy Nation: The Roots, the Spirit, and the Promise of Occupy Wall Street*, Todd Gitlin describes a number of Occupy Wall Street ritualized practices that I also saw at environmentalist gatherings, such as waving fingers as "twinkles" to agree with what someone says (New York: It Books, 2012).

116. Liz Pelly, "Anarchistic and Self-Trained, Are Street Medics the Future of First Aid?" *The Boston Phoenix*, February 15, 2012, http://thephoenix.com/boston/news/133998-anarchistic-and-self-trained-are-street-medics-th/?page=2#TOPCONTENT.

117. Michael Blanding, "Medic," *The Boston Phoenix*, February 20, 2003, http://www.bostonphoenix.com/boston/news_features/other_stories/multipage/documents/02704492.htm.

118. "Chicago Action Medical," https://chicagoactionmedical.wordpress.com/about/ (accessed June 10, 2015).

119. "Jews and the Civil Rights Movement," Religious Action Center of Reform Judaism, http://www.rac.org/jews-and-civil-rights-movement. Much has been written on the legacy of the Berrigan brothers. See Daniel Lewis, "Daniel J.

Berrigan, Defiant Priest Who Preached Pacifism, Dies at 94," *New York Times*, April 30, 2016. The study of youth and religion, like the study of children and religion in general, has been disregarded in both religious studies and youth sub-cultural studies. For a longer discussion of this and other issues concerning the study of youth and religion, see Pike, "Religion and Youth," 33–49.

120. http://www.peta2.com (accessed July 8, 2015).

121. James M. Jasper and Dorothy Nelkin, *The Animal Rights Crusade: The Growth of a Moral Protest* (New York: Free Press, 1991), 39

122. Daniel Keating, "Adolescent Thinking," in *At the Threshold: The Developing Adolescent*, ed. S. Feldman and G. Elliott (Cambridge, MA: Harvard University Press, 1990), 64.

123. I explore this dynamic in detail in "Dark Teens and Born-Again Martyrs: Captivity Narratives After Columbine," *Journal of the American Academy of Religion* 77 (2009): 647–72.

124. In *Huck's Raft*, Steven Mintz observes that Puritans' projection of their hopes and fears on the young is one of their lasting legacies.

125. Ibid., 29.

126. For a general overview of religions of the 1960s, see Robert Ellwood, *The Sixties Spiritual Awakening* (New Brunswick, NJ: Rutgers University Press, 1994). On the anticult movement, see Thomas Robbins and Benjamin Zablocki, *Misunderstanding Cults: Searching for Objectivity in a Controversial Field* (Toronto: University of Toronto Press, 2001).

127. Sarah M. Pike, "Witchcraft Since the 1960s," in *The Oxford Handbook of Religion and the American News Media*, ed. Diane Winston (Oxford: Oxford University Press, 2012).

128. According to Bron R. Taylor, "militant pagan environmentalism," in the shape of movements like Earth First!, came about in the 1970s as a "bricolage" of contemporary Paganism, New Age, Asian, and Native American beliefs and practices, which he discusses in "Earth and Nature-Based Spirituality."

129. Alan Nixon and Adam Possamai, "Techno-Shamanism and the Economy of Ecstasy as Religious Experience," in Donna Weston and Andy Bennett, eds., *Pop Pagans: Paganism and Popular Music* (London: Routledge 2014), 152.

130. In *Political Protest and Cultural Revolution*, Epstein describes the prominent role of contemporary Paganism in the antinuclear movement on 157–94. For an example of Starhawk's involvement with creating a ritual at an antilogging protest see Pike, *New Age and Neopagan Religions*, 159–60.

131. See Pike, *New Age and Neopagan Religions*.

132. Ibid.

133. http://www.llewellyn.com/product_publisher_reviews.php?ean= 9781567187250.

134. Luers was resentenced to ten years and released in December 2009.

135. Communication to author, March 5, 2007.

136. Berger and Ezzy, *Teenage Witches*, 212.

137. "About CAW," Church of All Worlds, http://caw.org/content/?q=about (accessed July 8, 2015). For CAW's connection to Earth First! see Otter and

Morning Glory Zell, "Who on Earth is the Goddess," http://caw.org/content/?q=node/68.

138. Chas Clifton, quoted in S. Zohreh Kermani, *Pagan Family Values: Childhood and the Religious Imagination in Contemporary American Paganism* (New York: New York University Press, 2013), 30.

139. Cherney calls himself a "Pagan" but embodies a kind of spiritual eclecticism that includes Hindu, Buddhist, and New Age practices as well as appreciation for some aspects of Islam, Christianity, and Judaism. His parents were nonobservant Jews and were "laissez faire," meaning that he was free to "check out a laundry list of spiritualities" (interview by author, February 17, 2015).

140. Vibra Willow, "A Brief History of Reclaiming," http://www.reclaiming.org/about/origins/history-vibra.html.

141. Letter to author, March 2006.

142. Craig Rosebraugh, *Burning Rage of a Dying Planet: Speaking for the Earth Liberation Front* (New York: Lantern Books, 2004), 20.

143. Clark, *From Angels to Aliens*, 5

144. The 2014 survey documented changes since an earlier survey in 2007. http://www.pewforum.org/2015/05/12/americas-changing-religious-landscape/ (accessed July 8, 2015).

145. "What matters" to activists, to borrow from the title of Ann Taves and Courtney Bender's book, is not necessarily captured by religious affiliation-disaffiliation or the secular-religious binary. In practice, Bender and Taves argue, a simple "secular-religious' frame" often breaks down and twenty-first-century Americans infuse their beliefs with a "reflexive awareness of paradox and ambiguity (Courtney Bender and Ann Taves, *What Matters? Ethnographies of Value in a Not So Secular Age* [New York: Columbia University Press, 2012], 2 and 29).

CHAPTER 3. CHILDHOOD LANDSCAPES OF WONDER AND AWE

1. "FBI: Eco-Terrorism Remains No. 1 Domestic Terror Threat," Fox News, Monday, March 31, 2008, http://www.foxnews.com/story/0,2933,343768,00.html (accessed March 29, 2010).

2. See for example, Dean Kuipers, *Operation Bite Back: Rod Coronado's War to Save American Wilderness* (New York: Bloomsbury, 2009).

3. Here I draw on political scientist Jane Bennett's description of landscape as an "'assemblage' or working set of vibrant materialities" (Klaus K. Loenhart, "Vibrant Matter, Zero Landscape: An Interview with Jane Bennett," *Eurozine*, http://www.eurozine.com/articles/2011-10-19-loenhart-en.html).

4. Interview by author, May 25, 2009.

5. Stephen Kellert, *Building for Life: Designing and Understanding the Human-Nature Connection* (Washington, DC: Island Press, 2005), 71.

6. 90% of the American environmentalists Louise Chawla interviewed credited their commitments to experiences in the wild or semiwild places where they played as children (Julie Dunlap and Stephen R. Kellert, eds., *Companions in Wonder: Children and Adults Exploring Nature Together* (Cambridge, MA: MIT Press, 2012), 9.

7. Interview by author, May 25, 2009.

8. Stuart A. Wright, "The Dynamics of Movement Membership: Joining and Leaving New Religious Movements," in *Teaching New Religious* Movements, ed. by David A. Bromley (Oxford: Oxford University Press, 2007), 195.

9. Paul L. Harris, "On Not Falling Down to Earth: Children's Metaphysical Questions," in *Imagining the Impossible: Magical, Scientific, and Religious Thinking in Children*, ed. Karl S. Rosengren, Carl N. Johnson, and Paul Harris (Cambridge: Cambridge University Press, 2000), 162.

10. Mark Bekoff refers to this tendency as "careful anthropomorphism" in *The Emotional Lives of Animals: A Leading Scientist Explores Animal Joy, Sorrow, and Empathy—and Why They Matter* (Novato, CA: New World Library, 2007), 126.

11. Chris Jenks, *Childhood: Critical Concepts in Sociology* (Abingdon, UK: Taylor & Francis, 2005).

12. For a similar dynamic in the context of contemporary Pagans, see Sarah M. Pike, *Earthly Bodies, Magical Selves: Contemporary Pagans and the Search for Community* (Berkeley: University of California Press, 2001), 155–81.

13. David Sobel describes this process in *Children's Special Places: Exploring the Role of Forts, Dens and Bush Houses in Middle Childhood* (Tucson, AZ: Zephyr Press, 1993), 109–10.

14. Tori Derr, "'Sometimes Birds Sound Like Fish': Perspectives on Children's Place Experiences," in *Children and Their Environments: Learning, Using and Designing Spaces*, ed. Christopher Spencer and Mark Blades (Cambridge: Cambridge University Press, 2006), 112.

15. Gary Paul Nabhan, *The Geography of Childhood: Why Children Need Wild Places* (Boston: Beacon, 1994), 28.

16. Priscila Mosqueda, "The Keystone XL Battle Comes to East Texas," http://www.texasobserver.org/east-texas-showdown/.

17. *Blockadia Rising: Voices of the Tar Sands Blockade*, directed by Garrett Graham, 2013.

18. Melanie Jae Martin, "Tar Sands Blockade Provides Training Grounds for Creative Tactics," November 15, 2012, http://wagingnonviolence.org/feature /tar-sands-blockade-provides-training-grounds-for-creative-tactics/.

19. For example, see anthropologist Anna Tsing's description of the multispecies landscapes where wild mushrooms grow in "Unruly Edges."

20. Alan Gussow, quoted in Sobel, *Children's Special Places*, 159. Also see Richard Louv, *Last Child in the Woods: Saving Our Children from Nature-Deficit Disorder* (Chapel Hill, NC: Algonquin, 2005).

21. Clearly many children grow up having these experiences, but my point is that they are emphasized by activists as having a direct influence on their environmental commitments.

22. Interview by author, December 22, 2014.

23. Email message to author, February 18, 2014.

24. Jay Griffiths, *Kith: The Riddle of the Childscape* (London: Penguin Press, 2013), 5.

25. See also Tim Ingold, *The Perception of the Environment: Essays on Livelihood, Dwelling and Skill* (New York: Routledge, 2011), 193.

26. Email message to author, February 18, 2014.

27. Peter H. Kahn Jr., "Children's Affiliations With Nature: Structure, Development and the Problem of Environmental Generational Amnesia," in *Children and Nature: Psychological, Sociocultural, and Evolutionary Investigations*, ed. Peter H. Kahn, Jr. and Stephen R. Kellert (Cambridge, MA: MIT Press, 2002), 100.

28. This aspect of young adult identity construction in the context of relationships with nonhuman species has been largely disregarded in psychological research on personality development. Not surprisingly, such research has tended to focus on interpersonal relationships between humans (Kellert, *Building for Life*, 65).

29. Kuipers, *Operation Bite Back*, 17–18.

30. Letter to author, February 24, 2007.

31. In *Biophilia*, biologist Edward O. Wilson argues that there exists an innate human urge to affiliate with other forms of life (Cambridge, MA: Harvard University Press, 1984), 85.

32. Rachel Carson, *The Sense of Wonder* (New York: Harper and Row, 1956), 42. For Carson, wonder encompasses many emotions, including "surprise, admiration, curiosity, awe, delight, reverence, humility, loneliness, and joy" (Dunlap and Kellert, *Companions in Wonder*, 2).

33. Carson, *Sense of Wonder*, 10.

34. Ibid., 22.

35. Lisa Sideris, "Fact and Fiction, Fear and Wonder: the Legacy of Rachel Carson," *Soundings: An Interdisciplinary Journal* 91 (2008): 357 and 335.

36. Patrick Beach, *A Good Forest for Dying: The Tragic Death of a Young Man on the Front Lines of the Environmental Wars* (New York: Doubleday, 2003).

37. Interview with Aaron, July 24, 2013.

38. "Interview: Film Maker Garrett Graham on the Tar Sands Blockade," http://earthfirstjournal.org/newswire/2013/10/23/interview-garrett-graham-and-blockadia-rising/#more-26230.

39. For activists, the ability to experience wonder does not decline with age and familiarity. Philip Fisher argues that such a decline is typical in *Wonder, the Rainbow, and the Aesthetics of Rare Experiences* (Cambridge, MA: Harvard University Press, 1998), 1.

40. See Dunlap and Kellert, *Companions in Wonder*.

41. In Louise Chawla's study of mainstream environmental activists and educators in the United States and in Norway, she found that the two most common reasons they gave for working to protect the environment were (1) special places in childhood and (2) family role models and mentors who shaped their attachments to place ("Childhood Experiences Associated with Care for the Natural World: A Theoretical Framework for Empirical Results," in *Children, Youth and Environments* 17 [2007]: 144–70).

42. "Support Eric," http://www.supporteric.org/statement.htm (accessed December 2, 2014). McDavid was released early in 2015 after a successful appeal that charged the government had withheld crucial evidence.

43. Letter to author, November 9, 2006.

44. Letter to author, February 24, 2007.

45. Dorothy G. Singer and Jerome L. Singer, *The House of Make-Believe: Children's Play and the Developing Imagination* (Cambridge MA: Harvard University Press, 1990), 4.

46. Interview by author, December 22, 2014.

47. Letter to author, November 2009.

48. Letter to author, March 5, 2007. Luers's sentence was later overturned and he was resentenced to ten years.

49. Letter to author, November 5, 2006.

50. Raffi Khatchadourian, "Neptune's Navy: Paul Watson's Wild Crusade to Save the Oceans," *The New Yorker*, November 5, 2007, http://www.thenewyorker.com/reporting/2007/11/05/071105fa_fact_khatchadourian.

51. Paul Watson, *Seal Wars: Twenty-Five Years on the Front Lines with the Harp Seals* (Buffalo, NY: Firefly Books, 2002), 47.

52. Hill, *Legacy of Luna*, 117.

53. "Julia Butterfly Hill Defends California Redwoods," Global Non-Violent Action Database, http://nvdatabase.swarthmore.edu/content/julia-butterfly-hill-defends-california-redwoods-1999 (accessed August 1, 2015).

54. Nabhan, *Geography of Childhood*, 7.

55. Gretel Van Wieren and Stephen R. Kellert, "The Origins of Aesthetics and Spiritual Values in Children's Experience of Nature," *Journal for the Study of Religion, Nature and Culture* 7, no. 3 (2013): 263.

56. Louise Chawla, *In the First Country of Places: Nature, Poetry, and Childhood Memory* (Albany: State University of New York Press, 1994), 160. Chawla points out that William Wordsworth believed that "naming and sympathetic knowing" were the "great endowments of early childhood" (160).

57. Kahn and Kellert, *Children and Nature*, xiii.

58. Email message to author, April 5, 2006.

59. Vegetarians and vegans are disproportionately represented in activist communities, although there are plenty of omnivores among radical environmentalists. Radical animal rights activists tend to be vegans.

60. Email message to author, February 18, 2014.

61. Griffiths, *Kith*, 82, and Akira Lippit, *Electric Animal: Toward a Rhetoric of Wildlife* (Minneapolis: University of Minnesota Press, 2000), 237.

62. Griffiths, *Kith*, 83.

63. Kay Milton, *Loving Nature: Towards an Ecology of Emotion* (New York: Routledge, 2002),149.

64. "Rebecca Rubin Sentenced to 5 Years for ALF and ELF Arsons," http://www.animalliberationfront.com/ALFront/Activist%20Tips/RubinSentenced.htm.

65. Sandro Contenta, "The Rise and Fall of Eco-terrorist Rebecca Rubin," http://www.thestar.com/news/insight/2014/02/02/the_rise_and_fall_of_ecoterrorist_rebecca_rubin.html.

66. Sue Donaldson and Will Kymlicka discuss this approach to animal rights in *Zoopolis: A Political Theory of Animal Rights* (New York: Oxford University Press, 2011).

67. Peter Reed, quoted in Val Plumwood, *Environmental Culture: The Ecological Crisis of Reason* (London: Routledge, 2002), 198.

68. Quoted in Jon Mooallen, *Wild Ones: A Sometimes Dismaying, Weirdly Reassuring Story About Looking at People Looking at Animals in America* (New York: Penguin, 2013), 6.

69. As Paul Shepherd puts it, "When the self is expanded to encompass the world, environmental destruction becomes self-destruction" (Cynthia Thomashow, "Adolescents and Ecological Identity: Attending to Wild Nature," in Kahn and Kellert, *Children and Nature*, 266).

70. My understanding of childhood narratives has been helped by Daniel Schacter's work, especially *The Seven Sins of Memory* (New York: Houghton Mifflin, 2001).

71. See for example, Mitchell Thomashow, *Ecological Identity: Becoming a Reflective Environmentalist* (Cambridge, MA: MIT Press, 1996).

72. Griffith dates the decline to the British Enclosure Acts of the eighteenth and nineteenth centuries that reduced the British Commons.

73. Howard P. Chudicoff, *Children at Play: An American History* (New York: New York University Press, 2007), 18.

74. David Orr, "Political Economy and the Ecology of Childhood," in Kahn and Kellert, *Children and Nature*, 291. In his book, *Last Child in the Woods*, journalist Richard Louv most famously blamed these trends for what he calls children's "nature-deficit disorder," which results in children's disengagement from the natural world. See also George Monbiot, *Feral: Rewilding the Land, the Sea and Human Life* (Chicago: University of Chicago Press, 2014), 167. In his essay "Eden in a Vacant Lot: Special Places, Species, and Kids in the Neighborhood of Life," biologist Robert Michael Pyle argues that he became a scientist and someone who "cares" about the environment as a direct result of playing in an urban canal when he was growing up (in Kahn and Kellert, *Children and Nature*, 324).

75. Pyle, "Eden in a Vacant Lot," 316.

76. Letter to author, February 4, 2007.

77. Griffiths, *Kith*, 300.

78. Letter to author, February 4, 2007.

79. Letter to author, February 4, 2007.

80. Email message to author, September 16, 2006.

81. Blackfire, "Common Enemy" in *Earth First! Journal*, March/April 2010, 21.

82. In *Feral*, journalist George Monbiot promotes mass restoration of lost wild food chains and wildlife corridors. But he couples these concerns with the fate of children's lives bereft of wild things and places (167–69).

83. Sobel, *Children's Special Places*, 125. According to Sobel: "As we bonded with our parents in the early years, we bond with Mother Earth in middle childhood," ("A Place in the World: Adults' Memories of Childhood's Special Places," *Children's Environments Quarterly* 7 (1990): 12.

84. Email message to author, November 29, 2013.

85. Letter to author, February 24, 2007.

86. Letter to author, April 5, 2006.

87. Letter to author, March 5, 2007.

88. Letter to author, February 4, 2007.

89. Letter to author, September 2006.

90. Letter to author, February 4, 2007.

91. Harvey, *Animism*, xi.

92. Email message to author, June 20, 2014.

93. Letter to author, November 5, 2006.

94. http://www.abolitionist-online.com/article-issue04_beyond.bars-christina.mclean.shtml (accessed December 6, 2009).

95. Letter to author, November 20, 2006.

96. Ibid.

97. Louise Chawla found in her interviews with environmentalists that loss of a favorite habitat was a motivating factor for many of them ("Childhood Experiences").

98. Psychologist Keith Oakley describes this process as one of "reactive emotions" in *Emotions: A Brief History* (New York: Oxford University Press, 2004), 4. Recalling emotional memories, such as grief at returning to a beloved woods to find it paved over for a parking lot, can affect current emotional states (W. Gerrod Parrot and Matthew P. Spackman, "Emotion and Memory," in *Handbook of Emotions*, ed. Michael Lewis, Jeanette M. Haviland-Jones, and Lisa Fedman Barrett [New York: Guilford, 2011]).

99. Letter to author, June 3, 2007.

100. Bernard Mergen, "Children and Nature in History," *Environmental History* 8 (2003): 646.

101. Louise Chawla observes that a common habit of childhood "is to animate nature and invest it with moral significance ("Spots of Time: Manifold Ways of Being in Nature in Childhood," in *Children and Nature: Psychological, Sociocultural, and Evolutionary Investigations*, ed. Peter H. Kahn Jr. and Stephen R. Kellert [Cambridge, MA: MIT Press, 2002], 202).

102. Letter to author, November 5, 2006.

103. In contrast, in the United States, "the many millennia of the domestic era effectively erased once-vital memories of animals and human-animal hybrids as mediators with or dwellers in the unseen spirit world." Bulliet, *Hunters, Herders, and Hamburgers*, 219–20.

104. Adrian Ivakhiv, *Ecologies of the Moving Image* (Waterloo, ON: Wilfrid Laurier University Press, 2013), 8 and 216–17.

105. *Asian Economic News*, February 3, 2003, http://findarticles.com/p/articles/mi_moWDP/is_2003_Feb_3/ai_97189336.

106. Related examples include *Captain Planet*, an animated series for children launched by Turner Broadcasting System (it ran until 1996 before going into reruns) and the first season of the ABC cartoon series *Superfriends* (1973). *Superfriends* episodes included the superheroes fighting villains who caused pollution and global warming.

107. Lorraine Daston, "Introduction," in *Thinking with Animals: New Perspectives on Anthropomorphism*, ed. Lorraine Daston and Gregg Mitman (New York: Columbia University Press, 2005), 8. Cary Wolfe discusses animal imitation in *Zoontologies: the Question of the Animal* (Minneapolis: University of Minnesota Press, 2003), 159.

108. Jenks, *Childhood*.

109. Loenhart, *Vibrant Matter*, xvii and 18.

110. Thanks to Robert A. Orsi for helping me articulate these points.

111. American studies scholar Jay Mechling describes boys' experiences at Boy Scout camps in his research on American boyhood as characterized by creating "different kinds of wild places in their hearts" (Mergen, "Children and Nature," 663).

CHAPTER 4. INTO THE FOREST

1. Dylan Kay, "Free Free: The Case of Jeff Luers," *Satya*, http://www.satyamag.com/jan04/kay.html (accessed August 7, 2015).

2. Jeffrey Luers, "How I Became an Eco-Warrior," http://freefreenow.org/index.html (accessed October 2, 2006).

3. Cheri Brooks, "Up A Tree," Forest Service Employees for Environmental Ethics, *Forest Magazine* (Sept/Oct 2000), http://www.fseee.org/index.php/ground-truth/200017 (accessed August 12, 2015).

4. "Fall Creek Latest Update," http://arlotec.tripod.com/fallck.html (accessed August 12, 2015).

5. Luers, "How I Became an Eco-Warrior."

6. Ibid.

7. Robert Pogue Harrison, *Forests: The Shadow of Civilization* (Chicago: University of Chicago Press, 1992), 169.

8. For example, according to Susan Zakin, three thousand people participated in Redwood Summer in 1990 (*Coyotes and Town Dogs*, 388). The protest was modeled on the civil rights movement's Mississippi Summer of 1964 and called on ecologically minded "Freedom Riders" to save the forest.

9. "Earth First! Hurls Civil Disobedience Into the Treetops," *Earth First! Journal* Lughnasad 2005, 32. According to Rik Scarce, the first tree-sits were in Oregon's Millennium Grove in 1985.

10. "Back to the Trees," *Earth First! Journal*, Lughnasad 2005, 33.

11. Wilson, *Biophilia*, 85.

12. See Helena Wulff, ed., *The Emotions: A Cultural Reader* (Oxford: Berg, 2007).

13. Peter H. Kahn Jr. explores the ways in which culture shapes biophilia in *The Human Relationship With Nature: Development and Culture* (Cambridge, MA: MIT Press, 1999), 42.

14. According to geographer David Sobel, making forts in the woods during childhood helps "to foster and shape the unique self that is born in adolescence" (*Children's Special Places*, 13).

15. Elizabeth Kenworthy Teather, *Embodied Geographies: Spaces, Bodies and Rites of Passage* (New York: Routledge, 1999), 3.

16. Derr, "Sometimes Birds Sound Like Fish," 112.

17. Letter to author, March 5, 2007.

18. Patsy Eubanks Owens, "Natural Landscapes, Gathering Places, and Prospect Refuges: Characteristics of Outdoor Places Valued by Teens," *Children's Environment Quarterly* 5 (1988): 18.

19. Interview by author, February 17, 2015 and Beach, *A Good Forest*, 54.

20. *If a Tree Falls: A Story of the Earth Liberation Front*, directed by Marshall Curry and Sam Cullman (Marshall Curry Productions, 2011).

21. Kevin DeLuca analyzes the derogatory treatment of environmentalists by mainstream media in *Image Politics*, 6.

22. Blake Ness, "Berkeley Protesters Bare All for Trees," *The Daily Caller*, July 20, 2015, http://dailycaller.com/2015/07/20/tree-huggers-at-berkeley-get-naked-with-trees/.

23. Harrison, *Forests*, ix.

24. Nash, *Wilderness*, 8–22. In the United States, according to religious studies scholar Evan Berry, wilderness has often embodied "radical alterity and afforded transcendental experiences" (*Devoted to Nature*, 72).

25. Harrison, *Forests*, 147–48.

26. M. Jimmie Killingsworth, *Walt Whitman and the Earth: A Study of Ecopoetics* (Iowa City: University of Iowa Press, 2010), 69.

27. Quoted in David Haberman, *People Trees: Worship of Trees in Northern India* (Oxford: Oxford University Press, 2013), 39.

28. Taylor, *Dark Green Religion*, 52. Also see Jane Bennett, Thing-Power" in *Political Matter: Technoscience, Democracy, and Public Life*, ed. Bruce Braun and Sarah J. Whatmore (Minneapolis: University of Minnesota Press, 2010), 37.

29. Jeff Goodell, "Death in the Redwoods," *Rolling Stone* 804, January 21, 1999, 60.

30. Ibid.

31. Paul Rogers, "A Decade After Headwaters Deal, Truce Comes to Northern California Redwood Country," *San Jose Mercury News*, March 8, 2009, http://www.mercurynews.com/ci_11844764 (accessed September 18, 2015).

32. Beach, *A Good Forest*, 8–18.

33. Ingold and Palsson, *Biosocial Becomings*, 8.

34. Beach, *A Good Forest*, 86.

35. David Abram, "Magic and the Machine: Notes on Technology and Animism in an Era of Ecological Wipe-Out," keynote address at "Wonder and the Natural World" conference at Indiana University, June 22, 2016.

36. Hill, *Legacy of Luna*, 227.

37. My views of how activists come to live with and develop within a community of species have been inspired by anthropologist Eduardo Kohn's descriptions of an "ecology of selves" in *How Forests Think: Toward an Anthropology beyond the Human* (Berkeley: University of California Press, 2013), 17.

38. Joan Dunning, *From the Redwood Forest: Ancient Trees and the Bottom Line: A Headwaters Journey* (White River Junction, VT: Chelsea Green, 1998), 9.

39. Goodell, "Death in the Redwoods."

40. Jim Hindle, *Nine Miles: Two Winters of Anti-Road Protests* (London: Underhill, 2006), 123.

41. Interview by author, October 1, 2015.

42. Interview by author, October 1, 2014.

43. Interview by author, October 1, 2014.

44. Interview by author, October 1, 2014.

45. Jay Griffiths, *Anarchipelago* (Glastonbury, UK: Wooden Books, 2007), 14.

46. Ibid.,18–19.

47. See Steve Baker, "Sloughing the Human," in *Zoontologies: The Question of the Animal*, ed. Cary Wolfe (Minneapolis: University of Minnesota Press, 2003), 148–49.

48. Vanessa Grigoriadis, "The Rise and Fall of the Eco-Radical Underground," *Rolling Stone* 1006, August 10, 2006, 75.

49. Anonymous zine, *feral, a journal towards wildness*, n.p.

50. Ibid., n.p.

51. Blackfire, "Common Enemy," 21.

52. *Earth First! Journal*, Eostar 2004, 5.

53. *Earth First! Journal*, Brigid 2014, 39.

54. N.d, n.p., published in San Francisco, CA.

55. *Earth First! Journal*, Beltane 2007, 29.

56. *Satya*, December 2006, 36.

57. *Earth First! Journal*, Beltane 2011, 26.

58. *Earth First! Journal*, Beltane 2011, 49.

59. *Earth First! Journal*, Beltane 2014, 1.

60. Hill, *Legacy of Luna*, 2.

61. Donna Haraway discusses "knots" of species "co-shaping each other" in *When Species Meet*, 49.

62. Hindle, *Nine Miles*, 147–48.

63. Ibid., 390.

64. Marten, email to author.

65. *Earth First! Journal*, Brigid 2013, 14–15.

66. Hindle, *Nine Miles*,102.

67. Ibid., 103.

68. Luers, "How I Became an Eco-Warrior."

69. Interview by author, May 25, 2009.

70. "A Commemorative History of the Minnehaha Free State and Four Oaks Spiritual Encampment" zine, July 2006, n.p.

71. *Earth First! Journal*, Eostar 2004, 3.

72. *The Sun*, April 2012, 5.

73. Luers, "How I Became an Eco-Warrior."

74. Ibid.

75. Randall Sullivan, "Hunting America's Most Wanted Eco-Terrorist," *Rolling Stone*, December 12, 2002, http://www.rollingstone.com/politics/story/11034035/hunting_americas_most_wanted_ecoterrorist (accessed January 15, 2007).

76. Goodell, "Death in the Redwoods."

77. Heather Millar, "Generation Green," *Sierra*, November/December 2000, 36–40.

78. *The Mountain Defender* zine, n.d, 15.

79. Field notes.

80. What psychologist Theodore D. Kemper calls "empathic role-taking emotions" put one individual in place of another who is suffering ("Social Models in the Explanation of Emotions" in *Handbook of Emotions*, ed. Michael Lewis, Jeanette M. Haviland-Jones, and Lisa Fedman Barrett (New York: Guilford, 2011), 53).

81. Beach, *A Good Forest*, 15.

82. Hill, *Legacy of Luna*, 66.

83. Letter to author, November 9, 2006.

84. In his study of Hindu tree worship, religious studies scholar David L. Haberman calls a similar personification of trees by Hindu worshippers, "deliberate" anthropomorphism (*People Trees*, 24).

85. Anthropologist Kay Milton observes that personifying nature is one of the many attitudes that renders nature as sacred and deserving of protection (*Loving Nature*).

86. *Earth First! Journal*, Brigid 2007, 35.

87. "Cuntree Folk: The Beltane Issue" zine, n.p.

88. Ibid., 61.

89. Ibid., 14–15.

90. https://www.youtube.com/watch?annotation_id=annotation_228884& feature=iv&list=PLmIqdlomtuSutOyd37cnjQPYoo4dyap85&src_vid=4IHRP9 Fiwoo&v=I8iooPHkyUo (accessed August 12, 2015).

91. I met a number of activists who had traveled to other countries to participate in protests. The *Earth First! Journal* and *Newswire* include significant coverage of environmental and animal rights protests outside North America.

92. Dunning, *From the Redwood Forest*, 216. Years later, the victims won a suit against the police (*Earth First! Journal*, Lughnasad 2005, 3).

93. Ibid., 26.

94. Many environmental protests have involved dressing up as nonhuman animals. At an action in Maine, activists dressed in animal masks and play-acted gagging to symbolize the effect on local wildlife of a timber plan (*Earth First! Journal*, Beltane 2009).

95. DeLuca, *Image Politics*, 56.

96. Tony Perucci, "What the Fuck is That? The Poetics of Ruptural Performance," *Liminalities: A Journal of Performance Studies* 5 (2009): 1.

97. I draw on Judith Butler's understanding of Arendt's "space of appearance." Butler describes these processes in the context of Tahrir Square during the Arab Spring in "Bodies in Alliance and the Politics of the Street," European Institute for Progressive Cultural Policies, http://www.eipcp.net/transversal /1011/butler/en.

98. Butler gives similar examples in "Bodies in Alliance and the Politics of the Street," http://www.eipcp.net/transversal/1011/butler/en.

99. Thanks to participants in my 2015 seminar on "Ritual, Pilgrimage and Environmentalism" at the Faculty of Theology at the University of Oslo and to Michael Houseman for pushing me to clarify this point.

100. David Seideman, "The First Spotted Owl War," http://archive.audubon magazine.org/incite/incite0901-webexclusives.html.

CHAPTER 5. LIBERATION'S CRUSADE

1. Peter Young, "The Price I Paid for a Priceless Awakening," *The Animals' Voice Magazine* (2008): 14.

2. "Support Peter," http://supportpeter.com/background.htm (accessed November 21, 2009).

3. http://portland.indymedia.org/en/2005/11/329205.shtml.

4. David Graeber, *Direct Action: An Ethnography* (Oakland, CA: AK Press, 2009), 258–59.

5. These conversion stories come from a variety of sources: letters from prisoners, interviews, accounts on websites and in zines, as noted in each case.

6. Liddick, *Eco-Terrorism.*

7. See, for example, Daston, "Introduction," 103; Wolfe, *Zoontologies*; and Bulliet, *Hunters, Herders, and Hamburgers*, 34.

8. Jasper and Nelkin (*Animal Rights Crusade*) locate this shift during the 1980s in the United States. Historian Diane Beers identifies the rise of animal liberation ideology from 1975 with the publication of Peter Singer's *Animal Liberation* (*For the Prevention of Cruelty*, 4).

9. Marjorie Garber, *Dog Love* (New York: Simon & Schuster, 1996), 35. For youth involvement see PETA's PETA2 site (http://www.peta2.com).

10. Bekoff, *Emotional Lives of Animals*, and Jane Goodall, *Hope for Animals and Their World* (New York: Grand Central, 2009).

11. Walter Bond, "The Importance of Straightedge—Vegan Hardline," http://www.animalliberationpressoffice.org/essays/2011-11-12_bond_straightedge.htm (accessed January 25, 2012).

12. Steven Blush, *American Hardcore: A Tribal History* (Port Townsend, WA: Feral House, 2001), 9.

13. Brian Peterson, *Burning Fight: The Nineties Hardcore Revolution in Ethics, Politics, Spirit and Sound* (Huntington Beach, CA: Revelation Records, 2009).

14. According to legend, Minor Threat's drummer was drawing a poster for a show with a wood ruler and told his bandmates that the ruler's straightedge was a metaphor for their lifestyle.

15. Haenfler, *Straightedge*, 59.

16. Beth Lahickey, *All Ages—Reflections on Straightedge* (Huntington Beach, CA: Revelation Records, 1998), xii.

17. Saadhya, email message to author, May 26, 2007.

18. Craig O'Hara, *The Philosophy of Punk* (London: AK Press, 1999), 142.

19. Ibid., 147.

20. Josh Harper, letter to author, June 2007.

21. Peter Young, letter to author, March 29, 2006.

22. http://www.peta2.com/outthere/o-earthcrisis.asp.

23. http://www.sing365.com/music/lyric.nsf/Biomachines-lyrics-Earth-Crisis/AA543E1E9E44EE7748256CF10027C5B1.

24. http://www.myspace.com/tearsofgaia, accessed May 20, 2009.

25. Letter to author, November 20, 2006.

26. Studies of ISKCON (none of which mention punk or hardcore) include *The Hare Krishna Movement: Forty Years of Chant and Change*, eds. Graham Dwyer and Richard J. Cole (London: I. B. Tauris, 2007) and E. Burke Rochford, *Hare Krishna Transformed* (New York: New York University Press, 2007).

27. Ibrahim Abraham, "Punk Pulpit: Religion, Punk Rock and Counter (Sub)cultures," *Council of the Societies for the Study of Religion Bulletin* 37 (2008): 3–7.

28. On the convergence of religion and punk see ibid.

29. O'Hara, *Philosophy of Punk*, 39. Curry Malott and Milagros Peña argue that "social protest was the most dominant theme in the 1980s and 1990s" (*Punk Rockers' Revolution: A Pedagogy of Race, Class, and Gender* [New York: Peter Lang, 2004), 99).

30. Quoted in James Wilson, "Punk Rock Puja: (Mis)appropriation, (Re) interpretation, and Dissemination of Hindu Religious Traditions in the North American and European Underground Music Scene(s)," (MA thesis, University of Florida, 2008), Chap. 2, 19.

31. Ibid., Chap. 3, 13.

32. See, for example, xCHIPxSem, "Krishnacore in the '90s," http://xstuckinthepastx.blogspot.com/2009/03/krishnacore-in-90s.html, and Erik Davis, "Hare Krishna Hard Core," http://www.techgnosis.com/index_hare.html. Wood's (*Straightedge Youth*) and Haenfler's (*Straightedge: Clean-Living Youth*) studies of straightedge include discussion of the influence of Krishna bands on straightedge, but hardly mention the animal rights connection.

33. Vegan Reich's Muslim lead singer Sean Muttaqi is an example. In 2012, imprisoned animal rights activist Walter Bond (Abdul Haqq) converted to Islam. On early twenty-first-century Muslim punk, see for example, Michael Muhammad Knight, *The Taqwacores* (New York: Autonomedia, 2005), and Evan Serpick, "Allah, Amps and Anarchy: On the Road with the First-Ever Muslim Punk-Rock Tour," *Rolling Stone* 1036 (2007): 20. On Jewish punks see Steven Lee Berber, *The Heebie-Jeebies at CBGB's: A Secret History of Jewish Punk* (Chicago: Review Press, 2006)

34. Blush, *American Hardcore*, 189 and John Joseph, *The Evolution of a Cro-Magnon* (New York: Punk House, 2007).

35. Joseph, *Evolution*.

36. Ibid., 418.

37. Norman Brannon, *The Anti-Matter Anthology: A 1990s Post-Punk and Hardcore Reader* (Huntington Beach, CA: Revelation Records, 2007), 4.

38. Haenfler, *Straightedge*, 320.

39. O'Hara, *Philosophy of Punk*, 148.

40. Wilson, "Punk Rock Puja," Chap. 2, 23.

41. Rochford, *Hare Krishna Transformed*.

42. Erik Davis, "Hare Krishna Hard Core," http://www.techgnosis.com/index_hare.html.

43. 108, interviewed by Saeed, Crucial Chaos, WNYU radio, April 30, 2009.

44. Vic DiCara, "I Was a Teenage Hare Krishna," http://krishnacore.com/biographies/108_bio.html (accessed November 3, 2009).

45. ISKCON Communications Briefings, October 1989, http://www.krishnacore.com/contents.html (accessed November 17, 2009).

46. Ravindra Svarupa Dasa, "With Shelter in Reading: The Scene at Unisound," *Back to Godhead*, http://www.backtogodhead.in/with-shelter-in-reading-the-scene-at-unisound-by-ravindra-svarupa-dasa/ (accessed February 1, 2016).

47. Ibid.

48. http://krishnacore.com/biographies/108_bio.html (accessed November 3, 2009).

49. Bhakta Vic, "Hardcore Hare Krishnas—The Straightedge Connection," *Back to Godhead,* May 1991, http://www.krishnacore.com/contents.html (accessed November 16, 2009).

50. Davis, "Hare Krishna Hard Core."

51. Ibid.

52. Haenfler, *Straightedge,* 13.

53. Stuart, *Bloodless Revolution,* xi–xii.

54. Ibid., xx–xxi.

55. Ibid., 298.

56. Stephen A. Kent, *From Slogans to Mantras: Social Protests and Religious Conversion in the Late Vietnam War Era* (Syracuse, NY: Syracuse University Press, 2001), 55–57.

57. Wood, *Straightedge Youth,* 57.

58. Peter Young, letter to author, November 20, 2006.

59. Letter to author, June 3, 2007.

60. Haenfler, *Straightedge,* 35.

61. Michel Foucault describes such spaces as "heterotopia" in "Of Other Spaces," *Diacritics* 16 (1986): 24.

62. Rosebraugh, *Burning Rage,* x.

63. Letter to author, May 5, 2007.

64. Sociologist Elizabeth Cherry discusses how punk rock subcultures help maintain veganism as a "lifestyle movement" in "'I Was a Teenage Vegan': Motivation and Maintenance of Lifestyle Movements," *Sociological Inquiry* 85 (2015): 62.

65. O'Hara, *Philosophy of Punk,* 92.

66. "Peter Young Interview," Animal Liberation Front, http://www.animal liberationfront.com/ALFront/Activist%20Tips/PeterYoungInterview.htm.

67. Letter to author, March 24, 2006.

68. Letter to author, November 20, 2006.

69. Adam Seligman et al. discuss "sincere" in contrast to "empty" ritual in *Ritual and Its Consequences: An Essay on the Limits of Sincerity* (New York: Oxford University Press, 2008).

70. John Lofland and Rodney Stark discuss this kind of orientation in "Becoming a World-Saver: A Theory of Conversion to a Deviant Perspective," *American Sociological Review* 30 (1965): 863–74.

71. Cultural studies scholar Lawrence Grossberg takes the perspective that "expressions of defiance are fabrications feeding complacency" in which "rage is disconnected from political articulation." See Neil Nehring, "Jigsaw Youth" in *GenXegesis: Essays on 'Alternative' Youth (Sub)Culture,* ed. John M. Ulrich and Andrea l. Harris (Madison: University of Wisconsin Press, 2003), 65.

72. Stacy Thompson, *Punk Productions: Unfinished Business* (Albany: State University of New York Press 2004), 21.

73. Lee Hall, *Capers in the Churchyard: Animal Rights Advocacy in the Age of Terror* (Darien, CT: Nectar Bat, 2006), 64.

74. Rosebraugh, *Burning Rage,* xiii.

75. http://planetgrenada.blogspot.com/2006/01/sean-muttaqi-vegan-recih-and-hardline-html (accessed March 3, 2008). Vegan Reich has also been controversial for its members' stands on LGBTQ issues.

76. Kelefa Sanneh, "Vegan Jihad: A Conversation With Sean Muttaqi," *Bidoun*, bidoun.org/articles/vegan-jihad-a-conversation-with-sean-muttaqi.

77. "Interview," muslimsforjesus.org (accessed April 4, 2008).

CHAPTER 6. CIRCLES OF COMMUNITY, STRATEGIES
OF INCLUSION

1. *Direct Action* zine, x.
2. http://greenmountainearthfirst.tumblr.com/.
3. Zakin, *Coyotes and Town Dogs*, 298.
4. "Insurrectionary Ecology" zine, 9.
5. See for example "Primitive Living Skills," http://www.hollowtop.com/pls.htm.
6. "Conserving Wild Nature in Virginia," in *Earth First! Journal*, Lughnasad 1999, 11.
7. *Earth First! Journal*, Brigid 2013, 25.
8. Email message to author, June 20, 2014.
9. Round River Rendezvous 2013 Welcome Packet.
10. Free Association, *Moments of Excess: Movements, Protests and Everyday Life* (Oakland: PM Press, 2011), 35.
11. Marten, email to author.
12. *Stop the ReRoute: Taking a Stand on Sacred Land*, Oak Folk Films, 2008.
13. Full Moon ceremonies at the spring continued for years afterwards even though the trees were gone. All quotes are from Elizabeth Marie Egan's zine, "A Commemorative History of the Minnehaha Free State and Four Oaks Spiritual Encampment," 2006.
14. Graeber, *Direct Action*, 266.
15. Ibid., 35.
16. Kera Abraham, "Flames of Dissent," http://www.eugeneweekly.com/2006/11/02/coverstory.html.
17. According to Grigoriadis and other accounts, Warner Creek was an experience that radicalized a number of people and where many of those who later were arrested for ELF arsons met each other ("The Rise and Fall of the Eco-Radical Underground").
18. "Free State Analysis: The Elliott Free State," *Earth First! Journal* 30th Anniversary Issue, n.d., 27.
19. Marten, email to author.
20. "Occupying the Montana Capitol Again," http://earthfirstjournal.org/newswire/2012/08/14/occupying-the-montana-capitol-again/.
21. Zakin, *Coyotes and Town Dogs*, 280.
22. Email message to author, August 9, 2015.
23. Darryl Cherney, interview by author, February 17, 2015.
24. Interview by photographer Lucas Foglia, "A Natural Order" (http://lucasfoglia.com/a-natural-order/).

25. Graeber, *Direct Action*, 248.

26. In *Sense of Place and Sense of Planet: The Environmental Imagination of the Global*, Ursula Heise argues that American environmentalists have been overly focused on the local and need to also pay attention to new forms of culture not anchored in place. Radical activists exemplify what she calls "deterritorialization (Oxford: Oxford University Press, 2008), 10.

27. Accounts in the *Earth First! Journal* and interviews with activists at the Earth First! Rendezvous 2013. For instance, see the *Earth First! Journal*, Samhain/Yule 2006.

28. http://greenmountainearthfirst.tumblr.com/.

29. Quotes from "An Open Letter to EF! Regarding Systems of Oppression and Centering Marginalized Voices," *Earth First! Journal*, Mabon 2016, 42.

30. "Who Bombed Judi Bari? Judy Bari Spoken Word," produced and edited by Darryl Cherney and Penelope Andrews of Environmentally Sound Promotions, n.d.

31. The concept of intersectionality is developed in Kimberle Crenshaw, "Demarginalizing the Intersection of Race and Sex: A Black Feminist Critique of Antidiscrimination Doctrine, Feminist Theory, and Antiracist Politics," *University of Chicago Legal Forum* 140 (1989): 139–67.

32. Brian, letter to the editors, *Earth First! Journal*, Samhain/Yule 2006, 5.

33. Email message to author, August 9, 2015.

34. http://earthfirstjournal.org/newswire/2015/12/20/monkeywrenching-the-misogynists-in-our-movements-a-historical-exploration-of-call-outs-and-anti-feminist-backlash-in-cascadia/.

35. The talking stick originated with indigenous cultures, such as some Native American tribes that used it in council circles, and the practice has been widely adopted by non-Native people in New Age, Neopagan, and other contemporary religious movements. https://www.acaciart.com/stories/archive6.html.

36. https://earthfirstnews.wordpress.com/articles/the-challening-male-supremacy-debacle-ef-rrr-2012/.

37. Email message to author, August 9, 2015.

38. Field notes.

39. All quotes from Sabitaj Mahal, "Fishbowl at Wild Roots, Feral Futures: Thoughts on Race, Identity and Solidarity," *Earth First! Journal*, Brigid 2013, 18.

40. Ibid., 17.

41. Quoted in "Decolonizing the Primitive Skills Movement," https://onstolenland.wordpress.com/2013/03/19/summary-and-response-to-decolonizing-restorative-justice-by-denise-c-breton/.

42. "Interview with Rod Coronado on Indigenous Resistance and Animal Liberation" in *Earth First! Journal*, Winter 2014. http://earthfirstjournal.org/newswire/2014/02/26/interview-with-rod-coronado-on-indigenous-resistance-and-animal-liberation/ interview.

43. 2013 Round River Rendezvous workshop on Black Mesa. Susan Zakin discusses a variety of groups resisting Black Mesa in the 1970s in *Coyotes and Town Dogs*, 48–49.

44. "Interview with Rod Coronado on Indigenous Resistance and Animal Liberation," *Earth First! Journal*, Winter 2014, http://earthfirstjournal.org /newswire/2014/02/26/interview-with-rod-coronado-on-indigenous-resistance-and-animal-liberation/ interview.

45. Ingalsbee, "Earth First!," 135. When I spoke with Earth First! activist Darryl Cherney, he recalled a sign at the entrance to one Rendezvous that read "This is not a healing gathering" and included a drawing of a person meditating with crystals" (interview with author, February 17, 2015).

46. Ingalsbee, "Earth First!," 203.

47. Ibid, 34.

48. Carbon, letter to author, September 2007.

49. *Earth First! Journal* collective, "Deep Green Transphobia," http:// earthfirstjournal.org/newswire/2013/05/15/deep-green-transphobia/.

50. Ibid.

51. Mahal, "Fishbowl," 20.

52. A Decade of Earth First! Action in the 'Climate Movement," http:// earthfirstjournal.org/newswire/2014/01/19/a-decade-of-earth-first-action-in-the-climate-movement/ (accessed December 10, 2015).

53. Widdow, "A Story of the Trans and/or Women's Action Camp and How It All Began," *Earth First! Journal*, Litha 2015, 31.

54. Ibid., 31.

55. The third annual TWAC in 2011 culminated in an occupation of the Oregon Department of Forestry office in solidarity with activist friends blockading a logging road in the Elliott State Forest.

56. https://twac.wordpress.com/page/2/.

57. "EF!'s COW is Born," *Earth First! Journal*, Samhain/Yule 2006, http:// www.environmentandsociety.org/sites/default/files/key_docs/ef_27_1_2.pdf.

58. Zakin, *Coyotes and Town Dogs*, 246.

59. F. Fox, "In Danger: Wolf Killing in Northern Minnesota and Wisconsin," *Earth First! Journal*, Brigid 2013, 23–24.

60. Interview with Aaron, July 24, 2013.

61. http://rampscampaign.org/about-us/.

62. *Earth First! Journal*, Brigid 2014.

63. *Breaking the Spell: Anarchists, Eugene and the WTO*, film online.

CHAPTER 7. RITES OF GRIEF AND MOURNING

1. I borrow the notion of "turning towards" from anthropologist Deborah Bird Rose (*Wild Dog Dreaming*, 5).

2. I develop many of these ideas in "Mourning Nature: The Work of Grief in Radical Environmentalism," *Journal for the Study of Religion, Nature and Culture* 10 (2016): 419–41. Bron Taylor discusses some ways that radical environmentalists are motivated by grief in "Evoking the Ecological Self," *Peace Review: The International Quarterly of World Peace* 5 (June 1993): 228.

3. Elizabeth Kolbert, *The Sixth Extinction: An Unnatural History* (New York: Henry Holt, 2014)

4. "In the World's Sixth Extinction, Are Humans the Asteroid?" NPR interview with Elizabeth Kolbert. http://www.npr.org/2014/02/12/275885377/in-the-worlds-sixth-extinction-are-humans-the-asteroid.

5. Dunning, *From the Redwood Forest*, 41.

6. Thom van Dooren describes how other species come to matter in *Flight Ways*, 139–40.

7. Rose, *Wild Dog Dreaming*, 22.

8. In her study of extinction, Melanie Challenger explains loss as "like shrapnel lodging in the mind as a permanent ache" (*On Extinction: How We Became Estranged From Nature* [London: Granta Books, 2011], 55).

9. Voice of the Voiceless, *From Dusk 'til Dawn: An Insider's View of the Animal Liberation Movement* (N.p.: Voice of the Voiceless Communications, 2008), 383.

10. Letter to author, June 3, 2007.

11. Robert Michael Pyle, *The Thunder Tree: Lessons from an Urban Wildland* (Corvallis: Oregon State University Press, 2011), 134.

12. Activists found themselves on both side of the debate over Makah whaling, with many activists arguing against the hunt and others supporting tribal sovereignty. The tribe itself was divided on the issue.

13. Rosebraugh, *Burning Rage*, 147–48.

14. *Earth First! Journal*, 30th Anniversary Special Edition, Samhain/Yule 2010, inside cover.

15. "The Hambach Forest Occupation," *Earth First! Journal*, Samhain 2014, 24.

16. Hindle, *Nine Miles*, 195.

17. Ibid., 213.

18. Ibid., 395.

19. Dunning, *From the Redwood Forest*, 250.

20. *Toward a Choice: Writings by Eric McDavid* zine, n.p.

21. Chris Jordan keynote, This Way to Sustainability conference, Chico, CA, 2013. See http://www.chrisjordan.com/gallery/midway/#about.

22. "The Dark Mountain Manifesto," http://dark-mountain.net/about/manifesto/ (accessed June 8, 2015).

23. Glen Martin, "Vandals Slash Giant Redwood," *San Francisco Chronicle*, November 28, 2000, http://www.sfgate.com/green/article/Vandals-Slash-Giant-Redwood-Tree-sitter-Julia-3302945.php.

24. Leif Utne, "Julia Butterfly Hill Tree Struck by Chainsaw," *Utne Reader*, November 29, 2000, http://www.utne.com/community/juliabutterflyhillstreestruckbychainsaw.aspx.

25. Paul Donohue, "Luna—17 Months Since Being Cut and Still Doing Well," http://www.pauldonahue.net/17_months.html (accessed May 8, 2015), and http://www.circleoflife.org/history.html (accessed May 8, 2015).

26. http://www.swans.com/library/art6/xxx051.html.

27. Freya Mathews discusses "the story of the biosphere told in miniature" in "Planet Beehive," in "Unloved Others," ed. Rose and van Dooren, special issue, *Australian Humanities Review* 50 (May 2011), http://www.australianhumanitiesreview.org/archive/Issue-May-2011/mathews.html.

28. *Earth First! Journal*, Eostar 2006.

29. All quotes from *Earth First! Journal*, 30th Anniversary Special Edition, Samhain/Yule 2010, 38–39.

30. Martha Lee, *Earth First! Environmental Apocalypse.* (Syracuse, NY: Syracuse University Press. 1995), 11.

31. "Ivory Bill Woodpecker," *Earth First! Journal*, Lughnasad 2005, 27.

32. Watson, *Seal Wars*, 33.

33. Dunning, *From the Redwood Forest*, 43.

34. Jennifer Jacquet, "Is Shame Necessary?" at "The Extinction Marathon," http://www.serpentinegalleries.org/exhibitions-events/extinction-marathon (accessed April 15, 2015).

35. In 1990 Christopher Manes called for a severe reduction in the Earth's human population in *Green Rage: Radical Environmentalism and the Unmaking of Civilization* (New York: Back Bay, 1991). From the 1980s on, a misanthropic faction was present in radical environmentalism (Turner, *Promise of Wilderness*, 306).

36. *Earth First! Journal*, Beltane 2009, 6.

37. http://www.paulkingsnorth.net/journalism/hope-in-the-age-of-collapse/.

38. Zakin, *Coyotes and Town Dogs*, 399.

39. "Down With Empire, Up with the Spring," n.a., n.d., 65.

40. Rosebraugh, *Burning Rage*, 20.

41. *Insurrectionary Ecology*, n.a, n.d., 3.

42. Watson, *Seal Wars*, 233–34.

43. Ibid., 234.

44. Ibid.

45. Email message to author, February 19, 2015.

46. *Memories of Freedom*, n.a., n.d., 68.

47. "How I Became an Eco-Warrior."

48. "A Letter from Rod Coronado" in *Memories of Freedom* zine, 71.

49. *Earth First! Journal*, Brigid 2014.

50. *Memories of Freedom*, 47–48.

51. All quotes from the zine, *Memories of Freedom*, 47–53 (n.d.).

52. Young, *Animal Liberation Front*. Actions claimed by ALF from 1979–2008: 4,934 animals released from labs, 128,314 animals released from fur farms, and 106 arsons, in a total of 1,353 actions.

53. See Bron Taylor's discussion of violence, including radical environmentalism's connection to Ted Kaczynski, "the Unabomber," in "Religion, Violence and Radical Environmentalism: From Earth First! to the Unabomber to the Earth Liberation Front," *Terrorism and Political Violence* 10 (Winter 1998): 1–42.

54. Rosebraugh, *Burning Rage*, 249.

55. See Tom Regan, *Defending Animal Rights* (Urbana: University of Illinois Press, 2001) and Gary L. Francione, *Rain Without Thunder: The Ideology of the Animal Rights Movement* (Philadelphia: Temple University Press, 1996).

56. Both quotes are from "Hypocrisy Is Our Greatest Luxury," *Satya*, March 2004, 22–23.

57. "Hypocrisy Is Our Greatest Luxury," 23.

58. http://www.animalliberationfront.com/ALFront/mission_statement.htm.

59. "Firestarter," 5.

60. "Hypocrisy," 22–23.

61. Rosebraugh, *Burning Rage*, 184.

62. Watson, *Seal Wars*, 107.

63. "The Turtle Talk," in *Herbivore* 13, n.d., 14–17.

64. "Earth First! of Humboldt County: Tools of the Trade," *Satya*, March 2004, 39.

65. All quotes from "How I Became an Eco-Warrior."

66. All quotes from "Home Demos and Traumatic Knowledge," in *Satya*, March 2004, 21.

67. "Working for the Clampdown: How the Animal Enterprise Terrorism Act became Law," in *Satya*, December 2006/January 2007, 12.

68. Jeff Barnard, "Fugitive in String of Eco-Terrorist Fires Surrenders," *Seattle Times*, November 29, 2012, http://www.seattletimes.com/seattle-news/fugitive-in-string-of-eco-terrorism-fires-surrenders/.

69. "Interview with Daniel McGowan" by *Earth First! Journal* Collective, *Earth First! Journal*, Samhain/Yule 2007, 22.

70. Kite, email message to author, September 16, 2006.

71. Funk, "Firestarter," 2.

72. Journalist Will Potter's *Green Is the New Red* documents the increasingly repressive government policies concerning animal rights and environmental activists after the terrorist attacks of September 11, 2001.

73. Tooker Gomberg, Angela Bischoff, and Ed. Press, "Alberta Explosion," *Earth First! Journal*, Litha 1999, 25.

74. *Earth First! Journal*, Brigid 2014, 23.

75. *Satya*, March 2004, 31.

76. "Warbler announces Hunger Strike. 4th Tree-Sit Goes Up," http://www.savelittlelakevalley.org/2013/03/28/warbler-announces-hunger-strike-4th-tree-sit-goes-up/.

77. https://www.indybay.org/newsitems/2013/04/03/18734637.php.

78. https://www.youtube.com/watch?v=YZcHa9zp2zs.

79. For two of many possible examples see Rosebraugh, *Burning Rage*, 189, and Voice of the Voiceless, *From Dusk 'til Dawn*, 442–43.

80. Rosebraugh, *Burning Rage*, 68.

81. Interview with author, July 24, 2013.

82. http://www.tarsandsblockade.org/onemonth/.

83. See the North American Earth Liberation Prisoners Support Network at http://www.ecoprisoners.org.

84. While many activists responded personally to my letters written to them in prison, one SHAC activist, Andy Stepanian, sent me a form letter, indicating he could not handle the volume of mail he received.

85. Voice of the Voiceless, *From Dusk 'til Dawn*, 511.

86. Ibid, 515.

87. Ibid, 539.

88. Ibid, 546–54.

89. In *The Palm at the End of the Mind: Relatedness, Religiosity, and the Real* (Durham, NC: Duke University Press, 2009), anthropologist Michael

Jackson explains that in acts of self-sacrifice, "value accrues to the *ideal* for which one ostensibly died" (205).

90. "Terrible Beauty: A Tribute to Brad Will," https://earthfirstnews .wordpress.com/for-fallen-warriors/. Will was shot while working as a journalist documenting the clash between paramilitary forces and the strikers and their supporters.

91. "Lament for a Bat, for the 10 Year Anniversary of Avalon's Death," *Earth First! Newswire*, http://earthfirstjournal.org/newswire/2015/12/21/lament-for-bat-for-the-10-year-anniversary-of-avalons-death/.

92. Grigoriadis, "Rise and Fall," 73.

93. A short memorial video, for instance, is online: https://www.youtube .com/watch?v=8yXYAKPasV8 (accessed June 1, 2015). As one viewer notes in the comments section: "Remember our fallen heroes-AND the snitches that kill and imprison our warriors!"

94. Hill was executed in 1915. Judi Bari, "Revolutionary Ecology," n.d, n.p.

95. "Remembering Bill Rodgers: Long Live Avalon!" www.catalystinfoshop .org; www.supportbill.org.

96. "Bill the Cat Heads Home," http://www.nocompromise.org/issues/29bill .html (accessed 4 March 2015).

97. http://earthfirstjournal.org/newswire/2012/12/17/remembering-avalon-on-winter-solstice/.

98. *Earth First! Journal*, Eostar 2006, 8.

99. "Beth aka Horehound, aka Dumpster Leg falls to her death from tree-sit at Eagle Creek, Oregon," http://slingshot.tao.ca/issue.html?0075011 (accessed May 31, 2015).

100. "Activist's death dampens Eagle Creek victory," http://forests.org /shared/reader/welcome.aspx?linkid=10114&keybold=rainforest+logging+ human+rights (accessed March 31, 2015).

101. "Activists Renew Perch on Mt. Hood," *Willamette Week*, July 17, 2002, http://www.wweek.com/portland/article-1140-activists_renew_perch_on_ mount_hood.html (accessed May 31, 2015).

102. http://portland.indymedia.org/en/2007/04/357488.shtml (accessed May 31, 2015).

103. http://earthfirstjournal.org/newswire/2015/04/25/healing-from-the-past-fighting-for-the-future-an-interview-with-loki/ (accessed May 31, 2015).

104. Literary scholar Mary Jacobus calls this kind of memory work, "the strange afterlife of mourning . . . that continues to honor the dead by talking to them" in "Distressful Gift: Talking to the Dead," *South Atlantic Quarterly* 106 (2007): 393.

105. Rosebraugh, *Burning Rage*, 148.

106. "The Political Becomes Personal," *Earth First! Journal*, Samhain/Yule 2006, 24.

107. Ibid., 25.

108. Interview with author, October 1, 2014.

109. Rebecca Solnit describes "hope in the dark" that works "against the tendency to despair" in *Hope in the Dark: Untold Histories, Wild Possibilities* (New York: Nation Books, 2004), 5.

110. Email to author, August 9, 2015.

111. See Taylor, "Religion and Politics of Earth First!" 261. As Taylor sees it, for radical environmentalists, "pessimism and optimism are two sides of the same tragic coin" (*Dark Green Religion*, 85).

112. "Protester Motivations," *Earth First! Journal*, Brigid 2014, 14.

113. Although I borrow the term "primal future" from Louis Herman's book *Primal Future*, other scholars have made similar observations. See Ingalsbee, *Earth First!*, 167, and Bron Taylor, "Earth First! From Primal Spirituality to Ecological Resistance," in *This Sacred Earth*, ed. Roger Gottlieb (New York: Routledge, 1996), 545–57.

114. Letter to author, March 29, 2006.

115. Zine, *reclaim, rewild: a vision for going feral & actualizing our wildest dreams*, 21.

116. Ibid., 6.

117. Ibid., 2.

118. Email message to author, September 16, 2006.

119. Thomas J. Elpel, "Primitive Living Skills," *Earth First! Journal*, Eostar 2006, 8, and Philip Weiss, "Off the Grid: Enter Government-Hating, Home-Schooling, Scripture-Quoting Idaho, the New Leave-Me-Alone America at Its Most Extreme," *New York Times Magazine*, January 8, 1995, 24–33, 38, 44, 48–52.

120. Letter to author, November 9, 2006.

121. *Earth First! Journal*, Brigid 2013, 72.

122. "The Butterfly Effect," an interview by Leslee Goodman, *The Sun*, April 2012, 8.

CONCLUSION

1. He took years away from activism to be with his family.

2. "The Resilience of the Wild: Talking and Stalking Wolves with Rod Coronado," February 13, 2015. http://www.blackandgreenreview.org/2015/02/the-resilience-of-wild-talking-and.html (accessed May 29, 2015).

3. https://ccrjustice.org/home/who-we-are/staff/gazzola-lauren.

4. Camilla Mortensen, "Former Ecosaboteur Returns for Ecstatic Dance Fundraiser," March 20, 2014, http://www.eugeneweekly.com/20140320/news-briefs/former-ecosaboteur-returns-ecstatic-dance-fundraiser.

Bibliography

Abraham, Ibrahim. "Punk Pulpit: Religion, Punk Rock and Counter (Sub)cultures." *Council of the Societies for the Study of Religion Bulletin* 37 (2008): 3–7.

Abram, David. "Magic and the Machine: Notes on Technology and Animism in an Era of Ecological Wipe-Out." Keynote address at "Wonder and the Natural World" conference at Indiana University, June 22, 2016.

Albanese, Catherine L. *Nature Religion in America: From the Algonkian Indians to the New Age.* Chicago: University of Chicago Press, 1991.

Alexander, Jeffrey. *Performative Revolution in Egypt.* London: Bloomsbury, 2011.

Arnett, Jeffrey Jensen. "Emerging Adulthood: A Theory of Development from the Late Teens Through the Twenties." *American Psychologist* (May 2000): 469–80.

Aron, Raymond. "Student Rebellion: Vision of the Future or Echo From the Past." In *The Seeds of Politics: Youth and Politics in America*, edited by Anthony M. Orum, 327–42. Englewood Cliffs, NJ: Prentice-Hall, 1972.

Ayers, Bill. *Fugitive Days: A Memoir.* New York: Penguin, 2003.

Bailey, Ronald. *Eco-Scam: The False Prophets of Ecological Apocalypse.* New York: St. Martin's, 1993.

Baker, Steve. "Sloughing the Human." In *Zootologies: The Question of the Animal*, edited by Cary Wolfe, 147–64. Minneapolis: University of Minnesota Press, 2003.

Barad, Karen. *Meeting the Universe Half-way: Quantum Physics and the Entanglement of Matter.* Durham, NC: Duke University Press, 2007.

Beach, Patrick. *A Good Forest for Dying: The Tragic Death of a Young Man on the Front Lines of the Environmental Wars.* New York: Doubleday, 2003.

Beers, Diane L. *For the Prevention of Cruelty: The History and Legacy of Animal Rights Activism in the United States.* Athens: Ohio University Press, 2006.

Behind the Mask. Directed by Shannon Keith. Uncaged Films, 2006, DVD.

Bekoff, Mark. *The Emotional Lives of Animals: A Leading Scientist Explores Animal Joy, Sorrow, and Empathy—and Why They Matter.* Novato, CA: New World Library, 2007.

Bender, Courtney, and Ann Taves. *What Matters? Ethnographies of Value in a Not So Secular Age.* New York: Columbia University Press, 2012.

Bennett, Jane. "Thing-Power." In *Political Matter: Technoscience, Democracy, and Public Life*, edited by Bruce Braun and Sarah J. Whatmore, 35–62. Minneapolis: University of Minnesota Press, 2010.

Bennett, Jane. *Vibrant Matter: A Political Ecology of Things.* Durham, NC: Duke University Press, 2010.

Berber, Steven Lee. *The Heebie-Jeebies at CBGB's: A Secret History of Jewish Punk.* Chicago: Review Press, 2006.

Berger, Helen, and Douglas Ezzy. *Teenage Witches: Magical Youth and the Search for the Self.* New Brunswick, NJ: Rutgers University Press, 2007.

Berger, Dan. *Outlaws of America: The Weather Underground and the Politics of Solidarity.* Oakland, CA: AK Press, 2006.

Berrigan, Daniel. *The Trial of the Catonsville Nine.* New York: Fordham University Press, 2004.

Berry, Evan. *Devoted to Nature: The Religious Roots of American Environmentalism.* Oakland: University of California Press, 2015.

Best, Steven, and Anthony J. Nocella, eds. *Terrorists or Freedom Fighters? Reflections on the Liberation of Animals.* New York: Lantern Books, 2004.

Bird-David, Nurit. "'Animism' Revisited: Personhood, Environment, and Relational Epistemology." *Current Anthropology* 40 (1999): S67–S91.

Bliwise, Robert J. "Flagging Faith," *Duke Magazine* (November/December 2011): 45.

Blockadia Rising: Voices of the Tar Sands Blockade. Directed by Garrett Graham, 2013.

Blush, Steven. *American Hardcore: A Tribal History.* Port Townsend, WA: Feral House, 2001.

Bogad, L.M. *Tactical Performance: The Theory and Practice of Serious Play.* New York: Routledge, 2016.

Brannon, Norman. *The Anti-Matter Anthology: A 1990s Post-Punk and Hardcore Reader.* Huntington Beach, CA: Revelation Records, 2007.

Breaking the Spell: Anarchists, Eugene and the WTO. Film online.

Bronski, Michael. *A Queer History of the United States.* Boston: Beacon, 2012.

Bulliet, Richard. *Hunters, Herders, and Hamburgers: The Past and Present of Human-Animal Relationships.* New York: Columbia University Press, 2005.

Burrough, Bryan. *Days of Rage: America's Radical Underground, the FBI, and the Forgotten Age of Revolutionary Violence.* New York: Penguin, 2015.

Butler, Judith. "Bodies in Alliance and the Politics of the Street." European Institute for Progressive Cultural Policies, http://www.eipcp.net/transversal/1011/butler/en.

Carson, Rachel. *The Sense of Wonder.* New York: Harper and Row, 1956.

Challenger, Melanie. *On Extinction: How We Became Estranged From Nature.* London: Granta, 2011.Chawla, Louise. "Childhood Experiences Associated with Care for the Natural World: A Theoretical Framework for Empirical Results." *Children, Youth and Environments* 17 (2007): 144–70.

Chawla, Louise. *In the First Country of Places: Nature, Poetry, and Childhood Memory.* Albany: State University of New York Press, 1994.

Chawla, Louise. "Spots of Time: Manifold Ways of Being in Nature in Childhood." In *Children and Nature: Psychological, Sociocultural, and Evolutionary Investigations*, edited by Peter H. Kahn Jr. and Stephen R. Kellert, 199–226. Cambridge, MA: MIT Press, 2002.

Cherry, Elizabeth. "'I Was a Teenage Vegan': Motivation and Maintenance of Lifestyle Movements." *Sociological Inquiry* 85 (2015): 55–74.

Chudicoff, Howard P. *Children at Play: An American History.* New York: New York University Press, 2007.

Clark, Lynn Schofield *From Angels to Aliens: Teenagers, the Media, and the Supernatural.* New York: Oxford University Press, 2005.

Crenshaw, Kimberle. "Demarginalizing the Intersection of Race and Sex: A Black Feminist Critique of Antidiscrimination Doctrine, Feminist Theory, and Antiracist Politics." *University of Chicago Legal Forum* 140 (1989): 139–67.

Daston, Lorraine. "Introduction." In *Thinking with Animals: New Perspectives on Anthropomorphism*, edited by Lorraine Daston and Gregg Mitman. New York: Columbia University Press, 2005.

Davis, Flora. *Moving the Mountain: The Women's Movement in America Since 1960.* New York: Simon & Schuster, 1991.

DeBenedetti, Charles. *An American Ordeal: The Antiwar Movement of the Vietnam Era.* Syracuse, NY: Syracuse University Press, 1990.

Delattre, Roland. "Ritual Resourcefulness and Cultural Pluralism." *Soundings* 61 (1978): 281–301.

Deleuze, Gilles, and Félix Guattari. *A Thousand Plateaus.* Minneapolis: University of Minnesota Press, 1987.

DeLuca, Kevin. *Image Politics: The New Rhetoric of Environmental Activism.* New York: Guilford, 1999.

DeLuca, Kevin. "Unruly Arguments: The Body Rhetoric of Earth First!, Act Up, and Queer Nation." *Argumentation and Advocacy* 36 (Summer 1999): 9–21.

Derr, Tori. "'Sometimes Birds Sound Like Fish': Perspectives on Children's Place Experiences." In *Children and Their Environments: Learning, Using and Designing Spaces*, edited by Christopher Spencer and Mark Blades, 108–23. Cambridge: Cambridge University Press, 2006.

Donaldson, Sue, and Will Kymlicka. *Zoopolis: A Political Theory of Animal Rights.* New York: Oxford University Press, 2011.

Dunlap, Julie, and Stephen R. Kellert, eds., *Companions in Wonder: Children and Adults Exploring Nature Together.* Cambridge, MA: MIT Press, 2012.

Dunning, Joan. *From the Redwood Forest: Ancient Trees and the Bottom Line: A Headwaters Journey.* White River Junction, VT: Chelsea Green, 1998.

Dwyer, Graham, and Richard J. Cole, eds., *The Hare Krishna Movement: Forty Years of Chant and Change.* London: I. B. Tauris, 2007.

Ellwood, Robert. *The Sixties Spiritual Awakening.* New Brunswick, NJ: Rutgers University Press, 1994.

Epstein, Barbara. *Political Protest and Cultural Revolution: Nonviolent Direct Action in the 1970s and 1980s.* Berkeley: University of California Press, 1991.

Feuer, Lewis. "The Sources and Traits of Student Movements." In *The Seeds of Politics: Youth and Politics in America*, edited by Anthony M. Orum, 365–85. Englewood Cliffs, NJ: Prentice-Hall, 1972.

Fisher, Philip. *Wonder, the Rainbow, and the Aesthetics of Rare Experiences.* Cambridge, MA: Harvard University Press, 1998.

Fishman, Jacob R., and Fredric Solomon. "Youth and Social Action: An Introduction." In *The Seeds of Politics*, edited by Anthony M. Orum, 247–52. Englewood Cliffs, NJ: Prentice-Hall, 1972.

Flacks, Richard. "The Liberated Generation: An Exploration of the Roots of Student Protest." In *The Seeds of Politics*, edited by Anthony M. Orum, 258–70. Englewood Cliffs, NJ: Prentice-Hall, 1972.

Foucault, Michel. "Of Other Spaces." *Diacritics* 16 (1986): 24.

Francione, Gary L. *Rain Without Thunder: The Ideology of the Animal Rights Movement.* Philadelphia: Temple University Press, 1996.

Free Association. *Moments of Excess: Movements, Protests and Everyday Life.* Oakland: PM Press, 2011.

Freedman, Estelle. *No Turning Back: The History of Feminism and the Future of Women.* New York: Ballantine Books, 2003.

Fudge, Erica. *Animal.* London: Reaktion, 2002.

Garber, Marjorie. *Dog Love.* New York: Simon & Schuster, 1996.

Gilmore, Lee. *Theatre in a Crowded Fire: Ritual and Spirituality at Burning Man.* Berkeley: University of California Press, 2010.

Girard, René. *Violence and the Sacred.* Baltimore, MD: Johns Hopkins University Press, 1979.

Gitlin, Todd. *Occupy Nation: The Roots, the Spirit, and the Promise of Occupy Wall Street.* New York: It Books, 2012.

Gitlin, Todd. *The Sixties: Years of Hope, Days of Rage.* New York: Bantam, 1993.

Goodall, Jane. *Hope for Animals and Their World.* New York: Grand Central, 2009.

Graeber, David. *Direct Action: An Ethnography.* Oakland, CA: AK Press, 2009.

Griffin, Susan. *Woman and Nature: The Roaring Inside Her.* Berkeley, CA: Counterpoint, 2016 [1978].

Griffiths, Jay. *Anarchipelago.* Glastonbury, UK: Wooden Books, 2007.

Griffiths, Jay. *Kith: The Riddle of the Childscape.* London: Penguin, 2013.

Grigoriadis, Vanessa. "The Rise and Fall of the Eco-Radical Underground." *Rolling Stone* 1006, August 10, 2006.

Grimes, Ronald. *Deeply Into the Bone: Re-Inventing Rites of Passage.* Berkeley: University of California Press, 2002.

Haberman, David L. *People Trees: Worship of Trees in Northern India.* Oxford: Oxford University Press, 2013.

Haenfler, Ross. *Straightedge: Clean-Living Youth, Hard Core Punk, and Social Change.* New Brunswick, NJ: Rutgers University Press, 2006.

Hall, Lee. *Capers in the Churchyard: Animal Rights Advocacy in the Age of Terror*. Darien, CT: Nectar Bat, 2006.

Haraway, Donna. *When Species Meet*. Minneapolis: University of Minnesota Press, 2008.

Harris, Paul L. "On Not Falling Down to Earth: Children's Metaphysical Questions." In *Imagining the Impossible: Magical, Scientific, and Religious Thinking in Children*, edited by Karl S. Rosengren, Carl N. Johnson, and Paul Harris, 157–78. Cambridge: Cambridge University Press, 2000.

Harrison, Robert Pogue. *Forests: The Shadow of Civilization*. Chicago: University of Chicago Press, 1992.

Harvey, Graham. *Animism: Respecting the Living World*. New York: Columbia University Press, 2006.

Hays, Samuel P. *Beauty, Health, and Permanence: Environmental Politics in the United States, 1955–1985*. Cambridge: Cambridge University Press, 1987.

Heilbronner, Oded. "From a Culture *for* Youth to a Culture *of* Youth: Recent Trends in the Historiography of Western Youth Cultures." *Contemporary European History* 17 (2008): 575–91.

Heise, Ursula. *Sense of Place and Sense of Planet: The Environmental Imagination of the Global*. Oxford: Oxford University Press, 2008.

Herman, Louis. *Future Primal: How Our Wilderness Origins Show Us the Way Forward*. Novato, CA: New World Library, 2013.

Hill, Julia Butterfly. *The Legacy of Luna: The Story of a Tree, a Woman, and the Struggle to Save the Redwoods*. San Francisco: Harper San Francisco, 2000.

Hindle, Jim. *Nine Miles: Two Winters of Anti-Road Protests*. London: Underhill, 2006.

Houseman, Michael. "Refracting Ritual: An Upside-down Perspective on Ritual, Media and Conflict." In *Ritual, Media, and Conflict*, edited by Ronald Grimes, Ute Huesken, Udo Simon, and Eric Venbrux, 255–84. New York: Oxford, 2011.

Houseman, Michael. "Relationality." In *Theorizing Rituals, Volume I: Issues, Topics, Approaches, Concepts*, edited by Jens Kreinath, Jan Snoek, Michael Stausberg, 413–28. London: Brill, 2006.

If a Tree Falls: A Story of the Earth Liberation Front. Directed by Marshall Curry and Sam Cullman. Marshall Curry Productions, 2011.

Ingalsbee, Timothy L. "Earth First!: Consciousness in Action in the Unfolding of a New-Social-Movement." PhD dissertation, University of Oregon, 1995.

Ingold, Tim. *The Perception of the Environment: Essays on Livelihood, Dwelling and Skill*. New York: Routledge, 2011.

Ingold, Tim, and Gisli Palsson, eds. *Biosocial Becomings: Integrating Social and Biological Anthropology*. Cambridge: Cambridge University Press, 2013.

Ivakhiv, Adrian. *Ecologies of the Moving Image*. Waterloo, ON: Wilfrid Laurier University Press, 2013.

Jackson, Michael. *The Palm at the End of the Mind: Relatedness, Religiosity, and the Real*. Durham, NC: Duke University Press, 2009.

Jacobus, Mary. "Distressful Gift: Talking to the Dead." *South Atlantic Quarterly* 106 (2007): 393–418.

Jasper, James M., and Dorothy Nelkin. *The Animal Rights Crusade: The Growth of a Moral Protest.* New York: Free Press, 1992.

Jenks, Chris. *Childhood: Critical Concepts in Sociology.* Abingdon, UK: Taylor & Francis, 2005.

Johnston, Lucas F. *Religion and Sustainability: Social Movements and the Politics of the Environment.* Bristol, CT: Equinox, 2013.

Joosee, Paul. "Elves, Environmentalism, and 'Eco-terror': Leaderless Resistance and Media Coverage of the Earth Liberation Front." *Crime Media Culture* 8 (2012): 75–93.

Joosee, Paul. "Leaderless Resistance and Ideological Inclusion: The Case of the Earth Liberation Front." *Terrorism and Political Violence* 19 (2007): 351–68.

Jordan, Chris. Keynote, This Way to Sustainability conference, Chico, CA, 2013. See http://www.chrisjordan.com/gallery/midway/#about.

Joseph, John. *The Evolution of a Cro-Magnon.* New York: Punk House, 2007.

Kahn Jr., Peter H. "Children's Affiliations With Nature: Structure, Development and the Problem of Environmental Generational Amnesia." In *Children and Nature: Psychological, Sociocultural, and Evolutionary Investigations*, edited by Peter H. Kahn Jr. and Stephen R. Kellert, 93–116. Cambridge, MA: MIT Press, 2002.

Kahn, Jr., Peter H. *The Human Relationship With Nature: Development and Culture.* Cambridge, MA: MIT Press, 1999.

Kahn Jr., Peter H., and Stephen R. Kellert, eds. *Children and Nature: Psychological, Sociocultural, and Evolutionary Investigations.* Cambridge, MA: MIT Press, 2002.

Keating, Daniel. "Adolescent Thinking." In *At the Threshold: The Developing Adolescent*, edited by S. Feldman and G. Elliott, 54–89. Cambridge, MA: Harvard University Press, 1990.

Kellert, Stephen. *Building for Life: Designing and Understanding the Human-Nature Connection.* Washington, DC: Island Press, 2005.

Kemper, Theodore D. "Social Models in the Explanation of Emotions." In *Handbook of Emotions*, edited by Michael Lewis, Jeanette M. Haviland-Jones, and Lisa Fedman Barrett, 45–58. New York: Guilford, 2011.

Kent, Stephen A. *From Slogans to Mantras: Social Protests and Religious Conversion in the Late Vietnam War Era.* Syracuse, NY: Syracuse University Press, 2001.

Kermani, S. Zohreh. *Pagan Family Values: Childhood and the Religious Imagination in Contemporary American Paganism.* New York: New York University Press, 2013.

Killingsworth, M. Jimmie. *Walt Whitman and the Earth: A Study of Ecopoetics.* Iowa City: University of Iowa Press, 2010.

Knight, Michael Muhammad. *The Taqwacores.* New York: Autonomedia, 2005.

Kohn, Eduardo. *How Forests Think: Toward an Anthropology beyond the Human.* Berkeley: University of California Press, 2013.

Kolbert, Elizabeth. *The Sixth Extinction: An Unnatural History.* New York: Henry Holt, 2014.

Kuipers, Dean. *Operation Bite Back: Rod Coronado's War to Save American Wilderness.* New York: Bloomsbury, 2009.

LaDuke, Winona. *All Our Relations: Native Struggles for Land and Life.* Boston: South End, 1999.

Lahickey, Beth. *All Ages—Reflections on Straightedge.* Huntington Beach, CA: Revelation Records, 1998.

Lasch, Christopher. *The New Radicalism in America 1889–1963: The Intellectual as a Social Type.* New York: W. W. Norton, 1997.

Latham, Rob. *Consuming Youth: Vampires, Cyborgs, and the Culture of Consumption.* Chicago: University of Chicago Press, 2002.

Latour, Bruno. *The Politics of Nature: How to Bring the Sciences Into Democracy,* translated by Catherine Porter. Cambridge, MA: Harvard University Press, 2004.

Lee, Martha. *Earth First! Environmental Apocalypse.* Syracuse, NY: Syracuse University Press. 1995.

Lesko, Nancy. *Act Your Age! A Cultural Construction of Adolescence.* New York: Routledge Farmer, 2001.

Liddick, Donald. *Eco-Terrorism: Radical Environmental and Animal Liberation Movements.* Westport, CT: Praeger, 2006.

Lippit, Akira. *Electric Animal: Toward a Rhetoric of Wildlife.* Minneapolis: University of Minnesota Press, 2000.

Lofland, John, and Rodney Stark. "Becoming a World-Saver: A Theory of Conversion to a Deviant Perspective." *American Sociological Review* 30 (1965): 863–74.

Louv, Richard. *Last Child in the Woods: Saving Our Children from Nature-Deficit Disorder.* Chapel Hill, NC: Algonquin, 2005.

Luhr, Eileen. *Witnessing Suburbia: Christian Conservatives, "Family Values," and the Cultural Politics of Youth.* Berkeley: University of California Press, 2009.

Luhrmann, Tanya. *Persuasions of the Witch's Craft: Ritual Magic in Contemporary England.* Cambridge, MA: Harvard University Press, 1989.

Malott, Curry, and Milagros Peña. *Punk Rockers' Revolution: A Pedagogy of Race, Class, and Gender.* New York: Peter Lang, 2004.

Manes, Christopher. *Green Rage: Radical Environmentalism and the Unmaking of Civilization.* New York: Back Bay, 1991.

McKanan, Dan. *Prophetic Encounters: Religion and the American Radical Tradition.* Boston: Beacon, 2011.

Mergen, Bernard. "Children and Nature in History." *Environmental History* 8 (2003): 643–69.

Miller, James. *Daoism and the Quest for A Sustainable Future.* New York: Columbia University Press, 2017.

Miller, Lisa. *The Spiritual Child: The New Science on Parenting for Health and Lifelong Thriving.* New York: Columbia Teachers College, 2015.

Milstein, Cindy. *Anarchism and Its Aspirations.* Oakland, CA: AK Press, 2010.

Milton, Kay. *Loving Nature: Towards an Ecology of Emotion.* New York: Routledge, 2002.

Mintz, Steven. *Huck's Raft: A History of American Childhood.* Cambridge, MA: Harvard University Press, 2004.

Monbiot, George. *Feral: Rewilding the Land, the Sea and Human Life*. Chicago: University of Chicago Press, 2014.

Mooallen, Jon. *Wild Ones: A Sometimes Dismaying, Weirdly Reassuring Story About Looking at People Looking at Animals in America*. New York: Penguin, 2013.

Nabhan, Gary Paul. *The Geography of Childhood: Why Children Need Wild Places*. Boston: Beacon, 1994.

Naess, Arne. "The Shallow and the Deep, Long-Range Ecology Movement: A Summary." *Inquiry* 16 (1973): 95–100.

Nash, Roderick. *Wilderness and the American Mind*. New Haven, CT: Yale University Press, 1967.

Nehring, Neil. "Jigsaw Youth." In *GenXegesis: Essays on 'Alternative' Youth (Sub)Culture*, edited by John M. Ulrich and Andrea l. Harris, 59–78. Madison: University of Wisconsin Press, 2003.

Nixon, Alan, and Adam Possamai. "Techno-Shamanism and the Economy of Ecstasy as Religious Experience." In *Pop Pagans: Paganism and Popular Music*, edited by Donna Weston and Andy Bennett, 145–61. London: Routledge, 2014.

Oakley, Keith. *Emotions: A Brief History*. New York: Oxford University Press, 2004.

O'Hara, Craig. *The Philosophy of Punk*. London: AK Press, 1999.

Orr, David. "Political Economy and the Ecology of Childhood." In *Children and Nature: Psychological, Sociocultural, and Evolutionary Investigations*, edited Peter H. Kahn Jr. and Stephen R. Kellert, 279–304. Cambridge, MA: MIT Press, 2002.

Orsi, Robert A. *Between Heaven and Earth: The Religious Worlds People Make and the Scholars Who Study Them*. Princeton, NJ: Princeton University Press, 2005.

Orum, Anthony M. "Introduction." In *The Seeds of Politics*, edited by Anthony M. Orum, 1–14. Englewood Cliffs, NJ: Prentice-Hall, 1972.

Orum, Anthony M. *The Seeds of Politics: Youth and Politics in America*. Englewood Cliffs, NJ: Prentice-Hall, 1972.

Owens, Patsy Eubanks. "Natural Landscapes, Gathering Places, and Prospect Refuges: Characteristics of Outdoor Places Valued by Teens." *Children's Environment Quarterly* 5 (1988): 17–24.

Palladino, Grace. *Teenagers: An American History*. New York: Basic Books, 1996.

Parrot, W. Gerrod, and Matthew P. Spackman, "Emotion and Memory." In *Handbook of Emotions*, edited by Michael Lewis, Jeanette M. Haviland-Jones, and Lisa Fedman Barrett, 476–90. New York: Guilford, 2011.

Perucci, Tony. "What the Fuck Is That? The Poetics of Ruptural Performance." *Liminalities: A Journal of Performance Studies* 5 (2009): 1–18.

Peterson, Brian. *Burning Fight: The Nineties Hardcore Revolution in Ethics, Politics, Spirit and Sound*. Huntington Beach, CA: Revelation Records, 2009.

Pike, Sarah M. "Dark Teens and Born-Again Martyrs: Captivity Narratives After Columbine." *Journal of the American Academy of Religion* 77 (2009): 647–72.

Pike, Sarah M. *Magical Selves, Earthly Bodies: Contemporary Pagans and the Search for Community*. Berkeley: University of California Press, 2001.

Pike, Sarah M. "Mourning Nature: The Work of Grief in Radical Environmentalism." In *Journal for the Study of Religion, Nature and Culture* 10 (2016): 419–41.

Pike, Sarah M. *New Age and Neopagan Religions in America*. New York: Columbia University Press, 2004.

Pike, Sarah M. "Radical Animal Rights and Environmental Activism As Rites of Passage." In "The Denial of Ritual," a special issue of the *Journal of Ritual Studies* (July 2013): 35–45.

Pike, Sarah M. "Religion and Youth in American Culture." In *Children and Religion: A Methods Handbook*, edited by Susan B. Ridgely, 33–49. New York: New York University Press, 2011.

Pike, Sarah M. "Witchcraft Since the 1960s." In *The Oxford Handbook of Religion and the American News Media*, edited by Diane Winston, 289–302. Oxford: Oxford University Press, 2012.

Plumwood, Val. *Environmental Culture: The Ecological Crisis of Reason*. London: Routledge, 2002.

Polner, Murray, and Jim O'Grady, *Disarmed and Dangerous: The Radical Lives and Times of Daniel and Philip Berrigan*. New York: Basic Books, 1997.

Potter, Will. *Green Is the New Red: An Insider's Account of a Social Movement Under Siege*. San Francisco: City Lights Books, 2011.

Potter, Will. "The Green Scare." *Vermont Law Review* 33 (2009): 671–87.

Pyle, Robert Michael. "Eden in a Vacant Lot: Special Places, Species, and Kids in the Neighborhood of Life." In *Children and Nature: Psychological, Sociocultural, and Evolutionary Investigations*, edited by Peter H. Kahn Jr. and Stephen R. Kellert, 305–28. Cambridge, MA: MIT Press, 2002.

Pyle, Robert Michael. *The Thunder Tree: Lessons from an Urban Wildland*. Corvallis: Oregon State University Press, 2011.

Reese, William. *The Origins of the American High School*. New Haven, CT: Yale University Press, 1995.

Regan, Tom. *Defending Animal Rights*. Urbana: University of Illinois Press, 2001.

Regnerus, Mark D. *Forbidden Fruit: Sex and Religion in the Lives of American Teenagers*. New York: Oxford University Press, 2007.

Ritvo, Harriet. *The Animal Estate: The English and Other Creatures in the Victorian Age*. Cambridge, MA: Harvard University Press, 1987.

Robbins, Thomas, and Benjamin Zablocki. *Misunderstanding Cults: Searching for Objectivity in a Controversial Field*. Toronto: University of Toronto Press, 2001.

Rochford, E. Burke. *Hare Krishna Transformed*. New York: New York University Press, 2007.

Rose, Deborah Bird. *Wild Dog Dreaming: Love and Extinction*. Charlottesville: University of Virginia Press, 2011.

Rose, Deborah Bird, Thom van Dooren, Matthew Chrulew, Stuart Cooke, Matthew Kearnes, and Emily O'Gorman. "Thinking Through the Environment, Unsettling the Humanities." *Environmental Humanities* 1 (2012): 1–5.

Rosebraugh, Craig. *Burning Rage of a Dying Planet: Speaking for the Earth Liberation Front*. New York: Lantern Books, 2004.

Rosewarne, Stuart, James Goodman, and Rebecca Pearse, eds., *Climate Action Upsurge: The Ethnography of Climate Movement Politics*. New York: Routledge, 2014.

Savage, Jon. *Teenage: The Creation of Youth Culture*. New York: Viking, 2007.

Scarce, Rik. *Eco-Warriors: Understanding the Radical Environmental Movement*. New York: Left Coast, 2006.

Schacter, Daniel. *The Seven Sins of Memory*. New York: Houghton Mifflin, 2001.

Seligman, Adam, Robert P. Weller, Michael J. Puett, and Bennett Simon. *Ritual and Its Consequences: An Essay on the Limits of Sincerity*. New York: Oxford University Press, 2008.

Sessions, George ed., *Deep Ecology for the 21st Century*. Boston: Shambhala, 1995.

Sideris, Lisa. "Fact and Fiction, Fear and Wonder: the Legacy of Rachel Carson." *Soundings: An Interdisciplinary Journal* 91 (2008): 335–69.

Singer, Dorothy G., and Jerome L. Singer. *The House of Make-Believe: Children's Play and the Developing Imagination*. Cambridge MA: Harvard University Press, 1990.

Singer, Peter, ed. *In Defense of Animals*. New York: Harper and Row, 1985.

Smith, Christian. *Soul-Searching: The Religious and Spiritual Lives of American Teenagers*. New York: Oxford University Press, 2009.

Sobel, David. *Children's Special Places: Exploring the Role of Forts, Dens and Bush Houses in Middle Childhood*. Tucson, AZ: Zephyr, 1993.

Sobel, David. "A Place in the World: Adults' Memories of Childhood's Special Places." *Children's Environments Quarterly* 7 (1990): 5–12.

Solnit, Rebecca. *Hope in the Dark: Untold Histories, Wild Possibilities*. New York: Nation, 2004.

Spira, Henry. "Fighting to Win." In *In Defense of Animals*, edited by Peter Singer, 194–208. New York: Harper and Row, 1985.

Stoll, Mark R. *Inherit the Holy Mountain: Religion and the Rise of American Environmentalism*. Oxford: Oxford University Press, 2015.

Stuart, Tristram. *The Bloodless Revolution: A Cultural History of Vegetarianism from 1600 to Modern Times*. New York: W. W. Norton, 2006.

Taylor, Bron R. *Dark Green Religion: Nature Spirituality and the Planetary Future*. Berkeley: University of California Press, 2009.

Taylor, Bron. "Earth and Nature-Based Spirituality (Part 1): From Deep Ecology to Radical Environmentalism." *Religion* 31 (2001): 175–93.

Taylor, Bron. "Earth First!: From Primal Spirituality to Ecological Resistance." In *This Sacred Earth*, edited by Roger Gottlieb, 545–57. New York: Routledge, 1996.

Taylor, Bron R. "Earthen Spirituality or Cultural Genocide?: Radical Environmentalism's Appropriation of Native American Spirituality." *Religion* 27 (1997): 183–215.

Taylor, Bron. "Evoking the Ecological Self." *Peace Review: The International Quarterly of World Peace* 5 (June 1993): 225–30.

Taylor, Bron R. "The Religion and Politics of Earth First!" *The Ecologist* 21 (1991): 258–66.

Taylor, Bron R. "Religion, Violence and Radical Environmentalism: From Earth First! to the Unabomber to the Earth Liberation Front." *Terrorism and Political Violence* 10 (Winter 1998): 1–42.

Taylor, Bron R. "The Tributaries of Radical Environmentalism." *Journal for the Study of Radicalism* 2 (2008): 27–61.

Taylor, Bron R. "Wilderness, Spirituality and Biodiversity in North America—Tracing an Environmental History from Occidental Roots to Earth Day." In *Wilderness in Mythology and Religion*, edited by Laura Feldt, 293–324. Berlin: DeGruyter, 2012.

Taylor, Dorceta E. *The Rise of the American Conservation Movement: Power, Privilege, and Environmental Protection*. Durham, NC: Duke University Press, 2016.

Teather, Elizabeth Kenworthy. *Embodied Geographies: Spaces, Bodies and Rites of Passage*. New York: Routledge, 1999.

Thomashow, Cynthia. "Adolescents and Ecological Identity: Attending to Wild Nature." In *Children and Nature: Psychological, Sociocultural, and Evolutionary Investigations*, edited by Peter H. Kahn Jr. and Stephen R. Kellert, 259–78. Cambridge, MA: MIT Press, 2002.

Thomashow, Mitchell. *Ecological Identity: Becoming a Reflective Environmentalist*. Cambridge, MA: MIT Press, 1996.

Thompson, Stacy. *Punk Productions: Unfinished Business*. Albany: State University of New York Press, 2004.

Tsing, Anna. "Unruly Edges: Mushrooms as Companion Species." *Environmental Humanities* 1 (2012): 141–54.

Tucker, Mary Evelyn, and John Berthrong, eds. *Confucianism and Ecology: The Interrelation of Heaven, Earth, and Humans*. Cambridge, MA: Harvard University Press, 1998.

Turner, James Morton. *The Promise of Wilderness: American Environmental Politics Since 1964*. Seattle: University of Washington Press, 2012.

van Dooren, Thom. *Flight Ways: Life and Loss at the Edge of Extinction*. New York: Columbia University Press, 2014.

Van Gennep, Arnold. *The Rites of Passage*. Chicago: University of Chicago Press, 1960.

Van Wieren, Gretel, and Stephen R. Kellert. "The Origins of Aesthetics and Spiritual Values in Children's Experience of Nature." *Journal for the Study of Religion, Nature and Culture* 7, no. 3 (2013): 243–64.

Vodovnik, Ziga. *A Living Spirit of Revolt: The Infrapolitics of Anarchism*. Oakland: PM Press, 2013.

Voice of the Voiceless. *From Dusk 'til Dawn: An Insider's View of the Animal Liberation Movement*. N.p.: Voice of the Voiceless Communications, 2008.

Watson, Paul. *Seal Wars: Twenty-Five Years on the Front Lines with the Harp Seals*. Buffalo, NY: Firefly, 2002.

Wilson, Edward O. *Biophilia*. Cambridge, MA: Harvard University Press, 1984.

Wilson, James. "Punk Rock Puja: (Mis)appropriation, (Re)interpretation, and Dissemination of Hindu Religious Traditions in the North American and

European Underground Music Scene(s)." MA thesis, University of Florida, 2008.

Witt, Joseph D. *Religion and Resistance in Appalachia: Faith and the Fight Against Mountaintop Removal Coal Mining*. Lexington: University Press of Kentucky, 2016.

Wolfe, Cary. *Zoontologies: The Question of the Animal*. Minneapolis: University of Minnesota Press, 2003.

Wood, Robert T. *Straightedge Youth: Complexity and Contradictions of a Subculture*. Syracuse, NY: Syracuse University Press, 2006.

Wright, Stuart A. "The Dynamics of Movement Membership: Joining and Leaving New Religious Movements." In *Teaching New Religious Movements*, edited by David A. Bromley, 187–209. Oxford: Oxford University Press, 2007.

Wulff, Helena, ed. *The Emotions: A Cultural Reader*. Oxford: Berg, 2007.

Wyn, Johanna, and Rob White, eds. *Rethinking Youth*. Melbourne: Allen and Unwin, 1997.

Young, Peter. *Animal Liberation Front: Complete Diary of Actions, the First 30 Years, 1979–2008*. N.p.: Warcry Communications, 2010.

Zakin, Susan. *Coyotes and Town Dogs: Earth First! and the Environmental Movement*. Tucson: University of Arizona Press, 1993.

Index

Note: Some activists are known only by first names, or by adopted "forest names"; additionally, some trees have been given names. For clarity, these are indicated by "activist" or "tree" in parentheses. Page numbers for figures are followed by *fig*.

Anderson, Kiera "Loki," 179, 222
Anderson, Tristan, 41
Animal Damage Control (ADC) Predator
Research Facility, 210–13
Animal Liberation Front (ALF), 159*fig.*;
animal releases, 137–38; early years,
48–49; ecoterrorism labels, 2–3; growth
trends, 27, 140; hardcore punk rock
and, 141–42; Operation Bite Back,
210–13. *See also* sabotage
animal rights movement: growing support
for, 21–22, 140, 232–33; history of, 42,
45–50; kinship with nonhuman animals,
73, 86–90, 135, 251n28; warrior
mentality, 207–13, 219–20, 224–26,
232; welfarist/liberationist debates, 46;
women, 178. *See also* hardcore punk
rock; nonhumans; veganism/vegetarian-
ism; *specific groups and actions*
animals. *See* nonhumans
animism, 96, 100–102. *See also* nonhumans
Anishinaabeg people, 191
anthropomorphism: in art, 120–22; cultural
trends, 99–101, 141; heightening of loss,
106, 128–29; kinship experiences, 73,
86–90, 105–6, 127–30, 135, 196–98,
251n28; sacredness, 258nn84–85
anticapitalism movements, 59–60, 143,
174–75, 263n26
antinuclear movement, 61–63, 67
antioppression movement, 176–80,
186–95
antiroad movements, 40, 67, 118, 123,
201
antivivisection movement, 46
apocalypticism: collapse, 197, 207, 224–29;
in hardcore music, 154; hope within,
224–29; sense of grief, 197, 204–7;
warrior mentality, 207–13, 219–20, 232
Arendt, Hannah, 133
Arrow, Tre, 125–26
arson, 27–28, 90, 104–5, 160–61. *See also*
violence
art: anthropomorphism in, 120–22; hope
for future, 228; mourning, 196–97,
203–6; performance, 33, 47, 131,
258n94; popular culture, 77, 82–83,
99–101, 141; rewilding in, 112*fig.*,
120–21, 121*fig.*
ASPCA (American Society for the
Prevention of Cruelty to Animals), 46
atheism, 96–97
Avalon (activist), 215, 220–21, 223
Ayers, Bill, 54, 55

Back to Godhead (magazine), 148, 150
Bambi (film), 100
Bari, Judi, 178
Beach, Patrick, 128
becoming, 6, 113–20. *See also* conversion;
identity construction
Behind the Mask (film), 49
"Behind the Wire" (song), 154
Belalia, Henia, 77
Bennett, Jane, 102
Bentham, Jeremy, 130
Berrigan, Daniel, 56
Berrigan, Philip, 56
Beston, Henry, 90
betrayals, 223–24
Bey, Hakim, 171
Bhaktivedanta Swami Prabupada, 145
Bilston Glen tree-sit, 40
Biophilia (Wilson), 108–9
"Birth First" (Geddon), 206
Black Mesa Defense Fund, 45, 183–84, 191
blockades, 19*fig*, 33, 34–36, 79*fig.*, 170–72,
172*fig. See also specific groups or actions*
Blockadia Rising (film), 77, 82–83
*The Bloodless Revolution: A Cultural
History of Vegetarianism from 1600 to
Modern Times* (Stuart), 153
Bookchin, Murray, 62
"Born Caged" (anonymous), 119
boundaries, behavioral: sharpening,
186–90; softening, 183, 190–95
Boy Scouts, 255n111
Brannon, Norman, 147
"Brave Hearts Forward" (Western Wildlife
Unit), 209
Britain. *See* United Kingdom
Brower, David, 44
Buechner, Karl, 144
Butterfly (activist). *See* Hill, Julia Butterfly

call-outs, 179
Cappo, Ray (Raghunath das), 142–43,
147, 148
Carr, Sean, 120
Carson, Rachel, 44, 81
Cascadia Free State, 171–72
Catonsville Nine, 56
CAW (Church of All Worlds), 68
Chain, Bridgett, 116
Chain, David, 82, 116–17
Chain, David "Gypsy," 113–15, 126
Cherney, Darryl, 68, 110, 128, 208–9,
249n139
Cherry, Elizabeth, 141

Paganism: childhood roots of, 96–97; influence on environmentalism, 9, 40, 66–70, 109–10, 248n128
Palestine, 41
Palsson, Gisli, 6, 114
Parsons, Talcott, 51
People for the Ethical Treatment of Animals (PETA), 21, 47, 48, 65, 241–42n9
performance art, 33, 47, 131, 258n94
personification, of nonhumans: in art, 120–22; cultural trends, 99–101, 141; heightening of loss, 106, 128–29; kinship experiences, 73, 86–90, 87–89, 105–6, 127–30, 135, 196–98, 251n28; sacredness, 258nn84–85
PETA (People for the Ethical Treatment of Animals), 21, 47, 48, 65, 241–42n9
physical bodies: feral states, 113–20, 174–75, 227; purification practices, 148, 155; tattoos, 118, 155
Piaget, Jean, 75
poetry, 203–6, 228
popular culture, 77, 82–83, 99–101, 141
population control, 206–7, 266n35
Post-Scarcity Anarchism (Bookchin), 62
Potter, Beatrix, 99
Potter, Will, 3
The Practice of the Wild (Snyder), 80
primal future, 24, 227–29
primitive skills, 167–69
professionalization, 44
property destruction. See sabotage
proselytizing, 65–66, 148–50, 248–49n119
protest rites, 133fig., 134fig.; definition of, 2; forest blockades, 19fig; identification with nonhumans, 130–32, 258n94; mourning, 198; as mourning, 202–4; news media coverage, 59, 111, 223; sacredness, 170
Proteus (activist), 127
punk rock. See hardcore punk rock; straightedge punk movement
"Purity Politics: How Animal Liberation Is Keeping Us from Animal Liberation" (Conroy), 57
Pyle, Robert Michael, 92, 199

Quakers, 56, 62
queer community, 177

Rabbit (activist), 15, 64, 118, 122, 224
Rachel (activist), 123–24
Rachman, Paul, 142
racism, 181–86, 187–88

"Rad Babies" (Geddon), 206
Radical Action for Mountains' and People's Survival (RAMPS), 6, 45, 192
Radical Faeries, 68
radicalism, 8–10, 47–49, 55–57, 110–11
Raghunath das (Ray Cappo), 142–43, 147, 148
RAMPS (Radical Action for Mountains' and People's Survival), 6, 45, 192
Ravindra Svarupa dasa, 149
Red Cloud Thunder Fall Creek tree-sit, 105, 127
redwoods, 48
Redwood Wars, 114
reincarnation, 152–53
religion: apocalyptic vocabulary, 208; martyrdom language, 217–24, 267–68n89; movements as holy wars, 45, 217–20; nature as, 7, 9; radicalism, 55–57; rejection of, 67, 70, 95–97, 249n145; use of conversion language, 20–21; youth as potential converts, 65–66, 248–49n119. See also spirituality; specific religions
rewilding: in art, 120–21; disidentification with dominant society, 136; fear of, 111–12; feral states, 113–20, 174–75, 227; of planet, 120, 225; primitive skills, 167–69
rewilding, of humans, 94
risks: acts of identification/disidentification, 131–32; downplaying of, 79, 82; to families, 79; isolation, 126–27; tree-sitting deaths, 218–19
rites of passage: actions, 173–74; forest experiences, 136; gatherings, 173; inclusivity through shared action, 192–95; isolation from outside world, 107. See also conversion
rituals: conversion to activism, 15–16, 19–21; functions, 108; identification with nonhumans, 130–32, 201–2, 258n94; influences on activism, 9; memorials, 220–24; protests as, 16–18, 75, 170–71; role in commitments, 7. See also conversion; grief and loss; spirituality
Rizana (band), 224
Rodgers, William "Avalon," 215, 220–21, 223
role playing, 190
Roman Catholics, 56
Rosebraugh, Craig, 156, 213
Roselle, Mike, 27

154; motivations, 97; rejection of
Christianity, 157–58; Weather
Underground, 53
youth: definition, 4, 237n9; exposure to
anarchism, 59–60; growth of Paganism,
66, 68–70; hardcore punk rock, 141–45;
influences, 22; introduction to activism,
49–50; nomadic, 174–75; paths to
activism, 38–41; as potential converts,
65–66; religious dissatisfaction, 70,

157–58; social significance of place,
109, 155–57; spirituality of, 21; spread
of Krishna Consciousness, 148–49;
teenagers as social group, 51–53;
trivializing of, 66, 158–59
Youth of Today (band), 152

Zakin, Susan, 174
Zell-Ravenheart, Oberon (Tim), 68
zines, 13, 14fig